P9-CMT-944

"IT RIVALS TRUMAN CAPOTE'S *IN COLD BLOOD*
. . . A STORY OF UNMITIGATED HORROR."

—Willie Morris

MONEY, MADNESS, MURDER: A FAMILY ALBUM

NUTCRACKER
SHANA ALEXANDER

"Miss Alexander's skills are on display again. She spins
this yarn with brio, keeping the narrative rolling along,
holding the reader's interest with deft infusions of telling
detail."

—*The New York Times Book Review*

"A Chekovian family tragedy . . . Alexander's compelling narrative builds in intensity around this uniquely
twisted woman."

—*The Washington Post Book World*

"Shrewd insights. . . ."

—*Newsweek*

"Straightforward readability . . . you may not forget
the Bradshaws as soon as you might have wished."

—*The Wall Street Journal*

"Chilling reading . . . leaves the reader stunned."

—*The Kansas City Star*

MONEY, MADNESS,
MURDER: A FAMILY
ALBUM

NUT-CRACKER

SHANA ALEXANDER

A DELL BOOK

Published by
Dell Publishing Co., Inc.
1 Dag Hammarskjold Plaza
New York, New York 10017

For Kirk and Scott Thompson, and Joyce

For Kirk and Scott Thompson, and Joyce

Contents

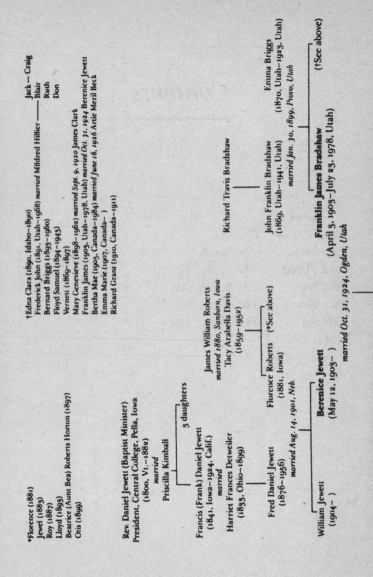

*Florence (1881)
Jewel (1885)
Roy (1887)
Lloyd (1893)
Beatrice (Aunt Bea) Roberts Horton (1897)
Otis (1899)

†Edna Clara (1890, Idaho–1890)
Frederick John (1891, Utah–1968) *married Mildred Hillier* ——— Jack — Craig
Bernard Briggs (1893–1960)   Blair
Floyd Samuel (1894–1943)   Ruth
Vernett (1865–1897)   Don
Mary Genevieve (1898–1962) *married Sept. 9, 1920 James Clark*
Franklin James (1905, Utah–1978. Utah) *married Oct. 31, 1924 Berenice Jewett*
Bertha Mae (1905, Canada–1984) *married June 16, 1926 Artie Meril Beck*
Emma Marie (1907, Canada–)
Richard Grant (1910, Canada–1911)

Rev. Daniel Jewett (Baptist Minister)
President, Central College, Pella, Iowa
(1800, Vt. –1882)
married
Priscilla Kimball

                    3 daughters

James William Roberts   (*See above)
married 1880, Sanborn, Iowa
Tacy Arabella Davis
(1859–1952)

Francis (Frank) Daniel Jewett
(1841, Iowa–1924, Calif.)
married
Harriet Frances Detweiler
(1853, Ohio–1899)

Florence Roberts
(1881, Iowa)

Richard Travis Bradshaw

John Franklin Bradshaw
(1865, Utah–1941, Utah)

Emma Briggs
(1870, Utah–1923, Utah)
married Jan. 30, 1899, Provo, Utah

Fred Daniel Jewett
(1876–1956)
married Aug. 14, 1901, Neb.

Berenice Jewett
(May 12, 1903–)

Franklin James Bradshaw
(April 3, 1903–July 23, 1978, Utah)

(†See above)

married Oct. 31, 1924, Ogden, Utah

William Jewett
(1904–)

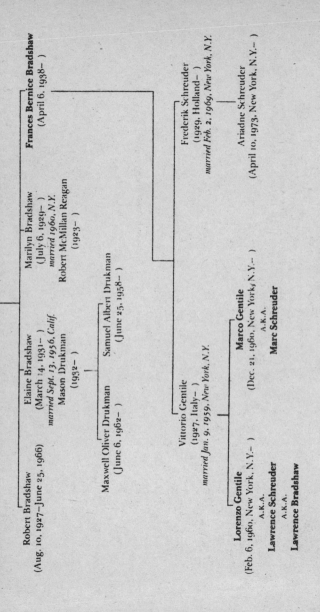

Robert Bradshaw
(Aug. 10, 1927–June 25, 1966)

Elaine Bradshaw
(March 14, 1931–)
married Sept. 13, 1956, Calif.
Mason Drukman
(1932–)

Marilyn Bradshaw
(July 6, 1929–)
married 1960, N.Y.
Robert McMillan Reagan
(1923–)

Frances Bernice Bradshaw
(April 6, 1938–)

Maxwell Oliver Drukman
(June 6, 1962–)

Samuel Albert Drukman
(June 25, 1958–)

Vittorio Gentile
(1927, Italy–)
married Jan. 9, 1959, New York, N.Y.

Frederik Schreuder
(1929, Holland–)
married Feb. 2, 1969, New York, N.Y.

Ariadne Schreuder
(April 10, 1973, New York, N.Y.–)

Lorenzo Gentile
(Feb. 6, 1960, New York, N.Y.–)
A.K.A.
Lawrence Schreuder
A.K.A.
Lawrence Bradshaw

Marco Gentile
(Dec. 21, 1960, New York, N.Y.–)
A.K.A.
Marc Schreuder

NUT-
CRACKER

Foreword

I HAVE BEEN ACTIVE as a writer and journalist for nearly forty years. But the number of great reporters I have run across in that time would make, as they say, a slim book. Without question, the top man on my list would be Tommy Thompson.

In October 1982 I was in my Long Island kitchen when Thompson, the best friend I then had in the world, made one of his frequent Sunday calls from his home in Los Angeles. Since we were both professional writers, these chats began with the ritual greeting of our trade: *How's the book going?* Tommy chided me for not yet having sent him galley proofs of the one I had just finished. I told him a set was already in the mail. He would surely have it in a day or two.

"Pamper me," Tommy said. "Dig up another set, and send it to me in Texas first thing tomorrow morning." He was catching a plane to Houston that night, and had just reserved "the most expensive suite I could get in the fanciest new hotel in town."

"I've decided I can use a little pampering," he said. "The doctors here now think they've found cancer cells in my liver."

I knew that Tommy had suffered intermittent bouts of hepatitis for many years; I remembered when he had first contracted it in New York after a "routine" blood transfusion. His experience since then, he told me, had suggested that doctors didn't really know very much about the liver, and therefore he had "made up my mind to fight" this latest diagnosis.

"But I think I can fight it better from Houston, where I know everybody," he said. "They've got all kinds of wonderful new diagnostic procedures down there, some of them not very pleasant. So what I've decided to do is check into this incredibly expensive hotel, then go to the hospital every morning and let them give me the works. But at night I go back to my fancy suite, order myself up a glorious dinner, put on my new silk pajamas, and climb into my king-size bed. Then all I'll need is a really great book to read. That's where you come in."

Oh, shameless Tommy!

I knew that when he mentioned "knowing everybody" in Houston, Tommy wasn't talking about all the rich and powerful real-life Texans he'd described in his blockbusting book *Blood and Money*. Nor was he thinking of his recent, even more successful Houston-based novel, *Celebrity*. The book he had in mind was *Hearts,* an earlier bestseller Thompson had written soon after leaving his staff job at *Life* magazine. *Hearts* is a meticulous account of the ferocious *mano-a-mano* between Houston's two world-famous heart surgeons, Dr. Michael DeBakey and Dr. Denton Cooley. The book was the product of a year-long, relentless investigation by Thompson of big-money miracle medicine as it had come to be practiced in his native state in the early 1970s, and from the day it was published, *Hearts* had assured its author permanent folk hero status throughout the Houston medical community.

Tommy had been a hero of my own since the late 1950s when I first saw him scrunch his big frame down behind an office typewriter and, not even breathing hard, start tapping out a story on deadline, captions and headlines included, at Gatling-gun tempo, all of it word-perfect the first time out. It was a nerveless performance, the journalistic equivalent of a high-wire front somersault without a net, especially dazzling to a stammering writer like myself, Queen of False Starts. Much later I learned that I was a kind of heroine of his. That was the time he called to say he hoped I wouldn't mind that he'd used me as a model for a character in his first novel, "suitably disguised," he hastened to assure me, "as a gorgeous, six-foot-tall, redheaded playwright." Come to think of it, it was the one time I can remember Tommy sounding nervous. I gave him my queenly permission.

Back in the glory-struck heyday of *Life* magazine—the 1950s and early 1960s—Tommy and I had worked side by side for a decade, star writers on the richest, biggest and best mass magazine in the world. It was a great adventure, a nonstop journalistic carnival, and while it was going on we tended to think of those times as our own best days as well. It was Tommy who had had the courage to jump ship first, an act most of the others on staff viewed as equal to leaping blindly from the first-class deck of the *Queen Mary;* and it was he who had encouraged me to jump next, and had held out his hand.

By that time, unknown to each other, both of our personal lives had begun to unravel. Whatever glorious voyage we were on must have seemed less than glorious to our spouses, and certainly it had stirred up the home lives of three young children—his two sons, my daughter. It was only long after our divorces were accomplished that Tommy and I could laugh about our early, painful days as single parents—the children's beach picnics we had organized, and the Thanksgiving and Christmas "family feasts" we had staged at Hollywood's most expensive restaurants. The three kids, rebelling against our softheaded sentimentality, usually behaved like unbearable brats, attacking where it hurt most: the tender guilt zone that lies below the belt line of every divorced parent. But the kids survived, and out of it all had grown a rock-sturdy devotion between Tommy and myself, mostly unspoken, but rooted nonetheless in the deep heart's core.

"I think I can probably win this fight," he was saying now on the telephone. "I certainly intend to give it my best shot. But whatever happens, Shana, I feel absolutely certain that you and I have *already* savored all the best things life can offer. We've been every place, we've seen every thing, we've covered all the best stories, and we've met the most interesting people of our times. We've had the most fun. How could life get any better than it's already been?"

Tommy's casual conversation that afternoon, I realized later, had been more carefully prepared than it appeared.

Tommy never read my book; I doubt he even got it. Liver cancer was already fighting him back. Three weeks later Tommy Thompson, 49, was dead.

It was five months after that before the promotion tour of my book brought me back to California. I telephoned Tommy's sons and suggested they come round to my hotel for lunch. An hour later, two young men filled my doorway, each one even taller and more rugged-looking than their father had been.

We went downstairs and ordered lunch in the familiar El Padrino Lounge, where Tommy and I had shared so many lunches long ago. The room was jammed, and when I remarked that the service seemed slower than it used to be, one of the boys said, "I'll go find out what's holding things up."

How like the father! I thought, as I watched the son extricate himself from our booth, politely but firmly shoulder his way past several startled waiters and busboys, and stride directly out into the hotel kitchens. When Tommy said *find out,* he meant that he would *personally* find out. He would go there himself, and ask questions, and look around. There was no place he feared to go, no question he was too respectful to ask, no gambit he hesitated to use to find out whatever he thought he needed to know. He was totally unselfconscious about this extreme directness—I remember my own astonishment at hearing Tommy inquire of a billionaire we had just met precisely how much money he had. Yet Tommy's manner, his charm, the utter sincerity of his wish and need to find the answer, and his persistence and energy and resourcefulness in digging for it had made him a reportorial force impossible to resist or long deceive.

His sons had the same easy manner, the same good-natured charm. I had not seen Kirk or Scott Thompson since their weedy, impossible teenager days; lunch was turning into a very agreeable surprise. Over coffee came a bigger surprise still. "We've been talking a lot lately about Dad's new book, the one he'd just started on before he died, and we've decided that you are the person Dad would have wanted us to turn over his notebooks to. He would have wanted you to be the one to write it."

Only the very young, and very loving, could ever be so certain what the dead "would have wanted," I thought, fumbling for my sunglasses.

Tommy Thompson was Fort Worth born and bred, the older son of a high school principal and a high school English teacher; his younger brother, Larry Thompson, became one of Houston's most capable trial lawyers. I don't know whether Tommy would have had the patience to study law. His taste was for speed, action, adventure, drama. He had put his talents, his energy and his great generosity into the service of taking the reader along.

He called himself a "born headline junkie," and recalled as a boy sitting on the family front porch before dawn waiting for the paperboy to arrive. He had started his own newspaper at eight; edited his high school newspaper even though he had to quit the football team to do it; majored in journalism at the University of Texas, graduated with honors in journalism in 1955, and become the star reporter on the Houston *Press* and the youngest city editor of a major daily in the country by the time he was twenty-three years old.

Then and later, Tommy was quite simply the best reporter anybody had ever seen. He was extremely surefooted, always racing and always setting new records. And, like every natural-born reporter, Tommy was eternally convinced that the story he had just stumbled upon was the best one yet.

One morning in the spring of 1982, in Las Vegas, where Tommy was then living in order to do research for his new novel, he had picked up the newspaper, at dawn as usual, and read about a murder case in nearby Salt Lake City. Nearly four years after the shooting down of a rich old man in a seedy old warehouse, two suspects finally had been arrested and charged. One was the victim's seventeen-year-old grandson. His accomplice was his mother, "a Manhattan socialite." She was still in New York City, fighting extradition. The boy was in custody in Utah, where his trial was about to begin.

Thompson put down the newspaper, picked up the phone, and reserved a seat on a flight to Salt Lake. Then he called his publisher in New York and said that, with the publisher's permission, he was temporarily putting aside his new novel in favor of what he knew best: true-life crime stories. Yes, he was sure he had just found the best one yet.

When Tommy found the news item in the paper about the upcoming trial, he not only knew he had to write a book about it, he knew the title: *Mama's Boy.* Tommy was right. That was the best possible title for what the story then appeared to be. But many things have happened since. Two months after the first trial, perhaps sooner, illness forced Tommy to stop work. More than a year passed before the story's climactic trial. There would turn out to be three of them. The third one was Mama's own.

By then the story had not just moved forward and expanded, it had changed shape. Its color and texture were different. The focus had altered. And so the present book is not a continuation of Tommy's book. *Nutcracker* is my book, reported and written by me alone, in my way, in accordance with my particular interests. But it could never have come about without Tommy's interests, Tommy's instincts, Tommy's love and counsel and example over more than twenty years; without the confidence and tact and skill of Tommy's family, his friends and publishing associates. Most important, part of the work is built on a solid foundation of Tommy Thompson's original notes.

These arrived on my doorstep one morning in early summer, 1983, firmly tied up with tape in several directions in an accordion-pleated lawyer's file. Inside it were all of Tommy's trial

notes, and a score of individual interviews typed up by Tommy
on his beat-up Olivetti the night of whatever day he wrote them
down. Later, when I had an opportunity to compare his typed
notes with the trial transcript, I realized that Tommy's extraordinary aquamarine eyes had not missed a single legal curlicue in
some exceedingly strange legal proceedings.

Engrossing though it was, the story seemed maddeningly incomplete. Yet, as soon as I had untied the file and begun to read,
Tommy had me back where he kept all his readers: in his lap,
held there securely for as long as it might take him to tell the tale.
He had had millions of us as readers, and a very few fortunate
ones of us had him as a friend. Now I felt triply bound to him: as
a reader, as a friend, and as a sort of trustee. As time passed and I
dug deeper into the story, I came to feel like Scheherazade. Tell
us a story, he'd said, handing me the opening pages.

Before I do that, I want to add a word about my own working
methods. In August 1983 I wrote to the "Manhattan socialite,"
Frances Schreuder. I told her that I had agreed with a publisher
to write a book about her and her family, and had begun work. I
said that I'd be in court in Utah the next month when her trial
began, and requested a meeting beforehand. The book would be
my third attempt to describe in full what happens when someone
gets caught in the public eye while at the same time embroiled in
that clanking, overworked, unpredictable machinery we call "the
criminal justice system."

I did not expect my letter to result in a publishable interview.
Like the subjects of the previous books, Patty Hearst and Jean
Harris, she was a criminal defendant on the eve of trial. I wanted
her, and her lawyers, to know my own ground rules for undertak-
ing projects of this kind. Under separate cover I sent her a copy
of my last book, and settled down to await a reply. Eventually the
certified and registered letter was returned unopened. I don't
know what happened to the book.

But on my first day in Salt Lake City I got an opportunity to
declare my intentions to her eighty-year-old mother, Berenice
Bradshaw. Thanks to Thompson's notes, I had recognized her
sitting in the courtroom during pretrial hearings, and that evening I found her in the phone book. She invited me to come right
over. It turned out she had admired both Tommy's books and my
own, and had even sent her daughter a copy of my latest one.
Could this be the reason I felt so drawn to this sprightly old

woman? I don't think so, but I mention it now in view of the way things turned out later.

An honest book about a real person pleading Not Guilty to a real crime can only work one way, I explained to her: *It must be my book, not yours, not your daughter's, so no agreements in advance, no payments, no promises of any kind. I hope you will cooperate, because that will probably make it a better book, and it will certainly make my own job easier. But I intend to write the book either way.* At this point I usually remind the almost certainly hostile lawyers and clients that people are powerfully attracted to certain true-life crime stories, and books about the case are inevitable. I will try very hard to understand what happened, and get the story straight. So she can cooperate, in hopes of making the inevitable better, more accurate, more comprehensible—or she can stonewall. Since I find this hard-nosed approach impossible to carry off in person, I normally resort to doing so by letter. But in Berenice Bradshaw's case, that was not necessary. This lively lady could scarcely wait to tell me about herself, her family, her troubles, and to introduce me to as many of her lawyers as possible.

We spent much of the next two weeks together, while her daughter's lawyers were making pretrial motions and a jury was being selected. Quite properly, the press was barred from these *voir dire* proceedings. By the time the lawyers had picked a jury, Berenice Bradshaw had told me the story of her life, given me her own and her husband's "autobiographies" to read, shown me her house, her family photo albums, taken me on a picnic and tour of her old neighborhood, and invited me to a Sunday brunch she was giving for her lawyers and their wives on the eve of trial.

The morning her trial began, Frances Schreuder pressed a crumpled note into my hand: *"Confidential. Please tell NO ONE. I am in room #501 at the Marriott Hotel. You must understand what I'm suffering. Where can you be reached?"* She was registered at the hotel under an assumed name. I called her that afternoon. As she requested, I told no one, including her mother. We spoke several more times by phone but could not meet while her trial was in progress. She mistrusted her lawyers, she said, and feared their disapproval. Every day after court during the seven-day trial I called her mother. As a potential witness, Mrs. Bradshaw was barred from the courtroom, and was avid for a running account of the struggle taking place behind Judge Baldwin's locked doors. After the verdict, Frances Schreuder invited me to her locked hotel room where we spent one very long afternoon together.

Eventually I was able personally to interview at length almost all of the people who appear in this book. With the exception of Frances Schreuder's young daughter, all names are real. Many valuable sources, however, talked to me on condition that their names not appear. Some were being protective of themselves or others; some were fearful of retribution. In all, more than three hundred people helped me to accumulate the information that appears in these pages. Understandably, a number preferred to speak anonymously, and I must thank them in like fashion.

Of the others, I must thank first my tireless and caring editors, Sam Vaughan and Jim Moser, and my literary agents and dear friends Joy Harris and Robbie Lantz: without the unflagging support and various navigational skills of these four people, this book could not have come about. Invaluable expert help was rendered to me by Alec Dubro, Dr. Erika Freeman, the Honorable Betty Friedlander, Abraham Halpern, M.D., Betty Prashker, Richard Stolley. Great assistance was received from Ann and Fred Hart and Jean Smart. There would quite literally be no manuscript without the many meticulous professional attentions of Millie Becerra and Kathy Alexander, my ever brave and honest first reader. The unflagging encouragement I received along the way from Maya Angelou, Ann Bronfman, Richard Craig, Gloria Jones, Mary and John Lindsay, Kennett Love, and Jean Harris was a source of continual wonder and nurturance. Most of all, I thank Eleanora and Michael Kennedy and Laurel and Wray Bentley for assistance personal and professional beyond measure.

The past two years of researching and writing have been variously a trial, an adventure, a workout, and what is called on talk shows a "growth experience." Endings are always harder than beginnings. Getting out of something is always harder than getting in. The only way out of this one for me was to write my way out.

So here it all is, Tommy: The story of Mama's boy, *and* of Mama. And of her other children, and of her parents, Granny Bradshaw and Gramps, and of the Bradshaws' other children, and of all the friends and enemies, cops and judges, psychiatrists and lawyers—more than forty of those—who play a part in the tale.

Part One

Overtures

. . . THE GREAT GOLD HALL ablaze with lights, the red velvet seats alive with children . . . rows and rows of children's faces, all upturned, a Christmas candy box of nougats, cherries, caramels, peppermint creams, and almost all of them the shining, scrubbed faces of little girls . . . delectable would-be ballerinas, brushed and shining and trembling. For one month every year during the holiday season, such is the impression looking down from the balcony into the orchestra section of the New York State Theater at Lincoln Center when, night after night and every matinee, the New York City Ballet puts on its Christmas classic, *The Nutcracker.*

Lights darken, noises dim, Tschaikovsky's overture pours fourth in creamy swirls of sound, audible Nesselrode. The gold curtain pleats upward in damask swags to reveal a gay party in nineteenth-century Germany—mothers in hoopskirts, dashing, mustached papas, daughters in ball dresses, little boys in velvet suits—all rushing happily about the stage, bowing, curtsying, whirling with glee.

A crooked old man enters, leaning on a stick. The children flock around him. He is Herr Drosselmeier, and he has brought to the party with him a very special Christmas gift, a magic nutcracker. Soon he will tell them a story about it, an elaborate and cracked tale first penned by E. T. A. Hoffman: that is his nutcracker suite. But first he distributes nuts, real nuts, to the eager children. In the Balanchine staging, a restaging of the master's own dream of magical childhood, seven tiny girls in mauve pantaloons cluster around the old man's knees. In fact they are seven infant ballerinas, rigorously chosen, the *crème de la crème* of very young students at the ballet school which trains many of the dancers who will one day join the Company's *corps de ballet,* one of the best the world has known.

The seven child ballerinas tease, plead, twirl, cajole. The candy box of audience children holds its sweet breath. To which one of

the seven will Herr Drosselmeier present his very first nut? The
child ballerinas themselves do not know. Indeed, they have made
it a game, a very secret game, just between themselves and the
gnarled old man. *Which one will he choose tonight?* they wonder
as they dart enchantingly about. Lately, though, the game has
gone flat. Lately he always chooses the same dancer. He always
gives the first nut to the tiniest one of them all. She is a grave
child who never smiles. She is eight years old. Her name is Ariadne.

. . . AT SIX FORTY-FIVE Sunday morning, Berenice Bradshaw heard the ancient Ford pickup cough and gargle in the
driveway and knew her husband was leaving for work. Mrs.
Bradshaw was seventy-five years old, and slightly deaf. She did
not actually hear the old man leave his small room just across the
hall from her own, or run his tepid bath. She did not hear him do
his thirty-one pushups, or stir up his breakfast of oatmeal with
evaporated milk, or hack off and brown-bag the chunk of her
meat loaf that would become his lunch. But she knew he had
done each of these things. The Bradshaws had moved into the
bungalow on South Gilmer Drive one April day in 1937, and
every single morning since then Franklin Bradshaw had followed
precisely the same routine, Saturday and Sunday mornings included: 15,055 tepid baths, 15,055 pots of oatmeal.

Franklin Bradshaw would not return home from the disheveled old Bradshaw Auto Parts warehouse, hard by the Union
Pacific railroad tracks, until after nine o'clock. Time was when he
did not get home from work until ten or eleven or even midnight,
but he was seventy-six now, and lacked the energy he once had.
By the time he came home she would have eaten supper and be
down in her small split-level basement office, pasting snapshots
into her photograph albums or working on her genealogy charts.
He would warm up his own supper: more meat loaf, which she
had prepared for him during the day, and Jell-O with fruit, and
perhaps a homemade bran muffin. While he ate, he would read
his newspaper. 15,055 copies of the Salt Lake City *Tribune*.

Weekdays or weekends, year in and year out, the routine never
varied. So on this particular Sunday morning, July 23, 1978, when
she heard Franklin's old blue Courier truck starting up, Berenice
Bradshaw did what she had done on so many other identical
Sundays: she rolled over and went briefly back to sleep. At 8:30
A.M. Mrs. Bradshaw got up and went down to the basement to
awaken her seventeen-year-old grandson Larry, who was spend-

ing the summer with his grandparents. She warned him not to be late for his ten-thirty flying lesson out at Skyhawk Aviation, near the Great Salt Lake. Larry was never easy to awaken, and this morning it took longer than usual. Larry had worked at the warehouse with his grandfather the evening before, the only time this summer the boy had set foot down there. The rambunctious Schreuder grandsons, Larry and his brother Marc, were not popular with the other employees. Last year, after the two sixteen-year-olds had spent the summer working at Bradshaw's, some employees had threatened to quit. That was why this summer Granny Bradshaw was paying $3,500 for Larry to take flying lessons instead.

A few minutes past ten o'clock Mrs. Bradshaw's doorbell rang. On her front porch was a police officer accompanied by a Mormon elder and Doug Steele, manager of Bradshaw Auto Parts and her husband's oldest friend. She asked them in and the elder told her to sit down. He knelt down beside her. "We hate to do this, Berenice," he said. "We've had a tragic accident. It concerns your husband . . ."

"I don't understand." She turned to Doug Steele. "What's he trying to say, Doug?"

"Berenice, Frank's been shot. He's been killed."

"Oh, my God! My God!"

"Now, help us out, Berenice. I know you've got some tranquilizers around here. Where are they?" Steele brought the pills and some water and Mrs. Bradshaw calmed down somewhat and the policeman said it looked like a robbery. The cash register was open, Frank's wallet and some coins and credit cards were scattered on the floor.

"What'll we do, Doug? What'll we do?"

The grizzled manager put his arm around her heaving shoulders. "We have to reach out for the family now, Berenice. Get hold of the girls."

All day long Mrs. Bradshaw, assisted by her grandson, tried to reach her three married daughters, two in New York City and one in Oregon. But this was July and a Sunday. Nobody was at home. It would be past midnight before she spoke to them all.

At 5:45 P.M. Mrs. Bradshaw and Larry went down to the Hall of Justice to give their statements to the police. No gun had been found, they were told, and there were no witnesses, no clues of any kind. The old man had been ambushed, shot in the back. It could have been anyone.

"I believe in capital punishment, so help me," Mrs. Bradshaw said. The widow answered all the police officers' questions. She told them her daughters' names and addresses. She described her husband's work habits, his business, his employees, "all very, very fine . . . wonderful men . . ."

They asked about her husband's will. She had not yet had time to look for it, she said. "Nothing but callers and phones all day." But she thought a copy was somewhere in her basement files. "I've seen it . . . but my family didn't like it, and he didn't like it. And so it is still there, but nobody likes it."

"Was your husband a rich man?"

"He told me we were poor."

The murdered man was far from poor. Bradshaw was by training a geologist who in 1929 had been shrewd enough to go into the auto parts business at the dawn of the cross-country motoring era, and to set up shop at the edge of the worst stretch of automotive badlands between the Atlantic and the Pacific. One store soon became a chain, and the stores pulled in a small river of cash. Bradshaw was determined to sequester every dime from the hated Bureau of Internal Revenue. Over the years his money had been quietly and extremely wisely invested, and reinvested—first in the stock market and in the successful chemicals company he founded, but finally and most extensively in federal oil and gas leases on the public lands which constitute seventy percent of the state of Utah. When he had leased as much land as the law permits a single individual to hold in a single state, 200,000 acres, he branched out to other states. Slowly, and almost invisibly, Bradshaw built up a one-man archipelago of oil and gas rights that spanned every state between the Mississippi River and Hawaii. Because of the 200,000-acre limit, the leases were held not just in his own name but in the names of his wife, his children, his grandchildren. It had all been done in a very low-key manner, and by the time of his murder the old man owned twenty-eight automotive stores and unknown millions of acres of oil land. Single-handedly, he had accumulated the largest estate ever probated by the state of Utah. His net worth was estimated by the Salt Lake City *Tribune* to be at least $60 million, and some knowledgeable sources said that, when all was counted, the figure could exceed $400 million.

. . . THE FUNERAL could not be scheduled until noon on
Wednesday. The day after the murder, Monday, July 24, was
Pioneer Day, the biggest holiday on the Mormon calendar. It
commemorates the arrival of the Mormons, after years of hardship and persecution, in Zion, the Promised Land, and on that
day the entire city shuts down so the Latter-day Saints can attend
the big LDS parade up Main Street to the Mormon Temple.

One of the handful of people to go to work on Pioneer Day was
Dr. Serge Moore, Medical Examiner of the State of Utah. He
commenced his autopsy of Frank Bradshaw at nine o'clock Monday morning and finished about two hours later. The old man
had been shot twice, both times at fairly close range. One bullet
had entered the middle of his upper back, the other the base of
his skull. Either would have been fatal. The killer had used
hollow-point, copper-jacketed Remington-Peters ammunition—
bullets whose copper-sheathed nose peels back on impact into
equal segments, like a lily.

The damage was fearful. The back of the skull and brains had
been blown away. Police photographs of the scene, which the
surgeon kept beside him for orientation as he worked, were almost surreal. On a worn and dirty floor, a skinny old man lay on
his back in an attitude of terror. A penumbra of bright blood
haloed his head and shoulders. His mouth was stretched wide in
its final scream. His lower plate had come loose and dangled in
the mouth opening. The eyes, also open, were wild. The arms
were upflung in surprise or fright, but the open palms bracketing
the gaunt gray face at ear level were in an attitude of benediction,
and long strands of gray-white hair floated out across the surface
of the crimson puddle. The agitated, red-edged figure resembled a
sixteenth-century cardinal painted by El Greco.

But the portrait's ecclesiastical quality stopped abruptly at
shoulder level. The body on the dusty floor was dressed in a
ragged orange polo shirt with penguins on it, and cheap black-
and-white-checked trousers. The front pockets had been pulled
inside out. From the neck down it looked as if some elderly dere-
lict had wandered into camera range, collapsed, and died.

Dr. Moore sealed the two bullets into plastic bags to turn over
to Homicide, cleaned up, and went home to get ready for the big
parade.

. . . WEDNESDAY JULY 26 broke bright blue and blazing, another furnace-like day of desert heat baking the high Wasatch Valley. By eleven o'clock, an hour before the service, the large parking lot at Eastman's Evans & Early mortuary, finest in town, was completely filled with the kind of sturdy, Detroit-built automobiles favored by Frank Bradshaw's relatives, friends and employees. These people, and their children, now sat sweltering and quietly fanning themselves on rows of pale blue folding chairs. For the first time any of them could remember, Bradshaw Auto Parts was closed in the daytime.

As more and more mourners arrived and overflowed the main chapel, attendants seated them in a backup funeral parlor where they could at least hear the service over loudspeakers. Even the first arrivals, in the main chapel, had nothing much to look at— no casket, no altar, just the stiff floral tributes massed at the front of the long, blue room, and a small wooden lectern. When it was time to begin, the immediate family members would be seated in a blue-draped semiprivate niche off to the left, shielded from the larger public view. Organ music played softly.

Marilyn Bradshaw Reagan, the eldest daughter, had planned her father's memorial service, reviewing with the undertakers the many available options, choosing the details she and her mother preferred, always mindful of certain tensions within the larger family. The Bradshaws are an honored Mormon dynasty. Franklin Bradshaw was one of the ten children born to John Franklin and Emma Briggs Bradshaw between 1880 and 1910. The family homestead was in Lehi, a pioneer Mormon settlement a few miles south of Salt Lake City, and from there Bradshaw uncles and cousins had prospered and branched out variously in banking, real estate, insurance, and farming.

As the youngest and last surviving brother, Franklin had inherited the position of family patriarch. But Frank was not much like his churchly, conservative brothers. He rarely attended family weddings or funerals, let alone regular Sunday services. He did not wear holy undergarments. Certainly Frank Bradshaw did not tithe ten percent of his earnings to the church. He was in fact known as something of a tightwad, a man who toured his auto parts empire by Greyhound Bus, a man who preferred to reoutfit himself, when it became absolutely necessary, at the Army-Navy store.

It is questionable whether he believed in the beautiful life eternal, life everlasting, which is the foundation of the Mormon faith. His wife Berenice said not; that he had just pretended to go along in order to keep peace within the devout Bradshaw clan. Bertha Beck, his deeply pious baby sister, said she knew better. "He told me he looked forward to meeting Mother again!" she huffed.

Certainly Franklin Bradshaw would have approved his wife and daughter's decision to have him cremated, that being both the most efficient and cheapest way to deal with an autopsied corpse. But the choice was viewed with disfavor by the Bradshaws. The entire edifice of the Latter-day Saints' belief rests on the certitude of a Second Coming, and as daughter Marilyn said later, "Whereas you don't *have* to have a body to come back to, it's considered definitely better if you do."

Most of the delicate problems in planning his memorial stemmed from the fact that Frank Bradshaw had married outside his faith. Idaho-born Berenice Jewett Bradshaw was regarded by the Bradshaws as a gentile—the Mormon term for all non-Mormons. Her husband's family, though always polite, had never fully accepted her. Berenice, serene and proud in the knowledge that her own ancestors were Huguenots, and that she was a direct descendant of Maximilian Jewett, a Yorkshireman who had settled in Rowley, Massachusetts, in 1638, did not particularly care what the Bradshaws thought of her. Her outspoken scorn for their religious views made that clear. "They believe the sky up there is all full of little invisible angels!" she would hoot. But she had bitterly resented the semiostracism accorded her children when they were growing up in Utah. To punish small children for their mother's intransigence was unfair and cruel.

It was nearly noon. Marilyn Reagan waited with her mother and two sisters in the stuffy family anteroom. On the whole, she was pleased with the way things were going. The ivory-colored programs had been nicely printed up, and the hired soloist would sing her mother's two favorite hymns. Berenice had studied voice before her marriage, and her children often heard her singing and accompanying herself on the family upright: "Oh, I come to the garden alone, While the dew is still on the ro-oses . . . And He walks with me, and He talks with me, and He tells me I am His own . . ."

But all that was long past. Franklin and Berenice Bradshaw had had four children. The firstborn, Robert, had died twelve years ago, and long before that his three sisters had scattered to

lead their own lives. Even the old parlor piano was long gone
. . . After the hymn, Marilyn had asked her father's kindly
cousin Wayne Hacking to be the first speaker, followed by Franklin's handsome young nephew, Craig Bradshaw. When Craig was
finished, the soloist would sing "Going Home," and then the
bereaved family would hasten back to Gilmer Drive to receive
the numerous condolence callers who were expected. Aunt Bertha Beck was at the house now. She had volunteered to stay
behind to answer phone calls and set out the many platters of
food. Aunt Bertha didn't mind missing the funeral. She already
felt very close to God, and to her brother Franklin. She certainly
didn't need any memorial service to remind her of either one.

All of the roast meats, salads, casseroles, pies, cakes, cookies
and punch had been contributed by the dead man's employees
and their families, more than one hundred and fifty people. They
had asked to do this as a way of expressing and dealing with their
own grief. Working for the old man had been like being part of a
big family, and many employees had been with him more than
twenty years, some more than thirty. Frank did not pay much,
but he always had time to listen to their problems. He found
summer jobs for the kids who needed them, and pregnant women
knew that whenever they were ready to come back to work,
Frank would have held a place for them. As they sliced and
kneaded and basted and garnished his funerary foods, many wondered what the boss's home would look like. Since none of the
Bradshaw daughters had been married at home and the Bradshaws did not entertain, it was going to be the first social event at
Gilmer Drive that anybody could recall.

The organ music reached a crescendo, died away, revived
again—the signal that the service was about to begin. Lynx-eyed
Craig Bradshaw looked like one of the unflappable Mormon
males who are often used by the Secret Service to guard the
President. But right now Craig was uneasy. His Uncle Frank had
always told him, "Craig, remember that the most important
thing in life is your family." Yet when he had dropped over yesterday to Gilmer Drive to pick up some pointers from Frank's
family on how they would like to hear him eulogized, they had
mentioned everything *but* what a good husband and father he
had been. That subject, they had made clear, was just as well
avoided.

A side door in the blue niche opened silently. Frank's immedi-

ate family was coming in now, the women first, the men following, and all of them walking as stiffly as playing-card figures.
Leaning forward slightly, Craig could see them from his front-
row seat.

Frances, the youngest daughter, entered first. She was forty
years old, with a stocky, boyish body, dark hair, intense eyes, and
a Lily Tomlin face. Yesterday, meeting her for the first time ever,
he had found her "striking-looking, but not attractive." Today he
could not see her features, but thought her oddly dressed. She
was clothed head to toe in black. "Even a hat!" he would say
later. "With a *big veil,* and long black gloves. *We* just don't do
that. I don't mean LDS. I mean *Utah people* don't do that."

Mrs. Bradshaw came in next. Craig was glad to see Berenice
"looking okay." Bright blue sunglasses hid her eyes. But her
curly gray hair was freshly waved, and her heart-shaped face
composed and impassive. Then Craig noticed her hands. Her grip
on Frances's black-gloved fingers was so tight that the old lady's
freckled, suntanned hands were milk-white at the knuckles.

Elaine Drukman, the middle sister, was truly petite, by far the
smallest of the four women now seated in the front row. She was
also the only daughter who resembled her mother. She had the
same in-the-bone prettiness, and tightly curled Orphan Annie
hair. But she looked worn, even weatherbeaten, compared to the
older woman.

Marilyn Reagan was amply proportioned, moon-faced, and be-
spectacled. Not so much as baby Frances, but more than middle
sister Elaine, Marilyn bore the family's genetic hallmark, the
powerful, slablike Bradshaw jaw. She reminded Craig of a kindly
head nurse, and he thought it a great pity that Marilyn was childless. She seemed to him to be the warmest and most motherly of
the four women. Craig had no idea how carefully Marilyn Reagan had prepared herself for the inevitable day of her father's
death, no idea of her years of daytime work as a paralegal specialist in wills and estates, no idea of her twelve years of night-school
study of inheritance tax law, no idea of her long, quiet campaign
to be named executor of her father's estate and one day to replace
him as owner-manager of the Bradshaw empire.

In the second row of the niche, behind the four bereaved
women, sat the men—a son-in-law and three of the four grandsons. The man was Elaine's husband, Mason Drukman, a slender, high-domed, good-looking Oregon professor of political sci-

ence. He sat squeezed between his two hulking, bushy-haired sons, Sam and Max Drukman, ages twenty and sixteen. Marilyn's husband, Robert Reagan, was not present. He was a lawyer employed by New York City to work on family court cases, and had felt compelled to remain behind in New York City.

Frances Schreuder, the youngest daughter, had no husband; she was twice divorced. Her first husband had been Vittorio Gentile, an Italian-born pearl importer and the father of her two teenage sons, Lorenzo and Marco, now known as Larry and Marc. Larry was here today, seated with his two Drukman cousins. Like them, he was dark-haired and powerfully built, but large, staring blue eyes gave his face a softer aspect. Again, there was no mistaking the famous Bradshaw jaw. Marc had been asked to stay home in New York City and look after his baby sister.

Frances's second husband, Frederik Schreuder, had been Dutch. Several years after their divorce he perished in a plane crash. But he had given Frances a daughter who was the jewel of her existence, her reason for living. The child was the greatest joy of Berenice Bradshaw's life as well—her first and only granddaughter. The little girl was now barely five years old, far too young for funerals, so Frances had left her at home in the care of her half-brother, Marc. Her name was Ariadne.

Cousin Wayne had finished speaking. It was Craig's turn. "I have heard it said that each of us, as we walk through the sands of time, leaves some kind of mark," he began.

Five minutes later he was reading the Twenty-third Psalm, all six verses, and then it was over. Out in the sweltering parking lot, Craig noticed Frances Schreuder one more time. Cousin Wayne was holding tight to her black-gloved hands and telling her how very much she reminded him of her dear, dead father. He could not see her face, but from under her black cloud of veil, mascara flowed like lava down her ashen cheeks.

1985

. . . UTAH IS UNIQUE among the fifty states. It is literally a church-state, a theocracy inside a democracy, and Salt Lake City —heart of the church-state—is a holy city just as Mecca is. Understanding this is key to understanding what happened to Franklin Bradshaw, happened both before and after the old man was found lying dead on the floor of his warehouse with two bullet holes in his back.

In Utah, the American melting pot is unstirred. Three out of four people are Mormons, and they are all here in this bleakly beautiful sanctuary "behind the Zion Curtain" because of religious persecution. For a nation that boasts it was founded on principles of religious freedom, the treatment of the Mormons has been harsh indeed. Only African slaves and native Americans fared worse. Before they reached their Promised Land, the Saints were tarred and feathered, lynched, massacred. They were hounded and mercilessly ridiculed by fellow Americans from the same Nordic and Anglo-Saxon Protestant backgrounds, from the same families, the same blood. The memory lingers. Xenophobia is endemic here.

But Mormonism is more than a religion. "To get the feel of what the Mormon church is all about, you have to see the Mormon church not as a church in the ordinary sense at all, but as a *society*—a society and a culture that is *built around religion.*"*

The society and culture that has evolved behind the Zion Curtain is not just unique among religions of the earth, it is uniquely American. What other nation could support a faith at once so fundamentalist and so optimistic as to preach eternal life, eternal marriage, eternal chastity and—fortunate under the circumstances—eternal upward mobility?

---

* University of Utah history professor Sterling McMurrin, dean of Mormon intellectuals and former U.S. Commissioner of Education, quoted in the Denver *Post* Special Report, "Utah: The Church State," Nov. 21–28, 1982.

The first revelation came to the young farm boy Joseph Smith in 1820, when God and Jesus spoke to him in a grove of trees outside his home town of Palmyra, New York. Two years later the Angel Moroni appeared in his bedroom, and led him to the hill of Cumorah where he found hidden a Bible made of solid gold plates—the Book of Mormon. Here too the angel gave him the magical stone spectacles, the Urim and Thummim, which enabled Smith to read and to translate the plates' "reformed Egyptian" hieroglyphics into English. They told the wondrous story of a band of Hebrews who, in 600 B.C., had made their way to the New World and become the aboriginal forebears of the American Indians. After Christ's crucifixion He had visited His American flock, and He now promised Joseph Smith that if the people would return to the simple gospel ways of the early Christians, God would return once more and guide His flock with divine revelations here in the latter days.

The spectacles disappeared, but Smith translated further revelations by staring at a magic "seer stone" he held hidden in his hat while scribes on the other side of a blanket wrote down what the young prophet said. Smith's original Mormon doctrines were modified by later prophets, in particular Brigham Young, and zealous missionary work began.

The new faith scrapped the concept of original sin and replaced it with the more American idea of man's eternal perfectibility. "As man is, God once was, and as God is, man may become." Hence divinity is progressive. Gods, angels, and men have progressed to different levels. God Himself—Themselves?—was once a man; Jesus is a kind of older brother. (Devils exist too. They are rebellious spirits, cast out for all eternity. Eternal vigilance is essential since a hundred devils exist for every living man, woman, and child.)

The Mormon belief system unites curiously American pairs of opposites. A relish for the dog-eat-dog practices of the marketplace goes hand in hand with the stern obligation to "Help thy neighbor." Saints do more than tithe at least ten percent of their income; they entirely look after their own. No Mormon need worry about food, housing, or medical care. The Mormon belief in the sanctity of the family coexists side by side with the Mormon doctrine of blood atonement: certain crimes—adultery, apostasy, murder—are so evil they can be paid for only by the shedding of the sinner's own blood.

Once one accepts the notion that the soul never dies, and that even the dead may be baptized and thereby forever saved, it becomes urgent to find out who one's ancestors are. *All* one's ancestors. Theoretically, at least, it should be possible to trace them back to Adam and Eve. Mass proxy baptisms of the dead take place regularly in the subterranean baptismal fonts, borne on the backs of twelve oxen, that are housed in the basement of every Mormon temple. By 1984 the church had built forty-seven temples around the world, including twenty-two in the United States, seven in Utah.

The urge to locate these ancestral legions of literal "lost souls" has made the Mormons into fanatic genealogists. The Salt Lake City skyline is dominated by two structures. One is the Mormon Temple, which shares a huge, ten-acre-square block amid lavish gardens with the glitter-domed auditorium of the Mormon Tabernacle Choir. This Temple is the symbolic heart of the entire church and, like all Mormon temples, entirely off limits to Gentiles. It is a structure to make pharaohs weep—huge, six-spired, fantastically turreted and built of deeply crenellated black stone. Its finial is a giant gold-leafed statue of the Angel Moroni blowing his heavenly trumpet out across majestic, snow-capped peaks.

The other building, a towering white marble skyscraper, is open to all. This is the World Center for Ancestors, an ever expanding genealogical library with the capability of listing on microfiche the name of every person who ever lived on this planet. Well over a billion names already are on file here. Carloads of new, or rather old, birth and baptismal records collected by the faithful from churches and town halls around the world arrive daily. Library visitors are taught how to look up and record their own family trees, using the library's five hundred microfilm reading machines available for public use. Mormonism is at once newfangled and extremely archaic, a form of computer-aided ancestor worship in modern, polyester dress.

In Mormon society and culture, highest values are placed on hard work, thrift, clean living, obedience to the elders and, above all, on the importance of the family. The best-known Church rubric is "No Success Can Compensate for Failure in the Home." Mormons perceive the family as a quasi-sacred entity which must be protected from the evils of society. Good for the family are plenty of group work, group play, and plenty of (marital) sex. Music and dancing are also good, and Salt Lake has long been renowned as a cradle of American ballet and symphonic arts, as well as for its Mormon Tabernacle Choir. Bad for the family in equal measure, and regularly denounced from the pulpit, are premarital sex, abortion, the Equal Rights Amendment, homosexuality, pornography, and women who work outside the home. These attitudes have given Utah a divorce rate only one third the national average, and a birth rate double the norm.

Mormonism is a male religion, a dream of prophets and patriarchs. The Saints are organized according to strict patriarchal principles, and sternly watched over by white-bearded elders who have renounced polygamy relatively recently, for reasons less doctrinal than political—not because polygamy is intrinsically such a bad idea, and perhaps it is not; but because the federal government declared it illegal. Still, it might be remembered that once you renounce monogamy, eternal chastity in marriage is a less drastic idea.

Joseph Smith declared Blacks the children of Cain, "cursed by God," and, until 1978, any trace of Negro blood made one ineligible for the Mormon priesthood. Women still are ineligible. Women and Blacks aside, the religion is extremely democratic. Any male convert over age twelve has a chance not just to enter the priesthood, but to better himself spiritually, to progress through this life and the next until he actually reaches the status of a god himself. What the faith offers his eternal wife—formerly read "wives"—beyond the attractions of *being* a god's wife, is not spelled out. Finally, as in every male tribal group, be they Mormons, Masons, college fraternity brothers, or cannibals in New Guinea, the church has plenty of secret rites and closed doors—the whole mumbo jumbo of Keeping Others Out. Secrecy is never so appealing as in a free society.

One last thought: In a society and culture devised by old men sealed for eternity into marital chastity, even *serial* marital chastity, the essential male-female bond may remain the one between husband and wife. But the essential male-female *tension,* the trilling wire in the blood, becomes the one between Susannah and the elders, between father and daughter.

. . . ÏT IS MORE THAN five years after Franklin J. Bradshaw's death. At long last the murderer has been found, tried, and convicted.

"No clues," the cops had said the day it happened. There *were* clues, but not the kind police usually look for. The clues were hidden within the dead man's family. To a degree they had been covered up *by* the family. Franklin Bradshaw's family—as utterly, achingly ordinary a family as one can imagine—would appear to have nurtured at least one, and possibly two, or maybe even three criminal psychopaths: a mother and her two sons.

The mother's trial is to begin today, Tuesday, September 6, 1983. The sons already have been sent to prison, one of them for murder, one for attempted murder. Having convicted one son of the crime, the State now contends it can prove that it was his mother who forced him do it. Her motive was money. She feared her father was about to cut her out of his will.

The defense will challenge the State to prove its appalling contention. It will assert that this mother, far from being her son's accomplice, is the innocent victim of a monstrous family frameup. It will portray her son as a kid vicious enough to shoot his grandfather in the back, then rifle his pockets; a boy so evil that when finally cornered, he would attempt to lessen his punishment by blaming his own mother.

The proceedings will finally get under way at nine o'clock, the morning after Labor Day. It is the first day of school, and eastern visitors out walking down Main Street early on this bright morning, away from the Mormon Temple and toward the Hall of Justice, are struck by the extraordinary numbers of children on the streets. Shoals of children, mostly blond, flow along the avenues, the smaller ones in arms, in strollers, or toddling behind very young, hand-holding parents. Brigham Young had begun laying out his city of Zion on the very day of his arrival here, and the major thoroughfares are eight lanes wide, that being the space required for an oxcart to make a U-turn. Oxen, unlike horses, cannot be taught to back up.

Salt Lake City is acutely aware of its origins, and breathtaking in its setting—a long, green ribbon of valley between barren deserts at the foot of mighty mountains beside the Great Salt Lake. Numerous monuments decorate the broad intersections on the promenade between the temple and the courthouse. One bronze tableau depicts an entire Mormon family pushing a hand-cart across the plains. There are huge statues of honeybees, and sea gulls, creatures which became part of Mormon iconography by helping the first families of settlers to survive in the wilderness. Most memorable are the many idealized sculptures of boys and girls in stone and stucco and marble and bronze; so many children abound that the visitor half expects to come upon the Pied Piper somewhere up ahead. But at the end of the line of statuary, at the foot of the courthouse steps, there is only a grim reminder erected by the Elks Club, the one unsentimental monument in view: a polished granite scroll with the Ten Commandments deeply incised in black stone.

The Criminal Courts Building is a standard postwar municipal structure of landscaped glass and concrete, cozy as an airport. The third-floor courtroom is small, round, windowless, bright blue, and air-conditioned to bone-chilling temperatures.

The most interesting-looking man in the room is Mike Rosen, chief defense attorney. He has a deep tan, pale hair, perfect teeth, gorgeous profile, stocky body, cocky air, and a strong Brooklyn accent. He is from the New York law firm of Saxe, Bacon & Bolan, headed by the brutally powerful Roy Cohn. Cohn himself will not appear. He never does. He *always* works behind the scenes. How or whether he will manage this in Utah is unknown. So far, the Cohn office has unspooled a creative series of delaying tactics which has stalled the proceedings against its client for over a year, not an inconsequential achievement in a case wherein the victim, his wife, his cronies, friends, and enemies had all attained the biblical age of three-score years and ten.

As the trial begins, no one really knows how strong a case the prosecution has. The prosecutor himself is not sure. His two key witnesses have been granted full immunity in return for their testimony, a circumstance which will allow the defense to make much of the issue of "reasonable doubt."

The strongest corroborating witness against Frances Schreuder could be one of her sons—both their names are listed among the more than fifty potential prosecution witnesses—unless it can be shown that the son is also an accomplice. The law does not permit one accomplice to corroborate another.

The slim old lady sitting alone over there, smartly dressed in navy blue dotted swiss, hiding her face behind big blue sunglasses —surely she must be the defendant's mother. Berenice Bradshaw is a Mom cut from the lid of a Mother's Day candy box. She is eighty years old, and when she first stands up she lists slightly, and shuffles more than she walks. She is a bit deaf too. But behind her spectacles is a heart-shaped Claudette Colbert face, tanned and well preserved, framed by thick and curly gray hair.

On campus at the University of Utah, where Frank Bradshaw first noticed her, Berenice Jewett was considered a good-looker, and she is still astonishingly pretty for a woman of her years. How extraordinary that this otherwise average old lady, looking like a paper cutout of Mrs. Middle America, should find herself in such a wild predicament—waiting for the curtain to go up on a murder trial where she is at once the widow of the deceased, the mother of the defendant, the grandmother of the perpetrator, and the bankroller of the entire legal carnival.

On the eve of trial, Berenice Bradshaw has toted up her legal accounts and found she now has more than thirty lawyers on her payroll. The fee for the trial about to begin is a cool million dollars, payable in advance. It has been paid.

Two points of law are important. The first is the matter of "aiding and abetting." Like most other states, Utah considers anyone who aids and abets the murderer to commit the crime to be just as guilty as the person who actually pulls the trigger.

Pecuniary interest is also an issue. Utah, like most other states, regards murder for profit as a more heinous crime than murder committed in passion, whether that passion be love or hate. To convict Frances Schreuder of first-degree murder, the prosecutor will have to show that she had a "pecuniary interest" in directly soliciting her father's death. On the other hand, if the defense can show that Frances lacked pecuniary interest, they can get the charges reduced to second-degree murder, not a death-penalty offense.

Utah is unlike all other states in its attitude to capital punishment. Not just three fourths of the people but ninety percent of the officeholders and public officials in Utah are Mormons, more

or less committed—depending on the level of their orthodoxy—
to the old Mormon doctrine of blood atonement. This is why
Utah retains the firing squad as one method of execution. The
majority of Utah's citizens do not merely approve the death penalty, they *demand* it, the state religion demands it. The situation
has made people in Utah especially touchy about charges of bar-
barism. In the wake of Utah's last big murder case, the Gary
Gilmore circus, such charges were particularly stinging, and in
response the legislature modified the law so as to grant every
person charged with a capital crime a two-phase trial. In Phase
One, guilt or innocence is determined in the usual manner. If the
verdict is guilty, Phase Two determines whether or not the death
penalty shall be imposed, or whether life in prison is sufficient
punishment. Phase Two is essentially a referendum on the defendant's moral character.

Utah offers those persons who do receive the death sentence a
final choice: lethal injection instead of the firing squad. The state
used to offer a third choice, death by hanging, but so few people
chose the gallows that some years back this option was dropped
from the menu.

It is well to remember that a murder trial is not a window onto
reality. It does not show what actually happened. A trial is a
carefully constructed play for a carefully selected audience—
twelve people. Rather, it is two plays. Neither is "true." Neither
is "complete." Each is a version of reality, very heavily edited.
After the final curtains—the two summings-up by the opposing
lawyers—jurors are invited to vote their preference. To put it
another way: trials are designed to *exclude* as much as to *include*
information. The one about to begin will exclude plenty.

The prosecutor gets to his feet and begins speaking quietly. He
explains to the jury that the murder in question occurred more
than five years ago. His evidence will focus not on the individual
who has already been convicted of the crime, but on the person
who ordered the execution, his mother. The defendant sits beside
her lawyer, her back to the courtroom.

She is a small woman, expensively dressed in silk and camel's
hair, with chopped black hair. As the county attorney describes
the events leading up to the death of Franklin Bradshaw and the
ultimate arrest and conviction of his grandson, the defendant
appears to be gazing steadily at the jury except when she makes
notes on a legal pad with a gold-and-ivory pen.

"This is a woman driven by greed," the prosecutor concludes. "And power. And the desire for money . . . a woman who would destroy virtually anyone who got in her road, who blocked her access to money. This is a woman who ordered her own son —her own flesh and blood—to kill her own father."

Mike Rosen walks coolly to the podium. He introduces himself, spells out the name of his law firm, walks back to the table where his client sits and, standing directly behind her, places a protective hand on each shoulder and says, "I represent this human being. I represent no one else . . .

"Okay, now I am going to try to scare you. But what you are going to do here is probably the most serious thing you have ever done in your lives, outside of your own family . . . This is a capital case. They are going for the death penalty in this case. But . . . before they can do that, before they can put Frances's life on the line, they have got to convince each and every one of you individually that they have met their Constitutional burden, their burden which never shifts—*never*—and that is proof beyond a reasonable doubt."

He points to the empty witness chair. *"That's where it's coming from!"* he snarls, as if the chair were a poisoned well. But "Frances Schreuder as she sits here today is as innocent as you, me, His Honor and Mr. Jones . . . Her presumption of innocence protects her like a coat. Only if they *prove it* does her coat come off. Remember her plea: Not Guilty. Those are magic words in this country. Those magic words say: *Hey! Those charges—I say* no! *You prove it!* That's America . . . That's what this trial is all about. Will the system work? The system works when you get twelve people, and a judge who gives you the law, and a defense lawyer who is *not going to quit* until the truth comes out . . ."

This high-voltage Brooklyn lawyer is very different in style from the drawling Utah prosecutor. How will his intense manner go over with these jurors? Their faces—seven women, five men— are attentive, carefully composed, as unrevealing of their feelings as the statues in their streets.

"The prosecutor told you there was tension in the family. *Of course* there was tension in the family! *Of course* there were problems . . . I am not going to stand up here and insult your intelligence and say that a family, with brothers or with sisters, and with wealth—there are no problems! Would they be a human family if there *weren't* problems?"

A silence. He wants the full attention of his audience of twelve. One of them had, himself, expressed the matter best, the lawyer says, during the intensive *voir dire* questioning which took place last week out of public view.

"Look, Your Honor," the prospective juror had said, "you can pick your friends. But you sure can't pick your family!"

Part Two

The Family

. . . AT THE START, THE Bradshaws could well have graced the cover of *The Saturday Evening Post*. If Norman Rockwell had run across them in 1938, say, the year of baby Frances's birth, he would have been tempted to set up his easel right in the middle of Gilmer Drive. Big, handsome, talented, athletic Franklin Bradshaw was a Dad who had put himself through college on a football scholarship, and in his junior year had up and married the prettiest girl and best dancer on campus—eloped with her, in fact, on Halloween. By 1939 he was doing very well as an auto parts dealer, the business he'd had the foresight to get started in ten years before. Wasatch Chemical, the wholesale company he had set up while still in college, was prospering too, and he had begun to speculate—modestly, of course—in the stock market. Dad and Mom now had four sturdy-looking young children, all well-dressed, nicely behaved. Robert Bradshaw, their first, was twelve, very big and strong. Marilyn had just turned nine, Elaine was seven, and cunning little Frances was still in her bassinet. Except for the baby, the children all took piano and tap-dancing lessons. Their pretty mother made a lot of their clothes, cooked all the meals, kept a very neat house, even played the piano. The children helped her out, doing whatever chores suited them best. Marilyn, named for her mother's favorite movie star, the gorgeous Marilyn Miller, was turning out otherwise. The child "could not learn to hippity-hop," said her mother. She was chunky and solid, a Bradshaw, not a Jewett. But she was proving a wonderful "other mother" to the other three children.

The family scene Norman Rockwell might well have chosen was the Bradshaws' annual preparations for the Shirley Temple Look-Alike Contest at the neighborhood movie house. Mother would be cutting out and sewing pink Shirley Temple dresses for her daughters; big Robert would be helping in some comical way; and even the baby would be somehow involved. The daughters would have been coiffed in Shirley Temple curls, carefully tied up in rag strips by their beaming Mom. That not one of these toothy, square-faced kids looked the least bit *like* the adorable movie moppet—a fact of life obvious to everyone but doting Mom— well, that would be the artist's gentle joke.

There were cracks in the portrait of course, cracks in the real family picture, as there are in every family. But Norman Rockwell would not have seen these, or would have chosen to overlook them. Bob had started having epileptic seizures by then, and Marilyn was trying to care for him on her own, holding him down on the basement floor by the old zinc sink, sitting on him until the fit passed, so he wouldn't hurt himself. Elaine had already suffered her first bout with rheumatic fever; in two years she would be stricken again, be confined to bed for the next two years, and emerge a permanent heart cripple. Baby Frances often refused to go to sleep. Sometimes she howled all night. When the neighbors complained, the entire family—mother, father and three children—gathered around the infant's crib and sang to her for hours on end. Berenice had had some sort of nervous breakdown after Frances was born, crying and refusing to come out of her room for months on end. Franklin was so busy with his stores, he didn't come home until late at night, and he left before daybreak. Much of the care of the newest Bradshaw was therefore left up to the older children.

But no family is without problems, stresses, skeletons, ghosts of one kind or another, and in truth the Bradshaws were no worse than the average family, and a lot better than many. Yes, Berenice was lonely and overworked. Yes, Franklin had become a workhorse, cold, reserved, seldom home. But half the wives in America felt lonely, weary, and unfulfilled, many of them with far more cause than Berenice Bradshaw had. Doubtless half the husbands felt lonely too, if the truth were known. But generally speaking the truth was not known. Generally speaking, *nobody* saw the cracks in the picture, or nobody talked about them or acknowledged them in any way. Least of all Franklin and Berenice Bradshaw. Like millions of other Americans, most of them perhaps, the world according to Norman Rockwell was the only world the Bradshaws ever allowed themselves to see.

And when the cracks in the picture began to widen, and spread, and deepen into fissures, the Bradshaws continued not to see, until, little by little, the members of the family began dropping through the cracks in the picture and tumbling into the boiling chaos that lay just beneath the painted surface.

Who *were* Franklin and Berenice Bradshaw? Where did they come from? Seldom has any family not of royal blood been so fully documented. He was the product of a devout Mormon background, a religion based on the study of one's origins, and she was a dogged genealogist, a woman who sought solace and distraction from the dreary present in the study of the tangled skein of bloodlines that had brought her here.

Each one of them wrote an "autobiography." Each sent out family newsletters. Ordinary letters also were exchanged between daughters and parents and grandchildren as the family grew. Even the unfortunate son Robert wrote a few. And all of it, every scrap, was saved. If the members of this warring family share one common trait, it is that they all seem to have been born with the instincts of pack rats. For all the Bradshaws, the function of their vast correspondence was not merely to exchange news: their letters were also political instruments in the ongoing factional struggles within the family. A secret copy of a letter to one family member was often posted to another, with instructions to read and burn. Nobody burned anything. All was stored up, proof of erstwhile love or past grievance; or stockpiled perhaps as ammunition for future battles as yet unformulated. Its precise purpose scarcely mattered. What mattered most was to save it.

Mother and daughters each kept file boxes, hatboxes, shoe boxes, and strongboxes full of saved-up family correspondence. As for Franklin's dilapidated, block-square building on West Pierpont, over the years it had come to warehouse much more than auto parts. It was also the enormous personal storehouse of a man who single-handedly operated two sprawling business empires, one in auto parts, the other in oil leasing. Moreover, he was a man who long ago had become caught up in a terrible, shameful family feud which family members managed, by and large, to keep concealed from public view but which burned along underground for decades like some coal-mine fires—impossible to extinguish, impossible to see, snaking along on its own timetable, feeding on the buried veins of its own fossil fuel, until the day when finally it blew sky high.

Stacked up in Franklin Bradshaw's musty storehouse, among all the auto parts and parts catalogs, were geology texts, mining surveys, personal papers, letters, family archives, old magazines and newspapers in bundles, legal papers, canceled checks, and financial records of every variety. Instead of ordinary file folders and filing cabinets, the old man put documents into salvaged used mailing envelopes held together with rubber bands or string, and filed them in old orange crates. And some items, the really precious ones, were tucked away among the auto parts themselves. So that amid the seeming rubble, in hiding places that only he knew about and often—increasingly—forgot about, were negotiable stock certificates, oil leases, securities of all kinds, important legal papers, copies of his various wills, loose blank checks, and an uncounted but not inconsiderable amount of actual cash.

Berenice Bradshaw personally typed out an autobiography that takes 142 pages to cover the past hundred years. Franklin's book covers more ground faster. Both books employ the bland style and pastel shadings of greeting-card writers. The effect is first charming, then numbing. Franklin's story begins with his maternal great-grandfather, Samuel Briggs, born in 1826 in Nottinghamshire, England. At the age of twelve the boy was sent down to work in the lead mines, and as quickly carried out again, overcome by poison gas. Too ill to work, he was idling in the village street when some visiting Mormon elders arrived from America, preaching the new faith and describing the wondrous advent of the Angel Moroni six years earlier in Palmyra, New York. Young Sam heard, believed, and made up his mind to escape Nottinghamshire for the Promised Land as soon as possible. At the end of his long life, by then a respected Mormon elder himself, Samuel wrote that "It was just borne upon my soul that the things those men were saying was correct. I have never had occasion to doubt it from that day to this."

Although Samuel, fourth among ten children, was the only one of his brothers and sisters to leave England, once he settled in Zion he fathered five sons, staunch Mormons all. Samuel was twenty-three when he and his wife, Hannah Dean, arrived in New Orleans in 1849. They moved upriver to St. Louis, Missouri, then farther on to Council Bluffs, Iowa, and finally to a region so wild it was known only as Upper Crossing of Keg Creek. Here their first son, Samuel Briggs, Jr., Franklin's grandfather, was born in 1851.

The young family struggled on, farming and cutting wood, trying to raise enough money for the westward journey to the

Promised Land which Brigham Young finally had established, only four years earlier, in the barren valley at the foot of the mountains beside the Great Salt Lake. Samuel managed to build his family a covered wagon, but after the difficult joinerywork had been completed, no blacksmith could be found in those remote parts to "iron it." A visiting Mormon elder, Apostle Ezra T. Benson (of whom more elsewhere, in another dynasty's archives), advised the couple to be of good faith and to abide; God would ensure that all who wished to see Zion would find ways. In swift time an itinerant blacksmith appeared, and "together with a company of Saints, Samuel and his family commenced their journey across the plains, traveling by ox team over the trackless desert, endangering their lives many times being subjected to the wild savages and stampeding buffalo."

Once settled in Lehi, Utah, Samuel tended his stock, cut wood, fought the Indians when necessary, was always upright and devout and steadfast in his temple work, and eventually attained the rank not only of elder but high priest. At age forty-three he was married to Emma Thomas, one of five children in a Mormon family which recently had emigrated to Utah from Wales. At this point in the chronicles, Hannah, his first wife, disappears. Since there is no mention of her death, it appears that Samuel's union with Emma was a polygamous one. Certainly it was fruitful. This couple had twelve children, of whom the eldest, Emma Briggs, would become Franklin J. Bradshaw's mother.

The matriarch on Franklin's father's side of the family—that is, the ancestor of the Bradshaws—was Mary Wagstaff, eldest of eleven children in Bedfordshire, England, who in 1833 married one William Bone. Like the Briggses, Mary and William Bone were baptized into the new faith by Mormon missionaries visiting from America. They sailed from Liverpool in 1854, traveled by train to Nebraska, and by oxcart across the plains to Salt Lake City in 1861. Mary eventually brought over her old mother, Mary Bethsheba, who was buried in Lehi at the age of 101.

Mortality was dreadful in the great trek; orphan children were commonplace in the Promised Land. Passing through Nebraska, the Bones picked up a nine-year-old orphan boy, Richard Travis Bradshaw, born in 1845 in Cheshire, England. Richard was raised in Lehi by the Bone family, and he married one of the daughters, Mary Ann. This young couple both died in their twenties, leaving three more orphan Bradshaws to be raised in the Bone household. The middle child, John Franklin, eventually married Emma Briggs and became Franklin J. Bradshaw's father.

At the age of ten, the young orphan boy ran away from home. Shortly before, there had been a celebrated spiritual experience within the Bone family. One day Mother Bone and a daughter were doing their washing when they received a visitation from "one of the three Nephites—prophets of old, who are still living on this continent."

These three Nephite brothers, also known in Mormon folklore as "the peripatetic immortals," appear frequently. They are benign figures with flowing white beards and hair, considered to be the spirits of three of Christ's twelve apostles who elected not to join Jesus in heaven right away, but rather to await the Second Coming roaming the earth and doing random good deeds. They appear and disappear to the faithful without warning, and the one who knocked on the Bone family's door on washday was in the guise of a limping man with a stone in his shoe. The women invited him in.

What happened next is described most fully in "Pleasant Recollections of Granny Fowler." The author, the younger sister of the runaway orphan boy, was at the time of the visitation a fifteen-month-old baby lying in a basket on the floor. When the visitor took off his shoe to remove the stone, the women saw that his foot was transparent. When they offered him breakfast, he told them he did not live by earthly food. "You do not believe me, do you?" he said. "But I will give you a sign. You will live to see your apple tree blossom out of season." Then he disappeared. A few years later, after Granny Fowler's parents had died, Granny Bone used to take the three motherless children "out to see the apple tree that blossomed out of season. It verily came to pass as the gentleman said it would . . ."

John Franklin Bradshaw, the orphan runaway, was twelve when he got his first job, herding sheep in Montana for eight dollars a month. At night it was so cold the rivets in his overalls stuck to his skin. For food there was only dried-out flour and water paste cooked in a fry pan and smeared with molasses or grease. But nothing would persuade him to accept charity or return to the stern household of Grandfather Bone. At fifteen he became a cowboy, breaking horses in Nevada. He worked on the railroad; for a time he mined gold. He homesteaded in Idaho, and finally, by the time he had built himself his own log cabin there, he was eighteen years old.

"I now felt I had the cage but not the bird," he wrote. Longing for the genuine home life he had never known, he began to correspond with a Lehi girl he could remember only faintly—the gently reared Emma Briggs. In 1889, when Emma was eighteen and John Franklin Bradshaw was nineteen, they were married. They had ten children, of whom seven survived. Franklin J. Bradshaw, born in Lehi in 1901, was the youngest of their four sons.

John Franklin Bradshaw in his lifetime would make and lose several fortunes. But by the time of his death, in 1941, he had become Lehi's major banker and a prosperous farmer and landowner. Emma and John Franklin began their married life in Lehi. In 1903 a group of Mormon polygamists fled to Alberta, Canada, to escape religious persecution in the States. John Franklin wanted to join them, taking along his wife and five young children. Utah already was running out of grazing land, and Alberta was said to be a stockman's paradise. He persuaded Emma to "go pioneering" by making her a promise which they each considered generous: if she would "give him ten years in the wilderness," he would build her the finest house in town when they returned to the civilized splendors of Lehi.

Emma readily agreed. Neighbor women warned of the hardship ahead, but she replied that she had married a diamond in the rough, "and I don't think my diamond is fully polished yet."

All the family memoirs throughout this period speak with greatest enthusiasm of the coming of electricity, indoor toilets, radios, movies, automobiles with isinglass windows and the other wonders of twentieth-century life. These people grew up with America, worked very hard, and greatly loved their toilsome lives. What is noticeable too in these gentle billows of prose is a uniformly sunny-minded outlook. The golden glow of nostalgia burns away all remembrance of muddle, disorder, madness, despair. Everything happens for the best. God is always good. Family closets contain no skeletons. Truth has become permanently sanitized. An immaculate eternity is assured.

Emma Briggs Bradshaw lasted only seven years in the hellish Canadian winters before her health broke and in 1911 forced the family to return to Lehi three years ahead of schedule. Franklin built her the fine house anyhow, on land bought from Grandmother Briggs, who was by now well into her twenty-seven-year widowhood and firmly established as Lehi's reigning matriarch. John Franklin had his fine house decorated with genuine hand-painted murals executed by an itinerant French scene painter. He bought for his wife the second motorcar in Lehi, a Cadillac with folding chairs in the back. He even took her to Southern California during the harsh Utah winters. Still her health continued to decline.

Emma always hoped that her youngest son, Franklin, would go on a Mormon mission. But now the football coach at the University of Utah was telling the boy he was sure he could get on the varsity team. Franklin promised his mother that if she would let him play college football first, he would do his missionary duty after graduation. She agreed, and in gratitude for his pledge bought him his first automobile. The relationship between Franklin and his mother appears to have been extremely affectionate and close, as it was also with his grandmother and with his sister Bertha, younger by three years.

In 1923 Frank was a strong, good-looking college athlete and an outstanding student. He had graduated first in his class in high school and, now a junior and a geology major, he continued to be extremely serious about his studies. That year his mother died of a heart attack at the age of fifty-two. His Granny Briggs died the following year. Frank was one of the fifty grandchildren she left behind. The death of these two women left the young man feeling doubly bereaved, and literally homeless. Then his father remarried, this time choosing a stern forty-year-old spinster, Sylvia Bushman.

Had not these events occurred in close succession, Berenice Jewett might not have had a chance. Berenice, a pretty, popular, fun-loving co-ed at the university, had suddenly become hell-bent on matrimony. Her parents were moving on to California so that Berenice's mother could pursue her voice studies, and her vivacious only daughter was determined not to go along. The only way she could stay behind was to get married. She cast about for the most desirable prospect.

Frank Bradshaw was attractive and well-mannered, a good dancer, and popular with his fraternity brothers. He came from a respected family and appeared to have a good future. But he had little interest in girls, and certainly no thoughts of getting married. He had given his varsity football sweater to his kid sister,

Bertha. Many years later he told her, "Bertha, I never even once asked a girl out the whole time I was in college. Know why? They always asked *me!*"

"But our home was all broken up. And Berenice was attractive. Not a raving beauty, but attractive," says plain Bertha Bradshaw Beck. "And she went to work on Frank."

As Bertha tells it, Berenice Jewett was extremely persistent. Frank said he wanted to finish school before taking a wife. Berenice told him he could continue studying after their marriage. Franklin protested that he wanted to be established in business first. "You can still marry me and do that," she said.

Franklin finally gave in. But in the manner of his yielding to Berenice's demands, he set a pattern and flavor to their relationship which would endure to his death. When Berenice wanted something, she would keep at her husband, worrying him "like a dog with a bone," he often said, until he found it easier to say "yes" than to resist her any longer. So eventually he almost always did say "yes." Soon his "yes" would turn out to really mean "yes—but." So that when Berenice finally "won" whatever it was that she wanted so badly, the victory was a hollow and bitter one · that never brought her the satisfaction she had hoped for.

On October 31, 1924, Berenice and Franklin got into the new car his late mother had given him, and they drove thirty-four miles to Ogden, Utah, where they were married, without rings or attendants, by a justice of the peace. Franklin drove his bride straight back to campus, dropped her off at her sorority house, and returned to his fraternity to spend the night. Except for Berenice's parents, they told no one of their marriage. They continued these living arrangements until Franklin Bradshaw was graduated the following June.

The young couple moved first to California, then Oregon and Idaho, and Frank tried his hand at several jobs before returning to Salt Lake City in 1928 and going to work for National Auto Parts Association, the largest in the country. In the next year of dealing in fuel pumps and fan belts, mufflers and sparkplugs, Frank Bradshaw saw America's future. He saw that it was all on wheels, that people had gone car-crazy, that they loved to peer under the hood and crawl under the chassis and try to fix it themselves. He saw a lifetime's future in auto parts and, having put in a year studying how the new business worked, he was ready to go into it on his own. He borrowed the money from his father and chose Provo, forty-one miles south of Salt Lake City, as his first location because nobody else yet had. He decided that he and Berenice would live over the store, not only for economy but so that when necessary he could literally offer a stranded motorist twenty-four-hour service. "Quality and Service Come First" was his policy from the beginning, and he would willingly get out of bed at midnight to go downstairs to wait on a customer.

The man who knows the story best today is Doug Steele, Frank's employee and oldest friend. A couple of years after Frank's murder the family sold the business, but Steele stayed on as manager. A stocky, pink-faced, white-haired, crinkle-eyed and kindly man, close to sixty now, he is still down there all day and every day, just as Frank was. His door is always open and the electric coffeepot outside it is never allowed to cool. "Nineteen twenty-nine was a bad year for most things, but a helluva good time for an auto parts store," Steele recalls, tilting back his chair. "People were busy buying cars and they liked to work on 'em. In those days a lot of axles were getting broke, and people had lotsa problems with clutches and transmissions. Frank was right there. He had a large stock, bought from NAPA, and he grew quite rapidly."

The store generated cash. Bradshaw invested it in the stock market. "Frank was shrewd. Did his own research. Stuck to basics: pay the book value. Buy 'em out of favor, don't follow the crowd. Buy low, sell high."

The Depression notwithstanding, under Bradshaw's stewardship his auto parts business continued to grow. Then came World War II. "People were unable to buy new cars, so they tried to keep the old ones together with glue and spit. You could sell anything you could get hold of. Frank did real good. And *smart?* With Frank, you approach the border of genius. Talk about being a good businessman—why, Frank wrote the book! And foresight! He could not only look down the block, he could look around the corner! He had *vision.*"

By war's end Bradshaw's inventory was all paid for, and within a few years he had stores in thirty-one locations up and down the state. His business was organized into seven basic corporations with independent divisions, a structure modeled after General Motors' separate Chevrolet, Pontiac, Oldsmobile and Cadillac divisions, "so if there was a problem at one end, it wouldn't hurt the other end." One division, All Car Parts, was set up deliberately to discourage others from entering the auto parts business in towns where Bradshaw already had a monopoly.

The Utah lieutenant-governor's office, where the state's corporate records are filed, lists nineteen Frank Bradshaw-related corporations. Early papers filed as far back as 1940 show that he did have some partners, mostly family members, but that Bradshaw himself always retained the majority interest. His mulish independence is apparent too; Bradshaw was cited by the state every year for failure to file annual reports as required by law.

What Steele calls *vision* early led Bradshaw to diversify. While still in college, he and a partner had started Wasatch Chemical, a company that bought bulk chemical products—fertilizer, cleaning solvents, antifreeze—by the carload, and knocked them down into smaller lots to sell to consumers. By the time Wasatch sold out to Mountain Fuel in 1969, it had become one of the largest independent chemical companies in Utah.

Franklin's father had started American Savings & Loan, which prospered first in Utah and then boomed in the Mormon stronghold of Hawaii. Although Frank was a stockholder of the company, its president was his eldest brother, Frederick. When Frederick died, control was passed along to other Bradshaw brothers and to their sons. The members of the younger generation eventually developed what Frank called "expansionitis" and, finding themselves with insufficient capital, they issued more and more stock until the company became "a plum ripe for the picking." In 1973 Dan Ludwig, the reclusive Florida billionaire, quietly bought up the stock and took the company away from the family. It was one of the few times the Bradshaws were ever bested in a business deal, and it had taken the richest man in America to do it.

Like his father, Franklin Bradshaw always had a special fondness for mining claims, and he held them both in Utah and Canada. As a young man in college, he had worked summers in the gold and silver mines at Park City, now a ski resort, and had become fascinated by the science of precious minerals. But the major source of Franklin Bradshaw's fortune was oil leases. His original interest began with a desperation born of success. "They wouldn't have said it that way then, but Frank 'n' them was makin' too much money in auto parts," says Steele. "They needed to reinvest to alleviate the seventy percent tax bracket they was in." The move succeeded in reducing the taxable income and eventually made Bradshaw his fortune. At his death, although it could never be proved, many Salt Lake oilmen believed him to be the largest individual leaseholder in the United States.

Bradshaw's multimillion-dollar auto parts empire may have been organized like General Motors, but its corporate headquarters looks as if it had been organized by a set decorator for haunted-house movies. The crumbling façade of the block-square warehouse appears untouched, even by a paintbrush, since Frank bought the place more than half a century ago. It is located on the faded, peeling, decaying industrial edge of Salt Lake in an area of warehouses, tire dealers, paint companies, small factories. The Bradshaw block on the south side of West Pierpont Street has a row of old pickup trucks parked below the loading dock out front. Rotting stone piers hold up the elevated bare wood sidewalk. Scuffed wooden steps climb steeply to an old yellow-painted wooden door with bleary signs: PUSH and OPEN. The door's bottom boards are raggedy, as if rats had been gnawing them. The wood is splintered by thousands of kicks administered by the stout boots of the hurrying, hard-handed, thrifty workingmen who were Frank Bradshaw's customers.

In a city less honest and well policed than Salt Lake, the security problems in operating a business like Bradshaw Auto Parts would be insurmountable. The warehouse serves as a distribution depot for the chain of stores, and at any time contains an inventory of $750,000 to $1,000,000 worth of readily disposable items. The huge, dilapidated building has a total of ten doors—five on the front façade, five at the rear. All the doors are individually locked, most of them padlocked from the inside. During the workday one or two doors are left unlocked, as fire exits, the open padlocks hanging on the hasps. The remaining doors, except of course the front door, are closed during the daytime, open padlocks dangling, so that doors can be opened from the inside by employees whenever necessary to receive or ship merchandise. Frank Bradshaw's first act every morning was to unlock some of these padlocks. At night he closed them. During the day the keys were tossed casually into a drawer in the managers' desk. Only he and his two top men, Doug Steele and the late Clive Davis, had keys to the outside lock on the yellow front door.

Inside, the place smells of auto wax and rubber and grease and oil, and it has the old-fashioned air of a run-down country general store. Parts spill out of boxes, and harried clerks and customers in mechanic's coveralls paw through stock catalogs with greasy fingers. Each morning at a little before 7:00, Frank Bradshaw used to park his old Ford truck, climb the steep steps to the platform sidewalk outside his offices, unfasten the lock on the beat-up door, and retrieve the money bag he had hidden the night before in one of the thousands of boxes of auto parts stacked along dozens of cluttered, crowded aisles. The bag normally contained about $300. His system was faster and safer and easier, he said, than taking the cash to a bank each night. He tended the counter himself for the early customers. When his employees came in at eight o'clock, Frank went next door to his "oil office," a small, bleak room which he shared with his faithful country-girl secretary, Nancy Jones. It looked an unlikely place for the stewardship of millions of dollars. The only decoration was a bowling trophy once won by a Bradshaw employee. The boss sat at a battered old schoolmarm's desk. Piled on top of it were the orange crates, with their vivid labels still intact—Queen Bee and Santa Anna—into which he had stuffed his geological maps and land surveys. He busied himself most mornings poring over these papers, seeking to determine the worth of particular pieces of land.

At the rear of the immense warehouse he had another desk with a swivel chair so broken that nobody but himself could sit in it. "You had to plant both feet firmly on the ground to keep from falling off," old-time employees joked. Back there Frank had other makeshift files, mostly in shoe boxes, and an old U.S. Army war surplus Royal typewriter on which he often typed his own correspondence. At night, after the other employees went home at seven o'clock, Frank would lock the doors, hide the money bag, and then work another three or four hours, alone, in his front office next to the street. Friends and mechanics and customers all knew to rap hard on his window and Frank would be happy to unlock the door and sell them the needed part. He had set up the original inventory, and knew every part in the place.

Franklin loved to supervise his small engine-repair business down at the far end of the raised sidewalk. The shop fixed things like chain saws and lawn mowers, and Frank seemed to enjoy leaving the abstract world of stocks, maps, and oil leases to run next door and caress a carburetor or a magneto. Several times a day he looked in on doings at the shop, and he always ran there and back as fast as he could go. The old man was a health fanatic. He toted around bottles of dark brown Karo syrup which he swigged for energy and pep. He gobbled wheat germ and vitamin tablets. He did not smoke, and he sipped at a cocktail perhaps once a year at a geologists' convention. During his autopsy, the surgeon commented that the old fellow had a healthier heart and lungs than some men half his age.

Bradshaw was often called miserly, but it might be more accurate to say that he had no interest in, and got no pleasure from anything money could buy. Mostly, he was frugal with himself. He saw no sense in taking a plane if he could take a bus; in taking a bus if he could walk. When his watch was stolen in a burglary some years before his death, he saw no sense in replacing it. He had no use for the high-priced attentions of doctors, lawyers, and other "professionals." He was a loner, self-made and self-educated, who believed he could already do most things better than other people, and what he did not know he could learn. One of the few purchases he allowed himself were self-help books with titles like *How to Be Your Own Doctor,* and *How to Draw Your Own Will.*

Two things he did not begrudge money for were education and medical expenses for members of his family, though he considered medical attention for himself an utter waste. And he did not object when Berenice began to travel. When she became the travel agent's best friend, moving in ever wider orbits, signing up for every cruise folder on the counter, he paid the bills gladly. He even reminded his wife that she should always invite her fellow cruise mates out for dinner in a restaurant one night, and not to forget to leave a solid ten percent tip.

Nor was Bradshaw stingy with his employees, especially where his time was concerned. When he died there were 155 people on his payroll, and few if any complaints. He had set up a generous retirement fund, and employees could borrow against it to buy a car, or for other needs. Although salaries were not high, employees could make a good living if they worked as hard as the boss. He gave every kid who wanted one a job; all four of the Steele kids had worked at Bradshaw's while they were growing up.

"All four of Frank's children worked down here too, when they were in high school," says Steele. "Oh yes, the girls too. They all knew the place *very well.*" But the three daughters left town for good as soon as they finished high school, and Bob

Bradshaw went into the service at seventeen. "There was obvious tension in the home. Frank was a very private person, a very proud person. He never showed his emotions, wouldn't reveal his soul to anyone. But, listen: once in a while he'd break down and talk to me. Because he had to have *someone* to talk to. He'd spend eighteen of his twenty-four hours down here! Who else was he to talk to? Hch, hch. Once time he said to me, 'Doug, be careful. A man works his ass off and he dies young. Then his wife finds a younger man and spends all the money. Six months later she says, What was the name of that guy I was married to?' "

Long before the end of his life, Frank Bradshaw had taught himself to control his feelings the way an Indian fakir controls pain. He was an austere man who cared nothing for creature comforts, for culture of any sort, for any of the "finer things of life." He didn't care what time it was. He didn't even care what he ate. He read nothing but geology and oil texts, newspapers, newsmagazines and financial statements. Most of these he read on Sundays, in the public library, for free. Whatever his vices, they were not of the garden variety. He did not chase women. He abstained from tobacco, alcohol, gambling, even caffeine. He did not play cards, nor did he have other hobbies. His only play was his work. Franklin Bradshaw was an almost pathological workaholic, a loner, in no ordinary way gregarious, although always entirely available to his employees and customers alike.

Yet he did have a diffuse family feeling: strong ties of blood to other Bradshaws, concern for his daughters, and—most of all—tender feelings toward his grandchildren. If Franklin Bradshaw, by all modes of measurement a "hard man," had one weak spot, that was his deep fondness for his four grandsons. It would prove to be, literally, his fatal weakness.

As for Franklin's wife, no one would seem to have had deeper family feelings, longings, yearnings, attachments—not the most devout Mormon—than Berenice Jewett Bradshaw. She is a woman who will organize her entire life around her family, who will fight the aching loneliness of her present family life by writing a detailed, one-hundred-year history of her past family life, and who ultimately will sacrifice all on the high altar of motherly and grandmotherly devotion.

Berenice Bradshaw began composing her "Autobiography" some time in the late 1930s, as a diversion from the struggle to raise four children almost singlehandedly. By the early forties she had set her work aside, too exhausted by the rigors of living her life to find energy to write about it. Then, in the late fifties, all her children grown and gone—feeling drained anew, emptied this time by her own sense of emptiness—she got out her old typewriter, found the old pages, and resumed work, as if reaching for a sense of *having lived a life* through the very act of setting it all down.

She is a patriot and contrives for the "Autobiography" to span one hundred years, 1876 to 1976, so that it will coincide with and help to celebrate the nation's Bicentennial. The work's main character does not appear until 1903, when Berenice Jewett is born in Sioux City, Iowa. The early pages are based on a memoir by Fred Daniel Jewett, Berenice's father, which she persuaded him to write in his later years. Fred had been raised in Denver, where his mother died just as the boy was finishing high school. A few months later he met pretty Florence Roberts, a student at the Denver Conservatory of Music. One moonlit night on Florence's parents' front porch, as Berenice tells the story, the young couple impulsively decides to get married. The next day Fred borrows a horse and buggy, they cross the Missouri River into Nebraska, hunt up a judge, find a red-shirted, overalled farmer and his wife to serve as witnesses, and tie the knot that will join them forever. Driving back to Iowa in the rain, the newlyweds meet an Italian traveling with a dancing bear. They pause "to watch the bear dance in the rain." This one fleeting moment of gaiety behind them, their story descends at once to the level of gritty struggle on which it will thereafter remain.

One sentence after the bear, Fred writes that "The old grind began, no honeymoon, no money." He clerks in grocery stores, toils in meat-packing houses and labors for a cigar maker. Berenice is their first child. Three years later, in 1906, her brother Bill is born. Berenice picks up the narrative in her own voice in the spring of 1909, just as the little family is heading west to Idaho. Her father has hatched a harebrained scheme to find some cheap farmland and raise a quick-cash crop of cantaloupes, potatoes, and beans. As a woman, Berenice Bradshaw can be realistic; as a diarist she habitually reaches for rose-colored glasses along with her pen. She describes life in the open fields with no shelter but a raggedy tent, parents and children toiling seven days a week from sunup to sundown only to be wiped out at market time by a price drop that leaves them still deeper in debt, as "a rewarding family experience."

Berenice's earliest memory is of standing with her toddler brother on the soft, high banks of the "large and treacherous" Snake River roaring behind their parents' house. Pregnant Florence notices the children and makes "a frantic dash the full length of the long lot and grabbed us for fear the banks would cave in and carry us to our death in this wild, dangerous stream." When Florence's third child is stillborn, five-year-old Berenice and little Bill are told by their father that "the saving of our lives caused the loss of our baby sister." Father makes a little wooden box and buries the infant under an apple tree in the backyard.

The family moves on to Eagle, Idaho, and a house so poorly built "you could throw a cat out the cracks." Fred earns fifteen dollars a month as a general-store clerk. His wife and children gather spilled coal from the railroad tracks for fuel. Then Dad is caught taking home an overweight sack of sugar and loses his job. He finds work in a slaughterhouse but is too "kind and humanitarian" to "relish working in this atmosphere of killing." He winds up as an accountant at a music company in Boise, commuting from Eagle by streetcar. The reaction of his wife, the former belle of the Denver Conservatory of Music, to her grim new existence is nowhere mentioned in this book. But twenty years later, the same tale of impulsive marriage followed by lengthy, withering regret will be recapitulated by the Jewetts' daughter Berenice, and Franklin Bradshaw.

Berenice describes a happy small-town girlhood filled with barn dances, sleigh rides and box socials. "We made our own good times instead of depending on outside activity or sitting glued to a television set as folks are doing today."

Berenice's forebears are distinguished chiefly by their longevity. One paternal great-grandfather, the Reverend Daniel Jewett, an Iowa Baptist minister and college teacher, lives eighty-two years; Grandpa Detweiler, a druggist, dies at eighty-three. The sons of these men each lives eighty-three years. On her mother's side is Granny Tacy Arabella Davis Roberts. Tacy dies at ninety-three, and is the most beloved figure in the book. Tiny, fierce, and high-spirited, she has six children and plays a major part in raising her only granddaughter, Berenice. Florence, Berenice's mother, is Tacy's eldest child; Tacy's youngest daughter, Beatrice, is only six years older than her granddaughter. To Bere-

nice, her "Aunt Bea" always seems more like an older sister, and
the children become lifelong best friends. Half a century later,
when Berenice Bradshaw, now seventy-nine, finds herself dodging subpoenas from a Salt Lake County Attorney, the place she
chooses to hide out is the home of her eighty-five-year-old Aunt
Beatrice Horton, in a remote fishing village on the coast of
Maine.

Berenice was not just tenderhearted Tacy's first grandchild.
She was for twenty-one years the only granddaughter in the entire clan. As such, she was passionately and uncritically adored.
When Berenice's narrative gets around to describing the arrival
of her own only granddaughter, Ariadne, the same intensity of
devotion is focused, like sunlight through a magnifying lens, on
one single little girl. Ariadne's middle name, it will turn out, is
Tacy.

The story has something of the flavor of *Our Town*. Ordinary
people are born, live, and die in unremarkable ways. Life is hard.
Women tend children and men work at whatever jobs are available. But instead of Thorton Wilder in bond, the reader gets
ladies' magazine vanilla. Whatever individuality may once have
marked the characters has been scoured away, either by the limitations of the biographer or by her careful sense of propriety.
People all wear their Sunday best in her numerous family photograph albums, and all appear in their best light in her narrative.
It renders them uniformly respectable and dull. Save for
Florence's early music study and Berenice's later voice lessons,
no one is involved even marginally with the arts, or with any
form of intellectual endeavor; there is no awareness of the outside
world of events, or the inner world of imagination. Unlike the
Bradshaws' writings, not even religious zeal enlivens the pages.
After a while, one longs for a transparent foot to appear in the
doorway.

Berenice spends long, exuberant periods in the care of Grandmother Tacy. When Aunt Bea turns fourteen, she invites her
friends over for a slumber party. At midnight the giggling girls
sneak downstairs to make a freezer of peach ice cream. As soon
as the teenagers leave their bedroom, Tacy and eight-year-old
Berenice tiptoe upstairs and "french" the empty beds with frogs
and slime and cold spaghetti. The evening ends in a riotous pil-
low fight, a glorious swirl of feathers in lamplight with little Bere-

nice and her diminutive grandmother triumphantly holding the fourteen-year-olds at bay.

But by the age of twelve, Berenice is back living with her parents and brother in an apartment in Salt Lake. Her mother works full-time as a saleslady in an elegant department store, a job that enables her to keep herself and her daughter always fashionably dressed. "Mother liked fine clothes, and Father was a stingy man." When Florence is hospitalized with a grave but unspecified illness, Berenice comes home after school to wash the breakfast dishes and start the dinner, then wash the evening dishes. She cleans the entire house on Saturdays and does the laundry in the bathtub. She is dutiful and does these chores without being asked. But in her memoirs Berenice confides that she felt "robbed of girlhood" and abandoned by her mother, just as her own daughters will come to feel.

In high school, once again living with her grandparents, Berenice blossoms. She is lovely and lively and, thanks to Florence, "always the best dressed." Soon she is "swept off her feet" by Arthur Tuck, the school's very handsome "prize catch." The summer after Arthur's graduation he proposes to fifteen-year-old Berenice "in a most dramatic, romantic way, just like they do in the movies." But first he must fulfill his destiny as a college football hero. (He is such a superb all-round athlete that he once takes thirty-two first places at the Oregon State Track Meet and achieves immortality in Ripley's *Believe It Or Not* as the "one man who won an entire track meet.")

Time and space are not kind to the lovers and they drift apart. "Fast" sorority girls pursue the football star. Finally "the worst" happens when Arthur, en route home from a track meet in Belgium, stops off in Salt Lake to visit Berenice. The sweethearts go hiking in the mountains. While they are gone, her mother—already in the habit of snooping in her husband's pockets—rummages through Arthur's clothes and finds an unmailed envelope addressed to another girl.

"Being curious and having that mother instinct of wanting to protect her own," Berenice writes, Florence steams open the letter, "writes off" a copy and, saying nothing, hides her handiwork under the shelf paper in her daughter's bureau drawer. The epistolary time bomb does not take long to explode. When Berenice discovers the copied love letter in her mother's hand, addressed to an unnamed girl, she locks her door and cries for an entire day and night. Then she sends Arthur a sarcastic note and never hears from him again.

"A broken love affair is very devastating and it took me several years to get over this," she reports. But though she cries for Arthur every night, she conceals her true feelings from everyone, and spends hours alone practicing her piano. Between mother and daughter, the subject is never mentioned.

Oppressed and excluded by the clannish Mormons who predominate at Salt Lake City's public high school, Berenice transfers to Westminster, a small, strict, private Presbyterian junior college. Once more she is popular, active, something of a "flapper" and frequently involved in "daring" escapades. She graduates in a beautiful dress of "orchid georgette, all ruffled," made by her mother, long white kid gloves and a large-brim leghorn hat trimmed with lilacs. The photograph shows a willowy, dark-haired young beauty with a ravishing smile. She enrolls in the University of Utah, takes a business course but is disinterested in studying, very fond of music and dancing, and frankly out for a good time. The year is 1922.

The book portrays her father as sweet and kind but "very stingy." Berenice is like her mother, more grasshopper than ant. The other men are seen as likable but ineffectual. Grandpa Roberts, Tacy's husband, reminds Berenice of Andy in "Amos 'n' Andy": "He always had a big deal on or a scheme where by he was going to get rich over nite but they always fell thru. He slept from deal to deal." Later in the story, when the multitudinous Bradshaws appear, both sexes are portrayed as imperious and smug, people who accept the hospitality of others as their "due" and treat Franklin's young wife—as they do every young female —as a slavey and semiservant.

Amid the Bradshaws, Berenice is a Cinderella with no hope of a glass slipper. She has already found her prince and is married to him. Their first two or three years of married life are times of genuine hardship. Berenice and Franklin hopscotch over the western states in a series of broken-down automobiles, looking for work, living in mining camps or cheap hotel rooms, or tenting in public camp grounds. They wander across Idaho, Montana, Washington, sometimes sleeping in their car, sometimes pawning it, often going without food for several days. Franklin works in a Tacoma smelter until his lungs ache; together they toil as migrant fruit pickers.

The grimness of their lives is unrelieved. Berenice feels responsible. "Franklin thought he was marrying a breadwinner, but I
turned out to be a liability." At times she succumbs to crying jags
which, under the circumstances, do not seem unreasonable. Once
they find shelter in an abandoned building during a heavy down-
pour. They have partially moved in when they discover "the
ground covered with green slimy creatures that look like dill
pickles with legs."

Although Franklin's father is the influential president of the
Bank of Lehi and both of Berenice's parents are employed, "we
never wrote any of our problems to our parents. For all they
knew we were just on a gay jaunt, taking in the sights and having
a whee of a time." But with cold weather coming on, the forlorn
pair heads south to California where both sets of parents happen
to be spending the winter. Franklin is dressed in a half-burnt
overcoat he has used to put out a fire in their car. His shoes are
mended with cardboard and string. Ashamed, the bank president
buys his son new clothes.

But "my appearance didn't touch his pocketbook," so Berenice
must wait for new outfitting until they arrive in Los Angeles. "It
seemed so good to be with my parents and the Roberts clan once
more. They were 'fun' people to be around. Franklin's people
were religious, their customs and outlook on life were very different . . . My people were free from ritual living, no inhibitions.
They were clean, honest people and loved life."

Berenice gets a department-store job and one day glimpses Ru-
dolph Valentino. Franklin drives a truck. But he sees no future in
Los Angeles and after six months decides to return to Utah.
Berenice would have preferred to remain, but "I was married and
my place was with my husband." In Franklin's version of this
story, confided late in his life to a trusted daughter, he realizes by
now that he has been inveigled into marriage with a fundamen-
tally frivolous woman and tries gently to leave Berenice behind.

In the summer of 1926, the tar on the California-Nevada desert
road literally bubbles in the heat, and Franklin patches twenty-
one blowouts in one boiling afternoon. After a three-day journey
they reach Lehi and find fresh garden fruits and vegetables arrayed on the family dinner table. For a time, this all-Mormon
community again seems like the Promised Land. Bradshaw relatives help find Franklin a job, and let them rent a family-owned
house. But winter comes, the barn turns out to be rat-infested,

and at night huge rodents jump against Berenice's back door. Visits to the privy become a hellish ordeal.

The one member of Franklin's family who is kind to Berenice is his sister Bertha. Both young women discover they are pregnant, and spend the winter happily stitching baby clothes. A Bradshaw relative decides to earn extra money raising poultry, and soon the muddy yard outside Berenice's house contains two thousand chickens; a half-dozen manage to fly inside each time she opens her screen door. When her labor commences, Franklin drives her to the hospital, but then goes home to help his parents. Berenice is furious that he is not with her at midnight, August 10, 1927, when Robert Jewett Bradshaw is born.

As always, Franklin responds to fury with further withdrawal. When the next three children are born, he will arrange for his relatives to drive Berenice to the hospital and to bring her and the baby home. Of all Franklin's failures as a husband, nothing angers his wife so much as his indifference at these times.

Florence arrives to help Berenice care for the baby and is appalled at her living conditions: a coal stove, no indoor plumbing, the two thousand chickens. Then Franklin's stepmother drops in with a full bushel basket of peaches and plums which she wants the younger woman to can. She has not even brought Mason jars. At this Florence blows up and, with Franklin's blessing, shepherds her daughter and new grandson back to the comforts of Southern California.

Franklin gets a job in the copper mines. Berenice and baby rejoin him, the ordeal begins anew: no running water, no paved streets, no comforts of any kind. Bob is an irritable baby who cries a great deal. Franklin decides to spend the summer prospecting, and leaves his wife and son with the senior Bradshaws. Berenice learns she is expected to do all the housekeeping in the big home, prepare Sunday dinners for any Bradshaw relatives who drop in, wash up the dishes and—after all that—entertain the guests at the parlor piano.

Her Cinderella existence worsens with the onset of her second pregnancy. As soon as Bob can walk, he starts wandering away from home. Their house has a deep irrigation canal on one side of it and railroad tracks on the other, so his frazzled mother ties him in the front yard with a strong rope. Robert continually wriggles free and disappears. Neighbors criticize the frantic mother for roping a little boy. "I tied him up because I loved him," she says.

Franklin has by now completed his year-long self-apprenticeship to National Auto Parts, analyzed the future of the business, borrowed a little money for inventory from his father, and is ready to set up shop for himself. Since no auto parts stores exist south of Salt Lake, the family moves down to Provo. Six weeks later Florence arrives for the birth of her second grandchild; Franklin is once again busy minding his store. The new arrival, Marilyn, is plump and healthy, although "I can't honestly say she was beautiful. I never thought my babies were beautiful."

A year passes. "All signs inform me another baby was 'in the basket.'" By now the family is living above the store, and the one bedroom contains a double bed and three cribs lining the walls. It is 1931. Franklin's money is split between two banks, one in Provo, the other in Lehi, and both banks close in the same week. The family is once more destitute, and soon there will be five mouths to feed, and hospital and doctor bills to pay. Berenice daily sieves vegetables and scrapes beef for baby food. She reckons she has now literally washed diapers every day for nearly five years. When her devout Mormon neighbors object that she is ignoring the biblical injunction to observe the Sabbath, she says, "The baby does the same thing on Sunday it does the other six days."

Bob is still wandering off, now with chubby Marilyn toddling behind. One day when Berenice is "huge with Elaine," and her two children have not been seen since early morning, she loses her temper and goes hunting. Finding the children in a candy store, without their tricycle, she takes a stick and "whams Bob every step of the way home."

After this she is "so disgusted" she never goes searching for Bob again, just waits for him to come home. "When I quit looking, he quit running away. Bob was always a sweet boy, never did naughty things like other boys . . . But he was hard to raise. He was five years old before we could get him toilet-trained. One day Franklin put him in the bathtub and took the broom to his behind. Another time we went up the canyon on a family picnic. Bob messed his pants. Franklin took his clothes off and ducked him in the cold mountain stream. When I think of all the cruel things we did to that boy trying to toilet-train him, I just shudder.

"Those were trying days, three small children to care for. It was work, work, work. I loved my children dearly. I did everything I was told to do by the doctors for their health and well-being. I did not neglect them, ever. They were three of the cutest children and got prettier every day. Bob was absolutely handsome."

Passages such as this one begin to have a defensive sound. Berenice's voluminous family photo albums, each one neatly pasted and labeled in white ink on black paper, show page after page of ordinary-looking children and adults in typical box-Brownie situations: sunbathing, graduating, sitting on ponies, admiring new cars, gathered around Christmas trees. Nobody is especially "cute". Everybody is squinting in the sunlight; the children are weedy or tubby-looking, the men are large, strong, and rugged, their women decidedly plain. The only exception is Berenice herself. She is a knockout.

In Los Angeles Florence dies of a stroke, at the age of fifty-five, and is buried in the family's Masonic plot at Forest Lawn. As soon as they are alone, Fred Jewett asks his daughter, "Well, honey, what do you think has happened to her?"

"Nothing, she is just where we put her, in the ground. People are always talking about going someplace when they die. I don't know where there is to go. I do not believe in any form of life after death here or anyplace else. It is ashes to ashes, dust to dust, the end."

By 1934 Berenice has joined the Provo chapter of the Eastern Star. Eventually she will enroll in Job's Daughters, the Daughters of the American Revolution, the Daughters of Armorial Ancestry, the Huguenot Society, and as many other hereditary orders as she can locate. She is not by nature a clubwoman. These activities serve more to relieve her aching loneliness, and to affirm her own identity among these Mormons by whom she feels overwhelmed.

In 1935 Berenice brings all her children down to the Provo Tonsil Clinic and has three pairs of tonsils snipped at once, according to prevailing medical fashion. Elaine falls ill with rheumatic fever. Not realizing the seriousness of the illness, Berenice takes her children to visit her parents in San Diego and rents a seaside cottage. "We thought we were doing the right thing by giving Elaine this exposure to sunshine and play. The result of our ignorance and the doctors' failure to advise us left Elaine with a damaged heart for the rest of her life."

Twice a week Berenice drags the children to dancing school. Faithfully she sews costumes, has metal taps attached to Robert's shoes, ties up Marilyn's hair into corkscrew curls, and rehearses everybody in "Animal Crackers in My Soup," all to no avail. The children are hopelessly untalented.

By 1937 Franklin is eager to open a second store, in Salt Lake City, and compete with the big-time auto parts dealers there. He tries to move his family into a dilapidated one-bedroom bungalow in Salt Lake which the Bradshaws already own but Berenice is adamant, and for once her father-in-law is on her side. Instead they buy the two-bedroom dream house on Gilmer Drive. Berenice is eagerly looking forward to moving her daughters out of the parental bedroom, where they now sleep (Robert occupies his own closet-size room in the rear) and to the freedom, by autumn, of having all three of her children in school for at least part of the day. But by autumn Berenice is dismayed to discover that, seven years after Elaine's birth, she is pregnant once again.

"I had three babies in three and a half years. I had four babies before I discovered what was causing it."

Berenice describes her family's first Christmas on Gilmer Drive as "the bleakest I have ever known." The Depression is causing Franklin to work even later at night, and he is saving a bit more money by eating only two meals a day. "Franklin was so on edge that winter, he was horrible to live with." On Christmas Eve, with her last fifty cents, Berenice buys candy for the children's stockings, a doll for each daughter, and "a cheap little red wagon" for Bob. When Franklin sees the toys he berates her for not waiting until after Christmas, when they would have been half-price.

"Expecting a baby under these conditions was almost more than I could bear," she says. "I wanted to die many times." But the other children, now ages seven, eight, and ten, are thrilled to have a baby sister and Marilyn becomes known in the family as "Other Mother." There will be times in the baby's first years when she is left entirely in Marilyn's care. After the delivery of Frances Bradshaw, Berenice goes into a kind of blue funk, and spends six months weeping and refusing to come out of her bedroom.

Before Frances is two years old, Elaine is ill again. One day her teacher sends a note home saying Elaine has been falling down a lot, and "fidgeting" so badly she distracts the other second-graders. A doctor says this is "St. Vitus' dance," associated with a serious recurrence of rheumatic fever. The only treatment is complete rest. The child must be kept entirely in bed, even for meals, and carried back and forth to the bathtub and toilet. For two years her education is supervised by a visiting teacher, but her twenty-four-hour care is split between Berenice and Marilyn, who is now ten.

"Elaine remembers being alone much of the time," says Marilyn today. She sat in bed working on her collection of expensive "Storybook Dolls." These were the Ken and Barbie dolls of their day, although larger and more lavish. Elaborate sew-it-yourself doll clothing could be bought to suit the dolls' fairy-tale characters, and Elaine made dozens of silken gowns, satin cloaks, velvet capes, pearl-embroidered Juliet caps, beribboned doublets; she stitched wimples, veils, peignoirs, embroidered waistcoats, satin breeches. These are the very same dolls, says Marilyn, which today stand side by side, untouched, a ghostly company of fairy-tale princes and princesses, cramming the top shelves of Ariadne's closets. Marilyn knows about this from Berenice, who gave Elaine's old dolls to her granddaughter. Elaine and Marilyn have never seen these closets.

In her "Autobiography," Berenice scourges herself for not recognizing Elaine's symptoms in time to prevent permanent heart damage. Her guilts reawaken sorrowful memories of her stillborn baby sister, after the episode on the riverbank.

Berenice wistfully recalls her own childhood fun with Tacy's children, "sitting around the big old table with a dishpan full of popcorn playing games." She tries this with her children. "All they did was fight. I thought to myself: Okay, they don't know any better, and they will *never* know any better. And I never tried the second time."

While Elaine is still bedridden, "Bob's health began to show signs of future illness." This is a reference, her book's only one, to Robert's increasingly severe epileptic seizures which had commenced at puberty. And now that she desperately needs domestic help, none is to be found. Unemployed women have gone to work in wartime defense plants.

Frances has been particularly difficult to care for since birth, even harder to put to sleep than Robert was. At times neighbors hear the Bradshaw family singing loudly late into the night. In fact they are all—parents and three children—sitting in a circle around the crib attempting for hours on end to sing the fretful baby to sleep. Today Berenice will acknowledge that "Frances was always trouble to raise. She was my caboose," she sometimes adds, "and many's the time I wished I could have given her back." But she says this with a rueful grin. Then she adds, "But I'm needed. That family really needs me," and she smiles.

In her book she is less forthright, more sentimental, more self-pitying. "All this time Franklin worked from early morning until late at nite, seven days a week," Berenice writes of the family's World War II years. "The children were my complete responsibility and care . . . Sundays I would watch the neighbors go off in their cars with their families and picnic lunches. I had a car. I could have put my children in and gone off. But what fun or amusement would there be for *me* to take three small children and wander off somewhere? . . . Just more of the same. No freedom or pleasure for me. Many a Sunday afternoon for years I would throw myself on the bed and cry. Cry for someone to show an interest, to relieve me of my constant burden. In the last fifty years I have cried enough tears to float a battleship. The well has dried up now but the emotions are still there."

This said, Berenice files away her "Autobiography" and does not touch it for the next seventeen years. She resumes writing on August 17, 1959—Granny Tacy's one-hundredth birthday—and she now invites Franklin to read over her account of their family's early years. He is not impressed. "You didn't make it happy," he tells her.

"But it *wasn't* happy!" she replies.

Berenice is somewhat more inclined than her husband to call a spade a spade. She acknowledges two or perhaps three "nervous breakdowns," the term both she and her daughters use for her spells of deep anxiety or despair. Franklin, with his increasing distaste for doctors and for any frailty of mind or body, will say only that his wife is "an over-nervous person." Whatever the label, the depressions she describes during her seventeen-year silence all seem linked to her feelings of inadequacy to the task of trying singlehandedly to raise four children, two of them seriously ill, in what she experiences as a bleak and emotionally hostile climate.

The first "breakdown," after Frances's birth, would today be

termed a post-partum depression. The second occurs in 1942 or
'43 when Berenice begins to experience "nerve exhaustion." She
fears that the walls of buildings are about to fall in on her; she is
afraid of smothering. She dreads closing her eyes at night, tired as
she is, for fear of dying in her sleep. Franklin must spend hours
sitting up with his wife, trying to dispel her terrors. She shops
around for medical help but doctors find nothing specifically
wrong. They recommend less stress, so Marilyn and Robert are
sent off for a year to a boarding school in southern Utah. Elaine,
now recovered, is able to return to the neighborhood public
school, and Frances is old enough to begin nursery school. To her
mother's surprise, she is considered a model child, perfect in every way. "This struck me as phenomenal as she wasn't that easy
to live with at home."

At the doctor's suggestion, Berenice resumes her voice and
piano lessons, and even for a time sings with the Mormon Tabernacle Choir. She also began making regular visits to a local spa
for whirlpool baths and other forms of hydrotherapy—a regimen
she still continues. Within a few months she is feeling quite her
old self again.

As soon as Frances is old enough, the child begins to assert a
fanatic determination to be independent of her mother. Shortly
before her ninth birthday, for example, Berenice is secretly planning a surprise party. The surprise is on Berenice when she learns
Frances has found out and called every potential guest to tell
them the party has been canceled. Just as Berenice had once
given up trying to prevent Robert from running off, and later
given up making popcorn, she now vows that she will never again
try to give Frances a party. In fact, the mother-daughter relationship will develop into a kind of lifelong surprise party and Frances will find continual new ways of surprising her mother with
bad news, thirty years of frogs and slime and cold spaghetti.

A 1946 family outing to Yellowstone Park is not a success.
Franklin, the fanatic early riser, becomes infuriated by the children's late-sleeping habits, which he blames on Berenice. He demands they all return home at once, but his wife contrives a stop
en route at the restored Wild West town of Jackson Hole, and
introduces her older children, now ages nineteen, seventeen, and
fifteen, to the delights of saloons and gambling dens, while eight-
year-old Frances is left sulking in the car. Domestic hostility siz-
zles through the pages of Berenice's one-sided account:

Franklin was chasing around town so I took my 3 oldest into a cocktail lounge where they sipped their first liquor cocktail. They took to liquor like a fish to water. They were ready for "seconds" when their father showed up. Our next excitement was at the gambling tables. Bob wanted to stay in Jackson Hole and be a dealer in "Black Jack." The next day we were on our way back to Utah. The kids said: "Do we have to go back to that Sunday School State?" Life in Jackson Hole was right "up their alley." This was the only trip our family ever went on together.

The senior Bradshaws make a conscious effort to find a congenial pastime, and take up square dancing. Although they make a few friends and even have their picture in *The Deseret News* as First Square Dance Couple of Utah, the idea sputters and dies in the cold winds of their relationship. Berenice says her husband enjoys dancing with the other women, but not with his wife, "so . . . he would yank me around over the floor. We would fight all the way to the dance and fight all the way home. About what I don't remember."

By the time Frances is in the fifth grade at the neighborhood public school she is studying music, and is prey to hostile teasing attacks by the Mormon majority. When the other kids gang up on Frances, Berenice tears off her apron and rushes down to the principal's office to defend her youngest. She makes it clear she considers such confrontations not rightfully a mother's responsibility but a father's, especially when the father is himself LDS. But Franklin of course is never around. The two older girls are by now attending the University of Utah, and Robert has disappeared from the narrative.

Berenice begins to travel in ever widening circles as her children leave home. Eventually her travels will take her by bus, rail, plane, and ship all over Europe, the Far East, and South America. She will float the canals of Venice and Bangkok, hike the streets of London and Milan, window-shop in Rio and Amsterdam, sail on cruise ships several times the length and breadth of the Atlantic and Pacific, clamber over the pyramids of Mexico, the Andes of the Incas, and the Great Wall of China, flight bag over her shoulder, camera around her neck.

She does not much care to visit churches, or landmarks. "I've seen enough cathedrals and museums to last me the rest of my

life! What I like to see is *people.* I like to see *how people live!"* she
exclaims, as if desperate to find some working models and patterns for family life.

On September 13, 1956, in San Francisco, Elaine marries Mason
Drukman, a former fellow student at San Francisco State, in the
Unitarian Church. Franklin refuses to attend the wedding, perhaps because he disapproves of his daughter's marrying a Jew.
Berenice is very much on hand, chirping cheerfully about the
beautiful bridal gown, about Marilyn and Frances in their specially made bridesmaids' dresses of green silk, and the small
champagne reception which follows.

But the family wedding that really pleases her, and inspires an
ecstatic three-page "Dear Family" letter afterward, will come
two years later, when Frances gets married. In the interval, Berenice has a third nervous collapse. It happens in 1957, on her first
tour of Europe: Gibraltar, Greece, Rhodes, Turkey, Naples,
Pompeii, Capri, Rome—the whole tourist *insalata,* all in thirty-
one days. She cannot get along with her tour mates, informs the
others that she is not continuing on with them to Spain, gets back
to New York flat broke, taxis to Marilyn's apartment, and is
embarrassed to have to ask the driver to wait while she borrows
ten dollars from her daughter to pay his fare. "Altho I was not
aware of it at this time I was going thru a nervous breakdown."

Whatever else leads her to term this episode a "nervous breakdown" must be read between the lines. But by now her narrative
has made abundantly clear that the Bradshaws are not a family to
face up squarely to either emotional problems or physical illnesses. Berenice tends to become agitated and ineffectual; she
feels powerless to handle matters and demands more support
from her husband. Franklin concludes that his wife's restless flut-
tering is the *cause* of the trouble, rather than the result. His
letters repeatedly accuse her of unnecessarily "working up" other
family members. He reminds his daughters frequently that their
mother is "an over-nervous person," but this is the farthest he
will go in acknowledgment of her genuine distress. Franklin's
own solution to each new family crisis is to retreat further into
the cluttered recesses of his warehouse.

In December 1958 Berenice is thrilled by the sudden news from
Frances that she plans to be married January 9 in St. Patrick's
Cathedral on Fifth Avenue. The groom is Vittorio Gentile, a
refined and moneyed European businessman. Franklin again says

he will not attend. Frances, unperturbed, invites Uncle Chubb Horton, husband of Aunt Bea, to come to New York and give her away. She orders up a frightfully expensive, custom-made white satin coat and lace mantilla. Marilyn gets busy cutting and stitching the taffeta gown she will wear as her sister's maid of honor. Vittorio arranges a wedding supper at the Colony Restaurant and polishes up his Mercedes-Benz. Berenice, who has at once offered to pay for everything, shops for a new dress and, as a wedding gift, shines up her entire stock of "family silver"—in truth, a series of pitchers and trays which she and Franklin have received over the years at Christmas from grateful Bradshaw's employees.

Berenice Bradshaw seems nothing short of ecstatic at this sudden turn of events. "Thank God!" she exclaims when she telephones the good news to her first-married daughter, in San Francisco. "Now all our troubles with Frances are over!"

"No, Mother," says Elaine. "They're just beginning."

Once they left Salt Lake, the Bradshaw daughters developed into very different sorts of women. Elaine, the invalid, became a pitiless realist, Marilyn a sort of sentimental pragmatist. In her apartment high over West End Avenue in New York, matronly Marilyn Bradshaw Reagan seems today a fifties housewife caught in a time warp—a grieving female Hamlet in Butterick Pattern dress. She really enjoys making her own clothes and scrubbing her kitchen floor. She is slow-moving, myopic, sorrowful. Though she and Berenice no longer speak, she still yearns with little hope that someday a reconciliation will occur. "The bottom line is: she's my mother, and I have a lot of feeling for her . . . *and some of it is mixed!*"

Elaine today is tough and dry-eyed. Life has burned away all illusion and sentimentality. When still young, she made a life-or-death choice to put her family behind her in order to survive her family. But though she rarely saw him, Elaine Bradshaw Drukman was probably the woman who loved Frank Bradshaw most deeply of them all. When he was murdered, her heart literally broke. She is alive today because of a porcine transplant. In 1980 at Stanford University the heart valve of a pig was implanted in her chest.

The elder Bradshaw sisters do resemble one another, and their mother and grandmother, in one respect: each is the stronger partner in her marriage. It is not that Robert Reagan and Mason

Drukman are weak men; rather, they seem less vivid than their wives. Among Bradshaws, the female bird always has the showier plumage, and the louder if not the sweeter voice.

While Frank Bradshaw was alive, Marilyn was a paragon of dutiful daughtership. She visited her parents often and wrote home regularly. She worked as a paralegal by day, and took courses in tax and estate law by night, preparing herself for the time when she hoped to take over her father's business. Frank Bradshaw never discouraged his daughter's dreams; for eleven years he paid her tuition fees. He continued to pay them even after Frances loudly asserted, to her parents and later to their lawyers, that never but never would she tolerate any such an arrangement. Frances believed that childless Marilyn's real purpose was not to help her parents but to cheat her sisters, and ultimately to deprive the grandchildren of their rightful inheritance. Frances charged that Marilyn was motivated not by daughterly devotion but naked greed.

The murder that split the Bradshaw family apart in 1978 also brought the two older sisters back together. Their mutual resolve to nail their father's assassin was now an alliance of spirit, a telephone alliance, and a far cry from the old days on Gilmer Drive when all the Bradshaws had lived close as flies in a bottle. After tiny Elaine's catastrophic second attack of rheumatic fever, she had been permanently installed in the sunny corner room that had once belonged to her parents. Franklin and Berenice and baby Frances now all shared the other small bedroom, which had formerly belonged to the girls, and Marilyn moved down to the basement with Robert.

"I was Other Mother in those days," Marilyn recalls. "I would come home from sixth grade and B.J. would give me the instructions for dinner and be off to her hydrotherapy thing—I remember she told me they had a 'big whirlpool with a hammock in it' at one of the local hospitals." At home, the life of B.J. (for Berenice Jewett) began to feel like the whirlpool without the hammock: an unwanted and demanding new baby, a nervous breakdown, then severe illness for her children, first Elaine, then Robert.

Very early one morning Marilyn heard a crash and thud outside her room, and found thirteen-year-old Robert unconscious on the basement floor, breathing heavily and racked by convulsions. She shouted for her parents and together they watched as the fit subsided. A few minutes later Robert awakened, as from a deep sleep, seemingly unaware of what had happened. Certainly twelve-year-old Marilyn was unfamiliar with epileptic seizures. Evidently her parents were equally ignorant, and perhaps they were also too ashamed to consult a doctor about their son's attack. For a long time, his care seems to have been left entirely to his younger sister. "What was to be gained by telling the folks?" she says today. "There was no need."

Since Robert was too big for her to move, she looked after him wherever he lay. She would hear the crash, leap from her bed, wet a cloth and put it on her brother's forehead, watch him get red in the face and froth at the mouth, and wait for the seizure to end. Years after she had grown up and moved to New York City, the slightest noise in the night made her sit up wide awake at once, fearful that Bob was about to have another attack.

At first Robert's seizures occurred two or three times a year. His sister noticed that they seemed to coincide with the days when Robert had an important appointment, and she thought his fear of keeping appointments might be what brought them on. Soon they were happening more often. At the start of World War II, Bob managed to enlist in the Navy's V-12 program. But doctors at Great Lakes Naval Training Station discovered his disability, and within sixty days he was given a medical discharge. Robert's attempts to serve his country are still tenderly recalled by his family. His mother and sisters dwell on his postwar achievements as a Boy Scout troop leader at the Unitarian Church, and as an electronics instructor in the Utah National Guard. Marilyn shows visitors Robert's Navy middy blouse, lovingly stroking the scarcely worn blue fabric as she speaks about what a wonderful cartoonist her brother was, and recalls his sweet nature. "He was a really nice guy. My husband liked him too."

All of the Bradshaws have trouble sleeping, and as teenagers Robert and Elaine used to take long nocturnal rambles together through the quiet neighborhood streets. Thoughts of her troubled brother, his kindness and goodness, his intelligence and his terrible suffering can still make her weep today.

What none of the Bradshaws like to talk about, and perhaps do not understand, is the progressive disorganization of Robert's mind. He spent the last eighteen years of his life in and out of mental hospitals, diagnosed as an incurable schizophrenic.

In 1952, a prefrontal lobotomy was performed on Robert Bradshaw at Utah State Hospital. Afterward the doctors told his family, "We wish we'd had him sooner." Marilyn believes this statement gave her mother "false hope" that Robert had once been "curable," but that the family had waited too long. What Marilyn thinks the doctors meant to convey was that had they had him sooner, "they might have been able to improve him on medication—the current medication." (Robert's type of frequent *grand mal* seizures are rarely seen today. The widespread use of Dilantin has rendered them medically obsolete in this country, like rabies or polio or smallpox.) "But I don't think they would have ever been able to get him into a productive life."

Marilyn herself believes that Robert suffered from "self-induced epilepsy." This has caused her to conclude that each time he suffered a seizure, "he was in fact giving himself his own shock therapy." Since, prior to his lobotomy, "Bob had had bad shock therapy," he was thereafter "in an untreatable situation . . ."

The Bradshaws' overall medical ignorance is surprising, though perhaps not unusual for its day. No one in the family seems to have had rudimentary first-aid knowledge. Marilyn never did learn that it was important to put something in her brother's mouth during a seizure to keep him from biting his tongue. Long after Robert was a grown man, Marilyn recalls, "they had to trim his tongue because the edges had got so ragged."

None of the Bradshaws except perhaps Elaine appears to understand what prefrontal lobotomy entails: it severs the most highly developed portion of the brain from the rest and, in effect, amputates "feeling." The procedure is irreversible, and today is castigated but not alas outlawed for the cruelty and grossness of its assault. The technique was employed in the late nineteen-forties and early fifties by some large state mental hospitals as a last-ditch method, after electro-convulsive shock therapy had failed, to render chronic mental patients easier to handle.

When lobotomy was first being considered for Bob, a preliminary psychiatric examination was required and Doug Steele drove him up to McTeigh Hospital, in Ogden. After he was examined, Doug was invited into the doctor's office alone. When Doug identified himself as manager of Bradshaw Auto Parts, "This psychiatrist almost fell outa his chair. He sez: My God! Why do they put *you* in this position? This is the *mother and father*'s role."

Frank Bradshaw could never face his son's problems. When the lobotomy was decided on, Berenice had to sign the permission papers. Doug Steele understood something of how Frank felt. One of the Steeles' own children has suffered several nervous breakdowns, and "Right to the day we die, the wife and I know we're gonna take this problem to our graves. But at least we've faced it. Frank was a genius in business. But he sure didn't meet the problem with Robert head on. I think every time he tried to face the problem in his own way, he'd have cinders thrown in his path by Berenice. She'd always be workin' against him . . . *and* talkin' everything over with Frances!"

But in truth neither Bradshaw parent could really face it, and each looked for reasons to blame the other, and in matters of family blamesmanship there is no such thing as a statute of limitations. Says Berenice today, "Franklin was a coward . . . Franklin would never stand up for his children. Never! When Bob was in junior high, the teacher called on him, and because he took his time to get up, the teacher came back and knocked him to the floor. But would Franklin go down there and talk to that teacher? Nope!"

"I *know* the trauma Frank went through with Bob," Steele says. "One time I remember the phone rang at home, and it was Frank. Berenice was out of town. He said, I'm having problems with Bob. Can you come down and help me, Doug? I'm afraid he'll get violent. I went down there, and Bob *was* almost out of control. And, oh boy, he was big! Bigger'n Frank—six feet four, two-thirty, mebbe two-forty pounds. So I told Bob I'd like to take him for a ride.

"Far as Bob ever hitting anybody, or hurtin' anybody, I've never seen that. It was just he'd get so *agitated,* he'd be screaming, working himself up against Frank. And that time Frank got scared enough of him, he felt he couldn't handle him alone. That's the only reason he called me. We took him down to City and County Hospital that time, got him admitted to the psycho ward."

Franklin preferred to communicate with his son by letter. But Berenice went to see him regularly every two weeks for eighteen years. Robert eventually was unable to care for himself; his seizures occurred every few days, and doctors had told the family that release was out of the question. Each time his mother came to visit, Robert pleaded with her to let him come home. His

"Dear Dad" letters speak repeatedly of his determination to "cut-myself-loose-from-my-Mother's-skirts," as his father continued to recommend, and of his plans to set himself up in the auto parts business. "Another look at the situation also tells me that I have never been independent since I can remember! How's that for training a boy to become a man? . . . As Mother can tell you, about all I have in this new room of mine is a bed, some post-cards on the wall, no place to hang my clothing, and some pictures of a complete Chrysler engine (part by part) which I study till I think I am about to go nuts! (insensible)."

If Berenice Bradshaw had had "false hopes" for Robert, Robert too had false hopes. He once walked away from the hospital and hopped a freight train headed east. When he was apprehended, in Wyoming, he explained to the authorities that he had been on his way to New York City "to help Frances." Says Marilyn, "That was the one way he knew to be useful to Mother."

Franklin's hopes were even less realistic than his wife's. He gradually convinced himself that—despite his son's tragic history—if only he himself could take a crack at disentangling Robert from his mother's apron strings, he could still "straighten him out." Only a few years before Robert died, Frank Bradshaw confided a new plan to Doug Steele. He said he wanted to move his son to an apartment in "a little hotel, half a block away from here, get a room there himself, and work with Bob day and night. He said if Bob could only be with *him* all the time, Frank could get his thoughts straightened out!"

"My husband could not accept illness," Berenice says. "The psychiatrist told him he couldn't face reality. He would take my son for a walk around the block thinking that was going to *cure* him. And when my son died, my husband said, 'Don't tell anyone.' *Don't tell anyone!* I said, 'Look, he's not a dog.' "

Officially, Robert Bradshaw died of a heart attack. His death certificate lists "idiopathic [of no known cause] epilepsy" as a contributing cause of death. But Elaine believes that what really killed her brother was the lobotomy, because it "had killed all his passion, his feeling."

Robert Bradshaw had left instructions to turn over his body to the University of Utah Medical School. Berenice Bradshaw had saved her son's cartoons, his military discharge papers, his Boy Scout medals, his certificate as an electronics instructor and other mementos, in a locked briefcase. Eleven months after his death, as Memorial Day approached, she became concerned that Robert had no grave, hence there was no place to display the flag to honor his military service in World War II. She seemed to want to arrange some kind of burial.

"Robert had died at the VA Hospital," says Marilyn, "and the Medical School still had his bones. Mother wanted them. She went down to see Dad at the warehouse. She had done all her fieldwork, she had got her package together. But then Dad shot down the idea."

"He's dead. I thought we were through with all this," Franklin said. But Berenice could not let go. She wrote to other family members, soliciting more aid and advice.

"I believe in living memorials, not dead ones," Marilyn wrote back. She never received a reply, she says, and her mother was left with a locked briefcase to which she used to point sorrowfully and say, "This is all that remains of Bob."

In her "Autobiography," Berenice would write:

June 1966, on Father's Day, Franklin and I visited Robert at the Veterans hospital here in Salt Lake City. We took some ice cream and the three of us sat on the lawn and had refreshments. He was in good spirits. One week later, on June 26, at 9:30 P.M. the Veterans Hospital called to tell us our son had just passed away. He went to his room to lie down and just went to sleep, never to awaken, a heart failure. A memorial service was held in the Unitarian Church. Marilyn and Bob came home and helped us in our grief with the final plans. Robert was 38 years old, had spent the last 18 years in and out of hospitals. His poor health was a source of heart ache to us, and the saddest cross we had to bear. he was a dear, sweet son, loved by his family and friends. His hopes and suffering had come to an end.

"O death where is thy sting and grave thy victory"? The sting is in the hearts of those who loved—and stand in silent bewilderment and anguish for a life that has vanished and the victory belongs to Mother Nature, that selfish individual who demands a return of all that she gives.

This is his obituary.

Guilts about their children haunted both Bradshaws. They responded in different ways. Franklin withdrew more and more from his family. "The really sad thing," says Marilyn, "was going down to that warehouse to talk to Dad, and realizing that *that* was his home, and *that* was his family." Berenice's guilt moved her in the opposite direction. She began to share her troubles indiscriminately with anyone who would listen. Eventually she became a hopeless, helpless emotional flasher.

Frances Bradshaw seems to have been born with an instinct for turning her parents' guilt to her own advantage. In return perhaps for the pain of knowing she was unwanted, the gods had rewarded her with the powers of Moloch. For whatever reason, Frances from infancy seemed positively to flourish in a hostile environment. She was like brine shrimp that live only in the waters of boiling geysers.

Before she is a year old, Frances has her entire family huddled together around her crib singing lullabys. By the time she is three, her technique is refined. To hear the sisters tell it, twelve-year-old Marilyn gets home from school and starts cooking dinner. Berenice goes out to shop, leaving Elaine in bed contentedly working on her Storybook Dolls, and baby "Frankie" playing happily on the kitchen floor. But as soon as they hear Mom's car turning back into the driveway, Frankie begins to howl.

Mom rushes into the kitchen with the groceries, demanding to know what's the matter. Frankie whimpers that Marilyn has been teasing her again. Berenice snatches up her injured darling to her breast and furiously punishes wicked Marilyn. She does not seek Marilyn's side of the story. Marilyn gets no chance to explain that Frankie had been happy, or at least silent, until they heard Mom's car.

"Mother would accept Frankie's word for *everything*," Marilyn says. "And she's *still doing that.*"

"Frances as a child was extremely strong-willed," another family member recalls. "She always wanted to be the center of attention and she early found ways of doing so. She simply threw herself on the floor and kicked and screamed until her mother gave her whatever she wanted."

Frances says all this is just wicked-sister talk. In fact, her younger sister was in the bedroom and had no idea what was going on. Her older sister was a sadist who invariably shut the baby up in the closet the moment the mother left the house. *That's* the reason she screamed so loudly as soon as she heard the returning car. Her older sister made her life hell. When she was six, Marilyn drowned her pet kittens. When she was getting dressed for her first school party, Marilyn crept into her room to whisper how ugly she was. Someone should write a book about the horror story of her childhood, Frances often says, and call it *Sister Dearest.* "It would make *Mommie Dearest* read like Grimm's Fairy Tales."

Whatever the truth of these childhood allegations, none would deny that Frances all her life has been a difficult person for others to deal with. To say "yes" to Frances is an invitation to be steamrollered. To say "no" to Frances is to invite such dire consequences that few in her lifetime have dared utter the word.

Frances herself has no difficulty saying "no"; that is her habitual response. When she does say "yes," a price tag is attached. These traits date back to childhood. Franklin once visited her bedroom for a rare father-daughter chat. His purpose was to tell her how "hurt" he had been by her indifferent grades at the end of her freshman year at East High School. He knew she had the brains to get all A's. If only she tried, she could graduate at the head of her class, as he himself had done.

Frances promised to try harder if he would reward her with the kind of college education she wanted; she had no interest in following her parents and sisters to what she saw as the humdrum University of Utah. She wanted an Eastern education at a top-quality women's college. Franklin agreed: If she got the grades, he would pay to send her East. It would prove a Faustian bargain.

Franklin Bradshaw kept all his feelings to himself, his anger especially. Whenever the Bradshaw children had to be punished, Berenice would be the parent who got upset, although Franklin was forced to administer the punishment. "Dad was not abusive or even really angry," says Marilyn. "She would scream and yell at us and get all worked up and then, when Dad came home, she'd get *him* worked up. Then she'd make him punish us while she stood around wringing her hands and looking pitiful.

"The only thing that really made Dad angry was when Mother got upset. I understood him," she adds. "I never felt any resentment toward him."

Elaine Drukman lacks any odor of sanctimony. She is probably the most clear-seeing person in this tormented family. She believes she has ESP, and hears a kind of "ping" whenever someone tells a lie. "An alarm bell goes off," she says. As an example, take her famous 1952 meeting with Vice-President Nixon. On the mantel at Gilmer Drive are two photographs: a last portrait of Franklin, made only months before his death, and a 1952 picture of Elaine shaking hands with Richard Nixon. Berenice shows the picture to visitors to indicate that, before meeting the liberal-minded Drukman, her daughter was politically unblemished. But Frances says, "My sister married a Communist." And Elaine says, "My politics are *more* radical than my husband's." In 1952, it is true, she did belong to the Utah Young Republicans, "But the moment the Great Man walked in, my alarm bells went off. I felt: That man is in a *different reality* from other people. Ever since, my mental picture of Richard Nixon has been a man who walks through life holding a mirror before him, seeing no one but himself, hearing nothing but his own voice."

The image fits her sister Frances equally well. By now, in fact, it fits every member of this by-hatred-possessed family.

Elaine today is a small, harrowed-looking woman with a harsh, nervous giggle. Traces of beauty remain, and she has moments of touching tenderness when she speaks of her father, her brother, her sons. She and her husband have led lives of serious political commitment. Mason taught political science at Reed College, in Oregon, and together they were active in the anti-Vietnam war movement, and later published a magazine dedicated to exposing political corruption in local politics. They opened their own experimental school when they could not find one they deemed suitable to educate their sons. Sam and Max are both graduate students now, and also teachers of art and music in northern California. The Drukmans have never earned much money. Mason for several years has been at work on an authorized biography of Oregon's late senator, Wayne Morse.

When her Drukman grandchildren were younger, Berenice used to visit fairly frequently, happy to baby-sit and to help the family along financially, though not without pointing out to her daughter, "You *would* manage to find yourself the only *poor* Jew in America."

In the mid-seventies, dismayed with American foreign policy and afflicted with a sense of political burnout, the Drukmans moved to New Zealand where for three years they edited a magazine dedicated to the cause of enlightened consumerism. But the Wellington climate is harsh, the wind blows without letup, and the intense homesickness of the teenage sons, and eventually of their parents, brought the family back to the United States just a few weeks before Frank Bradshaw's murder.

Elaine believes her parents had an unbearable marriage between a woman who didn't really want children and a man who very much did. Although her father was not a practicing Mormon, his values were Mormon values. Her mother was a woman born before her time. Both of them were tragic figures, but her father had an out: he could substitute his success in his business, bury himself in his work. Her mother didn't have that.

Elaine saw her father as a man with a distinct feminine side, as being very tender, very loving, but somewhat timid and inclined to back off if he felt that asserting himself would hurt someone else. He was assertive in business because he had to be. He was the youngest of four sons, and among Mormons primogeniture rules. His oldest brother inherited his presidency of American Savings & Loan. Franklin had to earn his own success.

Mason Drukman says, "Frank was not a mean man, and not a cruel man. But he *was* extremely one-dimensional. Unless you were conversant with oil or with auto parts, there was just not much you could talk about with him. And he was extremely remote. He wrote letters to his daughters in the third person."

Marilyn says her parents "did not dislike each other, they hated each other! We didn't hear much fighting. Not even talking. But we heard the *silences*. Long, long silences. And Mother was suffering. So she began putting all of her affection into Frances. Hugging and kissing her, sitting her on her lap when she was eight, nine years old. We were all adult children by then, teenagers. We knew Frances was too big to be sitting on Mother's lap. Mother was *using Frances,* as a companion, just the same as Frances later used Marc. But then Mother would have a bridge party for her lady friends, and she would tell Frances: Now this is for *my* friends. You can't come. And she would shut Frances out. Frances would have helped her get ready for the party . . . and then she would be sent away. It was a case of a lonely woman using a little child for company. But she never understood."

Frankie Bradshaw came East to Bryn Mawr College in 1956. Her schoolmates were a remarkably accomplished, dynamic group of

young women, among them Dr. Matina Horner, President of
Radcliff College, the writers Renata Adler, Kate Stimpson, and
Eve Pell, the revolutionary Kathy Boudin, and the TV producer
Joan Shikegawa. They included numerous women who would
become doctors, lawyers, academics, and people in politics and
the arts. None of them can relate the woman in today's tabloid
headlines to the girl they knew a quarter century ago. Those who
remember her at all—and a great many say they do not—recol-
lect a high-spirited, fun-loving, hard-drinking, hard-playing girl
from somewhere out West, someone not in the traditional Eastern
preppy mold, someone with more verve, more daring. They mention Frankie's unusual friendliness and high spirits, her surpass-
ing intelligence, quick wits, hearty laughter, her expensive
clothes, gaudy jewelry, brilliant red lipstick, and "that wonderful,
great big jack-o'-lantern smile."

Then as now, Bryn Mawr was a crucible of female intellect. In
their high school or boarding school, most girls in the freshman
class had been valedictorians or class presidents or tops in the
honor society. What one of them calls "a harrowing self-selecting
process was going on. The competition was . . . well . . . so
unnerving, we were all a little bit nuts." One of Frankie's classmates, later a well-known public official, deliberately went to
classes for several months wearing the same cocktail dress, same
dead carnation corsage, tennis shoe on one foot, athletic sock on
the other. Another girl, now a professor of psychiatry, used to
walk around campus with half her mouth painted blue, the other
half green. Nobody said a word.

Madeleine Di Gorgonzo Fletcher, an English professor at
Tufts University, lived next door to Frankie during their freshman year and thought her "deeply intelligent, ironic, never
rowdy but with a nice strain of rebelliousness. She was a little
zany and I liked her a lot. A person of great *gusto* . . . the kind
who is hard to force into line. Willful, but rather wonderful.
That's the sort of person who went to Bryn Mawr then. She
always tremendously enjoyed herself—and one of the things she
enjoyed most was getting around the rules."

Frankie's frantic activity, her chain-smoking, the nonstop talking, the frenzied-seeming pursuit of fun were not seen as unusual
for their time and place. Neither was the drinking. Indeed, heavy
drinking was considered a mark of "maturity," and Frankie was
admired for her capacity to hold her liquor, even though she was

not in the same class as her favorite drinking buddy, a woman we'll call Diana Blue (now dead of alcoholism), who was greatly esteemed for being able to down seven martinis at a clip and still remain sober enough to sign in and get down the hall to the bathroom before vomiting and collapsing in the shower.

"We all knew Frankie had a drinking problem," says another dorm mate. "She lived in the room right next to the warden, on the ground floor, and our whole dorm thought it hilarious, and rather wonderful, that the warden never knew that she was—always—totally drunk!"

In the late 1950s senseless curfew morals still prevailed. Bryn Mawr girls had to be inside their dorms by eleven-thirty at night, unless they had dates with boys; then the sign-in hour was advanced to 2 A.M. In the words of one girl, "You could screw all night in some guy's car—nobody cared. You could drink all night. It was not considered a crime to be drunk—if you could hold it. Just so long as you got back to the dorm by sign-in time, nothing else mattered."

A few things did matter, of course, including criminal activity, or signs of real or potential mental illness. Two psychiatrists were available on campus, and "troubled" girls were urged to unburden themselves. Their option: talk it out, or get out. See the shrink, or face suspension and expulsion. The chats were supposedly entirely confidential; doubtless they were not entirely so. Part of the role of such doctors in any institution is to anticipate scandal and try to make sure that if it happens, it happens off campus.

Frankie's family knew nothing of her exciting new life, and she took pains to keep it that way. During her freshman year, Frankie called her Other Mother collect on Sunday nights. Marilyn, by then a New York City career girl working in advertising, listened patiently as her sister "talked about nothing for hours. I never interrupted, I never asked for reimbursement, I'd just listen. If you cut her off, she'd get mad at you."

On holidays and some weekends, Frankie "came home" to Marilyn's studio apartment on East Fifty-fourth Street. She insisted on traveling by taxi, disliked walking even a few blocks, and flatly refused to take buses or subways. When she had a car, she parked it wherever she wanted, undeterred by No Parking signs.

At Christmas, Marilyn took Frankie with her to visit friends in

New Hampshire and was much embarrassed by her kid sister's habits. "She wouldn't bathe up there because it was a strange bathtub, she said. She had her period, *and* she slept with her socks on, so she really got stinking. She just didn't care."

The summer following her freshman year, her parents were dismayed by Frankie's behavior in Salt Lake. She would scarcely speak to them, refused to answer any questions about college, spent most of her time sullenly watching television, and put $600 worth of dents and scratches into the family car. Still no one stopped her. No one said no to Frances.

By their sophomore year, says Dr. Helen Peemoeller, a professor of English at Reading Area Community College in Pennsylvania, "Frankie did have a reputation for being highly emotional, even wild. But you must recognize that we were all neurotic then. Probably a lot of people would have told you I was more unstable than Frankie at the time."

When her second year of college ended, Frankie did not return to Salt Lake. Instead, she took a room at the Barbizon-Plaza Hotel in New York City, intent on "having a good time." A week or two later, Camilla Jones—now Camilla Jones Tatem, M.D., director of medical services at a hospital in New York State—was surprised to receive a phone call from a younger girl, Frankie Bradshaw, whom she was but vaguely aware of, mostly as Diana Blue's drinking buddy. Camilla had just graduated and was packing to leave for a summer in Europe before entering medical school.

When Frankie suggested they meet for a drink, Camilla agreed, and the two girls chose a lively bar but blocks from Frankie's hotel. Gino Restaurant is a venerable, much-loved New York institution: small, deliberately unchic, it is famous not only for good food and fair prices, but for the crowd of good-looking women and moneyed men who can always be seen three-deep at the bar waiting for a table. Camilla remembers Frankie swiftly striking up a conversation with a "wealthy young man" at the bar who began urging the girls to come for a ride in his Mercedes-Benz convertible. Camilla was reluctant; fun-loving Frankie was determined. "Come on!" she shouted. "I don't want to go alone."

After a brief spin around town, they ended up in the man's apartment. "Mostly they were drinking," Camilla recalls. "I wanted to go home. Frankie didn't." The man began to press gifts on the girls. Camilla kept the chic, tweedy little cap he gave her for many years. All the same, she was uneasy. The gifts "bothered" Camilla; they signaled that "something was wrong," a signal Frankie either did not pick up or deliberately chose to ignore. "I couldn't reach her."

The man left the room to search out more presents. "Frankie, we should not *be* here," Camilla whispered.

"But we're having fun. Have a drink!" Drunk and getting drunker, in truth slipping out of control, Frankie insisted on behaving as if nothing unusual were going on.

Camilla went home. A few days later, Frankie telephoned her to describe her "whirlwind romance." The round of nonstop drinking, driving, eating, and sex was still going on. She'd never had so much fun in all her life, Frankie said.

Camilla heard nothing more of Frankie for twenty-four years, not until another Bryn Mawr classmate, now a newspaper reporter, called her attention to the headline in the evening paper: SOCIALITE MOM IN $400 MILLION RUBOUT! As for the man the girls picked up in the bar, he was—and is—one of Gino's most faithful and beloved regulars, a pint-sized pearl importer named Vittorio Gentile.

Just before returning to college, Frankie and Marilyn were both briefly in Salt Lake. Frankie bought a "trunkful of new clothes" and had them shipped to Bryn Mawr. Back in New York City, Frankie did more shopping, and Marilyn accompanied her kid sister to Philadelphia to see a couple of plays before Frankie returned to campus and Marilyn to New York. She found a letter from Berenice enclosing bills for thousands of dollars' worth of clothing from Saks Fifth Avenue, all charged to the Bradshaws in Salt Lake. Did Marilyn know anything about this? When she called Bryn Mawr, Frankie said the bills were for a lot of clothes that didn't fit, and she intended to send them back to Saks. But she never did.

"Salt Lake City clothes were no longer good enough for her!" Marilyn sniffs. "The thing that's always meant most to Frankie is *status,* and she was on her way."

A few weeks later, Marilyn got a phone call: her sister was being held in the college infirmary. Failure to obey dormitory regulations, academic failure, dormitory thievery, charge account fraud, check forgery, drug use, and threats of suicide all eventually were mentioned. Bryn Mawr believed Frankie was mentally ill and required professional help. Since she refused to accept it, her family was now being asked to remove her from campus as soon as possible. Other Mother escorted her sister home to Salt Lake, and Berenice summoned Elaine from San Francisco to help out with this newest family crisis.

Marilyn says Frankie was suspended from Bryn Mawr not only because of a nervous breakdown, but because "she broke the rules. She was going to see Vittorio for weekends and signing out that she was staying with me. But she *loved* that school. She used to tell me all the time, 'If I couldn't go to Bryn Mawr, I would just *die.*'"

The Salt Lake City psychiatrist recommended that Frances enter a mental hospital in Colorado Springs. But Franklin was away on a business trip, Berenice could not bring herself to commit her daughter, and Frances would not go voluntarily. They found a second doctor who said he could treat Frances on an outpatient basis, with two or three psychotherapy sessions a week.

"Dad came home and he agreed with Mother and Frankie." Her sisters were opposed. They knew Frankie had already seen psychiatrists both in Salt Lake City and at college. "Why continue the same sort of therapy which had not worked earlier?" they reasoned.

They went to see the latest psychiatrist and asked what the matter was with Frankie. Their kid sister suffered from a "psychopathic personality disorder which it is probably too late by now to treat," they were told. The Salt Lake City doctor entirely supported the Bryn Mawr doctors' recommendation: either hospitalize Frances as mentally ill, or allow her to be charged with the crimes she had committed—dormitory thievery, charge account irregularities, check forgery. It was time to "quit bailing her out," time for someone to say no to Frances.

But for once Berenice and Franklin put up a united front. They did nothing at all.

Elaine was disgusted. She determined to follow the same policy she had urged on her parents—turn your back on Frances. She returned to San Francisco and for a time, until she realized such pressure tactics were totally useless, she even stopped speaking to her mother. As for her younger sister, she did not see her again until their father's funeral.

While her family wrangled over her treatment, Frankie was

quite competently plotting her own escape. She had always functioned most efficiently when under greatest pressure. Now it was
happening again. Stealthily she visited the town's best stores,
bought herself yet another new wardrobe, charged everything to
her parents, and stored the clothes in airport lockers. She still
needed cash for a plane ticket back to New York City.

A good source was the family stock in Wasatch Chemical, the
company her father had formed while still in college. Frankie
knew, though her sisters did not, that, to minimize his own net
worth, Franklin held much of the stock in his children's names;
probably she had acquired the information the summer she
worked in the warehouse before starting Bryn Mawr. She knew
too that if she posted a "lost instruments bond," guaranteeing
that "her" stock had been lost, new negotiable stock certificates
could then be issued, with no one the wiser, at least for the time
being. Frankie called on her father's older banker brother, Uncle
Bernard Bradshaw, described the "lost" stock, and hoodwinked
him into signing the fraudulent bond.

"And all this while she was letting Mother plan a great big
Thanksgiving dinner in her honor!" Marilyn exclaims. But Berenice must have suspected something was up. She found evidence
of the bond in Frankie's purse and told Elaine. Elaine told her
father, and Franklin blew up. "One of the few times I've ever
actually seen him do it," says Marilyn. "Then and there he personally took her to the plane."

Frankie had no luggage—just three lockers stuffed with clothes
in plastic bags and no reservation. The airport was thronged
with Thanksgiving travelers, and the plane was fully booked. But
Frankie threw a full-blown tantrum, shouting, "I've got to get on!
I've got to get on!" until the airline clerks were so embarrassed,
they found room for her. Even American Airlines was learning
the discomforts of saying no to Frances.

It was a few weeks after that when Frances called Salt Lake
City to announce her wedding plans. Marriage is one of the tradi-
tional options available to a daughter in revolt against her par-
ents. Berenice had married Franklin in order to remain in Salt
Lake City. Frances was marrying Vittorio in order to stay in New
York City.

"Mother was in favor of the marriage because she thought now
Frances would get taken care of," Marilyn says. "She knew that
Vittorio lived well. He had a nice car. He taught Frances to cook.

But it was a bad marriage from the start. They had such different backgrounds, different temperaments." Vittorio, born in Torre del Greco, Italy, in the early 1930s, is shorter than Frances, and he has one walleye. "He couldn't be in the war because of his height and the eye. That's why he has had to prove himself. That's why he lifts weights and exercises. *He* has psychological problems too," says Marilyn.

The fact was, Frankie and Vittorio enjoyed drinking together; then they fought. Yet Marilyn is certain that Vittorio did love Frances. He was very distressed when she left, and once their protracted and bitter divorce was achieved, the couple got back in touch. Frances phoned Vittorio from time to time, and they continued to meet for lunch occasionally, even after each was remarried. But their marital fights were real. Marilyn's studio apartment was down the street from Vittorio's place at Fifty-fourth Street off Madison. "He'd take her out for a fancy dinner and drinks, and drop her off on Fifty-fourth while he parked his beloved Mercedes. She'd be afraid to go home, and would call me and ask if she could spend the night with me. It happened so often I hated to hear the phone ring after ten o'clock at night."

After one gala evening, Frances ended up in the hospital having her stomach pumped. During a spat, Vittorio had flushed his dinner down the toilet, and Frances, in retaliation, had swallowed a bottle of aspirin.

Frances certainly knew Vittorio's habits before she married him. She had in fact passed out in his apartment on their first date. That he did not then "take advantage" of her she regarded as proof that he was a gentleman. All the fighting was probably sexually stimulating, one psychiatrist told the family. She probably liked getting beaten up, the doctor surmised, because it was the punishment she felt she deserved for hating her father as much as she did.

The year 1960 was an eventful one for all the Bradshaws. The federal government announced its public oil and gas lottery, and Franklin plunged into the complex game that would occupy him the rest of his life. He also devised and nearly carried out his plan to "save" Robert by moving him from the hospital to a furnished room near the warehouse, thus disentangling him from his mother's apron strings. That same year the third Bradshaw daughter,

Marilyn, got married, and Frances bore two sons, one in February, a second in December.

During Christmas vacation, Marilyn had fallen over the balustrade of a ski lodge in Saratoga, New York, and suffered a severe concussion. She awoke five days later astonished and pleased to find Frances and Vittorio had made the long train trip to her Schenectady hospital room, despite the bitter January weather and the fact that Frances was eight months pregnant. "I don't know whose idea that was, his or hers, but I appreciated it very much."

"As the years go on, you'll notice a change in her," Frances says the doctor told her at the time.

In consequence of her accident, Marilyn met a young, sandy-haired, mild-mannered negligence lawyer named Robert McMillan Reagan. He was divorced, the father of two teenaged daughters, and a former Assistant U.S. Attorney for the Southern District of New York. Eventually he would become a trial attorney for the City of New York, prosecuting child abuse cases for the city's family courts, and later chasing down runaway fathers in an attempt to recover welfare funds. Six weeks after Reagan met the injured skier, they decided to get married, but Marilyn had no interest in participating in yet a third Bradshaw wedding fuss. Furthermore, her father could not refuse to come to her wedding celebration if she didn't even *have* one. Thus Marilyn, like her mother and grandmother before her, eloped into wifehood.

A short time later, the newlyweds visited the Bradshaws in Salt Lake City, and Berenice made a backyard barbecue. She learned that her new son-in-law's father was the founder and headmaster of a Quaker school in Poughkeepsie, New York, and his sister was a heroic teacher of remedial reading, now confined by polio to an iron lung. Hence, his family had never had much money. "Frankly," he said, "I'm out for all I can get." He added that he and Marilyn had already made out their wills.

"What did he need a will for? He didn't *have* anything!" Berenice sniffed, and concluded that this son-in-law, like her first one, Drukman, had only married her daughter for the money. Later, Berenice came to believe that Robert Reagan was "squirrelly," and she told people he had spent time in mental hospitals. Both Reagans say the story is entirely false. Like the story about Robert being a fortune hunter, and Mason being a Communist, Frances made it up and convinced her mother.

Marilyn's marriage gave her some much needed perspective. No longer did she feel so continually bruised by the struggle between her mother and sister. Today she says, "You know, my sister's an intelligent person. And it's too bad to waste a life. But by the same token she has *taken* one life, and ruined several others. I'm thinking of her two boys. And certainly she hasn't made Mother's life very pleasant." But though marriage put some space between herself and Frances, the relief was more illusory than real. Other Mother could not really extirpate her sister unless she was also ready to let go of her mother—Frances and Berenice were too tightly knotted—and this sacrifice she was still unwilling, or unable, to make.

The Bradshaws' first grandson, Sam Drukman, had been born in San Francisco in June 1958, the same month that Frances met Vittorio. Their second grandchild was Lorenzo Jewett Gentile, born February 6, 1960, at Doctors Hospital in New York City. After a solo bus trip through Canada, her first tourist adventure alone, Berenice arrived in New York that fall, eager to see Lorenzo and try to help out her daughter, whose second pregnancy already was well advanced. Marco Francis Gentile was born December 21, only ten months after his brother. Marilyn said, "Larry was a love baby. Marc was passion after birth."

From the beginning, the two boys were very difficult to manage together. They were noisy, unruly, hard to put to sleep, and quarrelsome when awake. In April 1961 Frances needed varicose vein surgery, and Berenice came to New York again to help with her difficult, hyperactive grandsons. The following year she made still another trip, timing her cross-country bus ride so she could also visit the Drukmans, who were now expecting their second child.

Franklin remained at home, overseeing his expanding empire and also attempting to manage the affairs of his daughter Frances by long distance. At year's end he concluded she had $18,000 in oil leases as a result of his tireless efforts to "build her up a profitable oil lease business." But her continuing extravagances had produced a $6,525 overdraft at her bank.

One evening in June 1963 Vittorio came home to find that Frances and their sons had vanished. The apartment was stripped of all its furnishings and contents. Swastikas, "Heil Hitler!" and "Heil Mussolini!" were scrawled on the bare walls. Later, Berenice said they had to leave stealthily because "if he'd known that she was going to leave, he would have beat her to death. He's a little fellow, but strong as an ox. When she was pregnant with Marc, he used to pick her up by her feet and bang her head against the wall."

When Frances decided to leave Vittorio, she again plotted and planned her moves well in advance. "She had everything nicely put away and fixed so that she *could* leave," says Berenice. "She had her sister Marilyn come over, and a colored cleaning lady, and hired a van, and by noon they had everything out of that house."

Marilyn today does not recall being present. She only remembers being "in on" the planning of the move. Frances says Marilyn supplied the maid and "drove the getaway car."

Frances says that when she was pregnant with Lorenzo, her husband stomped on her stomach and inflicted prenatal brain damage. Vittorio says Frances was not a good mother. He sometimes came home from work and found the babies unfed, unbathed, their diapers unchanged. Berenice says Frances was a devoted mother. "She never neglected her children. She could have left these two boys with their brute father and gone off and had a good life for herself. But no, she stuck it out . . ." Berenice says a social worker told her that "had Frances stayed with Vittorio Gentile another year, they would all end up in a mental institution." Vittorio says that Berenice is crazy. He says Frances once attempted to have her mother committed to a mental hospital by a New York psychiatrist, Arthur M. Perlman. Dr. Perlman says, "No comment."

Frances and the boys moved first to a stifling, cluttered one-bedroom apartment at 40 East Eighty-ninth Street. Marco and Lorenzo's first memories date from this summer of 1963. Marco says he recalls his mother holding him out the window of the tenth-floor apartment to show him something on the street below. Both boys remember a cat named Henry that Lorenzo had trapped in a bottle. They remember dumping out all their mother's perfumes into the middle of her bed and how, when Frances discovered it, she beat them until they bled.

Soon after moving out, Frances charged her husband with nonsupport and cruel and inhuman treatment. Vittorio told the court he still loved his wife very much and wanted a reconciliation. Frances did not. She said he was a drunkard, insanely jealous, and often beat up their sons, as well as herself. The case did not make the newspapers until she also said that Vittorio was "allergic to sex." Vittorio countercharged his wife with abandonment, and said he often went to work at 7:30 A.M. in order to come home in midmorning and satisfy his wife's "love moods." After several days of titillating tabloid testimony, Judge Wilfred A. Waltemade, of Bronx Supreme Court, said he believed all the charges and countercharges were "greatly exaggerated," and added that both parents demonstrated an immaturity that made them "unable to cast aside their own selfish interests . . ." Frances says Judge Waltemade was thrown off the bench.

Robert Reagan, a professional in the field of child abuse, says he doubts Vittorio ever beat his small sons, though there is no doubt he frequently battled with his wife. Marilyn recalls only that he drove the children around in his car at breakneck speeds. The fact is that the Reagans did not see much of the Gentiles while they were married. It was only after they broke up that Frances needed her Other Mother again.

Just a few blocks away from Frances's new home was the Unitarian Church at Eightieth Street and Lexington Avenue, well known then as a neighborhood gathering place for sincerely committed churchgoers and for particular kinds of lost souls. The church held regular "coffee hours" that attracted a fluctuating crowd, all of them more or less lonely, more or less well-educated, more or less well-heeled denizens of Manhattan's Upper East Side. They fell into three categories: shy people who could be comfortable only with others of their own class, single women hoping to meet interesting men, and well-mannered oddballs and ne'er-do-wells who preyed on the first two groups.

Among the regular coffee hour visitors that summer, two sisters from Utah are well remembered. One had "a short, mannish haircut" and "exuded no charm." The other was "extremely vivacious," with a broad jack-o'-lantern grin. The sisters got talking one afternoon to a strange, garrulous fat man, a sometime high school science teacher named Richard Behrens. Marilyn met him only once again, that same summer, when she brought Robert along to a coffee hour. Then she did not hear from him for seventeen years. But between Frankie Bradshaw and Dickie Behrens perfect friendship budded, blossomed, branched, endured.

Like Frankie, Richard Behrens was clever, articulate, eccentric, disorderly, and alone. Like her, he was obsessed by the money-eyed classes, and by the Eastern WASP Establishment in particular. He had an encyclopedic knowledge of how it all worked, who was really Old Guard, and who was merely rich. He knew not merely who "mattered," but how much. He scanned the Social Register like a horseplayer eyeing the *Racing Form*. He knew who was who in the best families, and how they were and were not interrelated. He knew who was born rich and who had married rich and what kind of divorce settlements people made.

As a schoolteacher, he was especially sharp on private schools: which were best, and which were second-best, and why. He had a Salinger-like comprehension of the preppy scene, and an O'Hara-like eye for New York clubland. He had surveyed and mapped the entire hidden terrain—Racquet and River, Knickerbocker and Colony, Cosmopolitan and Century, as well as Yale and Harvard. He approached the "Society" section of the Sunday paper like a lepidopterist advancing on butterflies, alert to precise markings and subtle shadings.

Richard Behrens was at best a fringe dweller in the social carpet. His father, Herman Behrens, was a respected physician who lived and practiced in Jersey City, New Jersey, and was known around his hospital as "Herman the German." But Richard's older brother, Robert Behrens, was in a different class. He had a distinguished war record in the U.S. Navy and impeccable academic credentials—B.A. and M.A. degrees from Haverford College, Pennsylvania, and a Ph.D. earned in Europe. He was well married, an excellent father, and a career State Department official who had already made a name for himself in Germany, Vienna, and Washington as a high-level figure in the United States Information Agency. Those who know the family speak of the brothers as being "like night and day." Richard Behrens both intensely admired and bitterly envied his brother Robert's accomplishments.

Richard Behrens claimed he had attended both St. Paul's and Phillips Exeter academies, and been kicked out of both. (In fact, he grew up in Jersey City, went to Blair Academy and Lafayette College.) His job résumé, which he carried around with him, was four pages long. He was knowledgeable about cars, weaponry, chemistry, machines. He had sold ballistics microscopes for Leitz, written science textbooks for Prentice-Hall, and taught science and biology at many private and public schools. He was an impressive applicant, but never held a job for any length of time. His brains and fast-talking charm worked well at first. But sooner or later he would become hostile or resentful, or sloppy in his work; then he would disappear on a drinking binge and be fired.

Behrens's ethnic background obsessed him. He had what seemed to one old friend "a love-hate relationship with his Germanness, and also with Jewishness." He is not Jewish and fears being mistaken for such. He is addicted to the telephone and sometimes leaves six messages in one day, in a German accent, from "Adolf," or "Mr. Schicklgruber," brilliantly weaving some imagined Hitlerian adventure into an event from the day's headlines. Behrens's relationships with women, other than Frances, were usually fleeting, and he never married.

A career woman who once dated Behrens saw Frances and Dick together often in the mid-sixties. "The apartment she lived in was not very pretty, not terribly clean. There was always a certain amount of disorganization around Frances. She never could quite get it together. I felt there were a lot of loose ends in her life. But I know a lot of people like that. She was quite organized in regard to her children. Very conscious of the 'right' schools; very, very status-conscious. Both she and Dick lived on the fringes of WASP respectability. Then one of them would get very drunk, say something outrageous, and never get asked back. One time I heard Dick tell the hostess her mother was a lesbian. Another time, with several gay men at the table, Frances launched into a terrible tirade against faggots. Both were heavy drinkers and liked plenty of casual sex. But their relationships with the opposite sex came to quite bad ends. The live-in person was always described as 'too demanding.' The truly steady relationship was with one another."

Behrens posed as an eccentric mittel-European genius who knew everything about everything—music, art, science, philosophy, the history of psychoanalysis. It is true he had lived for a time in Lynchburg, Virginia, and undergone old-fashioned Freudian psychoanalysis there. He worked then as a department store manager-trainee and is remembered chiefly for being "enormously resentful of his co-workers."

Says a Virginia neighbor of the time, "Dick is always jockeying for power, matching wits, evaluating his performance, and checking the action." He is like a racetrack tout whose inside dope is always slightly screwed up.

Most important, Richard Behrens is a man seething with resentments—against the rich, but more against the poor; against the world, in which he found himself increasingly unable to "make it" professionally and socially. But secondmost of all, he resented his successful brother, Robert. And above everything, Richard Behrens hated his father.

"Dick was always obsessed with his inheritance," recalls a longtime friend. "He described his father as 'a miser.' When his mother was still alive, his father had a girlfriend on the side, and perhaps a child, and Dick talked continually about losing his 'inheritance' to 'the slut.' He was very much threatened by this woman and he kept saying, 'Someone should get rid of them!' "

Dr. Behrens lived in a run-down section of Jersey City, but he also owned a house near a lake, "and Dick was forever fighting to get it, inherit it, keep it out of the hands of 'the slut.' He talked incessantly about the necessity to protect his inheritance by killing his father."

Frances Bradshaw was becoming a purposeful social mountaineer, determined to leave Salt Lake City behind, resolute about associating only with "better" people. She encouraged her mother's passionate interest in breeding and bloodlines. Membership in the Huguenot Society was for years her proudest affiliation, and she blackballed her own sister there in order to maintain her unchallenged supremacy in the New York chapter. Her husbands, both Europeans, allowed her to sustain the illusion that she was part of some vague international diplomatic and business community. In fact, though brilliant, she was too disorganized to be part of any community. But her children were growing up, and more and more she began to live through them. Pushing the children into the right schools would give them, and herself, the social standing she surely knew she could never hope to achieve on her own. Frances alone would always be an outsider. But through her children's accomplishments, and her father's money, doors might be unlocked to her that otherwise would remain forever closed.

As an expert on private schools, Richard Behrens had answers to her most pressing concern. He had a moody, excitable, eccentric temperament like her own. He had her tastes—for all-night drinking, all-night talk, endless conspiring and figuring and plotting—as well as her tolerance for extreme disorder. He had her intolerance for fools and for rules, and her total contempt for what both considered the lower orders. Most of all perhaps, he had *time* for Frances. This was a woman who was always late;

who talked incessantly, and always took an hour or more to come
to the point; whose mind raced ahead of her tongue; who had
difficulty getting up in the morning and in going to sleep at night;
who could spend three hours reading the morning papers, and
two or three or even six hours on one phone call. Frankie Bradshaw took up a great deal of other people's time, and Behrens
had that to give her.

Like Frankie, Dickie was an outsider, an eccentric, a solitary
fantast. Before they met one another, each had lived the lonely
life of a genie trapped in his own jar. But a genie's purpose in life
is to escape his jar and then to serve his master. When fate placed
their two jars side by side, each became the other's Aladdin.
Unstoppered, their volatile imaginations arose, expanded,
writhed, intertwined.

They lived in Yorkville, the old German district on the Upper
East Side, and always kept within easy walking distance of each
other. He inhabited one of the many cheap, grimy flats that line
the side streets, and she always dwelt in one or another of the big
new high-rises along East End Avenue or York Avenue in the
Eighties. From 1963 until 1969, when Frances remarried and
moved abroad, she and her children had a two-bedroom apartment at 85 East End Avenue. When they came back to the United
States, they lived at 75 East End Avenue. After Ariadne's birth
they moved to a $1,000-a-month apartment at 1675 York Avenue
—all in the same neighborhood.

Berenice came to visit several times a year, and Lorenzo—
Frances's first son—often lived with his aunt, Marilyn Reagan.
Yet, in seventeen years, neither the Reagans nor Berenice once
laid eyes on the strange man who served Frances as faithful ad-
viser, companion, confidant, and coconspirator in both of her
drawn-out divorce actions; who freely offered her his filthy,
gummy, roach-infested apartment as a repository for items Frances wanted to hide from her mother, or from lawyers and private
investigators; the man who was her relief errand boy and baby
sitter and dependable "Dear Abby" for all seasons; and who was
always known as "Uncle George" to the two "fatherless" little
boys.

Not long ago, between the time he twice testified for the prosecution, in two murder trials, and the time he put in for the
$10,000 reward offered by the family for information leading to
the arrest of the killer, Dickie Behrens sat in his favorite hangout,

the Midnite Express coffee shop on Second Avenue and Eighty-ninth Street, and reminisced about his erstwhile friend. "Frances is a genius. Don't underestimate her, she's very smart. She taught me all about the law. She learned it from her divorces. They said she was a spendthrift, but I wouldn't say that in court. She spent her money in binges. But she didn't own a summer house or some of the other things her sisters did.

"She had a very smart eye for investment. Not just stocks and bonds and real estate. Jewelry. She had a sixty-thousand-dollar sapphire ring, forty-thousand-dollar diamond earrings. She has Chinese paintings and carpets she bought for very little that are worth a fortune. She was crazy, but she wasn't stupid.

"She was manipulative, of course. Even now I believe she has private dicks on me. My phone rings on weekend nights, late; I pick it up and nobody's there. But that's how she's always been. Always checkin' up on people, always trying to get stuff on everyone.

"The thing about her personality was that she was incredibly changeable. I'd go over to York Avenue and hear her screaming through the walls at her children. The whole building musta heard her. Then I'd ring the bell, and she'd switch! She came to the door a different person, like the screaming never happened.

"Did I ever sleep with her? No. I mean: maybe. My memory's terrible. She knows that. That's why they were trying to screw me up on the stand. But I never went for her. You know why? No tits. That's the whole story. Sometimes I thought: Maybe I coulda married her. But then I'd think: Who needs that kinda trouble? I was always introducing her to guys, friends of mine. And I wouldn't get jealous when she took them in, shacked up with them. _I_ never did. It just wouldn't have worked out between us. She needed a man. But maybe she hated men—I dunno.

"I'll say it straight out: Frances was cuckoo, nuts, crazy. But the whole family was crazy. Marilyn, she's a little crazy too. Her husband is supposed to be nuts. She's the power in the house, and he just does what she tells him—that's what I hear.

"Frances's lawyers tried to say that I was queer with the boys. That was bullshit. I wasn't. I'm not. The thing about Larry was: I couldn't tell how crazy he was. Frances _could_. She'd tell me, 'I'm scared of him.' He has this condition—I don't know what they call it—but he barks. Yelps. There's a name for it. But I was never sure he wasn't doing it just to get a rise out of Frances.

"The whole family was crazy. Except Ariadne. You ever look at a litter of puppies or kittens? You can tell right off whether it'll be a good one or not. Well, with her you could always tell. She'll be okay."

When Frances walked out on Vittorio, he offered $900 a month to support Lorenzo and Marco. With Berenice's enthusiastic approval, Frances rejected the offer out of hand. Her refusal precipitated a four-year divorce fight during which Frances depended entirely on her parents for financial support. Vittorio's lawyer, Irving Erdheim, a ferocious Grendel of the matrimonial bar, sought to prove that Frances had far more money than Vittorio, and that she was simply trying to harass and punish his client by depriving him of his children and forcing him into bankruptcy. Frances was not just a rich man's daughter, Erdheim claimed; she was wealthy in her own right because of the stocks and the oil leasing business Franklin had put in her name, and in the names of his grandsons.

The legal skirmishing involved a prodigious amount of time, expense, claims and counterclaims, transcontinental accounting, and legal depositions. Her father, Franklin, repeatedly urged Frances to compromise and settle. "Vitro"—as close as Franklin could bring himself to spelling "Vittorio"—was not a wealthy man. The costs of the convoluted litigation would surely exceed the rewards. Franklin's letters strongly advised his daughter to seek work now rather than hope for dubious alimony pie in the sky. Gradually his advice turned into demands, then into threats: unless his daughter went to work, or returned to Utah, he would cut off her funds. Though the tides of battle fluctuated erratically, Berenice mostly sided with her daughter. The one thing father and daughter agreed on was that Berenice's "help" invariably made matters worse.

Frances was sometimes conciliatory, usually hostile, and always adroit at playing one parent off against the other. She remained constant on one point: her children came before everything. She could not return to Vittorio, as her father wished, because he beat the boys unmercifully. She could not go to work because she was too responsible a parent to leave her sons in the care of strangers. She could not return to Utah because the New York courts would not let her remove the children from their jurisdiction. When Vittorio in desperation suggested they compromise by each taking one child to raise, and even offered Frances first pick, she replied that she would not "for one instant consider splitting up my family."

Berenice backed her daughter with cash as well as moral support. Over the years she would gradually liquidate all her own assets—bank accounts, oil leases from Franklin, securities she had inherited from her parents, her fine furniture, her beloved piano—until she had rendered herself literally penniless in her efforts to meet Frances's insatiable demands. Haunted by an image of her daughter and grandchildren living in the streets and starving—a scene Frances was most effective at conjuring up—Berenice drove herself into greater and greater frenzies of compassion. At some point she began secretly plundering her husband's funds in order to keep sending money to her daughter. Just when this practice began is unclear. (The matter was brought up superficially in one trial; in the other it was kept out completely, by pretrial agreement. To portray the widow of the murder victim as a little old lady driven into a lifetime of larceny by her husband's extreme stinginess was not deemed advantageous by either side.)

Marilyn Reagan has always been frank to say that the first forger in the family was not Frances but their mother. How can Berenice feign ignorance, or surprise, at this late date, Marilyn wonders. "Why, Mother *taught* Frances to forge, taught her by example, since she was a little girl! Mother gave her the fundamentals—and then she just took off!"

Marilyn maintains that Berenice for years had counterfeited her husband's signature. "We kids all knew she forged Dad's signature from time to time. She'd just practice up for a little while, and then she could do it. It was just for little amounts at first, and not necessarily checks."

Franklin kept Berenice on a household budget of $400 a month. She was also family bookkeeper and each month wrote out the checks her husband then signed. It was no different in most families, except that Franklin Bradshaw abhorred credit and insisted on paying cash for everything, including automobiles. So, like other wives, Berenice found ways around her husband's rules.

"What Mother would do, when I was growing up—she would charge things at all the stores. But if it was something big, an amount that Dad would be surprised at, she'd pay for it on layaway. So much a month. Then she'd go back each month and charge a few small items, so that the total amount she made out the check for would be different each time, and he never knew she was buying on credit.

"Mother *taught* me that. If she told *me*, she certainly must have told Frances."

Frances's four-year divorce war was fought on two fronts: in the courts, where records are sealed because of the children's tender years, and in an extraordinary flood of correspondence by which members of this riven family sought to influence one another's behavior, and justify their own. The writers often sent backup copies of their letters to other family members; recipients shared copies of letters they had received.

One reason for the great volume of correspondence was the old problem of saying no to Frances. Berenice and Franklin could never do it. They tried to deal with difficult Frances at arm's length, rather than really confront her, and Franklin in his letters appears to be truly frightened of her. They also sought to prove to their other daughters, and to one another, that they were really "doing something about" Frances, when all they were actually doing was writing letters. And checks.

All the Bradshaws communicate in a kind of double-talk wherein oxymoronic ideas pursue one another down the page. "I will gladly do . . ." means *I will do most unwillingly if at all* . . . "I have every intention . . ." means *I have no intention.* Franklin will begin a letter to Frances: "There is one thing I don't like to do and that is criticize . . ." and follow it with three single-spaced pages of complaint. Marilyn lectures that her parents' spendthrift generosity is "hurting Frances," when in fact her sister is thriving. Franklin will on occasion send Frances three contradictory letters about family financial matters, and invite her to instruct her lawyers to use whichever one they find most helpful. The one writer among them who expresses her feelings directly is Frances. "I will never come back to Utah" means exactly that.

A troubling letter arrived from New York in July 1964 from a psychiatrist who had been seeing Frances. She had been referred to him by the psychiatric social worker attached to the domestic relations court which was handling the Gentiles' divorce. The doctor wrote to the Bradshaws that "her need for treatment is urgent—her problems are serious." However, in seven of her nine visits, Frances had assured the doctor that her mother would absolutely refuse to pay his bills, and he now wondered about the Bradshaws' true intentions.

Berenice hastened to New York to "help." Franklin wrote Frances urging her to "work her hard"—as if his wife were a mule. Frances told her mother she had no room for uninvited guests; her mother would have to sleep on the floor. She did.

In January 1965 Franklin typed out another of his strange third-person sermonettes to "Dear Francis," as he almost invariably spelled his daughter's name. Caspar Milquetoast could scarcely have put matters more gently. He said that everybody has good points and bad points; there was no such thing as a perfect person. He said he would tell Frances about some of her good points and bad points "in a constructive way." Her "good points" were her good looks. She was "an attractive person." Her bad points were that she did not keep promises, she never appreciated the things other people did for her, she was a "poor business lady," and, like her mother, she was nervous and highstrung. "Those kind of people often make poor decisions and don't meet reality, especially if they are the baby girl and spoiled."

The letter went on to accuse Frances of wrecking her oil operation by cashing in securities to get money for lawyers. When Frances did not bother to reply, and refused to accept his phone calls, her father's feeble riposte was to send her ten dollars' worth of free stamps.

Franklin sought solace from Marilyn, and suggested she slyly invite "Vitro" out to dinner and grill him about his true intentions. Franklin offered to pay the check.

In New York, Frances and her mother decided to hire private detectives to try to "get something" on Vittorio in order to destroy his business. Ultimately Berenice denounced her son-in-law to the FBI as a pearl smuggler. Franklin threatened to testify for Vittorio, not Frances. Vittorio happily invited his father-in-law, whom he had never met, to stay at his apartment rent-free. By early April the attorneys were in full cry, taking depositions and trying to determine the extent of the family's Utah assets. Upon hearing that the fearsome lawyer Erdheim was planning to visit Utah, Franklin suggested it would be cheaper if Vittorio came out himself and saw first-hand the vagaries and unprofitability of the oil leasing business.

Then Franklin issued an ultimatum: unless Frances went to work, or returned to her husband, or came back to Utah, he would cut off funds and testify against her. Inevitably, his threat simply set Frances to spinning like a top with the energy of her own rage. In one day she dashed off three furious screeds. It is impossible to read them without concluding that all parties in this correspondence are lying; that all are extracting the same promises which they are themselves breaking; and that all are to some degree, in Frances's words, "sick in the head," or to use her father's phrase, are "over-nervous persons."

She first threatens her father. She will take him to court if he repeats the vicious gossip reported to him by Berenice: that she has been spending nights in men's apartments and is a "whore." She is "disgusted" that her parents would believe such filthy charges, and also suggests that the "report from New York" is fictitious, made up by one of her own parents.

Franklin sent a copy of this letter to Marilyn, with a handwritten notation: *Marilyn—I heard a rumor that Francis was drinking. This letter makes you wonder.*

Frances's second letter to her father that day protested that she could not go to work, as he wished, without abandoning her children, and added that she refused to go back to a husband who was "mentally ill." She warned that she would go on welfare, and in the same sentence refused to come home to Utah and "take my children away from their father." She accused Franklin of ignoring the weddings of his daughters, of ignoring his grandchildren, and of beating her. She warned Franklin that the New York cops would be waiting if he dared to come to New York City and testify for her estranged husband. She accused her mother of snooping and scene-making, and threatened her with banishment. She asked Dad not to show her letters to Mom, and swore she herself never showed her letters from Dad to Mom.

But this was just a warm-up. Frances as usual had reserved her full fury for Berenice, who had just left New York for Utah. Her mother's sickening visits always made her want to vomit, she wrote. Berenice would be scared to death to go to Marilyn's house "and pull the shit you do with me . . ." How Frances longs for a mother who would be kind to her! Berenice doesn't give a damn about anyone's feelings but her own. In her frenzies of housekeeping, Berenice cares nothing for her daughter's feelings and happily throws Frances's personal things down the incinerator! She has no concern for her grandchildren's feelings either, and tells them "to their little faces" that they were "born bad and wicked."

Berenice tries to buy affection with money. No wonder she has a son in a mental hospital! Frances's most vivid childhood memories "are of being completely alone, listening to you <u>talk to yourself</u> like a maniac all day . . . You say I married a dego *[sic]* and ruined everyone's life. Who did you marry? How many lives did you ruin?" Berenice married an emotional cripple, a man who cares about *nothing but* money, a man too busy making more money to attend his own daughter's wedding! The rest of the world is shocked at his insanity!

"You say *I* ruined lives? Where's *your* son? You say I'm a bad mother. Thank God my sons aren't helplessly emotionally crippled schizophrenics locked up for life in a mental hospital . . ."

The sulfurous fulminations end with an augury of violence still thirteen years down the road: "Most fathers wouldn't talk or act the way Dad does even if their daughter was a murderess . . ."

Frances's letters have the desired effect. Dad rushed home as soon as possible after work and found his wife sobbing and in a complete nervous condition, and she was still sobbing late at night "when I went to bed . . . Your mother is a very nervous high strung person, of course, one third to two thirds of all mothers are . . . It is up to the children to understand those nervous traits . . ."

His letters show Franklin to be just as manipulative as the other Bradshaws, a man entirely unwilling to confront anybody head on. His family motto might be: *Only Wage: Never Engage.* But his mind, too, was racing, and when his kid sister Bertha, "the family historian," wrote to him from California requesting some "boyhood memories," the frantic man sat down at the old Royal in the rear of his warehouse and typed out *eleven* long, single-spaced letters minutely recollecting his rugged Canadian childhood. Weather reports, catalogs of farm animals, the names of the Indian children he played with—nothing was omitted.

As usual, Berenice's tears destroyed her only temporarily. Another sharp jab of rejection—this time, a follow-up call from Frances: "Mrs Bradshaw, you are not welcome in my house. I never want to see any of you again!"—restored her mother to her old helping self. She "knew" her daughter needed her, no matter what anyone said.

For an entire year, Berenice had been begging Franklin to go to New York, insisting that only he could straighten out Frances's financial mess. By now she owed $3,000 to Saks Fifth Avenue, as well as back rent, and Berenice's "family silver" and Vittorio's pearls were in hock. Furthermore, as Berenice knew but Franklin did not, their daughter was getting ready to sell her $12,000 worth of stock in the family-owned American Savings & Loan.

"Dad would be furious if she does this, and the family here would be terribly hurt and mad," Berenice confided to Marilyn. She had considered offering to buy up the stock herself, then put Frances on a monthly allowance. But Berenice no longer had the money, and even if she did, Frances would refuse to sell her stock if she knew she were to receive an allowance anyway. Berenice had therefore formulated a secret plan to come to New York, without Franklin's knowledge. She would repossess the valuables from "loan sharks," and invisibly backstop Franklin's efforts, since she "knows everybody" in New York, and Franklin had never been there. She was also fearful that Franklin's "violent temper" might erupt if Frances defied him, and "he might beat her too."

Begging Marilyn to "act surprised" if her mother walked through the door, she concluded in a burst of realism: "I'm so very worried about Frankie's condition. You know and I know Dad does not recognize mental illness and if she were raving mad he would say: 'If she would get a job she would be alright.' He used to walk Bob around the block and try to talk him out of his schitsfranic (can't spell it). We know this is ridiculous. He will be the last one to recognize she needs help. This is the main reason I feel I should be there. If you and I feel she needs help we will have to gang up against him. This has gone on too long . . ."

Nonetheless, it will go on for more than a decade, until it ends in murder. Already all the Bradshaws' patterns were well established, the family battle lines clearly drawn. Berenice would insist to Franklin that he must apply the pressure, that she was too weak. But as soon as Franklin attempted to put his foot down and cry *Halt!* Berenice would undermine him by finding new ways to dip into the family treasury and bail out their daughter. So the threats were all empty gestures, the pressure was always too little and too late, as no one knew better than Baby Frankie.

In a sense, it was all a game, the deadly game of family power politics, a give-and-take of theatrical gestures, each one overblown to its most melodramatic proportions: every teardrop a river, every hurt feeling a mortal wound, every warning a thunderclap, and every cherished scab picked till it festered anew. The Bradshaws had been playing the same game all their lives, and to some extent they knew they were gaming. But they could not stop; they were addicted, hooked. Then, one day, the for-so-long-imagined gun held real bullets. And the game was over.

Hence the Bradshaws wrote without communicating. It scarcely mattered whether or not letters were delivered. Franklin's scheduled day of departure for New York City came and went, but he did not leave. He continued writing letters, spinning his wheels, obsessed. "When you figure taxes, you have depleted my assets $50,000 in two years . . ." Three days and countless pages after he was supposed to arrive in New York, Franklin at last sent a very firm letter, the one he "should have written" two years earlier: there would be no more money, and no help of any kind, unless Frances and the boys returned to Salt Lake.

He had revised his estimates, and now figured that his losses "in economic waste" exceeded $100,000. To Elaine he wrote that "Frances used to put on these temper fits and run her mother for years. I am afraid she is putting on the same temper fits with her lawyer and judge."

Soon Frances was writing back that she had received another eviction notice. Even though she had no food, both she and her hungry children would starve to death before she would let her father force her to leave her children. If she were to bring the boys to Utah, as Dad wanted, their father would be sure to snatch them back to New York. Her children were legally wards of New York State, she claimed. "I can say no more. My grief is too great, and my tears are too abundant."

Berenice was in Miami at a White Shrine of Jerusalem convention, booked to continue on with a package tour to New Zealand, when she was paged on the public address system and told the latest bad news. Canceling New Zealand, she rushed to the rescue, paid the back rent, and was rewarded by accusations of extreme betrayal from her husband. Not only had she once more "hurt" Frances, but, in Franklin's wonderful coinage: "As soon as I give her stric orders, you buypass me . . ."

By May, Franklin was onto Frances's plan to sell her stock. He wrote Marilyn: "How she got these certificates I don't know unless it is thru your mother. Francis has used pressure on your

mother before and I have had two or three severe arguments with
your mother (over-nervous people's judgement is often very
poor)." In anticipation of the dread Erdheim's arrival in Salt
Lake City to take the Bradshaws' depositions, Franklin was also
poor-mouthing his own business, and inflating his own labors. "I
have been trying to increase my working hours from 16 to 20
hours but that doesn't work out, as for health reasons a person
needs those 6 hours sleep." A few days later he reported that
Berenice had checked with a New York court official and been
told that Frances had never even applied for permission to return
to Utah with the children. If she did apply, the official thought it
very likely her request would be granted.

In their depositions to Vittorio's lawyer, the Bradshaws said that
together they had given their daughter about $27,000.

Q: And did you voluntarily give these monies to her?
A: [by Berenice] Yes.
Q: And they were a contribution on your part, is that correct?
A: Well, she had to have something to live on.
FRANKLIN BRADSHAW: [interrupting] They were supposed to
be paid back!

By midsummer Franklin was feeling like a badger in a hole. He
told Marilyn he had "even threatened to beat up your mother."
To Elaine he confessed the truth: he had slapped his wife in the
face "several times on account of her over-nervous makeup."
What upset him most was Berenice's efforts to run the selfsame
show he was proving himself incapable of running. "Your mother
is trying to act as a father and mother of the family which she has
done for years and how we are going to stop her I just don't
know."

But Berenice did. When Franklin hit her, in an argument over
a thirty-dollar gas bill, she marched down to the courthouse and
filed for divorce. "I can't understand a woman putting up with it.
No self-respect! They'd never hit *me* the second time! Never!"

After dropping the divorce action, she decided it was time to
visit Elaine. Franklin quickly warned the Drukmans, "Whatever's on *her* mind, get her off the subject as quick as possible & for
heaven sake work her hard so she is physically tired at night . . .

Your mother just has pictures every night of Frances starving to death of no money."

He pleaded with Berenice that they work together as a team. "All other wives everyplace . . . they refer the child to the father. But not in our family. You have gone over my head continually now for the last 3 years."

This had merely shown Frances she need never account to her father, and could always "buypass" him for her mother, who required no accounting whatsoever.

Franklin had decided the real reason his daughter was seeking divorce was that she had tired of Vittorio; she wanted a more varied social life. He beseeched her anew to stop her spending sprees, and claimed he had been forced to borrow all the money he had sent her in the past. His own borrowing was at the "danger point," he said. If she wanted more money, she should get it from a bank, using her American Savings & Loan stock as security.

Privately, Franklin sent his son-in-law Reagan to look into the matter and learned that Frances already had borrowed to the limit on her stock, and the money had been sluiced away at Saks, Tiffany's, and Bergdorf Goodman along with all the rest. Worse, he discovered that Berenice had secretly borrowed $700 on *her* American Savings & Loan stock, and given that to Frances, too.

Details of Frances's domestic existence must of necessity be reconstructed from the recollections of other members of her always carefully locked and guarded household: children, ex-husbands, ex-servants, Behrens, and Berenice—her only visitors. Not the best of sources in any circumstances, especially these: any child's-eye view of a parent is no more objective than the parent's of the child. As Housman reminds us: "The night my father got me his mind was not on me."

In this particular family, distortions and gaps in the children's recollections may be greater than most. By the time Lorenzo and Marco were teenagers, mother and sons had formed a secret criminal gang, and despite the revelations at the ensuing trials, there may still be much to hide. From the very beginning, Lorenzo and Marco—now known as Larry and Marc—led extremely strange boyhoods, although neither boy appears to have recognized at the time the singularity of his childhood experience. Lacking a basis for comparison, all children accept their environments as normal. Abused children accept their abuse. It seemed quite normal to these boys, for example, that for as long as they can remember, Marc rarely left his mother's side, whereas Larry was never after the age of four or five permitted to remain at home longer than a few days or weeks.

To interview Marc Schreuder, as he is known today, you must visit him at "Resorts International," the inmates' name for the brand-new state prison opened in 1984 at Point of the Mountain, near Draper, Utah, just south of Salt Lake City. The state penitentiary is a raw-new jewel of prison architecture set behind a frizzle of barbed wire in bleakest desert sands. The spacious visiting room glows with the elegant colors of a Roman afternoon: steel-reinforced cement block walls painted a tawny ocher, an exposed network of fat round overhead air-conditioning channels painted a beautiful verdigris green. Several massive, near-silent sliding steel doors, painted a deep sanguine, are operated by near-invisible guards inside a control room of black glass that appears to contain enough electronic gadgetry to run a nuclear submarine. Out in the big visiting room, circular windows—cross-barred and cathedral-sized—have been set high up in the lion-colored walls to frame postcard views of distant mighty mountains and eternal snows.

Marc Schreuder is a disturbing young man, fattish, crudely shaven, very clean-looking, dressed in short-sleeved denims. His large, staring bright blue eyes have the same round blankness as the great ocular windows overhead. He works in the prison kitchens, and his plump forearms are scarred with burn marks. His body is very tense: the legs jiggle continually up and down, his roly-poly fingers busy themselves tearing any available scrap of paper into ever tinier shreds. His movements are rapid, his speech jumpy. Unlike his mother and brother, he is on no medication. He is always hungry, and any food that is put on the table—chocolate bars, cakes, bagfuls of pretzels—disappears immediately. He eats like Larry. Wolfishly.

One feels that the one thing that truly excites him, besides food, is money and—even more—the game of money. Like his grandfather, he hates to spend money but loves to play with it. His manner is amiable, puppylike; he laughs too much, and in the wrong places. His laughter is one sign among many that he is not always sure when to laugh, when to cry. Talking to him is like talking to smoke; he conveys a sense of nonsubstantiality. He is not just a perpetual gamesman, not just abused. He is scatty, shattered, incapable of much communication because his sense of identity seems so fractured. He is like the atomized, blown-away debris of a personality; the pile of dust that has settled after Mom, and murder, blew him to psychic smithereens. He makes one think of Maurice Sendak's children's classic, *Where the Wild Things Are*. Marc is both the phantasmagoric creatures of the nightmare and the little boy who dreams them.

In the fall of 1965 Frances enrolled four-year-old Marco Gentile at the Emerson School, a fashionable, conservative private school just off Fifth Avenue which had a red-painted front door. He went there for two years. Marco thought of it as "the red-door school," but whenever he called it that, his mother became enraged. Later he learned why: other mothers in Central Park might think he attended the Little Red School House, a well-known progressive school in Greenwich Village. Behrens said this was "a Jew-boy lower class school," whereas Emerson was upper-class.

Larry did not go to Emerson. He was sent somewhere else, Marc is not sure where. "Mom said he was in a mental hospital. She said he just went zonkers. Had a psychotic episode. Lost contact with reality. Started smashing his head against the wall. He was institutionalized. I don't remember the name, but it was a small, private, city place, not a big state institution. Some of the time he could sleep at home . . . it's like some of the time he *wasn't* living at home, sometimes he was . . . But I know Larry *was* in an institution because later, when I was in second grade, I remember him joking about it. I remember him being obsessed with this boy he met—Donny? . . . Johnny? . . . Danny? . . . he wrote it everywhere. Wrote it on the walls . . . damn! I can't remember . . .

"But I remember Mom saying he was in a mental hospital. And when he came back, Mom said, *I don't want you near him!* I was really scared, afraid Mom was gonna beat me up over it. She said to stay away from him because he was 'sick in the head' and 'diseased in the mind,' and if I went near him, I'd catch it too. It was supposed to be, like, *contagious.*"

Marco was never frightened of his brother. "I *liked* Larry! This was the problem throughout my whole childhood. I *loved* to play games with Larry. We'd have counting aloud contests. I'd drop out at about fourteen thousand, but Larry could go on forever. Or Stratego—my favorite! But I was scared to play with him. Because Mom really censured it, really looked down on him. So it was something I always wanted to do, but never really did." As he grew older, he learned to be clandestine and furtive about playing with his brother, he says, "and when I got caught, I'd have to bottle myself in my room till the tidal wave of the storm subsided. Mom would be very, very angry if I was playing games with Larry, the 'sick-in-the-head boy.'"

Lorenzo was referred to derisively by Frances as "the Chocolate Treat," Marc says, whereas his own nickname was "Bunny Dew." He was told repeatedly that his older brother was "crazy, handicapped, disturbed, and disease-brained," and that he had had to be sent away to a special school for "sick-in-the-head" boys. His mother terrified Marc, he says, and effectively controlled him by repeatedly threatening that he, too, would be sent away to "crazy school" if he misbehaved. "She used to scream and bellow at me, *If you don't behave, I'm gonna ship you to a mental institution and never let you out! A place where you'll be for the rest of your life!* Or else she'd tell me she'd send me to Papa—Vittorio—and let *him* beat me up."

Marc today often wonders whether he really was beaten, and if so, by whom. Neither boy recalls being beaten by anyone, but both have a kind of patchy amnesia about their early years. Larry Bradshaw, as he calls himself today, is a young man with computerlike total recall of numbers, dates, and places, and he is honest to a fault about his teenage history of mental illness. But he remembers no early childhood problems. At times Berenice, too, says she is unaware of any "handicap." The Reagans, with whom Larry later lived, say that Larry, although "difficult to handle," was not ever in any sort of mental institution. They add, however, that Frances never made any effort to treat her two sons equally. From infancy, she always had one favorite and one outcast. For the first three or four years, they say, she doted on Lorenzo. Then, inexplicably, she switched to Marco. School records show that Larry spent his entire childhood and adolescence in a series of boarding schools, camps, and foster homes. When he was little he was sent to Salt Lake City to spend the summer with his grandparents. In third grade he was left with them for an entire year. Marc says he was told Larry spent this year in "crazy school." Overall, Frances made a sustained, determined effort to keep her sons as far apart as possible as much as possible. She tried to separate them not just physically but emotionally, psychologically. In this effort, too, she was successful. Today her sons do not really seem to like each other much, and Marc, in particular, is exceptionally jealous of any attention paid to Larry.

Marc sometimes says he thinks his mother hated Larry because his grandmother and Aunt Marilyn "favored Larry over me, and Mom resented the fact. And yet I also figured that Mom, too, favored Larry—*in certain respects*. I don't know why. Mom expected a lot more of me, drove me much harder. Larry she kind of gave up on. But then sometimes she'd seem to respect Larry *more* than me. Like maybe she thought him, being the eldest, would be the more wiser. I dunno. It was *weird*.

"Then, when I was in my teens and Larry was going to military school," says Marc, "it seemed for a while he had a resurgence and became the favorite again. But most of the time she hated him. Because he was sick-in-the-head, like the black sheep in the family. He was a diseased creation—a monster."

"Larry is not handicapped," Marilyn says flatly. "His problem is that he would like to have his mother love him." Larry would always do anything his mother wanted. "He kept trying to get back into her good graces; he'd do just about *anything* for that. I talked to him recently. He sounded not quite so starved for love anymore."

"I've never seen any handicap," says Bob Reagan. "He certainly got A's in school, later on. When they were little, and together, they *were* hard to control." Berenice, on her frequent trips to New York, rode the bus back and forth between her daughters' apartments. The sisters rarely saw each other, now that Frances was again leading the life of a single woman. Bob Reagan remembers urging Berenice to let him help her out with her grandsons' care. "She was here, baby-sitting, and she didn't exactly know how to handle 'em. They were *wild*. So I hit 'em a couple of times, with my open hand, on the rear, which she . . . she really doesn't like! There's no doubt that's what they needed. But I got a peculiar reaction from her. Not only she really doesn't like it but, I give her credit, she tells me. Straight out."

Reagan never saw Vittorio with his small sons, but from the way Vittorio's five children—the grown-up Marc and Larry and the three children of his second wife—act with their father, Rea-

gan gets no sense that any of them ever feared the little man with
the Chico Marx accent.

Marilyn says that when the family moved to East End Avenue
and the boys had a bedroom of their own for the first time, they
fought a lot, but both otherwise "seemed all right." She recalls
having a long talk with Marc when he was four or five "about
how sometimes parents don't live together anymore. But it
doesn't mean they don't love *you*. It just means they're having
trouble living together . . . And I thought he seemed to accept
that. I'd say their behavior, outside of being rambunctious little
boys, hard to control, was okay."

But the truth seems to be that Frances had a lifetime fear that,
if left alone, Larry would try to kill Marc and might very well
succeed. She has always claimed that Larry made several such
attempts on his younger brother. Both boys laughingly deny this,
saying it is just more of Mom's wild imaginings. Marc says he
never feared his brother. The Reagans also deny the stories completely. But the Reagans also deny mistreating Larry when he
lived with them, in fourth grade. School authorities thought otherwise. Marc says the Reagans sometimes pinched *him* till he
bled. Perhaps Marc and Larry, like the old man who thought he
could "cure" his son Robert with walks around the block, are
masters of denial. Berenice Bradshaw did not know what to
think. She vacillated. Sometimes she seemed to share her daughter's terror. At other times, like Franklin, she denied and covered
up. But throughout the history, one can sense her at least trying
to deal honestly and rationally with an irrational situation.

Did Frances really believe Larry was crazy, and dangerous? At
least some of the time she probably did. But she also used her
son's mental problems as a further way to manipulate her parents
into giving her what she wanted; a way to prevent them from ever
saying no to Frances.

If the sons were uncontrollable, that was understandable. Certainly no one had ever been able to control their mother. After
she left Vittorio, what interested her most was men. She was
dating a variety of men, and when the boys were still only three
or four years old, neighbors told Marilyn her sister often left
them alone overnight. By the time they were five or six, Marilyn
had reported her sister to the police for child neglect. Unable to
reach Frances on the phone, she would go to the East End Avenue apartment and find the front door wide open and the place a

"dirty mess." One time the children were gone, and there was nothing in the refrigerator. Moments later the little boys returned eating chocolate cake and french fries. They had gone down to the corner delicatessen and begged for food. She phoned the police and took the boys to her apartment on Sixty-fourth Street. "About midnight, Frances showed up. The police had left her a note that we had the boys. I drove them home, and Frances made me so nervous, I scraped the paint off her car backing out of the garage."

Then Marilyn, an extremely frugal woman, had offered to pay her sister for the gas. When Frances demurred, Marilyn tried to stuff a few bills into her sister's pocket, saying, "Here. Take it for the boys."

Frances flew into a rage, screaming, "You! You never did *anything* for the boys!"

In 1966 Frances put herself for two years under the care of a Park Avenue psychiatrist named Herman Weiner, who seems to have encouraged his patient to stand up to her overprotective mother. Berenice was attempting to infantilize her, Frances decided. She told Marc that Granny had a neurotic need for "babies to smother," which could account for Berenice's intense dislike of the man.

Robert Reagan remembers Dr. Weiner arriving in court to testify for Frances, during the divorce proceedings, and Marilyn Reagan remembers that at one point: Frances owed her psychiatrist $3,000. "My understanding was that her problem was inability facing reality," says Marilyn. The huge unpaid bill made her sister think it might be the doctor who had this problem, not his patient.

That same year, in Utah, Robert Bradshaw died. Frances later explained to Marc that her brother had been "fed to death" by Berenice. "Mom said when he was in the hospital, Granny would feed him and feed him, until finally he died because he was so fat," Marc remembers. "It was like a way of killing people, to smother them by giving them food." Frances told her son she had acquired this insight from her psychiatrist. "Mom said it meant that Granny actually *hated* the person. And that Granny hated and despised all men, that she wanted them killed. And unconsciously, she was *going to try to kill them!* That's one of the reasons Mom didn't want me out there in Salt Lake later on, when I got older. Because Granny would try to destroy me. Because she was a man-hater."

The summer after Robert's death, Frances and her sons arrived in Salt Lake City en route to establish residence in Sun Valley and, finally, to obtain an Idaho divorce, simple in comparison to the tangles of New York law. Marco was left in Salt Lake with Berenice while Lorenzo went to Idaho with his mother. By now the boys were six and seven, and both mother and grandmother were prepared to acknowledge what Aunt Marilyn does not: together the boys were simply impossible to handle. It was more than continual fighting, misbehaving, lack of normal control. Neighbors and teachers say they did not know how to eat or care for themselves, how to wash and dress. They seemed completely wild.

That fall Marco entered first grade at St. Hilda's and St. Hugh's, a fine private school near Columbia University run by an order of Episcopal nuns. The sisters soon learned from the driver of the school bus, who had been told it by the elevator man, that six-year-old Marco was often pushed onto the elevator still in his pajamas and half-asleep, carrying his school clothes in his arms. The elevator man would dress the little boy on the way down, and later leave the pajamas outside his mother's always locked door. Another of the nuns noticed that Marco was one of those children who arrived at school without seeming to have had breakfast. First graders like Marco were not uncommon. Many alcoholic or neglectful parents sent their children off to school unwashed and unfed. The nuns dealt with the situation pragmatically, quietly teaching the child whatever simple elements of hygiene and nutrition he needed to know. But little Marco Gentile is a still-remembered special case. The sister who first showed him how to pour his cereal into a bowl, and then put his own sugar and milk on top, and how to brush his teeth afterward, got the impression that these were all techniques of which the little boy was entirely ignorant.

In February 1968 Marco and Lorenzo were abducted from the family's New York apartment. Who did it, and why, and whether the boys were indeed "kidnapped" or "rescued" are still matters of family contention.

For once in her life—the only time anyone can remember—Frances actually had a paying job. She was a clerk-typist at a mailing list brokerage house, and one day she returned from work to find her apartment empty.

Says Marilyn: "Mother decided to take the boys back to Utah without telling Frances. Frances came home, and Mother had left her a note. Frances flew to Salt Lake City, rented a car, slapped Mother around, broke some dishes, and repossessed the boys. She sent the bill for all of it to Dad."

Berenice admits it happened, but says Marilyn was the instigator. "*She* was the one that pressed me into doing it. I called her the night before, and she said, 'You've *got to* do it. You've got to take those boys!' She told me they were being neglected. Of course, I didn't live in New York, and I didn't know what was going on like she did.

"Frances gave me a real good cuff. We had a lot of rough days back then. After her divorce, in between husbands, Frances wasn't totally responsible. Runnin' around in circles like a mad person. Not down to earth. Things weren't goin' right . . .

"But Marilyn thought that family should be put out in the street! She was very, very opposed to any support from me. Kept at me constantly about it. It wouldn't have bothered Marilyn one bit . . . in fact, she *wanted* to see that family put out. Kept telling me Frances would have to get worse before she could get better. Wanted Frances put in a hospital. Course, I couldn't picture such a thing, so I would struggle all that much harder to keep them afloat . . . Frances's case is very difficult to understand. At times she seems so *normal.* At other times she sorta goes off the deep end."

Marilyn says it was only later that Berenice started blaming her eldest daughter for masterminding the abduction, "only after Frances told Mother she would never forgive her."

But Marc, who was seven, remembers something quite different. "I'll never forget it. It was in the middle of the morning. Mom had gone off to work. Me and Larry were just kinda wandering around the house, bored . . . and Aunt Marilyn suddenly showed up at the door. 'Come on, kids! How'd you like to go to Salt Lake?' she said.

"I said, 'You sure it's okay with Mom?'

"Marilyn said, 'Sure. It could be just for the weekend . . . pack some toys and an overnight bag, and come on, boys, let's go!'

"I remember it was a Friday, and like night when we arrived. We hadn't been there for so long, it was like an exciting adventure for us. And Granny making the oatmeal cookies, and those good orange cakes! We got tucked up good in the downstairs bedroom. Next day we did puzzles around the house. Granny kept saying: We'll go home tomorrow," Marc recalls. "But secretly, I was getting kinda suspicious. Because I knew Mom would be *angry* if I wasn't in school. I knew she *really cared* about school. By Sunday night I was asking myself: How come I haven't heard from Mom?

"Then, alluva sudden, I'll never forget—Mom burst through the door! '*Kids! Kids!*' she yelled. Granny tried to stop her. They were still right at the front door. Mom like slapped her aside, hard, and I heard: '*Marco! Lorenzo!* Come on! We're goin' home! Pack the stuff!'

"And then Mom slammed Granny up against the wall china cabinet. And then Mom hit her! All the plates started to come crash-smashing down. Mom had ducked around Granny, then Granny came around again, and Mom shoved her against the cabinet and the plates started breaking, and she was really pounding her . . ."

Frances shooed the boys into a rented car, all the time screaming and cursing, "How dare you take my children! *How dare you kidnap my kids!*" The scene ended with Berenice in tears and Frances pushing the children out the door and shouting that her mother would never see her grandsons again.

She told her children they'd been "kidnapped" because Granny was "sick in the head" and "desperate for a child." Granny said it was Marilyn's fault for talking her into acting—for her grandsons' sake. Marilyn says the boys were indeed neglected and abused, as she had reported to the police, but that the "kidnapping" was strictly Berenice's idea. Only afterward did she try to shift the blame to Marilyn, in hopes Frances would relent from the terrible retribution she now decreed.

On the office stationery that symbolized her new economic independence, Frances composed an extremely high-toned letter accusing her mother of taking the boys simply out of an irrational desire to have babies at home again. "In line with your continual statements that you had nothing to live for or go home to—apparently my children were in a neurotic fashion supposed to fill some sort of void in your life."

How could Berenice imagine that Frances would have fought five years to wrest her sons away from Vittorio only to permit them to be stolen by an even worse enemy? Then she begins to salt the wound. Granny can give the children only money and material possessions. What they crave—the love of their mother —is something only Frances can give. To arrive home from a hard day's work and find that her own mother "has chosen to deceive, lie, cheat, and sneak around and commit . . . the most horrible crime that any mother could against her daughter" will have dire consequences. Normally Frances would have been willing to send the children home to see their grandparents for vacations. But that is all finished now. Frances and sons will soon drop from sight forever. Letters from home will be torn up unopened, and "you will never be able to discover where in the world we are."

No such luck. The instant school was out, Frances shipped both boys off for the summer to Salt Lake City. Before Lorenzo's arrival the Bradshaws had received a carefully worded letter from the medical director of a New York City psychiatric clinic and school, a licensed state agency for the care of the mentally ill. Were the Bradshaws aware that their grandson Lorenzo was "a very seriously disturbed child whose sense of reality and of personal identity is so precarious as to warrant the diagnosis of psychosis"? What, therefore, is the grandparents' position regarding the child's overdue school fees? The school has been unable to collect even the cut-rate price of $480 agreed upon with Frances for the past year's care. She claims Vittorio is responsible for the debt, and he has left the country. And what about next year? The present uncertainty about his future at the school is "bad for Lorenzo and bad for his mother."

There are further problems. "Since his mother works," Lorenzo needs to come home to a warm, efficient housekeeper who will provide the child with "the nurturance . . . stability and support required at the end of our school day." Such care is quite expensive.

Franklin took the position that he was unwilling to send another dime to New York, especially when just the sort of "warm, nurturing, supportive, efficient" people the doctor ordered were

standing by in Salt Lake City. Eight-year-old Lorenzo arrived
there in sorry shape. A medical checkup showed him to be suffering from a strep infection, early-stage protein deficiency, an io-
dine shortage, mild to moderate anemia, bad teeth. Medications
and vitamins were begun. A dentist went to work on his five
cavities; Marco had none. A young Bradshaw cousin was pressed
into unpaid service to help Berenice care for the unruly boys.
Mornings, Marco was sent to play school at the Jewish Community Center. Lorenzo was evaluated by the chief of child psychiatry at the University of Utah Medical School and found to have a
high IQ but surprising deficiencies in reading and writing.

In Franklin's view, the only thing wrong with his grandson was
parental neglect. Lorenzo was overpushy, underdisciplined. "He
wants to do what he enjoys, and that's it." Gramps clearly enjoyed taking the boys in hand. Small boys seemed much easier to
deal with than difficult daughters had been. Every evening he
talked to them about the same subjects that interested him—
rivers and mountains, history and geography, coins and money
and automobiles. He brought them down to see his wonderful
warehouse. He taught them to spell.

The day he tried to teach them the names of all the western
states, Idaho and Colorado and Utah and Nevada, Marco learned
but Lorenzo balked. Gramps said if he didn't spend some time
each day studying and learning things, he would fall behind the
other boys, and Lorenzo snapped back, "I can spell things that
Marco can't! I can spell *Grandpa* and *Grandfather.*"

"Sure enough he could, and Marco couldn't," the delighted old
man wrote to Frances.

She wrote that she was working hard, even bringing work
home at night. She had a new boyfriend, "a member of the international diplomatic corps," she said, and she described a man
who had the same background and credentials as Richard
Behrens's brother Robert. In fact, the man was a Dutch national
who worked at a middle-level job in a firm of international management consultants. His name was Frederik Schreuder.

In Utah, the children thrived. Lorenzo joined the Cub Scouts
and went to YMCA camp. Granny arranged outings to amusement parks, and backyard sleep-outs. Neighborhood children
were always around, and the brothers had friends for the first
time in their lives. Gramps brought home saws and scraps of
lumber, and the kids built four tree houses in the backyard. Bere-

nice went so far as to order two tons of sand dumped into her garage so they could have their own sandpile. She lived in a happy flurry of housekeeping, washing, cooking, and cleaning and set up a basement playroom filled with toys.

"The boys spend a big part of their day in the sunshine and fresh air. Their bodies are brown as Indians. They have gained in weight and I feel sure they have grown an inch. Our lovely back yard with its lawn, shade and large tree is simply heaven to them," she wrote.

There were darker elements to the story. The children were as wild as ever. Sometimes they spent all day banging nails into the roof. They tracked the sand all through the house and broke the glass door. None of the other neighborhood mothers ever invited them over to play.

They were secretly shoplifting. "My first memory of the warehouse—stealing auto parts!" Marc recalls. "Little, cute auto parts. Like ball bearings. I *loved* ball bearings! I think Larry initiated the stealing, because he was older, and I tended to listen to him when Mom wasn't around."

They hid the loot back at Gilmer Drive. One day Larry was dragging wagonloads of sand all over the neighborhood. "He seemed to make friends a lot quicker than I did. I was scared, shy, and tended to stay only by the house. Larry started ordering me around, being bossy. 'I want you to take another load of sand down the street to my friend's house,' he said.

"I said, 'No, Larry. I'm tired of dragging sand.'

" 'If you don't do it,' he said, 'I'm gonna tell Grandpa about the auto parts that you and I stole.'

"I said, 'Well, you stole 'em too.'

"Granny heard us fighting. She didn't know what about, but she was mad about the sand and said she was gonna have Grandpa punish us when he got home. So we hid under his bed. When he got home, she told him we'd been bad, and then Larry told Grandpa we'd stolen the auto parts. I remember that it was the lightest little spanking I'd ever had!"

One afternoon Marco and Larry were returning from the park, unaccompanied, when Marco was hit by a car. *"Blam!* It seemed like a long time later when I woke up, because it was dark and I was under a blanket and a whole crowd of people were standing around. Then they took me to the hospital, put some kind of big bandage on. The man that hit me was there. He was a friend of

Granny's, and he felt so sorry and sad. And I remember Granny telling me, 'Never, never tell Mom about this!' She knew Mom would get *extremely* angry. That was one of the contradictions. Because Mom let me and Larry go anyplace alone in New York City."

Schooltime was approaching. Frances demanded $300 a month for a housekeeper and school fees for Lorenzo. The Bradshaws refused, saying the boys were better off in Salt Lake, even though they did miss their mother. Frances claimed the psychiatrist said the children needed to be with their own mother, not "two old folks in Utah." But Franklin held all the cards. He suggested an "experiment": leave the boys in Salt Lake at least until Christmas, or until Frances could "legally prove" she had the means to support them in New York. A Solomon-like compromise was arrived at. Lorenzo would remain with his grandparents, Marco would be shipped back to New York.

When he got off the plane, he saw a tall, slender, athletic-looking man standing beside his mother. He had sparse, gray-blond hair, a narrow face, and thin lips, and he spoke English with a faint "Swedish-sounding" accent. While the man went to collect the luggage, Frances whispered, "Ooh, I know you'll like Frederik!" Marco *did* like him, especially liked driving in Freddie's new red Delta 88 Olds, and he thought his mother was "very gushy . . . they were very much in love."

At the time Frances and Frederik met, he was employed by PA International Management Consultants, a sleek, glossy, worldwide outfit that specializes in all sorts of advanced technologies and in finding the people to run them. It maintains sixty-odd offices around the globe from Aberdeen, Scotland, to Wellington, New Zealand, with main headquarters in Princeton and London.

Freddie worked in PA's Park Avenue office and lived in a small flat in Flushing, Queens. Every weekend he drove to the Queens flat of his ex-wife, Gloria, to pick up their small son, Fritje, for his regular, court-ordered visitation. Even after Freddie moved in with Frances and Marc at 85 East End Avenue, in Manhattan, he continued faithfully to pick up Fritje, and he often took Marco along for the ride.

Fritje was a couple of years younger than Marco, a well-be-haved little European kid in short pants, and Marco liked him a lot. "That's where I first saw those big, violent scenes," Marc recalls. "Freddie would drive me out to collect Fritje, and I waited downstairs in the lobby while he went up. I always heard yelling, screaming. It happened five or six times. Once I actually saw her come racing down the stairs, her and Freddie still screaming. But after we moved to Europe, I never saw her or Fritje again."

One Saturday morning in February 1969 Marco and Freddie drove out in the big red car to pick up Fritje as usual, and on the drive back Freddie told the boys that he and Frances were getting married that afternoon. The wedding took place at Marble Collegiate Church on Fifth Avenue, and the only people there whom Marco knew were the Reagans, and Fritje. The other guests were Freddie's friends. Berenice had remained in Salt Lake looking after Lorenzo, who was now a happy, normal-seeming third grader in public school, his grandmother says. Marco, however, believed his brother was back in the state school for "sick-in-the-head" boys, the place he, too, would be sent if he misbehaved.

Frances told her family that Freddie was about to be transferred overseas, and she was delighted with the prospect of a glamorous new life in Europe. But then Gloria refused to surrender Fritje. When Frederik insisted on remaining in New York to continue the custody battle, he lost out on his promised new job. Frances was bitterly disappointed. That spring she was twice hospitalized by her physician, Benson Shalette, M.D., and Frederik later dated her Seconal addiction from this time. In Utah, Lorenzo broke his leg skiing, and a doctor refused to treat the boy without prior parental consent. When Berenice telephoned, Frances at first refused her permission. Granny was "just trying to usurp" the mother role, she charged.

School ended, Lorenzo returned to New York, and the Schreuders rented a summer house on Fire Island. Unemployed, Frederik spent a miserable summer fighting both with his ex-wife and his present one, and trying with little success to discipline his rowdy new stepsons. Alone, each boy was difficult; together they were unmanageable. They fought continually, though today both young men say they were merely roughhousing. Frances was again worried that Lorenzo might kill his younger brother. She had seen him try it several times, she said—once by drowning, once by pushing his head through a pane of glass, once by dropping him off a window ledge, once by shoving him in front of a subway train.

Both Larry and Marc deny the stories. "That's Mom's paranoia," Marc scoffs. "And Mom's hype. Bullshit! Poor Granny believes everything Mom says, and half of what Mom says is exaggerations, and the other half is a bunch of lies. Like that time me and Larry were playing in the ocean. I remember it. Pure *horseplay*. But Mom interpreted it as *sick Larry, disease-brained Larry! Trying to strangle me, trying to drown me.* We were *both* horseplaying in the ocean! I had no fear of drowning. I couldn't imagine why Mom was so angry. And so convinced! She started to scream at us: *Get out of the water! Larry! Get out! Don't you touch Marc!*

"And that time he tried to throw me through the window— that was because he was *very* angry. Larry's like Papa [Vittorio]. He's got a big temper, and sometimes it explodes. You don't see Larry angry often, but when you *do*—watch out!"

In fall 1969 Frances took a three-week trip with Freddie to Belgium and the Netherlands, ostensibly to look for housing once a PA job abroad opened up. Berenice had come East to look after Marco. Lorenzo now lived with the Reagans, and nightly vanquished Uncle Bob at the difficult war game Stratego. He had learned so much in Utah that St. Hilda's and St. Hugh's put him a class ahead of Marco. Berenice told Marilyn that Frances intended to dump Larry on the Reagans permanently when she moved overseas. The Reagans would not have minded, they say now. They felt sorry for the boy and liked having him around.

Separated in two households, the boys managed to make trouble in both. When Granny attempted to limit Marco's TV watching, the eight-year-old went after her with a butcher knife. Larry had taken to dropping on all fours and barking like a dog. At school, Marc imitated him, and the barking mania swiftly spread among the other third and fourth graders.

The Reagans tried to discipline Larry at home. The boy complained to the nuns that his Uncle Bob was beating him. Was he? Reagan comes from a family of educators and champions of children's rights. Marilyn today says she thinks the trouble was that Bob was hitting Lorenzo without the child really understanding what his Uncle Bob wanted from him.

Berenice wrote to Frances that the school was threatening to expel one or both of her sons. Frances rushed back from Europe, and—determined not to be late to an appointment at school to discuss Lorenzo's problems—she smashed up her car, lost her wallet, and commenced what became a day-long altercation with the crew of the moving van she had hit. For now she hurried on to school, where the nuns told her Lorenzo had tried to gouge out one child's eyes with scissors, and was asking little girls to take down their panties and show him their private parts.

From school, Frances returned to the accident scene, resumed her high-pitched battle, and called the cops. They hauled everybody in to the police station, where Frances called her lawyer. The moving men, now into triple overtime, were beginning to enjoy themselves. It was evening, and a third shift of police had come on duty by the time the cops were able to escort the enraged woman home. The escorting officers then and there urged Berenice to sign commitment papers which they had brought with them, so her daughter could be placed in a mental hospital for observation. Berenice acknowledged that her daughter appeared to be "off her rocker," but as soon as Berenice agreed to sign, Frances calmed down and the cops left.

Marco's mother had returned from Europe with wads of cash that she carried around in her purse—a lifelong habit whenever she was flush—and soon little Marco was helping himself to small amounts, tens and twenties. Thus his little life of crime, begun at age seven by stealing ball bearings from Gramps' warehouse, marched on.

On October 31 Berenice spent her forty-fifth wedding anniversary alone with her grandson, boggled by the systematic way in which the eight-year-old hit every single apartment in his large building for a Halloween handout.

One day in December Frances suddenly yanked nine-year-old Lorenzo out of school and, that very day, shipped him alone on a plane to Holland, where, after a six-hour airport wait, Frederik arrived to collect the little boy. Outrageous child abuse by her brother-in-law had forced her to act in this precipitate manner, she said.

Frances was able to leave New York City only with Marilyn's help. The first time the moving and storage men—not, alas, the same crew—arrived at her apartment, Frances was asleep and no one was able to awaken her. She asked Marilyn to supervise the next attempt, after her own departure. When Marilyn arrived, she discovered Frances had also employed an elderly private detective to supervise everybody else.

Before she left New York, Frances sent her father a docile letter assuring him of her intentions to repay some new loans he had made to carry her and Frederik through the period of his unemployment.

Frances's last act before leaving the United States was to obtain a court order changing her sons' names. With a stroke of the pen, Lorenzo and Marco Gentile legally ceased to exist. The two little blue-eyed boys who arrived in Holland dressed in the drafty European-style short pants insisted on by Frederik were now known as Lawrence and Marc Schreuder.

By January 1970 the Schreuders and Marc were shivering together in Frederik's unheated cottage on the shore of the North Sea. Larry had been placed in the International School at Vilstern, the Quaker-run Dutch boarding school where he would complete fourth grade, and fifth and sixth. Marc moved with Frances and Frederik to a tiny apartment in The Hague, enrolled in the new English private school there, and was soon top boy in his class.

Franklin Bradshaw was now sixty-eight years old and enormously though murkily rich. If he were to die intestate, the government would take most of it, and Berenice for some time had been attempting without success to persuade her husband to make a will. She thought he was probably too cheap to lay out the legal fees. But this spring she found a way. She was planning to go on a Mormon-sponsored Far East tour with her sister-in-law Bertha Beck. They would visit the Osaka World's Fair, then see the sights of Japan, Thailand, Singapore. Franklin was happy to pay his wife's way. Reluctant to undertake so vast a journey without first setting her affairs in order, Berenice called on an outstanding estate lawyer, David Salisbury, and said she wanted to make out her will. When the document was ready, she invited Franklin to witness her signature. Together they visited Salisbury's sumptuous tower offices, situated so that occupants sit eye-to-eye with the gold-leafed Angel Moroni himself. David Salisbury is an uncommonly shrewd and persuasive man and, as his elegant office walls attest, a Stanford University Law School classmate of Supreme Court Justices William Rehnquist and Sandra Day O'Connor. By the time the Bradshaws were ready to go home, Franklin had consented to have the same lawyer work out a will for himself. "I tricked him!" says Berenice.

Lawyer Salisbury's major concern in the spring of 1970 was to minimize taxes on the huge estate. The best way to do this was to

leave the broadest possible discretionary powers to Franklin's
widow. Accordingly, the will Salisbury drafted set up two trusts,
a marital trust and a family trust. Individual trusts were also set
up for each grandchild. The F & B Corporation, a limited part-
nership with Franklin and Berenice as general partners, and their
daughters and grandchildren as limited partners, was set up to
enable the grandparents to funnel as much money as possible
away from the IRS while they were still alive.

Under F & B, each of Franklin's daughters received income
from three irrevocable trusts. Two of these trusts were so-called
income accumulators, with the expiration date of Trust B set ten
years later than the expiration date of Trust A. Trust C paid
income only; the principal was untouchable. Each minor grandchild was in on Trust A and could cash out at age twenty-one if
he or she wished, and receive about $50,000, providing that Bere-
nice Bradshaw approved.

Frank Bradshaw signed his will April 13, 1970. May 12 was
Berenice's sixty-seventh birthday, and she spent the day alone on
Waikiki Beach. By June, F & B Corporation had made its first
distribution: 400 shares of Mountain Fuel to each of the limited
partners. Mountain Fuel is a utility company that invests in oil
leases; some years earlier in a stock swap it had bought out
Franklin's Wasatch Chemical. Mountain Fuel was then trading
for about $37 a share. Franklin Bradshaw elected to distribute the
dividends to his daughters and grandchildren but retain the stock
certificates. He cached these along with everything else in the big
warehouse.

Now that her children had trust funds, Frances could use the
income to pay for school, camp, and other expenses. Eventually
she would find ways to loot the trusts themselves. For now, summer was approaching, and the most pressing problem was the old
one of how to keep her two boys apart. Berenice had proposed
that Larry come back to Salt Lake. Frances at first accepted, then
decided a camp in Europe was preferable. Berenice's invitation
would only result in a long ocean voyage and grand tour of Europe for Granny and the boy, and an inevitable descent on the
Schreuders. Frances found good camps in Switzerland and Denmark and worked out plans to have one boy away at camp while
the other was home. Larry had become so attached to Freddie,
she told her father, that he refused to share his stepfather with
Marc. So the children had to be alternated. And either boy got to

feeling abandoned if he was sent away for more than a few weeks at a time. Frances offered to send her father photocopies of the high-pressure, secret communiqués she had been receiving from Berenice, and she urged that her own letters be destroyed. "Mother has for many years gone to the warehouse and found your hiding places and read your personal mail and then spread it around the family," she wrote.

When Berenice's father had died in 1956, he left her a bit of money, which she had invested in stock held in the joint names of herself and her eldest daughter. They had shared the dividends until Marilyn realized that her mother was selling off the principal to raise more money for Frances. It was time to claim her share of the inheritance before Frances got it all. She found a modest co-op apartment on West End Avenue in the Eighties that could be bought for $24,000, and asked her mother for most of the financing—$20,000. Today the Reagans still live in the same building, though not the same apartment. After the murder, and the unexpected money that resulted, they moved up to a higher floor.

When summer came, Larry was sent alone to camp in Denmark, and Marc moved with the Schreuders to Belgium. Frederik had finally obtained a good job as international marketing director for Europe for PA International. His title was larger than his salary, however, and soon he was writing to his father-in-law, whom he had never met, listing a catalog of debts and mentioning that winter was coming on and there was no money for warm clothes for the children. In his smarmy report on the grandsons, he wrote that "Marc too wants much attention, warm-hearted boy that he is . . ." while ". . . Larry is a more difficult boy . . . still torn by his chilhood [sic] experiences and the things done to him."

Larry's chief problem, Frederik wrote, is "that he cannot stand the presence of Marc. I love the boy, he knows it and thrives on it because he too needs a daddy, yet he will sometimes try to hurt me just out of sheer rebelliousness." Franklin responded generously. He offered to continue paying his grandsons' private school, camp, and medical bills, which came to several thousand dollars annually. He mailed Frances's choice Mountain Fuel stock certificates to Belgium and told her he thought the stock would double in value in the next three to five years, and she would be very foolish to sell. "But you can get a bank loan on it for $11,000 in any country in the world."

Frances's second marriage was proving no less turbulent than her first and followed the same pattern: a gradual crescendo of domestic discord, interrupted by bouts of physical and mental collapse. Frances's illnesses were never minor, her fights with Freddie never mild. In Marc's memory, all the crazy scenes of malady and mayhem have gelled into frenzied, frozen comic-book panels, scratched in white on black. He even makes comic book noises as he recalls them. "Okay, first the Hong Kong flu. Mom was *really* sick. Two weeks at death's door. She'd cough and cough. ARRGH! ARRGH! She wasn't supposed to smoke, but she did, and big gobs of goo came out. One time she was coughing so hard this little bony thing came out . . .

"Then something went wrong with her bladder line. She'd crawled out of bed dragging the blanket and she'd groan and pass out and sleep in the middle of the floor. I didn't know what to do." The next scene is a Brussels hospital. Marc arrives daily, does all his homework at bedside, plays Stratego. "One day I got there and saw tubes coming out. URK URK. She'd had the surgery and was all doped up. She wanted spaghetti to go. I went right out and got it—BLAM! And when I came back, Mom was out cold. I thought: *Damn!* I felt really hurt, you know? That I'd brought it, and she didn't even appreciate it."

Then "we were in some big old train station and Mom was late, of course, and the train was pulling out. The doors closed on Mom, *right on her surgery!* WHAP! She was really screaming. The conductor had to pry her out."

A second kidney operation became necessary and "me and Mom flew to London. DRZZH! DRZZH! Very fine hotel. Little old ladies fixing tea sandwiches. Mom was in the hospital two weeks." Once more Berenice came rushing to the rescue; again wallets disappeared, tickets and passports were lost, cars smashed. There were new sudden illnesses, new appeals to Franklin for emergency funds, more pleas from Berenice: "Her life is at stake." There was more trouble with Larry, more family fights, frenzies, recriminations, confusions, accusations. The parents were still oversleeping and failing to get the boys off to school. Only husbands and scenery had changed. Otherwise, the whole circus had just moved abroad.

Soon what Marc calls "the beat-up scenes" began: "Freddie

would smack Mom around, Mom would lock Freddie out. Then Freddie reversed it! Pulled a double switch and locked Mom out!" Sometimes the "beat-up scene" starred just Freddie and Marc. The first of these had occurred the summer after the wedding while the new little family was living in an exclusive Fire Island beach colony. Freddie discovered his new stepson playing with matches under the living room couch and accused him of deliberately setting fire to the rug. "He *really* beat me up. I felt bruised all over. To this day I say I'm innocent. But nobody would listen to me . . . Then, after the beating, I'd usually get locked in my room six hours or so. I can't remember . . ."

They were in Brussels, in a more elegant flat at 505 Avenue Louise, when his stepfather caught ten-year-old Marc smoking his first cigarette. "Freddie just beat me all over. Just . . . damn . . . he beat me *everywhere.* With those hard hands he has, he just kept on going and going and going. And I had to write 'I will never smoke again' a hundred times, even though Freddie himself smoked at least as much as Mom.

"Another time Mom and me were by my bed, on Avenue Louise, and Mom was talking to me in a really nasty way. We'd just come back from meeting all Freddie's relatives at his mother's funeral, in Holland, and Mom was whispering, *Nobody liked you!* Freddie caught her doing it . . . and she got real scared. Then he started smacking her around, pushed her back on the couch. Started giving her little punches—DZHHH! DZHHH! DZHHH! Like chewing her out, you know? I felt sorry for Mom. I really did."

Frances describes such scenes quite differently. She says Freddie would come into the room, glance over at the boy, and ask Marc, "Should I, or shouldn't I?" She says her husband invited her son to decide whether or not she was to be beaten that day. To punish or not to punish was Marc's whim, she claims, and Freddie merely the instrument.

Marc's descriptions of Mom's fights with Freddie have the same jagged, zany comic-book quality. He has given them titles: "The Lockout!" "The Double Lockout!" "The Beat-up Scenes!" As Marc talks in his odd, infantile, disjointed manner, it becomes apparent that his melodramatic stories of Mom's misadventures are recollected through Frances's self-pitying eyes, not his own, and that it is all part of a script learned a long time ago. Quite possibly they never actually happened, or happened differently.

No matter. By now they have become part of the ongoing Little Nell melodrama of Mom's life, as she shared it daily, freely, and entirely with her frightened, half-crazed sons. The question is: Who really wrote the script? Was it Mom or was it Marc? It is hard to imagine that he really "felt sorry" for Mom, or felt much of anything, beyond his terror of abandonment. His feelings have congealed at a very infantile level. The patchy amnesia—if that is what it is—keeps him from remembering more than fragments of scenes, reflections in a broken mirror. A scream, an oath, a burned pork chop thrown, a door slammed, the tinkle of breaking glass.

The Schreuders slugged it out through four furious summers in expensive rented beach houses at Fire Island, four freezing winters abroad, and innumerable trial separations and reconciliations. Freddie blamed his wife's erratic behavior on Seconal addiction, a drug that he said Dr. Shalette, her New York physician, had told Schreuder was necessary in order for Frances to "maintain her mental balance."

Often Frances Schreuder did seem truly unaware. During one of her Fire Island summers she invited Dickie Behrens and two women friends to come out for a day at the beach. The trip to Fair Harbor involves a three-hour car drive, an hour-long boat ride. The visitors arrived hot and famished. The hostess seemed not to notice. She offered them nothing to eat or drink—not out of stinginess, her visitors thought, or even lack of hospitality. She was simply "out of it." Two other things stayed in the visitors' minds: both women remarked that bikini-clad Frances projected "tremendous sexiness, the real high-voltage stuff" despite what would seem the handicap of being entirely flat-chested. The other thing they remember is that, all the long afternoon, the hostess and Behrens exclusively, compulsively discussed only one subject. They each kept talking about their "inheritance," and how they were going to get their hands on it. Said one: "I couldn't understand why they kept saying *inheritance?* Didn't they really mean *trust funds?*"

After the Schreuders' third summer at the beach, Freddie brought the boys back to Europe and Frances spent a month in Salt Lake. While she was still there, Franklin Bradshaw received a letter from his son-in-law asking for still more money for the children's care. Franklin wrote back with a counteroffer: he would take Marc, but not Larry, off their hands for a year, "if *that* will force Frances to go to work." He also demanded an accounting of the $3,000 Berenice had advanced Frances to cover her medical bills.

When the Schreuders came back from Europe the following summer, Larry was still kept at cautious arm's length. The marital fights were worse than ever. Frederik had taken to locking Frances out of the house overnight, and sometimes locking Marc out as well. This year, when it was time for school to begin, a significant change occurred. Frederik returned to Europe, taking only Larry with him, and Frances and Marc checked into a suite at the Plaza Hotel. The Schreuders had begun to split up. From now on, Frances would turn more and more to Marc, and rely on him as "the man of the family." She began calling him her "Strong Professor." He was not quite twelve years old.

For a couple of months, Marc lived like a male Eloise. He felt like the only child of a huge, adoring family. "Room service all the time, and I knew all the pages and bellboys. Pepe was my special friend, he'd always say, *'Oh, hello, Marc!'* It was just so *fun* there. Knowing everybody. The people at the Oak Bar, the coffee shops. They all knew me, and I wondered why. I guess people all know you, if you live at the Plaza."

The day that Marc was accepted to begin sixth grade at Allen-Stevenson School, Frances was truly overjoyed. Dickie Behrens had advised her that this Waspish, socially faultless one-hundred-year-old academy full of proper, blue-blazered boys was the right place for Marc, and had helped her fill out the forms. "Mom was fanatic about wanting the best for her children, especially schools. She detested public schools, which she said were filled with 'niggers and Jews and dirty white trash.' Mom emphatically told me, on myriad occasions, that public schools were bedlams where violence, disrespect, and any number of foul things occurred. Only at the best private schools could her children get the best education, and later attend the most prestigious private colleges."

Frances Schreuder was not a demonstrative mother. But the day her son was notified that he had been admitted to Allen-Stevenson was one of only three times in his life that Marc remembers his mother actually hugging and kissing him. These three moments of tenderness punctuate his account of his hobgoblin boyhood like three kisses from an evil queen.

Soon after school opened, mother and son moved from the Plaza Hotel back to an apartment in their old neighborhood, this one at 75 East End Avenue. Marc was proud to help with the moving. "Mom said I was 'man of the family.' She began confiding everything to me. She'd start by helping me with my homework . . . and, well, she'd just tell me everything that was going on. I remember one time she was missing some document, and she screamed to me hours and hours about this piece of paper. She never did that to me before. Anything that was wrong, I was blamed. I was supposed to be a man. Yet it seemed like I couldn't do anything right. It was very mixed up."

In this same stormy period, Frances Schreuder's longtime psychiatrist moved away to Canada. She turned to her twelve-year-old son as a stand-in. Marc says, "She was always telling me how helpless she was in New York, how people constantly were trying to take advantage of her. So she needed her 'Strong Professor' always around with her. Me. Apparently I was trying to fill her shrink's shoes, as well as Freddie's."

This was also the time that Marc began to sleep in his mother's bed. "Freddie was gone, see. It started that I was always doing my homework in her bedroom. She always wanted to monitor my homework, and soon I just was living in there. I didn't like to go to my room." Soon Marc was doing his homework in his mother's bed, then falling asleep there. "People make sexual connotations out of it, but there was nothing! She would sleep on one side. I would sleep on the other. I was just . . . very lonely. And Mom practically wanted . . . I mean she didn't really care. She wanted the comfort of having another person. Like nearby. Rather than me being . . . And Mom was . . . She was all I had, at that point. Larry was away in Europe. With Freddie. And . . . DRZSHHHH."

Marc says 1972 was also the year his mother started beating him up regularly, thrashing him with the buckle end of a leather belt whenever his school grades failed to meet her inflated expectations. "Mom beat me worse than Freddie ever did," he says, adding that his scalp is crosshatched with scars. Four years later, Marc Schreuder was graduated from Allen-Stevenson School with top honors in his class.

Marc says he was also beaten for "acting like sick Larry . . . or even playing with sick Larry. I was supposed not to go near him when he was home. Period. That's when I really learned to obey Mom. WHOOSH!" For a moment he must stop talking. He is breathing too heavily. Is it the memory of being beaten which is so upsetting, or of sleeping with his mother, or of being forced to act like a man yet berated for being only a kid? Are his stories even true? The breathlessness is genuine. But is it caused by the stress of lying or the stress of truth? No way to know. How can one even be sure about the marks under his hair? Marc later on acquired a girlfriend who says his scalp is indeed a network of raised scars. But Frances says that the little boy was savagely beaten by Vittorio, and by Freddie. Marc was also struck in the head by a car, and his head was pushed through a pane of glass by his brother. Berenice says she saw this. Marc says it never happened. Marilyn says that one day Frances called her and told her she was keeping Marc home from school because he had had his first wet dream. Whom and what does one believe in this family?

In prison, Marc has taken many college psychology courses and belongs to several psychotherapy groups. He often ponders the nature of his mother's illness. Sometimes he thinks that her paranoia, her rages, stupors, and other erratic behaviors and violent mood swings are evidence of manic-depressive psychosis, also called bipolar mood syndrome. It would please him if that were the correct diagnosis, since "that's what so many great artists have had." It is comforting to think of his mother in the same category as Van Gogh and Virginia Woolf, Handel and Berlioz, not to mention Byron, Shelley, Coleridge, Blake, Poe, Lowell, Balzac, Hemingway, Ruskin, Goethe, and Schumann. But if his mother *was* manic-depressive all these years, he wonders why none of her many psychiatrists treated her for this disorder. His abnormal psychology text books say that lithium carbonate has revolutionized treatment of this form of mental illness. One reason may be that his mother was never sick enough long enough. And when the real pressure was turned on, she was always able to calm down and behave in a rational manner. A brilliant intellect helped her. So did money. With endless money, it is not difficult to elude the punishment society awards to ordinary sinners, nor for abused children also to miss out on the protection and care it offers ordinary victims.

It is hard for Marc even to think of himself as an abused child, let alone to discuss it. Larry finds it impossible. Of his childhood he says only, "It was all right. It was okay."

Marc is quick to say he feels he "did not suffer as much as Larry. Physically, anyway. Maybe emotionally I suffered more. I don't know. I think emotionally I had a lot of abuse. Ninety percent of my abuse is emotional. I couldn't say no to Mom. It was just very difficult for me to do.

"She was always threatening me with some kind of emotional . . . blackmail. If I was good, she'd hold out the carrot. She'd love me. I was always trying to get her to love me. And she was very effective in turning the cold shoulder. If you did anything she didn't like, or that was even socially improper, according to *her* ethical standards—she would cut off the love. And as I became older, it seems like this became more unbearable, not less."

Locking Marc out was especially effective. She did it over and over; the technique always worked. She never permitted either son, or anyone else, to have a key to the apartment. Only she was doorkeeper, and she maintained absolute control. "Just to be out in the cold was basically saying to me: I hate you. I don't love you. It seems like, throughout my childhood, I was *always* trying to get her to love me, trying to be supergood, do everything superperfect. And it seemed like I could never quite do everything the way she wanted me to. It just never came out right."

When Freddie and Larry came home that Christmas, in 1972, Frances and Marc fled to Salt Lake. It would be Marc's last visit to "the Lake" for five years. Later his Mom would tell him she did not want him spending too much time around "sick Granny," he says. He remembers laboring over a history paper on the Wright Brothers over the holidays, and Granny driving him to the public library for research. He does not remember confiding his unhappiness with his mother to a diary, nor describing there the beatings with the belt buckle. In 1977, when he was raiding Granny's files, he was astonished to discover copies of his old diary pages hidden among her papers.

When Marc and his mother returned to New York after Christmas, Freddie was at home, Larry back at the Reagans'. On New Year's Eve, after a fight with her husband, Frances turned up at the Emergency Room of Lenox Hill Hospital "irrational and incoherent." She was treated with Thorazine and kept overnight for observation.

Frances Schreuder was discharged from the hospital on New Year's Day 1973 exhausted, ill, and six months pregnant. Frederik was not around, and Berenice was off on another of her tours, this one to Tahiti, Fiji, and New Zealand. Marc looked after his mother as best he could. Her morning sickness was so severe, he remembers, that her bed was often surrounded with "little pools of vomit." When Frances awakened, she would pick her way through the mess to the bathroom. Marc's job was to clean it up.

One afternoon she was in bed as usual when the doorbell rang. Marc unlocked the triple-locked front door. "And BLAM! He walked in! My first thought was: A midget Henry Kissinger! What's he doing at my door? Then he said—*Marco!* and I knew right away . . . Oh my gosh, *here's Papa!*"

The little man warmly kissed and embraced his son. Marc could scarcely believe it. Ten years had passed since he had seen or heard from his father. Vittorio was in fact remarried, with three children, but his new family still lived in Italy, he said, and he was on a business trip to the United States.

During the six weeks he stayed in Frances's flat, Vittorio did the shopping, cooked the meals, and tenderly looked after his ex-wife and son. As soon as Frances felt able to get out of bed, she went to Tiffany's and ordered three hundred expensive, engraved birth announcements for the new baby. She bought several thousand dollars' worth of deluxe nursery equipment and expensive handmade baby clothes. Then it was time for Vittorio to go home, and she lapsed into another despair.

One night Marc was awakened by thumping sounds. He found his mother in the living room, surrounded by tissue paper and ribbons. The floor was heaped with boxes of baby presents, dolls, and other bits of the expensive layette, and Frances was bringing more items from her bedroom closets into the living room.

"Mom was acting very strange. There was a thick slur in her voice and she said, 'That's right, Marc. I'm drunk . . . and I don't wanna live . . .' I'd never seen her drunk before. I *had* seen her slurred like that, talking in a thick, old voice from her Valiums or whatever she was taking to sleep with, to calm her down. But this time she kept saying 'I'm drunk!' and carting dolls and baby carriages and stuff back and forth. It was like: Ariadne hadn't even been born yet—and Mom was preparing for her birthday party already!"

Then Marc's mom began "acting really nutty. She started crying and hitting herself in the stomach with a large box—wham! WHAM!"

"Stop, Mom!" Marc yelled, grabbing the box away. It contained pieces of a collapsible crib or baby carriage. Frances cried harder, and Marc felt she was furious with *him*. He could not understand. This was the second time he had had to stop his mother from hurting herself. In all, he remembers five suicide attempts by his mother. Another time he came home unexpectedly and found her crying loudly in the living room. When he asked her what the matter was, she had shouted, "I want to die!" and leaped from the couch to the window of the seventeenth-floor apartment. She had flung up the sash and got her head out before Marc grabbed her around the waist. "I remember dragging her back and shouting, *'Mom! Mom! Please don't!'* "

Frances several times threatened to swallow pills. Once Marc walked into his mother's bedroom and found her in bed "acting very strange, crying and sobbing."

"Mom, what's wrong?"

"It's your grandmother! I don't want to live any longer!"

"Why, Mom? What happened?"

"I just *don't!*" she snarled, and again it felt to Marc as if he were the person she was angry at.

"Alluva sudden—I don't know why—she just jumped up and started screaming and ran into the bathroom saying, *'I'm gonna kill myself, Marc!'* And she locked the door.

"I said, *'Come on, Mom! Don't do that! Please!'* God, I was just begging and crying and screaming—crying so *hard!* A disaster was about to take place, and she had the door locked and I couldn't get in."

Marc pleaded for five minutes before his mother silently opened the door. "Something told me she hadn't really done it, hadn't taken anything. We sat in the bathroom and talked. I kept trying to find out what was the matter, because I knew Mom had gone through so much with her money problems and all. Each time it happened I talked with her afterwards for hours, because I was always afraid she was gonna make another attempt. I didn't want this on my conscience—no way! And besides, the idea of living without Mom was impossible."

The suicide gestures usually occurred in the daytime, Marc says, and they always followed a conversation with Berenice. "I think they happened, especially the later ones, because Mom felt she was so helpless. Because she didn't have control. Gramps had stopped sending her money. So she had to depend on Granny. Granny had her under her thumb. And she hated having to depend on Granny for money. Or anything. Hated it! Because that way, according to Mom, Granny had control. Granny could manipulate *her.* And Mom would describe how Granny so-called deliberately used her power.

"Mom said Granny deliberately sent little chunks of money at a time, to keep her always begging for more. But the real reason Granny was doing it—I understand now—was that Mom was such a spendthrift. Granny was fighting to space the money out, trying to hold back so Mom wouldn't blow it all, and so Granny would still have something left to send her. So Granny was really fighting to *keep our family alive!* But it took me a long time to get that figured out."

Frances Schreuder's third child was born April 10, 1973, in Doctors Hospital in New York City. Frederik was in Europe. Frances called her parents and told them she had named her new baby Ariadne Tacy Alexandra Schreuder. "Tacy" appears to have been an afterthought. The name did not appear on the engraved Tiffany baby cards. When the package came, says Marilyn Reagan, Frances tossed them away.

Marilyn's visit to Doctors Hospital recalls the advent of the godmother in *The Sleeping Beauty.* She peered at the infant through the nursery window, congratulated the mother, silently left a gift behind, and returned to West End Avenue. She never saw the child again. Asked why, she sniffs, "I wasn't invited."

A few days later, Berenice arrived in town, breathless with excitement. She could not wait to hold in her arms her first and only granddaughter, her very own "tiny baby doll."

The stakes in the family game had risen sharply.

Part Three

The Boiling Up

BERENICE STAYED IN New York for two months after Ariadne's birth. When she left, Frances took up a yellow legal pad and fired off two letters that make her previous communiqués to her parents seem sentimental. She told her father that her mother was incompetent, senile, disobedient, mentally ill, and so desperate to have a baby to care for that she had become an evil demon who "turns people into babies . . . She turned Bob Bradshaw into a helpless vegetable baby . . . She, Dad, and she alone put Bob into his grave . . ."

She scourged her mother for even daring to "discuss my daughter, whom you fought to have killed with an abortion," and for causing Elaine's broken heart. Frances's penchant for grotesque exaggeration was most apparent in her account of Marc's sprained ankle. "You let your grandson rot in pain and misery . . . while you went berserk . . . wallowing in self pity . . ." Berenice was lucky, said Frances, that her grandson was even alive.

During the three tempestuous years of her divorce from Frederik, Frances's separate furies seemed to fuse, her rage at husbands, parents, sisters, and sons all boiling up into one caldron of wrath. Frances had begun to spend much of her time in bed, fat, angry, or depressed. When she felt really low she sent Marc out for a quart of ice cream, poured the syrup in, and ate it out of the container. She had no money. Frederik sent nothing, and neither did Dad. Without her mother, she and the children would starve to death. The poorer and more dependent she felt, the more she ate. As she often said, "You have to be rich to be able to diet."

The noise of the Schreuders' three-year marital breakup was like the grinding of icebergs. Having concluded during her first four-year matrimonial war that Vittorio had found himself a lawyer even smarter and nastier than her own, she had decided next time, Erdheim would be working for her, not against her. As life with Frederik began to fray, Frances had retained her old adversary. By the time her second divorce finally was granted, in the spring of 1976, the ferocious Erdheim had surpassed even his own professional standards, and the thoroughly trounced and vanquished Frederik had seemingly disappeared from the planet. Frances described him as an even worse crook than Vittorio; she told people that U.S. Immigration authorities had permanently barred him from ever entering the country. Later she embellished the story with a description of Frederik's death in the much publicized airport runway collision on March 27, 1977, of a Pan Am 747 with a KLM 747 in the Canary Islands. Neither story is true. Frederik Schreuder is alive and well, remarried, and living in a far-off land. But for a decade he has found it preferable to give the United States a wide berth.

Frances launched her attack by charging that Frederik had deserted her during her pregnancy and refused to contribute to the support or medical expenses of mother and child. He had returned from Europe at Christmastime 1973, "without even a fifty-cent toy," and dropped a sudden karate chop on Frances's neck as she was holding her baby. She accused him of twenty more assaults, several requiring hospitalization, between then and the following February, when she finally obtained a temporary order of protection from family court to keep him out of their home and away from her children.

Frederik countercharged that his wife neglected her children and left Marc to fend for himself in the afternoons, roaming the streets, searching for food, sitting in stairwells alone, or sheltering in neighbors' apartments until she returned home and unlocked the door, sometimes as late as midnight. She forced her son to clean the apartment while she lay in bed. She kept him up until one o'clock in the morning "for company." She had failed to teach him proper personal hygiene or bathroom habits, and he stank so badly that neighbors and elevator men complained. She so neglected Marc and the baby that both children were marked with burns from accidents with cigarettes and boiling water. Doctors who had treated the children were named in the complaint. Neighbors had several times called police to report cries and screams emanating from the Schreuders' thin-walled apartment. Dates were cited. The baby often was left alone, allowed to fall off the bed onto her head, and allowed to put paper, glass, and nails into her mouth. Frances frequently attacked Marc "and on several occasions pounded the boy senseless."

Poor Frederik. His flights of exaggeration would prove no match for the combined talents of Erdheim and Frances. She composed a forty-seven-page answering affidavit accusing Frederik, among other things, of being a "criminal psychopath" so sadistic and vicious she was lucky to be alive. She described him stamping on her surgical scars, flinging her about the apartment, tossing her over the coffee table. "My son Marc . . . stood in horror watching his mother being so savagely abused. My husband continued in the presence of my son to beat me with his fists and smash my body around the apartment until he was exhausted. Virtually my entire body from head to toe, both front and back, was covered with welts, cuts and bruises." She also accused Frederik of child abuse, of stealing from his children, of sadomasochistic attacks on his wife and others; of embezzling funds from his employers, of income tax fraud, tranvestism, sexual perversion, international espionage, and a perpetual flow of green-black pus from his penis.

Frederik wrote back that his wife had been crazy since the age of six, and he gave the court the names of a dozen psychiatrists and institutions in the United States and abroad who had treated Frances over the years. He filed flurries of countercharges about his wife's longtime irrational and abusive behavior. He asserted, for example, that during their first summer in Europe, at the same time that Frances was writing reasonable letters to her parents about summer camps, she was also filing complaints with the Dutch police that the FBI was tapping her phone. She believed the FBI suspected her of clandestine romantic meetings with a Polish secret agent. Her complaint caused The Hague police to recommend to Frederik that his wife be put under psychiatric observation.

He said that one Sunday morning, while the family was still living at the Brussels Hilton and looking for permanent quarters, Frances was picked up by the police wandering half-naked through the streets. The following month, he said, after they moved to their tiny room-and-a-half apartment at 505 Avenue Louise, his wife had become convinced that a TV camera advertising a photography shop across the street was really a CIA spy camera trained on their apartment, and she refused to come out the door. He described a Saturday morning, after a fight at home, when Frances followed him to his office and "went berserk, severely damaging walls, doors & light fittings by smashing at them with the heel of her shoe . . . an incident hushed up by my company. Around that time her French physician Dr. Antoine Germain and his Swiss psychiatric consultant Dr. Will Adler strongly recommended to her that she place herself voluntarily under observation, but she refused."

He described how Frances attacked him in his sleep. He had called an ambulance . . . "whereupon the police, after consultation with her doctors, forcibly committed her to the Brugmann Clinic, a mental hospital managed by Dr. Ovieska and Dr. Fayersteyn. Struck with pity for her, I managed to override the authorities and obtained her release in my care . . ."

Frances pooh-poohed it all. Frederik was just up to his old tricks, she said. He had behaved the same way during his divorce from his first wife, also accusing *her* of being a slut, a druggie, and an unfit mother. Frederik had made these charges in letters in Dutch to his long-dead mother, in Holland. Frances had somehow acquired the letters. She turned them over to the court, along with her own typewritten English translations.

Nor was Frederik ever able to break the family court's order of protection, which barred him from the apartment as a danger to Frances and her children. He was never given a chance to answer the charges. Frances outwitted him through the simple device of obtaining five postponements of the hearing on the matter over the next nine months. When Frederik did get a court order allowing him to visit the apartment to collect his clothes and personal possessions, Frances threw such a tantrum, he said, that the cops accompanying him asked why he did not have her committed. But by then Frederik had lost all appetite for battle.

In contrast, Frances was in fine fettle. She now conjured up letters to each of her parents from her current psychiatrist, Dr. Maxwell Brand. Surely he was knowledgeable about her mental health. Originally Dr. Brand had been the court-assigned marriage counselor for the battling Schreuders. Dr. Brand now wrote to the Bradshaws that in his opinion Frances was not crazy at all. Indeed, he found her to be holding up remarkably well in a period of great stress.

Once more Franklin Bradshaw sided with a son-in-law he had never met against his own daughter. Secretly he sent Frederik letters of support criticizing Frances and Berenice. He said he did not believe in divorce, and that Frederik was unemployed only because his daughter had caused him to lose his job. Franklin

accused Frances of "bleeding me of my working Capital," forcing
him to take out over $100,000 in bank loans, and actually imperil-
ing the survival of his business. In short, Franklin once again
tried by every means he knew to "say no to Frances."

Frances retaliated by filing suit against her father in Utah, accusing him of refusing to turn over to his grandsons, and to her,
certificates for stocks and bonds that were in fact their property.
Franklin countersued, charging his daughter with a long history
of fiscal irresponsibility and unfitness, and of looting her sons'
assets for her own personal use. Franklin said that the bonds
Frances was now demanding that he surrender had been promised her not by him but by his wife, and over his near-dead body.
As for her claim that he owed her an additional $8,000 in Moun-
tain Fuel stock, he contended once more that this had always
been intended as a loan to cover other bad debts—not as a gift—
and had never been repaid.

Berenice jumped into the fray. From New York she wrote her
husband that Frederik was an even more abusive husband than
Vittorio. Her daughter's first divorce was the first ever granted in
New York State on grounds of cruelty to children, Berenice believed. "But that *Frederik*—he broke her jaw!"

Her Dutch son-in-law also had once shoved Berenice bodily
out of her own Zürich hotel room. She had heretofore kept quiet
about such disgraceful goings on, she said, not wishing to sow
seeds of marital discord. Now she wrote out long lists of
Frances's many serious illnesses abroad—two kidney operations,
major abdominal surgery, double pneumonia, back trouble,
bleeding ulcers, knee trouble, and severe influenza. She wrote to
her son-in-law that he had been guilty of gross medical neglect,
and she was now "fighting for my daughter's life." If anything
should happen to Frances, Berenice warned, the Bradshaws
would hold Freddie forever responsible and "point the finger of
shame."

The maddened Frederik, like a wounded bull, made a final
lunge before collapsing in the sand. He sent the court a long,
desperate letter describing additional episodes on York Avenue of
all-night screaming and bottle throwing that resulted in thirteen-
year-old Marc being locked out five hours "and in his emotional
agony defecating in the building's hallway." This in turn had
caused the building's management to fire off a series of Mail-
grams demanding immediate intervention in the Schreuder mat-

ter by the New York City police commissioner, the health commissioner, the three different judges involved in the case, the Society for Prevention of Cruelty to Children, and the Bradshaws. Relevant documents were attached.

His plea concluded: "I think that these are facts you should know, your Honor: three young children are being abused and neglected by a mother who is out of mental control but nobody apparently cares enough to break through legal niceties to act for the protection and welfare of these children."

Curiously, in view of the seriousness of his accusations, Frederik failed to file any charges. Possibly he feared reattracting the attention of his first wife; possibly he was as given to hyperbole as his second wife. In any event, by the end of the year Frances had obtained a paper from the New York State Department of Social Services saying they had investigated the child abuse charges against her and found them all to be unfounded. Much later, when Marc had grown up, he would claim that he clearly recollected being escorted down to the offices of the Society for Prevention of Cruelty to Children by the society's investigator, Ralph Manzi, and questioned about his home life. "I'll never forget, because Mr. Manzi was the first time Mom told me to lie to any stranger." She had warned him that if he told Manzi the truth, "I could never live with Mom again. Well, forget that! I really *loved* Mom! I loved her and I hated her. It just seemed I couldn't live without her."

Before it ended, in sum, the Frances/Freddie divorce war had been turned into another vast Bradshaw family game—like the money game, like Stratego—in which every member of the family played. And as the fight ground on, each of the players kept raising the stakes and bluffing. Nobody ever called the bluffs: that might have ended the game. Instead they just reraised and kept going.

The strain on the boys during this period must have been fearful, much worse than the first divorce fight, which they had been too young to understand. They both seem to have rather liked Freddie, despite his quick temper and European ways. He had given their chaotic home life a certain stability. With him out of the picture, husbandless, rudderless Frances turned more and more to Marc. If Marc was no longer his mother's bedmate, he was still kept busy as her chief confidant, cook, errand boy, dishwasher, doorkeeper, in-house shrink, all-star prep school achiever, and one man suicide prevention squad.

Toward the end of the '72–'73 term, Larry's Dutch boarding school had refused to keep him any longer without payment. Freddie told them to send the bill to the Bradshaws and brought the boy home permanently to the United States. Frances, Marc, and the baby were again at Fire Island. Larry stayed for two weeks, happily helping feed and change his adored baby sister. Then he was again exiled, this time to the New York apartment.

Before he left, the brothers had started playing a new game, "Stalingrad," which could go on for days. "It was a war game," Larry explains, "and you'd gain territory. Whoever got more of Mom's attention got more territory. Once I wound up with one small island in the Pacific and Marc had the whole world."

In the fall, Freddie drove Larry out to Eastern Military Academy, the Dickensian, decrepit and now defunct boarding school in Huntington, Long Island, where he would be dumped for the next five years. Larry coped with his increasing ostracism from his family in several ways. He first became an obsessive penny collector. In the summer of 1973, left alone in Frances's apartment, he took to roaming the streets of the Upper East Side and counted about fifty neighborhood banks. Each day he visited as many banks as possible, and in each bank he bought a thousand pennies for ten dollars. He sorted through them searching for rare "wheatbacks," pennies minted before 1959, then returned the discards for bills and change, and moved on to the next bank. In three years, working mostly summers and school vacations, he had netted some six thousand wheatbacks, valued at perhaps $200. By that time he was into his third year of residence at EMA.

In 1974 Larry started putting out his own one-man magazine. He called it *The Occupier: The Family Minded Monthly*. In all, he issued about sixty *Occupiers*, one every month until December 1979. He only stopped when he went to prison and the right kinds of paper and ink were temporarily unavailable.

Occupiers are one-of-a-kind documents, each one twelve or more pages. They are hand-written, handsomely illustrated in colored inks, emblazoned with flags of the world, and strewn with hand-drawn "ads," mostly for douches and maxi pads. The articles deal with world events, especially presidential doings—invariably seen from an ultraconservative viewpoint—as well as

sports, top-ten tunes, and the ongoing saga of Larry's sex life. But
the primary content is a detailed chronicle of the doings of every
member of the Schreuder/Bradshaw family.

Larry titled his magazine *The Occupier,* he explains, because
he started it to keep himself occupied. Psychiatrists say it "probably helps to tell Larry who he is." Certainly it is one way he
asserts his attachment to the family that keeps pushing him out.
Unfortunately for historians, and probably for the police, the first
forty *Occupier*s, up to midsummer 1977, were seized by Frances
after Larry's arrest. He believes she still has them, locked away in
a safe-deposit box. But *Occupier*s #40 through #60, covering
the years immediately before, during, and after Franklin Bradshaw's murder, are gone for good. They contained numerous stories about Larry, Marc, Frances, Behrens, Freddie, Granny and
Gramps, the Reagans, and Ariadne, and it is virtually certain
that they included many details of the murder plot as it boiled up
and finally boiled over. Larry says he kept these issues locked in a
typewriter case in the trunk of his car. Soon after his own arrest,
eighteen months after the murder, Larry's car was stolen from a
curbside parking space near Frances's and Behrens' apartments.
The theft was not reported to police; no attempt to recover the
car was ever made.

During the Schreuders' divorce, Berenice kept herself occupied
by travel abroad and remodeling at home. In three years she
visited Alaska, Tahiti, Fiji, New Zealand, Oregon, Central and
South America, Mexico, Washington, D.C., and New York City,
and by July 1976 she was rolling through China on a tourist bus.
Between tours she made over her house, added a safe and a sauna
in her basement, and installed air-conditioning throughout. She
kept her beloved maple furniture, the deeply ruffled lampshades,
the green wallpaper. As a present to herself for her golden wedding anniversary, she also bought a new car.

The car and the home repairs do not seem to have attracted
Franklin's undue attention. But when he found out she had borrowed money to finance these expenditures, he was horrified and
repaid the loan instantly. Withal, Berenice did not neglect her
maternal duties. In May 1975, a year before the Schreuder divorce
became final, she sent Frances still another 100 shares of Mountain Fuel, pointing out that she had sent a total of $21,000 in the
past six months, and politely requesting "an accounting."

Frances sent back a partial "accounting" and a full-throated denunciation. She said she felt as if her father had "purchased a marriage." She accused him of being such a male chauvinist that he actually expected Frances to repay her husband's debts to her father! She said she was beginning to feel as though she hated all men. Her fury increased until she sounded like a ventriloquist's dummy on Berenice's knee: "Those two men can go rot in hell before I will pay a penny for a debt of Frederik's! I'll fight Dad in court until he regrets it. Just what do these men think? I am paying for three fatherless children and if F.J.B. wants me to pay some more of Frederik's debts, he must have sawdust in his head instead of brains."

Franklin continued quietly slaving away in his unheated warehouse. "I don't know whether I can take another winter down there," he told the Reagans, so on a summer's visit they bought shelving and fixed him up an attractive at-home office. He never used it. Berenice had made it clear that his greasy work clothes and disorderly habits were not welcome in her tidy new basement.

By the early 1970s Richard Behrens had become an intermittent alcoholic. When he was drinking, old acquaintances often noticed him staggering in and out of First Avenue bars, unshaven, unwashed, muttering to himself, dressed in thrift shop clothes and carrying other clothes in a paper bag. When he was dry, he worked as a substitute schoolteacher. Behrens had also become an active player in the Bradshaw family game, the only non–family member to take part. But he was careful to keep his distance if Berenice was around, and the old lady saw him only once, very briefly, two years after her husband's murder.

The first time Marc remembers meeting "Uncle George" was early in 1974, when he took Frances and her son out to dinner at a little Italian restaurant in Little Italy, near Canal Street. "He acted *very* drunk, I recall . . . thick talk, unsteady movements." Marc remembers at least ten more meetings, most of them at modest Yorkville restaurants which offered the German-style cooking Behrens preferred. Frances brought Marc everywhere, and the boy listened while the adults for hours discussed world events and their family problems. Frances dominated the conversations, it appeared to Marc, talking incessantly of Frederik's unendurable, autocratic "Prussian" ways, and Granny's "smother love."

One February afternoon Marc was home alone, doing homework on his bed. Freddie returned early from his office and asked Marc in a strange, tense voice if his mother was seeing another man? Marc described the meetings with Behrens, which now occurred once or twice a week. Yes, occasionally they met in Behrens' apartment. But no, the two adults never went into the bedroom alone together, and they had never asked Marc to leave. Freddie was unconvinced.

When his mother arrived home, Marc heard screaming, slapping, arguing, and shouting in the living room. The next morning Frances instructed her son to triple-lock the front door; her husband, she believed, had keys to only two of the three locks. That evening, somehow, Freddie got back inside. Mom took Marc out to a restaurant for dinner and berated him for being a "Freddie boy," and for failing properly to secure the door. When they got home, Freddie had locked them out and refused to open up despite Frances's pounding and shrieking. She took Marc down to her car, and they drove around for a couple of hours, then parked in front of the Old Dutch Delicatessen at Second Avenue and Eighty-fifth Street, and sat with the heater running until the battery went dead. It was about midnight now and extremely cold. Frances sent Marc to a phone booth to call "Uncle George" and ask him to bring blankets and jumper cables. Behrens did, but the car was also out of gas. Marc spent a miserable night huddled under blankets in the back seat while Mom and Behrens talked quietly up front. At dawn Behrens was able to jump the battery. At the gas station he paid; Frances was also out of money.

Frances now drove to lawyer Erdheim's office, obtained the necessary papers and, by afternoon, she and Marc and some cops were back at the apartment door. Freddie would not open up until the cops commenced smashing the door down. Frances and her son walked in; Freddie packed his suitcase and left.

Frances frequently called Behrens "the old woman." But Marc is quite certain his mother and Behrens were never lovers, though he thinks Freddie would have been equally jealous of the friendship either way. In any event, after Freddie left, Frances began turning more to Behrens as a confidant, and to Marc somewhat less. They met only rarely in his disordered apartment. Usually he chose one of his favorite German restaurants. He smiled and said "Heil Hitler" as Frances and her son approached.

Save for Behrens, the Schreuders and Bradshaws were now playing in an all-family game, and the only family member who was not involved in it was adorable Ariadne, asleep in her expensive bassinet. The child *was* adorable: pretty, quiet, utterly beguiling. And she *was* asleep. She never showed the fretful wakefulness, the irritability, hyperactivity, and insomnia that plagued so many others in her family. Ariadne from birth has seemed an enchanted, and enchanting, child. She has impressed everybody who has ever known her—schoolteachers, ballet teachers, neighbors, other mothers, even other children, who can be a notoriously cruel cabal—as an exceptionally lovely child. It is almost as if she is under some sort of benign magic spell, as if a genuine Good Fairy presided over her birth. Those teachers, schoolmates, and others who are unaware of her troubled family background simply do not believe it is true. Those who do know the truth cannot understand how she has survived it. But from birth onward, Ariadne has seemed entirely untouched by, or at least unmarked by, the chaos around her. Her family life whirled along in a perpetual maelstrom, and the child floated on the surface as peacefully and prettily as Thumbelina in her walnut shell boat.

In August 1975 Berenice waited for a day when Franklin was out of town. Then she went down to the warehouse for a quiet visit with Doug Steele.

"How much are we really worth, Doug?"

"Berenice, if Frank started spending it right now, you could not get rid of it all in your lifetime. You couldn't even spend the *interest.*"

Flabbergasted, the old lady returned to Gilmer Drive, clumped downstairs past her display of Hopi dolls, Greek *efzoni* soldiers, koala bears, toy matadors, and Delft pottery to her little basement office, and typed out a two-page letter to her husband. It was Berenice Bradshaw's personal declaration of independence. Yet, in places, one can detect the authentic tones of Frances, as if Granny were now the dummy seated on her daughter's knee. Saying nothing about it to anybody, she tucked the sheets of paper into her husband's bureau drawer, just as her mother Florence had done to her many years before. When Franklin came upon the letter, he said not a word either, just took it down to the warehouse and filed it away along with everything else.

Aug. 30th, 1975

FRANKLIN:

Here are some correspondence for you to look over with this explanation. As I have told you I have one ambition left in these last days of mine and that is to see that my grandchildren are raised properly and well edicated.

We are rich people and there is no reason why we should not share our wealth with our own flesh and blood. The time to share with our family is now, when they need it not twenty years from now. The Drukman family seem to be doing a fine job on their own. They have never asked for help, they prefer to do their own thing in their own way. For 25 years money has been spent on educating Marilyn, I think she has had her share. We have three (3) fatherless grandchildren who need us and our help, personally and financially. Marc and Larry are now young men, a critical time in their lives. Now is the time for making the kind of high quality men of these young boys we want them to be. They have no one to look after them, to support and encourage them but us. They are looking to us for this guidance and developement. I'm dedicating myself to giving them my all, my best. The very least I can do is finance their education. You let them down last year (1974-1975) by not paying their schools. It was a desperate struggle for their mother, with no husband and no income, to keep these boys in these fine schools.

I finally got wise, it took a long time. You have told me many times, I cannot spend all my income. With this worthwhile interest in my grandchildren I want to share this "vast wealth" with them. Why should they suffer while we linger in our old age with more wealth than we know what to do with. Doug said to me: "You folks can't spend the interest on your money." What is to happen to all this wealth? Why can't we and our family enjoy some of the fruit of our whole-life's labors? We are in our 70's, how old do you have to be to "be old"? If I had my way we would sell everything we own and divide it up with our families and we start living and they enjoy life a little more. Now I know this will never be, you will not change and how sad. I think you are making a big mistake

---

All spellings, punctuation, and the language of all family letters is exactly as written, except for bracketed information.

not to liquidate the Auto Parts business. There is no one to carry on that business. As Doug says: "After the Mr. goes there will be a blood-bath". How well we both know. How sad to let this happen when it can be avoided by taking care of our business affairs *now*. I think everyone in the organization is wondering what is going to happen to the business and to them personally when you die. There is no feeling of security with three (3) violent, unfriendly daughters waiting to gorge the life-blood of our 50 years of work. I think about this, are you doing the right thing?

I promised my grandsons I would take care of their schooling. As you will see by the enclosed copies I have taken care of this years, 1975-1976. You offered me $5000 for my American Savings and Loan stock. If you can give me $5000 for my stock you can give me $5000 without my stock. You are choking to death in stock, still you have your hand out to take away from me any sign of property I might own. You don't want me to "own anything" or have "anything" of value. I'm just supposed to work up to my last day for my board and room. I intend to change that. My stock is not for sale.

I made a trip down to Lehi and went to the bank. I found my signature is as good as yours in that bank. Also I found my bank balance to be over $38,000. I had four cashier checks made; one for $3800 for Eastern Military Academy, one for $3200 for Allen-Stevenson school, two for $300 each for the boys some school clothes and $200 cash for myself. This leaves a balance of about $30,791.15.

I have a wonderful feeling knowing I have done the right thing. I intend to share my wealth and income with those I love,

Berenice J. Bradshaw
[Signature]

By Christmas Frances Schreuder was saying quite openly, "This family can't keep going much longer, not unless somebody kills my father." It was said in jest, of course, and understood as hyperbole, just one more of Mom's wild exaggerations. They did not speak of the matter when "Granny the bat" was visiting. But at other times Frances and Dick Behrens freely discussed the need to get rid of her father, and the boys joined the conversation

if they felt like it. Murdering Dad became the family "sick joke";
how to accomplish it evolved into a further twist of the Game. At
home, in the privacy of the night kitchen, there were no reservations, no constraints within the Schreuder family. There were
secrets of course, conspiracies, and plots galore. Each family
member had his own hiding places, spots to protect private trea-
sures from the ceaseless nocturnal raids of the others. But in one
another's presence, anything could be said or done. Nothing was
taboo. It was not necessary to close the bathroom door or the
bedroom door. The front door had triple locks. Behind it the
policy was—anything goes. If Mom wanted to spend the day in
bed, have a thirteen-hour phone conversation with Behrens, stay
up all night, sleep all day, or sleep two days, it didn't matter.
Marc was old enough to get back and forth to school by himself.
He could run down to the deli when they were hungry. He knew
how to buy a cooked chicken, make garlicburgers, feed and care
for the baby, clean house. Frances had no friend but Behrens and
seldom went out except to graze the aisles of expensive department stores. She never had guests, and the door was kept locked
and bolted. Except for the baby Frances saw no one but Marc
and Behrens, and more rarely Larry and Berenice. The five of
them rolled round and round in a closed circle, five serpents with
their tails in one another's mouths.

The Drukmans had by this time made their move to New
Zealand. Frances had stopped speaking to Marilyn. Her sister
had misappropriated her furniture, she said, while she was in
Europe, and when Marilyn sent Marc a card for his fifteenth
birthday, December 21, 1975, with a real wheat penny attached,
Frances made him send it back. During Berenice's annual Christmas visits, she commuted between her daughters' warring households. The sisters vied silently for her favor. Frances cooked a
Christmas dinner of stuffed bass with shrimp sauce, and Berenice
could not stop telling Marilyn how delicious it was. She bragged
to the Schreuders that the Reagans took her to the ballet to see
the annual Christmas production of *The Nutcracker.* On New
Year's Eve she and Frances and Marc and Larry sat down to play
Stratego. As dawn broke on January 1, 1976, all four of them were
still playing the game. As soon as Granny left, discussion of the
family joke resumed.

Berenice did not need to hear the joke to know that matters in
the Schreuder household were reaching a flashpoint. Franklin,

however, believed he had finally put his foot down: if people in this family want more money, he wrote, they can go to work like anybody else. But Berenice kept sending whatever she could, and Frances kept spending whatever she could lay her hands on. One spring day she lugged Larry's collection of six thousand hand-gleaned wheat pennies to the nearest bank and turned them in at their face value—sixty dollars.

In the night kitchen, the family joke was repeated and elaborated upon. The family had but two choices: take Ariadne to live in Harlem, or murder Gramps. "Harlem was a big subject with Mom," Marc says. "She kept saying that she would never let anybody make her and Ariadne live in Harlem. And at the same time she would say she'd *rather* live in Harlem than go back to Salt Lake and live under their thumb. Because she would *never* go back to Gilmer Drive. She would rather *die* than live with Granny."

More and more Frances Schreuder was talking about her need to "control my own life," even though a life so out of control is rarely seen. Rather than "lose control," she said, she would kill herself.

In retrospect one can see that by the time of Ariadne's birth, Berenice and Frances were a pair of mirrored female figures locked in mortal combat. Frances had become a complete parasite—entirely dependent on her parents, increasingly on her mother, for her very existence—yet a parasite who demanded total "control" and insisted on total independence. This insistence ultimately would turn parasite into parricide.

Berenice too had become a kind of parasite, dependent on her daughter for the emotional nourishment and excitement she could not find elsewhere. To escape the empty drabness of her life, Berenice was more than willing to leap into the boiling volcano of Frances's existence; she was eager. Thus her maternal concern became her justification for doing what she wanted to do anyhow. But her concern was genuine, not counterfeit.

The more viciously Frances abused her mother, the more tenaciously Berenice clung. Looking back at these two grappling female figures, it is hard to tell which woman is the oak and which the mistletoe, who is the strength and who the clinging vine slowly strangling the mighty tree. Only through Frances can Berenice have another baby, can she have fun in New York, can she *live*. "Life is so different here and there," says Berenice. "In New

York, I have friends but no relatives. In Salt Lake, I have relatives but no friends."

So Frances's frenzy is understandable. She *must* fight off this "zombie Mommie," as she sees her, this vampire who can live only on her daughter's blood. Hence her constant bad-mouthing of "evil Granny . . . Granny the bat . . . Granny the croc . . . sick-in-the-head Granny"—a nonstop brainwashing of which Berenice is entirely unaware. Entirely? Perhaps not. It might be more accurate to say that she must preserve her "ignorance" of Frances's bad-mouthing in order to go on with the Game.

All Frances's children appear to have been unusually attached to their mother. Can this be due only to their fear of her terrible wrath, to their craven desire to please Mommie because *Mommie bites?* Not at all. Frances had an uncanny ability to be a kid with her kids, to get down entirely onto their childish level. She did not belittle, did not talk down to them. She treated them as equals. "Out," they knew, meant *locked* out, but when they were "in" with Mom, they were in on absolutely everything. A long-noted empathy exists between children and fools, children and the mad, children and the blessed. Frances had such empathy in great abundance. The offspring of Frances Schreuder could count on an extremely seductive as well as dangerous childhood.

On July 3, 1976, Frances typed up a rambling, fifteen-page letter to David Salisbury, the lawyer who had drawn up her parents' wills; she charged Marilyn with meddling in her parents' estate planning and of "deliberate fraudulent misrepresentation and undue influence [on the Bradshaws] with the intent of benefiting for herself unduly and under false pretenses and misrepresentation at the expense of others without my parents' full understanding, knowledge, or comprehension." The letter clearly shows two important facts, in a case where hard facts are even harder to come by: (1) Frances did have knowledge of her father's will and (2) she very much feared he might change it to her own disadvantage.

In her letter she further accused Marilyn, "childless and always somewhat irrationally jealous of the grandchildren," of pressuring Berenice to provide for Robert Reagan in her will as if he were not a son-in-law but a natural son. Later she would accuse the Reagans of seeking to adopt Robert's two grown daughters from his first marriage so as to increase their proportionate share of the estate.

Marilyn has "always had a peculiar relationship with men," and is trying to "hold on to the love and affection" of Reagan by promising him a share of her inheritance, Frances told Salisbury. To avoid this evil scheme, Berenice, "against her better wishes," has been unfairly forced to exclude her daughters from her own will. Frances's anxiety becomes clearer when she explains that Berenice is now supporting herself and her children at a rate of $3,000 a month.

No sooner was Frances's divorce decree final, in the spring of 1976, than Marilyn was back in Utah trying to impress her father with her knowledge of estate planning. Congress had added a new wrinkle to the gift tax law which she thought could be used to the estate's advantage. Franklin knew better. "Get in the truck, Marilyn," he said. They drove to the University's law library, where without hesitation he put his finger on the right page of the right statute.

"Old Dad was sure up on things," she says. "He didn't say much because he was always trying not to make waves. He was living with Mother and trying to keep things happy and . . . er . . . calm. Dad was always in the middle, don't you see?" Her hazel eyes blink rapidly behind large, clear plastic spectacles. Marilyn still hoped to be named her father's executrix, and she had providently bought herself a Salt Lake City condominium at a good price. She could live here more economically than in a hotel on her visits to supervise the estate after he was gone. Franklin told her it was all a false hope. "Not because you are not competent, Marilyn. But because your mother and your sisters just wouldn't like it." Rather than "make waves," Franklin elected to sink Marilyn's boat.

At home Marc kept house. He was ever compliant, he says. On the rare occasions that Larry was home, "He was a little more recalcitrant than me. He'd say, 'Why do I have to run down to the store twenty-four hours a day for you? Why do I have to be your slave?' I mean, there's a difference between doing favors, being a helpful son, and just *using you* day after day! Mom was always quoting Dr. Brand at us then. Her psychiatrist. She'd say, 'According to Dr. Brand, I don't have to tell you why. You just *do it!* I'm your mother and that's it!'

"I thought that was a little strange. I couldn't *imagine* Dr. Brand would say that! At the same time I thought: *Well, damn! I guess Dr. Brand's right then. I guess I'd better shut up.*" So Marc

made garlic salad, cheeseburgers, chicken breasts. "Whatever
Mom would tell me, I'd do. Night after night we had the same
thing. She'd go out and buy it, and I'd fix it while she read her
paper or watched TV. She could sit in her bed cross-legged for
hours, reading her papers. Whenever her papers were cut off,
she'd make me steal papers from down the hall."

Stealing was not odious to this young man. In his last year at
Allen-Stevenson, he broke into and vandalized the chem lab and
stole a Nikon with a 50-mm lens, a 105-mm telephoto lens, and
other equipment. Marc says Frances stole the Nikon from him
and locked it into her special white cabinet. Marc says now that
the total value of his chem lab thievery was $200–$300. Allen-
Stevenson says it cost $1,500 to replace the equipment and repair
the damage. Berenice Bradshaw, who terms her grandson "a
born thief and a maniac for destruction," cites the correct figure
as $15,000. She was told this by her daughter.

Whatever the amount, there is no question but that Marc is an
accomplished thief. At home he stole from his brother, his
mother, and his grandmother with jaunty aplomb. Tape recorders, doodads, money, comic books, cameras, rare coins, teddy
bears—a whole kaboodle of kid's loot wound up in his secret
hiding places. Larry had his cache. Mom had hers. Loot flowed
as rapidly, bafflingly back and forth among the three of them as
the pea in a shell game.

Years later, from prison, Marc wrote a letter describing the
perpetual intrafamily shell game: "The white cabinet was an all-
purpose lockup, containing mostly whatever Mom deemed appropriate to lock up at the time, like jewelry—when she was in
her paranoid mood, thinking perhaps me or Larry or even
Granny might steal it. Like tapes, such as those Larry made in
the summer of '77; or my slides, like those I took during the
summer of '77; or documentations—the cabinet contained a good
deal of such paperwork; like letters—sometimes Mom locked up
letters from Susie Coleman, if she could find them, or other documents. [Susie, daughter of the neighborhood delicatessen owners,
was one of Marc's few friends. They have exchanged private
notes and letters for years; she still writes to Marc in prison. His
correspondence with Susie is one of the few areas of Marc's life
which he still tries to keep inviolate.]

"I managed to secure access to the cabinet by popping the nails
out of the two panels in the back, which I did on several occa-

sions when Mom left the house with Ariadne—or when I was alone and Ariadne was at school. The reason I continually (at least, on five or six occasions that I can remember) entered the cabinet was because of the contents: Most of them seemed to be [things of] mine that Mom had snatched or stolen from me. Sneaking into the cabinet provided me with an easy way to determine exactly what Mom stole from me (I was always surprised by what Mom managed to steal from either me or Larry) and let me steal at least some of my stuff back.

"Mom's primary lockup in [our next apartment on Gracie Square] was a closet right next to her bed secured with a Miva magnetic lock. This closet contained two locked red tool chests secured with two padlocks—Dynalocks, requiring curious round keys to open them. In these chests were documents mostly, with some other stuff of mine, like a rare half-dollar I found which Mom had heisted from the mailman, and she never even told me she had it—but I suspected, because a coin that expensive doesn't just evaporate.

"Outside of these red tool boxes, Mom kept her medications, jewelry, important documents and letters—so Granny would not get ahold of them—and anything else that should be kept out of either my or Granny's hands.

"Mom also maintained a safe-deposit box at the Manufacturers Hanover Trust Company at Seventy-second and Madison. The box was huge, and Mom maintained a vast quantity of documents, newspapers, and letters in here. Also Mom kept stuff like tapes, slides, silver coins, and other stuff.

"Ninety-eight percent of my stuff and a hundred percent of Larry's stuff was vulnerable to Mom's frequent raids. However, some time in 1976 I developed an ultra-secret hiding spot at 1675 York Avenue that probably still exists. I removed the panel of wood at the bottom of a closet wall, dug out some of the cardboard insulation, and used the tiny spot to hide mostly coins I had bought for myself, or Mom had bought for me. By hiding them, Mom would not either steal them back or ask me to sell them when she was broke and penurious (which was always). By the time we moved [to the next apartment] I had learned the advantages of safe-deposit boxes, and I paid for several at various banks around Manhattan, hiding stuff like comics (which Mom *loved* to destroy and destroyed on numerous occasions when I was a boy); slides (which Mom loved to steal); and other stuff which I wanted to survive Mom's myriad maraudings."

At Marc's next school after Allen-Stevenson he would successfully loot the chem lab, and would twice clean out the school store. Both times he was eventually caught; both times his crimes were minimized and hushed up as much as possible. Prosecution of white-collar schoolboy crime—kleptomania and vandalism—reflects poorly on the reputation of any institution. Better when possible to play down such pranks.

In Marc Schreuder's case it always proved possible. At the Allen-Stevenson graduation ceremonies, the gymnasium was packed with parents, relatives, and guests. Frances sat proudly in a front-row seat, with the beautifully dressed Ariadne on her lap, watching the blue-blazered ninth graders parade onto the stage. And when the honor boys were asked to step forward and receive their special certificates of academic excellence, Marc was among them. Afterward, other parents congratulated Mrs. Schreuder on her son's brilliance, her daughter's loveliness. They told her how fortunate she was to have two such outstanding children. Not a soul among them knew she actually had three.

That fall, outfitted in his all-new Hush Puppies, gray socks, corduroy trousers, and jacket and tie, Marc Schreuder went off to the prep school which Behrens had helped his mother to find at the eleventh hour. Early that spring, after numerous conferences with Behrens, Marc had applied to two boarding schools and one day school: Choate and Hotchkiss in Connecticut, and Trinity School in New York City. Behrens was the acknowledged family authority on boarding schools, Frances the expert on private schools in Manhattan. Her personal favorite was St. Bernard's—all the best Allen-Stevenson boys went there—but she sadly rejected it for her own son as being "a little too Jewish." Then both boarding schools rejected Marc, and Trinity put him on its waiting list (and eventually rejected him).

Undaunted, Frances enrolled Marc in the Hotchkiss summer tennis camp, sent Granny the bill, and when the day came, drove him up to camp in the big red Delta '73 Olds she had acquired from Freddie. Although she usually got lost on the small, winding Connecticut roads, she knew the way to Hotchkiss. "Uncle George" Behrens had driven all three of them up to the school on the occasion of Marc's initial interview.

By the time Marc got home from tennis camp, Frances an-

nounced she had found a new "great school." Her researches had
discerned a small prep school with a faculty "loaded with degrees
from Princeton, Harvard, and Yale." Mother and son set off for
their interview at Kent School near the village of Kent, Connecticut. They were several hours late—Frances got lost again—but
Mr. Gowan took them on a tour of the campus, interviewed
Marc, and accepted him that very day. It was mid-August. Three
weeks later Marc moved into his dormitory and began tenth
grade.

In Salt Lake Berenice received an emergency phone call from
Frances's attorney: the landlord at 1675 York Avenue was again
threatening eviction. Granny rushed to New York, money in
hand, paid the back rent, swabbed and scrubbed and cleaned up
Frances's disheveled apartment. But she stayed at the Reagans.
Frances was refusing to speak to her.

Four days before Christmas, in anticipation of President
Jimmy Carter's new tax laws, Frank Bradshaw's accountant Herman Wood began making distributions through the F & B Corporation and its three trusts to the Bradshaw children and grandchildren. At the same time Frank's nephew Craig Bradshaw, the
upright young insurance man, learned that he had been named
without prior consultation as F & B's unpaid trustee.

Snow mantled the frozen Wasatch range, subzero winds ripped
the valley floor, and icicles fringed the draughty warehouse. In
the midst of this savage season, Frank Bradshaw received a rare
and intensely affectionate note from his grandson Marc. Two
years later, after his death, Berenice turned over a copy of the
note to police as proof that the boy was devoted to his grandfather and could not possibly have wished him harm. She made
many copies and passed them out to Bertha Beck, to Marilyn,
even to casual acquaintances. She saw the note as an icon of filial
piety, and it became a rare source of personal comfort during her
bereavement. Much later, in prison, Marc said his mother had
stood over him as he typed it, dictating every word.

Dear Grandpa,

I hope you are feeling better today! Generally sleep is the best
cure for any illness or desease. The longer you sleep the
sooner you get well. The best way to get rid of a flu as in your
case would be to get really warm, under the covers. Taking

vitamins is also good for a flu because they help you get better quicker.

   If you aren't well today you shouldn't press your body on through hardships but STAY IN BED! If you don't, you'll become sicker than you were before and you won't be able to do ANY work at all!

   I love you VERY MUCH! ! !

   I hope you get better soon!

   You are the sweetest grandpa a boy could have!

   You are the sweetest, kindest, generous, nicest, most loving, <u>BEST</u> grandpa in the world! ! !

   I am so lucky to have a grandpa as nice as you!

   Billions and billions of hearts, hugs, lovies, and kisses!

                                        LOVE marc!

   Throughout 1976 Frances's conversation dwelled increasingly on the family joke. "It would come up *every day!*" Marc says. "It seemed like she wasn't just preparing me—she was trying to prepare herself for it." The question is: when did the boiling pot boil over? At what point, and how, did the longtime family joke become the working family agenda?

   By the spring of 1977 Frances Schreuder had become preoccupied with God. Inspired by the wondrous goodness that Ariadne had brought into all their lives, she had sought out formal religious instruction. By early June she and her little daughter were ready to be received into the Episcopal Church. Granny was rhapsodic. On the Sunday of their baptism, she wrote to her daughter and granddaughter that she was "deeply impressed [that] you both are taking unto yourselves a religion, especially the Episcopal Church. I'm pleased [that] my dear, darling granddaughter has drawn you to commit your lives to something inspiring, something higher than man . . ."

   Despite her own lifelong atheism, or perhaps because of it, Berenice Bradshaw confessed her envy of those who find help and strength through religion, and expressed her passionate hope that Frances would finally find happiness in life, "now that Ariadne has shown you the way."

   Whatever her spiritual motivation, it is possibly relevant that of all the private preschools in Manhattan, the toniest is probably

Episcopal School, at Sixty-ninth Street off Park Avenue, operated by St. James' Episcopal Church. Certainly it has the most impregnable waiting list. Many potential students are registered at birth. Most are not just the children but grandchildren and even great-grandchildren of previous graduates. One of the four-year-olds accepted by Episcopal in the spring of 1977, to begin school in the fall, was a golden-haired child named Ariadne Schreuder.

When his wife told Franklin Bradshaw the wonderful news, it triggered a new variation on a worn theme: work cures all ills. If Ariadne was old enough to go to school, then she was old enough to be sent away to summer camp. So if Frances would also agree to send her grandsons to Salt Lake City, she herself would be free to go to work at last. He offered both boys summer jobs working in his warehouse at $4 an hour. Granny would provide free room and board on Gilmer Drive.

"Absolutely *not!*" said Frances when her sons told her. For two solid weeks she refused even to accept a phone call from Salt Lake City. Marc and Larry were shattered. The boys were dedicated consumers, avid capitalists. They yearned to gorge themselves on *things,* products, the stuff of TV commercials. Their longings—like everything else about them—were infantile. They articulated their wishes in a kind of babytalk. "My real buy-buy goal was a big ole' Nikon." They were like giant babies gurgling for very expensive toys. Their notion of heaven was to be turned loose in a Crazy Eddie store.

"Working for Gramps was a chance to make good money. Four bucks an hour! I mean—now you could buy *anything!* Larry could buy . . . cars! To me it was . . . cameras! We were just *yessing* Mom to death, we wanted it so bad."

For two weeks the Bradshaws tried every night with no success even to get their daughter to come to the telephone. Either no one answered or one of the boys picked it up and said that their mother was out. Then one evening Frances herself picked up the phone. She said she was so sorry to have missed their earlier calls. Yes, her sons had indeed told her about the invitation. She thought it was a perfectly wonderful idea. Marc and Larry would fly out to "the Lake" the moment they finished school.

The Bradshaws were overjoyed. So were Marc and Larry. The boys had always been wild about money. Cash and currency excited them physically They liked to hang out at banks, to hear the chinking sound of coins, to feel the heavy warmth of a pocketful of change, the electric crackle of new bills. They could name all the faces on all the denominations. And both were avid coin collectors as well as knowledgeable readers of the financial pages. But neither boy had ever been given any money of his own. Not only had they never held jobs, but unlike their schoolmates, neither of them had ever received an allowance. The only way they knew to get money was to steal it. Now they had been offered a chance to *earn it!* Visions of motorbikes—and tape decks and TV sets—danced in their heads.

A different vision danced in Frances's head. Did she dream it up all alone? Or did the boys contribute? And what about Behrens? Perhaps it was a shared vision boiled up out of four fevered brains—two troubled adults, both obsessed with killing a father to protect an inheritance; and two unstable adolescent boys. It was a vision of a tiny band of latter-day Robin Hoods: a pair of bold and slick-fingered young desperadoes directed by a female master criminal with a shadowy, part-time *Führer*/adviser. The gang had a name, the Good Old Schreuder Household, or—alternatively—the Fifth Avenue Crowd. It had a set of written rules and a single objective: The gang's target was a lying, sneaky, cold-blooded old miser with an evil, addled wife. The gang's objective was to steal as much money as possible and to bump off the wicked old man so as to make it look like an accident. The money was not just for the gang's own use. Once their immediate wants were taken care of, the gang had a higher purpose. A child was in mortal danger. Unless they ransomed her, saved her, a golden-haired little girl they all adored was certain to be starved out of her snug home and forced to live in Harlem.

How much of this "vision" did each one of them really believe? No way to tell. "One thing you gotta understand," says Marc today, "is that the reason Mom was sending us to Salt Lake, and the reason we were going there, were entirely different. We wanted the four bucks an hour. Mom was sending us . . . no, *allowing* us to go, because we were supposed to bump off Gramps." Of course it would have to look like an accident. Over the next few weeks Frances considered and discussed several methods, Marc says. Dropping an electrical appliance into his morning bath would be one way to do it. Another way would be to burn down the warehouse. Finally she decided that the safest way was to lace his morning oatmeal with sufficient amphetamines to induce a heart attack.

"Basically, Mom sent me and Larry out to Salt Lake City in the summer of '77 to poison him with amphetamines. She said if we put 'em in his oatmeal every day, eventually he'd have a heart attack." Marc claims he is "foggy" on how Mom obtained the "black beauties," fat black capsules filled with tiny white beads. "Black beauties" is the street name for 20-mg Biphetamine capsules, made by Pennwalt Company. They contain fillers, and it could take a cupful or more to make a lethal dose in a pot of oatmeal.

Larry today denies knowledge of any plan to poison Gramps. "Kill him? I know we stole, but I never heard anything about killing him." But he also seems knowledgeable about the source of the drugs: "I heard Mom and Marc went up to Harlem, or maybe Forty-second Street, and copped 'em from some black guy."

Marc says his mother always had a large supply of black beauties, diet pills, and many other medications on hand. He says he and Mom crushed the drugs together, removed the stuffing from a green-cloth toy mouse—"cute little mouse, with a tail, and everything"—and replaced it with the crushed drugs.

This occurred in Mom's bedroom during what Marc calls "the Prelims," two nights before the boys left town. "I was sitting at Larry's typewriter, which Mom had expropriated for her own use, installed it in her own room. When Mom wants anything, she kinda takes it over. She doesn't care who it belongs to. *You don't tell Mom no.*"

Larry's old typewriter was set up on the end of the bed. Together the gang members worked out a list of rules to follow in Salt Lake City. "We were all discussing it together," says Marc. "I was just typing down the feedback. It was like":

1. How to deal with Granny and not become brainwashed by Granny.
2. How not to become infected by Granny's sick ways.
3. Don't ever let Granny follow you.
4. Be sure to get up in morning and administer dosage.
5. Be polite to her, but also be able to say no.
6. Don't eat Granny's chocolate cakes. Don't let her fatten you up!
7. Don't let her domineer you!
8. Don't let her twist you round her little finger!
9. Don't let her have you doing all her errands.

10. Do what *you* want to do. Don't let her boss you around!
11. Phone home daily, always from pay phones, and make Progress Report to Mom.

Marc can no longer remember every one of the rules, he says, but his mother has a copy of the document in her safe-deposit box. "Basically the idea was—Mom was giving us *permission* to be insolent to Granny. To *defy her!* The idea was: Granny's a very sick person. Don't let her boss you around. Don't let her take you anywhere. If she wants to drive you down to the warehouse, and you have your own sneaky plans to do something down there—like steal some stocks or bonds—tell her, *no.* The idea was not really to make her life miserable. We were supposed just to be polite but stand firm."

Marc admits that this goal "somehow got lost when we got out there." Things did not work as Frances planned because she did not have two slick-fingered desperadoes, but two clumsy, excitable kids. It was a mess. To the unsuspecting Bradshaws, it must have seemed as if a pair of criminal Katzenjammer Kids had come to stay.

The summer passed in a nightmare montage, its lunatic cast of characters—the elderly Bradshaws, their criminal grandsons, a warehouseful of hard-working Mormons, and mad, manic Frances—all caught up in a surreal tangle of larceny, hooliganism, madness, and murder. To disentangle the real from the hallucinatory, let alone truth from lies, is no longer possible.

The boys arrived in mid-June and started work immediately. Gramps assigned Marc to work under Doug Steele's supervision, and apprenticed Larry to his number-two aide, Clive Davis, the Mormon elder. Doug put Marc to work classifying brake parts at a desk alongside his own. When the noon rush came, Doug went out to the counter to help wait on customers. In early afternoon, as usual, he sent his fourteen-year-old daughter—another temporary summer employee—to the bank with the cash receipts. Then Doug's phone rang. The bank said the money bag was $1,400 short.

Doug took his new assistant upstairs to an isolated spot under the warehouse roof and questioned him alone for three solid hours; Marc simply stonewalled until the grilling ceased.

Before anyone realized what was happening, the Good Old Schreuder Household was in full cry: the brothers were looting blank checks, cash, and securities from both house and warehouse and sending it back to New York in a steady stream. Their demonic energy was fueled by a murderous competition for Mom's approval. They stumbled and fell over one another in gleeful, greedy frenzy and at the same time held back as much as they dared, both from Mom and from one another. Their pace was so headlong, so heedless that discovery at the earliest possible moment was inevitable. The pattern of their thievery was established early. When Marc got back to Gilmer Drive with his $1,400 haul, he waited until Granny and Gramps were asleep. Larry had gone to a porno movie. Marc removed one of Granny's new air-conditioning vents and taped $500, perhaps more, inside. He rushed the remaining $900 to Mom, who had been crying on the phone "that she needed an immediate infusion of cash: her phone was gonna be cut off, Con Ed was gonna turn off her lights, the rent was due. I thought: She'll *love me* for this!"

But Mom was angry. Already Marc had tipped their mitt. The gang's presence was now known. He should have been more "sneaky." The next night he sneaked into Granny's basement office, found a box of her personal checks, and sent Mom a handful. But Larry had already sent Mom an entire brick of warehouse checks "in a manila warehouse envelope. He really outdid me . . ."

Marc, more of a homebody, cleaned out everything he could find from Gilmer Drive. Larry was bolder and did most though not all of the warehouse thievery. Their loot in securities came to $150,000 in common stocks, "Martin Marietta, GE, IBM, all Fortune 500 stuff," says Marc. "It was hidden in twenty-five-year-old *Life* magazines he had secreted in his cabinets. Couple of bricks of $100 bills in there too. Larry found those. It was like a competition that summer—who could do the best job stealing and getting money for Mom. It was like a game to us . . ." It was a game of Stratego for real, and much of the time Marc felt he was losing to Larry. "He was smarter than I was. I was too attached to Mom."

One day they found $30,000 in Mountain Fuel stock certificates belonging to Elaine Drukman and sent them off to New York. Frances at once set up a false identity. She opened two bank accounts and a stock brokerage account in the name of Elaine Drukman, and obtained a phony Elaine Drukman driver's license, all in preparation for cashing in the stock. Later she would say she had learned these tricks from Richard Behrens.

At Gilmer Drive the brothers' competition was both savage and clownish. Larry clicked on his tape recorder whenever he heard his grandparents having an argument. Marc snapped Granny's picture from behind whenever the old lady bent over to sweep the floor or to pick up her grandsons' dirty socks. If his camera was unloaded, he clicked the shutter anyway, just to taunt her. Then, when she got angry and started swearing, Larry switched on his tape recorder. At summer's end the boys returned from "the Lake" with a wealth of pictures and tapes of the Bradshaws at home, which Frances subsequently used both to blackmail Granny and as a bizarre form of family entertainment. Frances loved them so much, her sons say, that she ultimately stole them all.

Marc and Larry seemed incapable of honest work. When they weren't busy looting and thieving, or triple-punching the time clock, or goofing off and sleeping in the back of the warehouse, or tormenting Doug and their grandfather, they hung out at porno movie theaters. One morning the sink in the warehouse ladies' room was discovered filled with human excrement. But the most fun was taunting Granny. She did all the boys' laundry, bed making, and housework. No one had ever done these things for them before. In a way they were grateful; they enjoyed her "mothering." But they resented the griping and nagging that came with it. They were used to being ragged, dirty, and smelly, used to looking after themselves, and in many ways they preferred it to Granny's eternal criticism. Frances, in their daily phone calls, encouraged her sons to defy and torment Granny at every opportunity. When they knew she was making a dinner for them, they would fail to turn up to eat it. Or they would let her spend all day cooking, then deliberately gorge at McDonald's and come home saying they were full.

Larry had more caution than Marc, and more sense. Marc would do simply anything his mother said, and he was more vulnerable to her pressure. Midway in the summer Frances refused to communicate with Marc for two or three weeks. She would deal only with Larry, Marc says, "because I was not coming through with the big stuff, so she was threatening me. I was having trouble finding any more stocks and bonds and stuff. So I wasn't calling Mom every day. Larry kinda took over from me. Mom got really angry and told me, 'Don't ever come home! You can go live in Salt Lake!' I was terrified, really depressed by that.

For two weeks I was like in limbo. I believed her threats, believed she was gonna leave me in Salt Lake alone. Forever. That I'd never go back to Kent. Cause that's what *she said*. That I wasn't really pulling through for her. Especially with the oatmeal. It came out that we *weren't* really doing it every day. We were disobeying her orders. She was giving orders to increase the dosages. And we weren't giving him any dosages at all! But we were telling Mom every day on the phone that we were getting up very early every morning and putting it in his oatmeal. And Mom would say, 'How's he doin? Tell me what he's like! Tell me his physical symptoms!' I'd make up the stuff, because Larry isn't very good at that. I tend to be more imaginative. So I'd say, 'He seemed a little more jumpy and nervous today . . .' And I guess I wasn't that good of a liar. And she was getting mad because I wasn't trying hard enough! I wasn't stealing enough! I couldn't find the will. I was being lazy!"

The fact is, Marc says today in injured tones, "I was too busy working at Bradshaw's, making an honest living. Instead of stealing for her. And she got mad at that, making me incommunicado. Which she knew I hated. We got back together when I finally did find some more stocks. At the warehouse. Like in another cabinet. It was like 'Okay, now you've come through with more money for me. Now I will talk to you again. I will give you love now. Whooooeee!' "

On one point Marc is clear, or at least consistent. "That mouse —we never even unsewed it! Later, after we got fired from the warehouse, I took the drugs out and flushed them down the toilet."

Did he? Berenice says she knows the boys tried to poison her husband's oatmeal. "They also tried to poison the air in his bedroom. One night I was awakened by a scream. I got up to see what it was, and Marc had gone in my husband's room and was filling the air with something to choke him. I don't know what it was, but it woke him up, and my husband was screaming, 'Marc, get out of here! Get out!' "

Later that day at the warehouse, Frank vomited several times, Doug Steele says. Warehouse employees say that on several occasions that summer the boss was so jumpy he could not sit still. On Marc's own tapes—the ones he says Frances stole from him for her own delectation, and he stole back again—one can hear him and Larry laughing together about the times when "Gramps was running up and down stairs like a speed freak."

Did this really happen? Was there a mouse stuffed with black beauties? Did a family murder plot really exist that summer, or is this more of Larry and Marc's comic-book imaginings? A crabby old lady's paranoia? The envy of two jealous sisters? Maybe Gramps was running because he was an exercise freak, not a speed freak. One cannot know all the truth. But in hindsight, one truth is clear. By August 1, when the Schreuder Household was exposed and put out of action, the raiders were $200,000 ahead. Moreover, long before that time, certainly both Franklin and Berenice Bradshaw knew that their grandsons were stealing them blind. They knew that not just pilferage but major theft was occurring. And they knew that their daughter was centrally involved.

On the morning of August 1, Frank's faithful, plainspoken secretary, Nancy Jones, was at her desk in the rear of the warehouse going through the morning mail. She opened the July statement from Walker Bank & Trust. The July withdrawals seemed a bit higher than usual, and she riffled through the canceled checks. Two checks, for $10,000 apiece, were made out to cash and signed "F. J. Bradshaw"—a crude forgery of her boss's signature. She looked on the back. Both checks had been endorsed in large, flowing script, "F. Bradshaw," and deposited to Frances Schreuder's account. Nancy recognized the handwriting.

She hurried to the front of the warehouse and showed the checks to Doug. "We'd better tell the Mister right away!" Frank was working behind the counter when Doug and Nancy called him aside and handed him the two checks.

"Oh my God!" he shouted. Then the old man burst into tears.

Franklin told Steele to call the bank. Steele reported the two forgeries and several smaller checks which also appeared to have been forged, and said Bradshaw's did not intend to honor them. He asked that the funds be replaced.

"No problem, Mr. Steele, we will have the monies in your account within twenty-four hours."

But there was a problem. Check forgery is a federal offense. Before the monies could be restored, it would be necessary for Mr. Bradshaw to sign a complaint. The bank would be happy to send the necessary papers down to the warehouse right now. But this was family. Frank balked.

"No go, Doug," he said. "No go." Then, aware that still other stolen checks, as yet uncashed, might be floating around, the old man told Steele to close out the account and open another with a different number.

But even now that the Bradshaws knew and suffered the humiliation of having their employees know the truth about their daughter Frances, and her sons, still they could not acknowledge the truth and could not confront it. Some combination of shame, fear, and family pride, with perhaps an added amalgam of bewilderment and compassion, made the Bradshaws unwilling and indeed incapable of filing criminal charges against Frances or their grandsons. On this point, if on few others, Berenice and Franklin were always in accord. The fact is that after forged checks totaling $22,000 were discovered on August 1, and after Franklin openly broke down and wept in front of his employees, fired the boys, and grimly instructed the bank to honor no more checks that might be returned from New York City—a week or two later, very quietly, he gave each boy his job back.

Larry was rehired first, to work weekends only, when no one else but Gramps was about. Marc was forced to wait longer. Six years after the murder, the memory of favoritism toward Larry still sets Marc gnawing on ancient wounds. He broods about "the extra hint of guilt on me, the *extra taint*," because Marc had done the original $1,400 robbery. Even though it was Larry who invented the way to triple-punch the time clock, a way he refused to share with his brother, "that still made Larry look just a little bit more honest than me, in their eyes . . . And Larry was the eldest. *And* he was definitely their favorite. So of course they took him back before me."

But Marc had the last word. Larry had invested the fruits of his labors in a 1962 Impala, the first car—the first *anything*—he had ever owned. Now he intended to drive it alone cross-country to begin his senior year at EMA. The Sunday night before he left, Larry drove down to Bradshaw Auto Parts, let himself in with pilfered keys, and stole as many tools, tool kits, flares, and small, valuable auto parts as he could cram into the Impala's roomy trunk. He went home and stowed his packed suitcases in the back seat, parked his car in Granny's new garage, and retired early to be certain of a good night's sleep. At three o'clock Marc crept upstairs from the basement where he and Larry slept and awakened the Bradshaws. He told them what his brother was up to, and now Marc, Granny, and Gramps all tiptoed out to the garage. Marc had pocketed Larry's car keys, and together the three of them silently unloaded the trunk of Larry's car. Larry left at daybreak, and he did not discover the loss until several miles out of town, when it occurred to him that his car felt strangely light in the rear end. That same Monday morning, "by invitation," Marc was back at work at the warehouse.

By the time Marc got home, Frances was spending the loot. For $35,000 she had rented Dragon's Hall, a famous old mansion in Southampton, Long Island, originally built by the DuPonts. It has three floors, twenty-five ornately furnished rooms, a ball-room-sized library, a fully equipped, restaurant-sized kitchen, a night-lit, palette-shaped swimming pool, acres of landscaping, its own dock and jetty, and an imposing entrance marked by red-painted dragons on white pillars.

Frances had been careful not to tell her mother anything about the mansion, so Granny had only bought Marc a plane ticket as far as New York City. He had to do the last hundred miles by the Long Island Rail Road and taxi, arriving at about midnight. He was apprehensive riding up the long driveway. He felt he had done nothing right that summer and expected his mother to be cold and angry. Instead he found her deliriously happy. She hugged and kissed him warmly, as she had done only once before in his life, when he was admitted to Allen-Stevenson. This was the second kiss from the Evil Queen.

Bubbling joyfully about her luxurious Southampton summer, Mom guided Marc to a plush sofa in a vast living room lit by antique sconces and decorated with dark paintings of shipwrecks and tempestuous storms. Cantaloupe balls, caviar, and tiny toast squares had been set out, and as his mother chattered gaily and fed him on "toasts liberally smeared with caviar," he "got the distinct feeling that she was treating me like a little boy who had fucked up a little bit, but all in all had done a good job looting, stealing, insulting, and raiding his grandparents."

The person Frances seemed to be angry at was Larry—so angry that from the summer of 1977 onward, Larry was locked out for good. When winter came on, he would scratch at the apartment door, beg, and plead to be let in. Frances would not open, and she refused to let Marc open it. As far as Frances was concerned, Larry had officially ceased to exist.

When Larry came home on weekends from EMA, he literally

had no place to go. Until it got too cold, he slept in his car. Occasionally he slept at Behrens's place. Eventually he would be back scratching and pleading at the Schreuders' door. Frances was adamant. Larry knew how to gain admittance to the building at 1675 York Avenue, but he could not get into the triple-locked Schreuder apartment. Roaming the back fire stairs, he eventually found a bare space, a landing leading to a door to the roof, which was unused in winter. For an entire year whenever he was "home," weekends and vacations, Larry slept up there like a dog, wrapped in the New York *Times* and curled into discarded cardboard cartons he found in the trash and hauled up to his hideaway. Sometimes when Larry came scratching at the door, Marc was able to hand his brother a few clean clothes, a sweater, or best of all, a blanket. But only if his mother was out or asleep. Otherwise Larry was firmly and permanently barred.

What had he done? It was more a matter of what Larry had not done: He had not put the black beauties in the oatmeal. He had betrayed the gang. As Marc said later, "She finally got sick of Larry because Larry was bungling everything. He wasn't putting the stuff in. Turned out she never really wanted me to do it . . . she thought *I* was gonna bungle it. So putting the pills in Grandpa's bowl—that was supposed to be Larry's job."

Once Larry Schreuder "ceased to exist," Marc and his mother were alone together, entirely dependent on one another—"like husband and wife," the trial psychiatrist would say. Ariadne was left in the care of a young and proper "English nannie" whom Frances had engaged for the season. She appeared to be a pleasant and refined young woman who adored Ariadne, and she swiftly taught her the exquisite good manners which have since impressed so many. "Usually the nursemaid has to buck the mother," says a former caretaker at Dragon's Hall, a person who has observed scores of the grinding nanny-versus-mommie power struggles which mark the Hampton summers. "But this girl got a free hand, *no* interference at all! And the child was very, very intelligent, talked very well . . . a really sweet little thing! But the mother was weird. Wacko. You could just look at her and see how eccentric she was."

Later Marc wrote to a friend: "Mom showed me pictures of that 'nice English nanny' without a bra on or panties. Mom claimed that this nanny was into pornography, and that was why she fired her. In my opinion, she was nice, but she did spend an excessive amount of time on the beach toasting herself a lovely hue of amber."

A neighborhood woman was employed by the owners of Dragon's Hall to do the housekeeping. She had her own key and arrived at the mansion by bicycle several times a week. The strange tenant chattered to the housekeeper for hours. "She talked a lot about Eastern schools. She knew the 'good' schools, the 'best.' She always talked about 'the best.' I thought: From the way she spends money, I guess she can *have* the best. But all she had was coffee and cigarettes. I don't ever recall seeing her eat food. I never once saw her near the pool."

The family had no cook. Ariadne was fed by the English nanny. Marc seemed to fend for himself. No meals were ever served. "I used to feel sorry for her, she seemed so lonely. She talked about getting ready for big dinner parties. I remember once she ordered a case of Dom Perignon. Another time she told me she had a date that night with David Rockefeller." But she never had the party. The champagne sat there all summer. She tried to give the housekeeper a bottle. The woman knew there were no dinner parties because there were never any dishes in the sink and no leftovers in the fridge. Nothing.

One day Frances showed her cleaning woman a five-month-old newspaper story about the plane crash in which her husband had perished. He had been very wealthy, she said, and loved her very much, and had left her a great deal of money.

The village woman also served as "upstairs maid," and she soon discovered that Frances rarely got out of bed. Her closet was stuffed with expensive negligees, but she wore the same two garments almost all summer long. "I don't think she was very clean. She never used the tub."

Frances had let it be known that she was interested in buying Dragon's Hall. The woman from the real estate office who came around to discuss it was surprised when the potential buyer opened the door wearing "a filthy sundress, covered with spots."

Of Marc the housekeeper recalls only that he had "an eerie look in his eye" and spoke very little. One day she was cleaning a leopard-skin loveseat in the library, after Marc and Frances had been sitting there, and discovered a pair of soiled women's panties tucked behind the cushions. Tactfully she left them where she found them. The next day they were gone.

One morning the village woman was unable to open the door.

She later learned that Mrs. Schreuder had accused her of stealing and had ordered all the locks changed.

Before he went west in the summer of 1977, Marc had learned from Mom to think of Granny as "mostly bad . . . but Grandpa really still seemed benevolent, benign, fatherly . . . a distant, *distant* figure." When Marc returned, Frances had turned up the heat of her rage. Now it seemed to Marc that she said the same words to him every day: *"He's a miser and a dirty, sneaking liar. He is very cold-blooded. He was never a father to me. He wouldn't even pay for Elaine's heart operation. He tried to help kill my brother Bob!"*

"She'd tell me these horror stories every day about how evil he was," Marc continues. "How he used his money to try to destroy people. How he ruined a lot of people in business, to get all their money. And that a lot of people hated him. And that he hated *her* too. Because he was letting her starve. With Ariadne. Go in the gutter! How he didn't have any feelings for any one of us!"

With these words ringing in his ears, Marc was buying new school clothes and getting ready to return to Kent to begin eleventh grade. Meanwhile out in Salt Lake City, Frank Bradshaw had stopped speaking almost entirely. The boss had never been loquacious, but Doug had never known him to be so silent as he was in the weeks after Marc left town.

One morning when Doug Steele arrived at the warehouse, Frank handed him a half sheet of paper. At first glance, it appeared to have been Xeroxed from one of the pages of his will. It was in fact a revision of his will which the Boss had asked Nancy Jones to type up the day before, and it named Doug and Marilyn Reagan as coadministrators of his estate. Across the bottom of the page, Frank himself had typed in: "1/3 of my estate to Berenice J. Bradshaw, 1/3 to Marilyn Reagan, and 1/3 to Elaine Drukman." And that was it. All of it. He had not even signed the change, merely typewritten his initials *above* the added line. Frances was not even specifically disinherited. Like Larry, she had simply been declared nonexistent.

Could this feeble gesture be the old man's sole response to a $200,000 rip-off? Only this phantom fist, this poison-pen letter written in disappearing ink? Just as curiously, a dozen Xerox copies of the document later turned up scattered all over the vast warehouse. Perhaps it was a gesture intended more for his ware-

house family than his real family, not meant as a show of force to
Frances but a show of guts to his employees that, despite his
humiliating tearful outburst, he did not intend to be pushed
around by his bossy wife, hooligan grandsons, and criminal
daughter. If the message was intended for Frances, it was even
more remote than one of his vague, third-person letters of re-
proach. But even this pale threat was threat enough. When word
of his note reached Frances, it triggered her determination to
assassinate him.

Almost certainly that word was passed by Berenice. At once
some sort of murder plot began to boil. Frank had typed out his
timid threat at the end of August. In early September, if Behrens
can be believed, Frances already was speaking to him about obtaining a gun. She also mentioned looking for a "hit man." By
October he had found and introduced her to a barroom acquaintance, one Myles Manning. In November Frances gave Manning
$5,000 to kill her father, he says. He took the money, but then
told Frances he had been arrested in Salt Lake City before he
could carry out his assignment.

Undeterred, Frances continued her own efforts to obtain a
weapon, Marc and Behrens say. New York has stricter gun laws
than its neighbors, so Behrens says she sent him to try to buy a
gun in New Jersey and Virginia. He was unsuccessful. Meanwhile, says Marc, Frances was buying stacks of gun magazines
and sending away for mail-order gun catalogs. She took Marc
with her on shopping tours of sporting goods stores. These were
gleeful expeditions which often ended in shoplifting sprees.

When Frances was feeling good, feeling flush and high, shoplifting was her favorite pastime, Chinatown her preferred play-
ground. She loved racing through Chinese gift shops scooping up
cheap tourist gimcracks. What she took was unimportant; the fun
was the act of stealing. If her impulse to shoplift was urgent, she
would go down to the deli and filch flavoring extracts, expensive
bottles of vanilla and cherry. Forging, stealing, shoplifting, lying,
cheating, blackmail—all were made into a Game, all were varia-
tions on the same sport, the sport of Getting Away with It.

Tuition was now due at three schools—Kent, EMA, and Episcopal. Frances demanded that Berenice pay it all. It did not matter that Frances herself now had more money than ever before in
her life. Unless Berenice paid the new crop of school bills, Frances vowed never to speak to her mother again. So once again

Berenice's "help" consisted of forging her husband's signature to pay her daughter's bills. Was this demand merely another variation of Frances's Game, or were the new forgeries extracted as a kind of insurance? Entrapping Berenice now in current Schreuder larcenies would ensure that she remained vulnerable to further blackmail at some future date. As it worked out, the forged tuition checks were to serve quite a different purpose.

Once the tuition checks were signed, Frances had no further use for Berenice, and she immediately severed all communications with Salt Lake. She forbade her children to write or to accept phone calls. She returned cards and gifts unopened. For ten months Frances totally cut the Bradshaws out of her life. Now *they* were "nonexistent." Frances had plenty of money. She could live life as she chose, could drain it to the lees without interference from parents or husbands. She spent thousands on new clothes, trinkets from Tiffany's, including $20,000 diamond earrings, later replaced by a pair that cost $40,000. She paid off thousands of dollars worth of backed-up psychiatry bills to Dr. Brand, whom she continued to see. She hung onto Dragon's Hall until January, and she and Marc and Ariadne spent several long fall weekends out at the mansion. In New York she hired a daily maid, Jewolo, to clean and keep house, and to deliver Ariadne to Episcopal Nursery School each morning, now that Marc had gone back to Kent.

Frances's own mornings were passed in an hours-long routine which had to be followed in an unvarying way. It left little time for anything else and often made her one or two or even three hours late for subsequent appointments. Sometimes she was unable to get there at all. When she awoke, at nine or ten o'clock on weekdays, the routine required her to read and digest all of the New York *Times* and *Daily News* before getting out of bed. The process took several hours, fueled by endless pots of black coffee and interrupted by the day's necessary phone calls, any one of which might last an hour or more. The routine was carried out in a chain-smoking haze. Getting through the papers in this manner took so long that often the routine had to be interrupted by the press of other events, in which case the unread papers were stacked near the bed for future completion. Breakfast, on a tray, was two or three poached eggs, three or four or six slices of whole wheat toast, more coffee, and cigarettes. Now the metabolic tempo began to pick up. Frances had always been a "nighter," and as afternoon and evening wore on, the nicotine and the gin-and-tonic, which by now had replaced the river of caffeine, induced a state of increasing wakefulness which lasted until the wee hours and could be extinguished only by sleeping pills, until the cycle began anew. Thus although Frances did not "do" anything in the conventional meaning of the term, she was always very "busy" and almost always late.

As much of the routine as possible—all the reading, eating, drinking, and phoning—happened in or on her big bed, a kind of large, untidy nest which was shared first with Marc, later with Ariadne, and on rare, brief occasions with Larry. Although the children had their own rooms, they preferred to spend as much time as possible with their mother, doing homework, reading, playing with cats and toys, or watching TV from their own side of the bed. Ariadne slept with her mother until she was eight or nine and got a nightly nursing bottle as well. Granny did not approve, but domestic tranquility required her to look the other way unless Frances was out of town and she was temporarily in charge of the household.

On school days Frances had herself up and dressed in time to pick up Ariadne. Most of the youngsters were picked up after school by maids or limousines, so the few parents who came in person to collect their offspring got to know one another slightly. Frances Schreuder is remembered by them as extremely shy, withdrawn, "almost frightened. You had to really work at it to get her to talk at all." Mrs. Schreuder did manage to convey, however, that she herself was a graduate of Miss Hewitt's Classes —a Manhattan finishing school of highest gloss. And though she declined to join Episcopal's PTA or participate in other school activities, she was prompt and generous with cash gifts for any school project. Aside from her "otherness" and lack of physical allure—made the more striking by Ariadne's loveliness—Frances is chiefly remembered for looking "much too old to be Ariadne's mother." Ariadne had been born four days after Frances's thirty-fifth birthday. She was a "late baby," just as Frances herself had been.

On weekends Frances slept until noon, sometimes longer. Ariadne's favorite plaything had become a pair of Frances's old ballet slippers, from her high school days, made of faded pink silk trimmed in white lace. The child took to wearing the slippers around the house. Once or twice Frances put Tschaikovsky on the record player and showed Ariadne a few steps. Weekends were also the times when Larry tried to sneak back home. Marc's job was to guard the door. But he felt sorry for Larry, and if his mother was asleep or out, Marc would sometimes let Larry in. "Then," Marc says, "Mom would find out he'd been here and threaten to lock *me* out if I did it again."

So at other times, Marc says, he would stand absolutely still just inside the door, not making a sound, just watching Ariadne playing, on one side, listening to his brother begging and some- times sobbing on the other side, and pounding some metal object against the heavy Medico burglar-proof lock.

One time, when Frances was home, Larry pleaded with Marc for over an hour to open the door, while Frances screamed from her bedroom, "Don't you *dare* let him in!"

"Come on, Marc! Just let me in! Just let me get some of my stuff! Please let me in! Please!"

It was early afternoon, bright sunshine, Marc recalls, when he finally opened the door. Larry dashed toward their bedroom. Frances came out of her room shouting, "Okay, get back out! *Get back out, Larry!* GET OUT!"

Larry, in their room, was frantically tearing blankets off a bed, grabbing pillows, coats, shoes, sweaters. Frances was yelling, "Leave my house immediately!"

She turned on Marc, and her voice grew low, menacing. "Okay, Marc. You get him out. Or you're locked out too!"

Marc pleaded for time. "Come on, Mom! Why don't you just let him get his stuff!"

"Marc . . . *I warned you* . . ."

Marc approached his brother. "Come on, Larry! You gotta *go*, Larry. *Please!*" Now Marc was doing the begging, and Larry was becoming more methodical in collecting his belongings.

"Marc, I'm calling the police!" Frances shrilled.

"Come on, Larry, you've *got* to leave now," Marc whined, and he began trying to shove his brother and his jumble of bedclothes out the front door again while shoes and caps tumbled to the floor.

Frances decided she and Marc and Ariadne should spend Christmas vacation out at Dragon's Hall. When Marc got home from Kent, he spent most of one day and night helping his mother and Jewels prepare for the journey. "Packing or moving is always a horrendous and excruciating ordeal for Mom," he explains. "She has to pack thirty dresses, ten pairs of shoes, and all the massive bundles of paperwork, newsprint, and other documentation she never has time to sort out, read, or throw away."

Shortly before they were ready to leave, Marc made a comment about Berenice which enraged Frances. She accused him of "calling Granny on the sneak," which he denied. "She'd been harping on that ever since summer," he says, accusing him of having been "brainwashed by Granny," and acquiring "all of Granny's bad habits. I had come back *fat*. 'Ewe, you're just like Granny! Ewe!' "

Marc did not think he was fatter; the kids at school had said nothing. "But Mom kept saying I was behaving and talking just like sick Granny, and had picked up all of Granny's nasty, filthy habits, and she didn't want me to live around her, if I was gonna act like sick-in-the-head Granny." Shouting now that he was "a Granny ass-licker" and "ball-less wonder," Frances said she intended to punish Marc by making him spend Christmas all alone in the apartment. She insisted on carrying the suitcases down to the underground garage without his help, and when all was stowed, she and Ariadne drove off.

It was twilight in the midst of the holiday rush-hour traffic on the Triboro Bridge when Frances ran out of gas. Later she would blame both Marc and Behrens. She had left her gas tank full, she claimed, but Behrens had pinched her car keys the night before and taken Marc out joyriding. Now Frances managed to coast to a stop, two hundred yards from the nearest emergency phone. Leaving Ariadne in the front seat, Frances got out of her car and darted across two lanes of whizzing traffic to a police call box. It was out of order. As Frances tells the story, she was back in the big red Oldsmobile, singing Christmas carols with Ariadne while they waited for help to arrive when—wham! wham!—they were rear-ended, hit and hit again, by a drunk driver. Ariadne was thrown to the floor. Frances's head slammed the windshield, and she passed out twice while the cops were extricating her from the wreckage. "Each time I came to," she says, "my only thought was: *Is Ariadne alive?*"

Half an hour after his mom had stormed out, Marc got a call from the police. His mother and sister had been in a car wreck and were now in the emergency room at Metropolitan Hospital Center, on 1st Avenue and 97th Street—almost Harlem after all! Marc raced uptown and found his sister with a slight concussion and his mother with an injured back and bruised head. He spent the next five hours consoling Mom, talking to cops, and scavenging the wreck to recover its precious cargo—Mom's luggage, and literally scores of Christmas presents, their wrappings torn and scattered.

Marc's most urgent assignment was to hire a car and driver from a limousine service so they could immediately resume the journey. Eventually Mom and Ariadne were bandaged and released from the hospital; luggage and Christmas presents were stowed aboard the limo, and everybody including the now forgiven Marc piled in for the long drive out to Dragon's Hall. They arrived at four o'clock in the morning. Ariadne was fine. Frances wore a neck brace for a while, and the car was totaled; they did not even bother to collect the wreck from the police parking lot. Frances warned her children repeatedly: never, never disclose the accident to Berenice. All the presents turned out to be for Ariadne, says Marc. For his own combined Christmas and seventeenth birthday present—December 21—his mother gave him what they each prized most: cash.

Larry spent Christmas in New York, alone.

The Reagans visited the Bradshaws in Salt Lake City over Christmas, and one day Berenice caught her daughter snooping through her basement files. Marilyn knew all about the half-page will memorandum which her father had Xeroxed and spread around his warehouse, and Berenice surmised her daughter was searching for a copy of the new will itself, as proof that she was now coexecutrix and Frances was eliminated entirely. Nonsense, says Marilyn. When the year-end dividends of F & B Corporation had been handed out that Christmas, Frances and her sons, but not Ariadne, had been pointedly omitted from the distribution. This was sufficient proof to Marilyn and everyone else in the family of her father's state of mind in regard to the Schreuders. As for her activities in her mother's office, they simply reflected her ongoing sense of responsibility to keep herself fully briefed on estate matters at all times. Nonetheless both Marilyn and Elaine believed, and continue to believe today, that Franklin Bradshaw had executed a new will, one which reflected his new state of mind regarding the Schreuders. They are convinced that someone found and destroyed the new will on the day of their father's murder, or perhaps the night before.

By the time Marc had gotten home from Kent for Christmas

vacation, he says, the $200,000 loot from the previous summer was almost gone. Now Frances was saying that—her efforts to hire a hit man having failed—Marc himself was going to have to kill his grandfather before the evil old man carried out his threat and starved them all into submission.

Sometimes she wheedled; other times she raged. Marc tried to say nothing at all. It was always least painful to himself, if he could summon the fortitude, to keep silent and let his mother's emotional typhoons simply blow themselves out. But once he lost his temper and shouted, "Why don't *you* do it!"

"I would do it," he says she replied. "But then who would take care of Ariadne? What am I supposed to do—bring her along with me?" When Marc said he would take care of his sister, Frances jeered, "Oh, come off it, Marc!" and turned away.

In January Frances received still another eviction notice. There must then have been some communication with Salt Lake, because one day as Franklin was eating his meat loaf sandwich, he told Doug Steele he had a new plan: if the Schreuders would agree to come back to Salt Lake, he was going to give them the house on Gilmer Drive; make them a present of it. He and Berenice would buy a little condominium, closer to the warehouse.

Berenice yearned to inform Frances of all she was doing in the Schreuders' behalf, despite Franklin's opposition. But Frances refused her phone calls. She tore up her mother's letters unopened. So Granny began sending copies of her letters to the boys at boarding school. Marc sided with his mother and remained incommunicado. But lonesome Larry wrote back. A clandestine correspondence began. Berenice begged her grandson to destroy her letters, of course. She dreaded what would happen if they should fall into the wrong hands, Frances's hands. But Larry was a Bradshaw, and Bradshaws throw nothing away. By the time the Bradshaw case came to trial, these letters, like Granny's forged tuition checks, had fallen into the hands of the law.

Sunday, Jan 29th, 1978

Dear Frances:

I think I have some good news for you . . . Yes, at 74 I'm going to work, for your family . . . It is strange the minute I mentioned "work" he [Dad] lit up. I've decided you can "catch more flies with honey than vinegar." . . . I call him "the slave driver."

. . . I'm telling Dad you and your family need your inheritance now not 20 years from now. I wrote to Marc and told him to have his school bill sent to Grandpa. We have never heard from Marc since her left here, not even a note to thank his grandfather of his Xmas and birthday checks. We have had many letters from Larry and he thanks us for everything we do for him . . .

. . . If you want to spend the rest of my life hating me you are only hurting yourself . . .

. . . Because your financial problems concern Marc and Larry I'm sending them a copy of this message. Both boys are very worried about how their family is going to live . . .

All my love, Granny

Feb. 14th, 1978

Dear Larry:

. . . we are paying for a dead horse . . . [Frances had allowed her car insurance to lapse before the Triboro Bridge accident.]

. . . the Xmas present I sent to her [came back] "unopened". If she had taken a club and beat me over the head she could not have hurt me more . . . I can't sleep, eat, I cry half of the day. I believe if you boys had let me know about her horrible accident I could have . . . patched things up . . . I had a feeling it would take a disaster for get us back together again, we had the disaster but I did not know about it . . . I can't understand, every timne she is sick, in the hospital she refuses for me to know until she is well. Why??? Why, does she hate me? . . . Marc has all the same hated feelings towards me his mother has because she has thoroughly indoctranated him with her feelings . . .

. . . She intendes to turn my granddaughter against me (she told me so) Why? Why should Ariadne be taught and told to hate her grandmother when she has no cause to hate me. Her mother has poisoned her her against her grandmother . . .

. . . I'm her only source of income how can she treat me like this . . . Never once has she ever thanked me . . . Larry destroy this letter so no one with ever see it.

All my love, Granny

Monday Feb. 20th 1978

Dear Larry:

You have been very faithful about writing to us and we appreciate it very much. If you didn't write we would never know what is happening to your family . . . You are <u>our</u> family and we are concerened about all of you. "Blood is thicker than water" and you don't errase blood ties.

. . . We are her only source of income, without us your whole family would perish and yet we are treated like the "scum of the earth" by her . . .

Your mother is causing all of you to suffer because she wants to punish us . . . Last summer was a nitemare to Grandpa and me but we are not being revengeful or hostile instead we are digging down trying to keep your family from sinking . . . I'm never allowed in her house (the door will be bolted shut she says), she intends to turn Ariadne against me by leting her hear the tapes (what is on those tapes I don't know) . . .

Grandpa paid her car insurance . . . If you mother is ever in the hospital again, and she will be, please let me know maybe at such a time I can bound some sense in her head and make her understand she needs me . . .

. . . Why don't you apply to the Forestry Service for a summer job? . . . I don't think you could possibly earn enough to support yourself in N.Y. . . .

Your grandfather is still working his long hours but he is ageing and is not well. He hardly eats anything is is getting thinner and thinner . . .

Larry please destroy all my letter, I don't want them to get back to your home . . . I woyld never take Marc into my confidence. He is an "old blabber mouth". Tells all. When handling family difficulties you have to use discretion. I'm afraid I did not use discretion in things I said last summer and our family fury is the result . . .

Sunday April 9th, 1978

Dear Larry:

. . . I dread getting Marc on the phone, he is like "talking
to a vegetable". Everything I ask him the answer was and is:
"I don't know". Your mother has Marc so brainwashed he
doesn't dare say "his soul is his own." . . . He did let me
talk to Ariadne once for a few minutes but she started caling
me "offensive names" so I hung up, I was totally shocked
. . . I called back a few minutes later and asked Marc who
taught Ariadne to call me names and he siad: "I don't know".
He said you boys were going to get Easter dinner. I said:
"What are you preparing for dinner?" He said: I don't know"
. . . see what I mean about talking to a vegetable . . .
    Thursday was your mother's birthday . . . Did you get
the $100 check I sent to you for Easter? Before Easter I sent
your mother $1,000 and each of you kids I sent $100 for Easter
and vacation money. Sent a check for $1,100 for Dr. Nelson
her dentist. Last week I set her another $1,000 plus $100 check
from Grandpa for her birthday and $100 for Ariadne's birth-
day which is tomorrow. That makes a total $3,600 I have sent
to her within the month. Never does she write or call . . .
    . . . I put in 3 to 5 hours [a day] at the warehouse. I get
paid $4 an hour, that brings me in around $200 twice a
month. Every cent, plus my $200 Social Security I send to
your mother. I got a check from F & B for $2,400 and every
cent was sent to your family . . . If it wasn't for financing
your family I would be traveling. Your mother knows how
much I like to travel. I haven't had a nice trip for several years
because your family need my money and help . . . I wil be
75 in May. I keep up my home, keep Grandpa's food prepared, clothing washed, go to the Spa at least 5 times a week
have spent a little time doing genealogy . . . Grandpa "purrs
like a kitten" when I go down there to work. He is looking
very old and so tired. He still goes to work at 6 A,M, and home
between 8 and 9 P.M. every day . . . Monday April 3rd he
was 76. Not one in your family sent him a birthday card . . .
The warehouse gave him a huge, beautiful, delicious
cake . . .
    The IRS is on our back to pay tax on money we have given

your family to live on in 1976. Your mother reported her income from us as a gift now the government is on our back to pay "them" a gift tax . . .

I think you should contact your grandfather regarding your college financing . . . Your grandfather says he does not plan to finance you and Marc's college education. He says you boys are to earn your way thru college . . . All these years your mother has stuck her kids in expensive private schools and sent us the bills . . . She plans to put Ariadne in expensive private schools but she never asks us if we will pay for it . . . Your family does not have a dime of income coming in except from ME . . . It is incredible that your family should live in a $1,000 apartment with all the normal monthly expenses and no one works and yet you have no you have no income. No one else in this whole world lives like this.

. . . I think your mother has had a very sad life, she has such poor health also. Your family is on my mind constantly. I love Frances very, very much I feel so very sorry for her. I just wish I could help her physically but she will never let me in her home . . .

Today is Ariadne's birthday. How much I would like to be there to share it with her. I sent her a lovely figurine from the store, cost $45 and also a check for $100 and a lovely birthday card but I don't think your mother will tell her it is from "Granny". Your mother refuses to acknowledge me as her mother. How horrible. Between you and me I think she is suffering from a mental breakdown . . . She hates her parents and every relative she has . . .

. . . Once more I suggest you destroy my letters if they get in her hands she will only hate me more. So for my sake see to it my letters do not get back to her, PLEASE.

[undated; approx. April 19, 1978]

Dear Marc and Larry:

. . . We are so very proud of both you boys, Larry for his ROTC scholarship and Marc for the honor rolls . . .

. . . My social security check goes right off to your mother, also my pay check down at Bapco [Bradshaw Auto Parts] . . . I earn between $400 and $500 a month, social security $200 and I get an oil check that amounts around $100 so this makes about $700 a month I send to your mother. I got a check from F & B Investment in March for $2400 . . .

I tried for months to get your mother by phone. I called all day on her birthday [April 6], all day on Ariadne's birthday [April 10] but she never answers. Finally one evening last week I just decided to try once more and she answered. I was surprised and pleased. She talked 1 1/2 hours . . . She tells me how much Ariadne loves her dancing. Her dancing lesson fell on her birthday but she prefered her dancing lesson to a birthday party. I'm so pleased Ariadne has taken to dancing. It is unusual for a girl so young to take to an artistic activity such as dancing. I wanted to be a dancer . . .

. . . Now that spring is here the house needs cleaning . . . I do get in a little social life. Sat. I went to the "Ice Follies."

Sunday, April 26, 1978

Dear Larry:

. . . First we are all thrilled and pleased over your scholarship . . . It must be a great relief to you to know for the next 8 years at least your life is all scheduled for you with no financial worries . . .

. . . Grandpa and I . . . can't understand why you say you need money for Lehigh application? We will send you the money if you can explain to us what you did with the other Lehigh check we sent you.

We are pleased you have a part time job. Your mother and Marc should be earning some money.

Grandpa and I are concerned and worried about your home conditions. We can't understand why your mother keeps denying you to come home . . . She says you eat and drink, (milk and orange juice) Ariadne's foods . . . As I said in my last letter your mother is suffering some emotional and mental problems . . . She is now 40 and has accomplished nothing. Grandpa and I have been nagging her for years to make something of herself . . .

Larry I want you to know you can come to our home any time. Our home is your home. There is no need of you going to your own home if you are not let in and welcomed. Never

again do I want you and Marc in my house at the same time
. . . I will never forget the volgular names Marc called
me . . .

. . . I'm glad you admit and realize how wasteful you were
with your money last summer . . . It made me sick to see
you boys throwing your money around when I knew how
desporately you would need money for the coming school year
. . . The vacation money I sent to Marc, he gave most of it to
his mother, I will give Marc credit he does look out for his
mother in a financial way which You don't . . .

. . . We will send you the money for a bus ticket any place
you want to go to get work . . .

Your mother says the insurance company is furnishing her
with a car. I don't think she should be driving a car. She can't
afford the gas to run it.

All for now, Let us hear from you

Lots of love, Granny

Cut off from the Schreuders, Granny spent her free time that
spring researching her family tree in Salt Lake City's huge Genealogical Library and traced her Huguenot roots all the way back
to Charlemagne. Invisible to Granny, life in the Schreuder's New
York household had reached a rolling boil. Several grand designs
were growing at once, expanding and overlapping. One day Frances was seen lunching at La Côte Basque, one of Manhattan's
most fashionable restaurants. Her guest, a Bryn Mawr alumna,
truthfully did not remember anybody named Frankie Bradshaw.
But the woman had been out of college twenty years, and Frankie
had named several classmates she did recall. Now the woman
was on the boards of several educational institutions, and Frankie
had said on the phone that she wanted to discuss her own passionate commitment to quality education. Her belief in stricter
schools and higher academic standards had developed, she explained, while she was living in Europe as the wife of a wealthy
industrialist. Her husband had recently died, and now she wanted
to make certain endowments in his memory. The conversation
was resolutely high-toned, but Frankie made it clear that her son
attended Allen-Stevenson, and she wanted a letter of recommendation to a good girls' school for her daughter.

The next day, calling herself "Elaine Drukman," Frances was

seen opening a checking account in an East Side branch of the Manufacturers Hanover Bank. Her son Marc accompanied her.

A few days later Richard Behrens was seen in New Jersey making inquiries about buying a gun. Then Frances and Marc were seen in a bank. Together they forged and cashed a $323 IRS tax-refund check which had arrived in the mail for Larry. Frances was frequently seen that spring in her psychiatrist's office. What they discussed is unknown, but she paid a portion of her medical bills with a forged $720 Franklin J. Bradshaw check. Frances was also seen at at least four Manhattan private schools —Spence, Hewitt, Chapin, and Brearley—making inquiries about enrolling a daughter and hinting broadly that she would like to offer endowment and scholarship funds to the school.

Frances dragooned her Bryn Mawr friend into another lunch, this time at the chic Café Des Artistes. For two hours she debated whether the school letter for Ariadne should be handwritten or typed, and whether personal or business stationery created a better impression. She had drafted a letter which said something like "I have visited many fine homes, and rarely have I encountered such an atmosphere of culture and refinement as exists in the Schreuder family." The friend, who had never been inside the Schreuders' door, thought this sounded pretentious and silly, but she too proved unable to say no to Frances. As it had to so many others, it seemed preferable by now to be rid of Mrs. Schreuder by saying yes.

Frances was next seen by the woman's Park Avenue doorman. She had dropped off a small package which turned out to contain an effusive thank-you note—handwritten on fancy Tiffany stationery—and a $900 Tiffany wristwatch. The woman telephoned Frances again, trying to say no, she could not possibly accept. Frances insisted until the woman decided it was easier to keep the watch than continue the conversation.

One day Frances was seen back at Gino Restaurant, having a long, voluble, high-spirited lunch with Vittorio. As they were leaving, Vittorio says, Frances told him with a laugh that if her family was going to survive, somebody was simply going to have to murder her father. "I'm probably going to have to put out a contract on him!" she giggled as they pushed their way out into the fine May sunshine on Lexington Avenue.

Larry graduated from EMA in June. Behrens drove Marc out to Long Island for the big occasion; Frances did not attend. The

band played, cadets marched, and Larry Schreuder was the un-
disputed hero of the day. He was the only graduate to win a full
college ROTC scholarship for "having demonstrated exceptional
leadership potential," in return for four years of military service.
He was also named top boy in the school, and class valedictorian.
He won varsity letters in wrestling and track. He was honored as
editor of the school newspaper, which he himself had founded,
and as president of the Stamp and Coin Club, which he had also
founded. He was champion of the chess squad. But Larry had
ridden to victory on a dying horse. Eastern Military Academy
was by then in such an advanced stage of decay that as soon as
the diplomas were handed out and the folding chairs stowed, the
school was closed for good, shut down by New York State for
over seventy health and safety code violations. Marc took many
pictures of the graduation ceremonies with his new Nikon,
bought with last summer's stolen money. He and Larry could
hardly wait to send them to Salt Lake. They wished they could
see the faces of their proud grandparents as they examined the
photographs. The pictures emphasized the fact that most of his
classmates, said Larry, were "big, thick-lipped niggers, real jun-
gle bunnies!"—a great joke on the snooty Bradshaws, both brothers agreed, and they giggled with Behrens about it all the way
back to New York.

Granny had already sent homeless Larry a $75 Trailways bus
ticket, good for any destination in the United States. Larry chose
"The Lake." He had told her he had no where else to go. But
nobody wanted him down at the warehouse. So, within a week of
his arrival, he had conned Granny into $3,500 worth of flying
lessons, a small price to get him out of her house. Before the
summer ended, Larry had earned his pilot's license, and had
pretty well memorized the aerial topography of eight western
states. In early July Behrens made another trip to Virginia, and
was again unsuccessful in obtaining a gun. Ironically the easiest
place to buy a weapon would probably have been Salt Lake City.
Utah then required no fingerprinting, no ballistics testing of new
weapons, no waiting period. The same kind of weapon that was
to be used to kill Frank Bradshaw is readily available in K-Mart.

At about the time Behrens returned empty-handed from Virginia, Frances compelled Marc to make three phone calls. Inconsistencies, evasions, and lies cloud the accounts of this period
given by Marc, Larry, and Behrens. But three years later a mas-

sive records search by Utah authorities nailed down certain critical airline and telephone dates. On July 13 Marc called Jon Cavenaugh, a Kent School acquaintance who lived in Midland, Texas,
and said he was on his way to Utah to see his grandparents and
maybe to go on a hunting trip. He might come by way of Texas
and try to buy a gun there. "No problem," Jon said, but Marc
sounded so vague that Jon didn't really expect him to turn up.

That same day Behrens received a twelve-minute collect call
from Salt Lake City. The only person Behrens knew in Utah was
Larry. "It's gonna come down soon now," Behrens would claim
Larry said. "Wow! I'll stay close to home, then," he said Larry
replied.

The same day, Marc talked Granny into persuading Gramps to
send the Schreuders a last $3,000. Their rent was now $1,200 a
month, and his mother had received a second eviction notice. If
Gramps would come through just one more time, Marc promised, none of the Schreuders would ask him for anything ever
again. Ultimately the old man agreed. But as if to underscore the
object of his compassion, Frank Bradshaw told his secretary
Nancy Jones to draw the check in Ariadne's name. Some of this
money would be used to buy a plane ticket and gun.

And the same day, July 13, someone also called United Airlines
in New York City and made a plane reservation from Salt Lake
City to Dallas to New York in the name of "L. Schreuder." That
reservation was never picked up, nor the caller identified. But it
looks very much as if someone was trying to frame Larry.

The big $3,000 check was cashed in New York as soon as it
arrived. Marc says that by the time he was ready to pick up the
plane ticket, July 19, not enough money was left in the kitty to
cover both it and the gun. Frances told him to hock his new
camera and recording equipment. He took them down to Olden
Camera, on Broadway, and raised another $300, which he turned
over to Mom. Then he went to the Plaza Hotel, his old home,
and gave the clerk at the American Airlines branch office in the
lobby the cash for a round trip New York-Texas-Utah-New York
ticket made out in the name of "L. Gentile."

Young Jon Cavenaugh was away at work at his welding job
July 20 when Marc rang the doorbell of the large, two-storey
house on a tree-shaded street in Midland, Texas. When his
mother said Jon was not at home, Marc "expected to have a cold
door slammed in my face." Instead, astonishingly, Mrs. Cave-

naugh invited him in and started fixing him lunch. After he had eaten, she showed him to the guest bedroom. Marc could not believe it. He had never stayed overnight with a school friend, he says, and had no notion of normal family life. Now, simply because he was a friend of Jon's, the Cavenaughs were making him part of their family. "The whole attitude of the family seemed so genial and happy!" he said later. He was surprised when Mrs. Cavenaugh went out to do the grocery shopping. He had assumed that Jon ran down to the store whenever his family got hungry, just as he did.

When Jon got home from work, Marc told him he wanted to buy a gun, and they discussed the comparative merits of rifles, shotguns, and handguns. Marc knew nothing about weapons, Jon could tell, but since his friend lived in New York City, Jon decided he "might as well" buy a revolver. It would be a useful item to have at home as well as on the road, Jon thought. Since Marc was technically underage—not, evidently, a serious matter in that part of the world—Jon arranged the purchase through a former boss, a gas station operator named Malcolm McPhail. He knew a woman named Sharla Vestal, then the wife of a deputy sheriff, Jerry Register, who dealt in guns on the side. On Saturday morning Marc and Jon met with Register and McPhail in the lobby of the Commercial Bank Tower, and the deal was indeed "no problem." Jon and McPhail examined the weapon, and when they pronounced it good, Marc peeled off $175 of his grandfather's money. Register was surprised. He had thought one of the Texans was the buyer. But that was "no problem" either, and Marc took possession of the big, new .357 magnum Smith & Wesson "Policeman's Special" still in its original box. "That oughta take care of anything you run into back-packing in the mountains," someone said. A few dollars more, to McPhail, bought Marc a box of bullets. The affable gas station owner instructed him how to get the weapon through the airport security and aboard the plane: Simply check it in his suitcase. Marc obeyed. He did not even take the blue-steel weapon out of its box.

While he was in Texas, Marc says, he loved playing Monopoly with Jon's two little brothers. He also enjoyed the family dinners, sitting around a real table while Jon's mother served and nice Dr. Cavenaugh carved. Marc claims he knew this sort of behavior only from TV. At his house either he did the cooking or they had

TV dinners and takeout food, and they almost always ate in Mom's bedroom.

"That was the one point when I *really* didn't want to go through with this whole insane plan—bumping off Gramps," Marc says. "I thought: *Wow! Wouldn't it be nice to just stay here!* I was just fantasizing. *Boy! I love this family! The mother's so warm and friendly . . . and the father. They're so normal! The house is so neat! Not a pigsty. They seem so happy! They're having so much fun here. God, I wish I could just stay forever!*

"It would just be a little fantasy. Then I'd come back to reality. *No, I gotta get this job done. No, I gotta gain Mom's love back.*" Marc did stay over in Texas one extra day; he was supposed to leave Friday evening, the twenty-first. "Mom wanted me to have more time at the Lake. To prepare myself."

What does he mean by "prepare"? Are Marilyn and Elaine right—*was* there another will? If so, it would positively have to be destroyed before it could fall into police hands. A new will would not only disinherit the Schreuders, it would show police the motive for the crime which was about to occur.

Marc Schreuder did not leave Texas until Saturday afternoon. He arrived in Salt Lake at 9:50 P.M. After he recovered his bag, he walked out into the desert wasteland around the airport, opened his suitcase, opened the gun box, took out the weapon, pointed into the dark, and fired a gun for the first time in his life.

Earlier that same evening, July 22, Larry had worked at the warehouse with his grandfather for the only time that summer. At about six-thirty, Berenice picked him up for supper and took him to the Spaghetti Factory in Trolley Square.

Did Larry return to the warehouse later, after Frank Bradshaw had gone home? Did he open the inside padlocks for Marc? Alone, or perhaps with Marc, did he spend the night tearing apart the old warehouse, knowing it was the last time they could quarry hidden treasure from this disordered Ali Baba's cave? Was this the night that the original 1970 will disappeared from the warehouse, the will that could not be found after Frank Bradshaw's death? Did Larry or Marc perhaps also find a new will— one disinheriting them all—and destroy it before they destroyed its author?

Marc says that when his plane landed in Salt Lake City, he took a taxi to the motel his mother had recommended, registered under the fake name she had recommended, and then called home collect and told her he could not go through with it. Their conversation lasted an hour-and-a-half. He was crying much of the time, but Frances was implacable. "She told me, 'Okay, Marc. If you're not gonna do it, don't bother coming home.' She said that in a really gutterlike nasty voice which I can never forget. 'Don't bother coming home. Me and Ariadne will live in a Harlem tenement and collect welfare. And the door will be locked forever. Doors can be opened. And doors can be closed.' "

Marc still hears the dreadful voice today. Remembering, he says, "At that point in my life that was torture for me. I was *never* gonna let myself get on Mom's bad side, like Larry got on her bad side, and get locked out permanently. I would do *anything* to avoid getting locked out then. And it *would have happened!* I know it. To this day I'm sure of it. And Mom *would* have been evicted! Because Gramps was not coming through with any more money. And I would have been *blamed* for her eviction. Blamed for every misfortune that came *after* that. I was pretty sure Mom would have hated me for ever and ever. And I couldn't stand that idea. Here I had spent so many years trying to fight for her love. Trying to do everything just perfect, just right for her. And here I blow it . . . just because of one . . . well . . ." his twitchy voice drops. "Just because I won't bump off Gramps. You know?"

The staring blue eyes look down. There is a long silence. "I feel funny talking about this . . ." But Marc cannot stop talking about it. Very early the next morning, still following his mother's instructions, he says, he taxied to the warehouse, and hid across the street. He saw his grandfather arrive. He followed him inside. "And in the warehouse, even when I was talkin' to him, I was still thinking: *God, I have to ki* . . . I was still talking myself *into* it, it seemed like. It was running through my mind: Why don't I just throw this gun in the river? And just go home and live with Granny?

"But I just couldn't. Just couldn't! I said to myself: 'Mom will never love me again. I've gotta get with Mom.'

"I was actually talking to him. But my mind was thinking completely different. My mind was racing. Trying to think of excuses. Trying to think of *anything!* I wasn't even conscious of what I was saying. I could only hear my thoughts, not my voice.

"My mind said: *Fuck this, man! FUCK THIS, MAN! I'm gonna go live with Granny*. It was that clear! But it was like a fantasy also. Then I'd bring myself back to reality again: *I hadda do it! I hadda do it!*

"It was like, as if . . . when I was doing it, as if . . . I was going through a third person. Like I was above myself and looking down. As if I was seeing all of it through a frosted glass. I wasn't really aware of what I was doing. AHRRGH! I don't know what the hell was going through me, y'know?

"Then the voice that said, *Fuck this! I'll go live with Granny,* it got SQUASHED. By things like: *What happens if Mom kills herself? Yes: Mom will kill herself. And I'll get locked out. And I'll never see Mom again. Mom'll never see me again. I can never live with Mom again. Mom's my only friend! . . . Granny's evil. Granny will smother me. Granny will kill me by feeding me to death. Like she did Mom's brother."*

Marc does not know what would have happened if his grandfather had not turned away. He does not recall how long they talked, nor what they were talking about. They stood three to four feet apart. "But he [Gramps] *had* to turn . . . Because I couldn't do it in his face. Sneaky to the end. I just couldn't do it . . . I just felt . . . God! I just felt so *guilty.* If he hadn't turned around, I never would have done it on him. I *think* what I was doing . . . I was *desperately waiting for somebody to come in.* So I could give Mom an excuse. So I could say, 'Well, *he* came in, and I couldn't do it.' I was looking for ways to buy time, it seems like.

"But then I thought: *God! I'll get home! AND MOM'LL WANT ME TO DO IT AGAIN!*

"Then I thought: *Okay, buy time . . . and wait for Mom to kill herself!* And this was a very real thought with me. Mom had tried it before. And this time she really would. Because she'd *never* live in Harlem. She'd *never* move back to live with Granny. Ever. She'd sooner kill herself. And I knew that *would* happen. And I knew I would not be part of her life. Especially after that phone call . . . that phone call I'd had the night before, from the hotel, was *reeling* through my head. Still is. I think if I hadn't called her that night . . . I'd of never done it. That phone call is *key.* Because that call put the fear of God in me, man! It was just like: I was gonna lose everything! I was gonna lose Mom; I was gonna lose everything I knew and loved. Mom and Ariadne. She *was* everything, you know. I wasn't willing to do that. Wasn't willing to have her committing suicide. Wasn't gonna take that chance . . . Because she'd done it before, y'know? *G-O-D!"*

. . . The two shots were ear-splitting.

Marc easily caught his nine o'clock flight back to New York, he says, the gun again checked in his suitcase. He was very nervous, and amazed not to be arrested at the airport. In the air he had an intense fantasy that Gramps was not dead, only wounded. On the taxiride home from JFK, he retrieved the gun from his suitcase and put it in the wallet pocket of his plaid jacket. He arrived at 1675 York Avenue with less than eight dollars in his pocket. Mom had figured his expenses very sharply. He went through the lobby, past the doormen, up in the elevator. It was about five o'clock, a hot Sunday afternoon in July. No one was home. Locked out again, he went to the deli and ate a couple of sandwiches, not because he was hungry but because he had some vague notion of establishing an alibi. Susie Coleman, daughter of the owners, was a close friend.

When he got back to the apartment, Mom had just returned from Jones Beach. It appeared that she and Ariadne and "Tricky" had spent the day together. When the door opened, Marc says he saw all three of them in the foyer, standing on Mom's zebra-skin rug, still clutching their beach paraphernalia. Mom had her damp bathing suit on under her clothes. Behrens wore a funny-looking pair of shorts and rubber sandals. Ariadne held her little pail and shovel.

"Mom said, 'Did you do it? Where's the gun?' I said, 'Yes, I did it.' Mom said, 'Oh! Thank God!' "

Then Frances Schreuder threw her arms around her son and hugged and squeezed and kissed him hard, and this was the third kiss from the Evil Queen.

Part Four

The Boiling Over

. . . ELAINE WAS THE first daughter to arrive. Berenice Bradshaw and her grandson Larry were waiting at the airport Monday morning when the plane from Oregon landed at Salt Lake City International Airport. The newly widowed Berenice, and Elaine Drukman, were back waiting at the airport when Marilyn landed at noon; she had got the last seat on the seven o'clock flight out of Newark. The sisters decided not to stay at Gilmer Drive but at Little America, the town's newest luxury motel. When Frances showed up, they thought, it was best that she and her mother have a chance to be alone.

No one knew which plane Frances would be on, so throughout that day and evening, and the next, Berenice met every flight from New York. Frances was not on any of them. She did not appear until Tuesday evening, when she turned up at Gilmer Drive in a taxi. Because the flights were overbooked, she had flown to Salt Lake by way of Los Angeles, she said. She had fourteen pairs of shoes in her luggage. When her sisters suggested she sleep in her father's bed, Frances declined; she preferred to share Larry's room in the basement.

Many matters needed to be discussed before the memorial service and at-home reception the next day. Marilyn told Frances about the funeral arrangements. Privately, Frances told her mother she would soon be needing more money for rent. Berenice warned Elaine always to watch her purse at Gilmer Drive. Larry was "a terrible thief." The widow was also worried about the future of the family business. "We just can't let Marilyn take over! We *can't!*" she whispered to Elaine.

Marilyn certainly knew that her father's half-page memo making her co-administrator of his estate was not a legal will, that it had not been properly signed, witnessed nor executed. Still she regarded it as an expression of his intent. Furthermore, she believed that a new and properly-drawn will stating these intentions did exist.

Berenice announced to her daughters that, despite the tragic circumstances which had reunited them all, she was happy to have her family together once more, the Drukmans newly returned from three years in New Zealand, both girls here from New York, and three of her five grandchildren. Tomorrow night, after all the guests had left, Granny wanted to take everybody out to a private dinner, just her immediate family. She knew the perfect restaurant, The Jail House. It had private dining rooms only; you just called up and reserved a "cell."

The Bradshaw murder was front-page news, and the police were filing reports and taking statements from everybody. All of the interviews were conducted by Detective Joel Campbell, a young and not very experienced policeman usually assigned to juvenile cases. Berenice Bradshaw and Larry had given their statements Sunday evening. On Monday Doug Steele and other top-level employees were interviewed. All of them mentioned the Bradshaws' difficulties with the Schreuder family, the thefts and forgeries of the previous summer, the fact that Franklin had failed to prosecute, and that one of the thieves had in fact come back to live with his grandparents a few weeks before the murder. Clive Davis, Doug Steele's right-hand man for thirty-one years, said flat out that simple robbery *could not* be the motive. A robber would strike in the dark, not daylight; he would strike at the end of a business day, when there was money in the till, not on a Sunday morning. But the Schreuders had forged $40,000 in checks that he knew of in 1977, he said, and he felt either they or an assassin hired by them had to be behind it. "There isn't anybody in Salt Lake that I know of that would want to do that to Frank Bradshaw," he told police. Davis, who died in 1983, was a respected Mormon Elder, and his words carried special weight.

On Tuesday afternoon Marilyn was interviewed and spoke of forgeries totaling $20,000 to $30,000. She said they had caused her father to write a new will disinheriting Frances. She termed her sister "irrational" and advised police to "handle her carefully."

Elaine, interviewed directly after Marilyn, was the most blunt. "Assuming that it was not a robbery," Detective Joel Campbell asked her, "is there anybody anywhere in any situation that would want to take him, hurt him like that?"

"Well, when I first found out *how* my father died, something did flash into my head. Because there *is* one person who would want to hurt him . . ."

"And who is that?"

"My sister Frances. And what flashed into my head was: *Oh my God—Larry's* there!"

Elaine said the Schreuders' thefts the previous summer totalled $55,000. She added that she suspected her mother of protecting Larry. Berenice had first told Elaine she heard Larry leave the house "shortly after" Dad. Later she changed and said the time was ten o'clock. As soon as she had time, Elaine volunteered, she intended to feed her mother a couple of glasses of wine and try to force out the truth. Then she broke down and wept.

By Tuesday even the Bradshaw relatives were doubtful that it had been a simple robbery. Don Bradshaw, nephew of the dead man and president of the family-owned American Savings & Investment Corporation, is a personable, candid man in his midforties. His hobby is raising cherries, and he had been high up on a ladder tending his cherry orchard Sunday morning when he got the news.

Don and his wife Jean had been the first family members to reach Uncle Frank's house on Gilmer Drive. It was 10:20, or 10:30 at most, he said later, and Larry was at home. The strange young man did not speak a word but silently stalked in and out of the room "like a cat" while they tried to comfort his grandmother. They recall Berenice telling them then that she had got up and made Larry's breakfast about half an hour after she heard Frank leave the house.

By 11 A.M. Doug Steele had returned from the warehouse, where he and Clive Davis had been scrubbing the bloodstained floor. Other relatives had begun to arrive. So Steele asked Don, as a senior male relative of the dead man—he is a son of Franklin's older brother, Frederick—to return with him to the warehouse and help search for hidden cash.

"You know who did this, don't you?" Steele said as they got into the car.

But Don Bradshaw knew nothing whatsoever about the Schreuder family's crime spree in the warehouse the preceding summer. Bradshaw males are stern and proud; they do not tell one another their troubles. Frank had never once seen fit even to mention his grandsons to his nephew Don, no more than Don would have thought to discuss with Franklin the suicide of his brother Jack, despite the fact that Jack had spent his entire life in Frank's employ. Jack Bradshaw had always wanted to work alongside his own branch of the Bradshaw family, in the insurance business, but his psychiatrist advised against it. Jack was "mentally troubled." His first breakdown had occurred at nineteen, in Africa, where he had gone on an LDS mission to try to please his mother. He had never got along with his uncle Franklin the entire twenty-five or thirty years he had worked for him as manager of his Richfield store. There had been several more breakdowns, and then one Sunday morning, on Mother's Day, when he was about fifty, Jack blew his brains out. Such matters were best left unspoken.

On Pierpont Street the two men parked at the foot of the loading dock and climbed the wooden stairs to the beat-up yellow door marked "Push." Steele had barely touched his key to the lock when the door swung open.

"My God!" He turned to Don, white-faced. "I'm pretty shaky . . . but I'm *sure* I locked up here when I left half an hour ago!" They were standing just inside the door now, right in front of the counter where Frank had been killed. The older man seemed to be in shock. "Don, did I just *dream* that door was unlocked?"

"No, Doug. You just put the key up to it, and it pushed open." They had walked in a few steps farther and were behind the counter when suddenly Doug said, "Hey! Let's get out of here fast! Now I *know* someone's in here!" A fire door was open, the one they always kept closed.

"You're *really* crackin' up, Doug," Don said as they retreated back out to the loading dock. But Steele was already hailing a passing police car. "I'm *dead certain* someone's been in that building since I left!" he told them, and the police kept watch until Steele got a locksmith to come over and change every lock in the place.

While the men were at the warehouse, Don's wife Jean had fixed Berenice some breakfast and done up Larry's dishes. Berenice had started to cry again when she saw Frank's cereal bowl, so Jean started talking about the Great Reunion she and Frank would surely have.

"I don't believe in any of that!" Berenice said. "But we're gonna have great problems. *Right in this house.*" She had become quite agitated, and when Don returned, he and Jean together tried to calm her down. Don and Marilyn Reagan had once been schoolmates, and he knew of her intensive paralegal training and her efforts to help her father. He now advised Berenice to "rely on Marilyn."

"That seemed to excite Berenice worse," he said later. "The girls didn't get along, she told us, and she started accusing Marilyn. *Marilyn will take over! She'll do what she wants.*"

Don had seen Frances only once since she was a toddler. That had been a day, ten years before, when she had marched into the American Savings & Loan offices demanding to see the stock record books. She was trying to trace her father's stocks. Don's older brother Blair Bradshaw was then president, and "Blair accommodated her, had her sit down at a desk, gave her the books. I went over and introduced myself, but she wouldn't have anything to do with me. Acted like she couldn't possibly be interested in anything I had to say."

Don was curious about her because of an unseemly letter she had sent to his wife just after Jean was appointed regional western director of the National Junior League. "You may not know me, but I'm your cousin and I desperately want to be admitted to the New York City Junior League. Would you mind proposing me and sending me an application?" Since Don and Jean indeed did not know Frances, they had no qualms about tossing her cheeky request into the wastebasket.

Now they wished they knew Frances a bit better, so they could advise Berenice. They felt great compassion for Frank's widow and had no doubt she was suffering deeply. But, even today, seven years after the crime, they do not believe her story that Larry left Gilmer Drive at ten o'clock for his flying lesson. Cherries are a finicky fruit. They need to be picked at the moment of maximum ripeness. "All that day, no matter what else was going on, I always kept one eye on the watch," Don Bradshaw maintains. "I always knew the time almost to the minute. It was Sunday, you see, my day off, and I knew that in spite of all I couldn't wait another week. I still had to get those cherries picked today."

Frances Schreuder was the last member of the family to give the police a statement. By the time she arrived at the Hall of Justice, at four-thirty Wednesday afternoon, after the funeral, she appeared to be the last person in Salt Lake who still believed Frank Bradshaw had been done in by strangers.

Q: Okay, what have you heard about your father's death?
A: He never knew what hit him.
Q: Pardon?
A: He never knew what hit him.

She spoke of the "bad neighborhood . . . pretty sleazy . . . drunks on the streets . . ." When Detective Campbell mentioned he'd heard there had been a "bit of a problem" the previous summer, when her sons worked for their grandfather, Frances said, "I was furious at them." But when he asked her straight out about the stolen and forged checks, she implicated Berenice.

Q: Okay. Now tell me what that was all about.
A: No. Because my mother has done it for years.

That night at the Jail House restaurant, Berenice was again "so happy to have the family together," even under these circumstances, that she brought her camera along to record the family reunion in their private cell.

Another record, or version, of that same family reunion is provided by a tape recording which Marc says he made about a month after the murder, in Mom's bedroom. Both boys are in Mom's bed. Larry is drunk and sleepy but wakes up when Frances begins telling her sons that Berenice does not wear underwear. Like many of the family conversations Marc would choose to record, this one is preoccupied with excrement:

MOM: You ask her, "How come you don't wear panties, Granny? Why don't you wear a brassiere? Why don't you wear underpants?"

"Oooh . . . [mimicking Berenice, in a flutey voice] I like to feel *free! Ahh-h-h-h!*"

MARC: Mom . . . Mom! Mom, *tell* Larry.

MOM: I don't think Larry knows.

MARC [excited]: Larry, ever hear about maxipads or minipads by Kotex? . . . Well, you see, instead of Granny going to do pee-pee in the toilet, see . . .

LARRY: Oh, God . . .

MARC: She does pee-pee in these minipads and maxipads.

LARRY: You're crazy! That's impossible! . . .

MOM: . . . She changes them in front of me! . . . I mean, it's *awful!* She pees in them and changes them about ten times a day.

LARRY: Like a diaper!

MOM [gleeful]: Every time she comes to New York, she sits on my sofa, and there's a big spot!

LARRY [incredulous]: She just pees them!

MOM: I say, "Granny, what's that?" "Oh, just a little accident. I forgot to change my pee-pee pad."

LARRY [laughing]: Her pee-pee pad! . . . Remember the time she shitted all over herself?

MARC [thrilled]: Where was *this?*

MOM: At the Jail House. The night of Grandpa's funeral . . . All of a sudden she just disappeared. She had Montezuma's Revenge.

LARRY: And she just splattered. All over herself!

MOM [laughing]: The whole wall of the toilet, and everything!

LARRY [giggling]: The whole bathroom was *splattered.* Totally!

MOM [gleeful]: It had to be *cleaned. She* threw up, and *we* should clean it! It was pretty embarrassing . . . They had to send up a cleaning crew. When we left, there were two women in there with these huge buckets of sterilizer, scrubbing the *walls! She had the shits!*

MARC [thrilled]: You mean—she had Montezuma's Revenge all over the damned walls?

MOM: Are you kidding? . . . She hadda take everything off! Everything was covered with shit! She had no clothes to wear! She was hiding out in the car!

LARRY: It was *my* car, too! And boy, it took a long time to clean the stink! Ugh! Disgusting!

MARC: The smell. The lovable smell of shit!

MOM: . . . Then she couldn't find her glasses and camera . . . So I had to go back in . . . I went to the bathroom. That's when I saw the cleaning crew. Then I said, "My mother." They said, "Ahw." They said don't worry, they'd clean it. I said, "I'm so sorry. My mother was a bit sick. You know, her husband died."

With the assassination of the patriarch, all the game plans had to be revised. Franklin, in his zeal to avoid taxes, had left control of his fortune entirely in his wife's hands. The sisters would now

fight one another for control of Berenice. Berenice would fight to
hire professional management: she did not want any member of
her family in charge of the others. She knew them all too well.
Once again only Frances would get her wish.

Thursday morning, the day after the funeral, the widow and
her three daughters showed up first at the accounting firm of
Peat, Marwick & Mitchell to hear from Franklin's tax man, Herman Wood, about the workings of F & B Corporation. Next they
had an appointment with the bank attorney handling the estate,
Stephen Swindle. Marilyn had prepared herself for these meetings by reviewing the nineteen-month-old F & B limited partner-
ship agreement. At that point, Marilyn says, Frances had no clear
grasp of estate matters. She simply sat beside her mother muttering "Get a copy! Get a copy!" as each document was discussed.
At one moment it seemed to Marilyn as if Frances and Berenice
might be plotting to ask Mr. Wood to become executor. To forestall this Marilyn raised the question herself: Would Mr. Wood be
available? Not surprisingly, the old man said no. It is possible
that he recoiled in horror.

But the suggestion had enraged Frances. "Where did you *ever*
get that idea?" she sputtered all the way down in the elevator. By
the time they hit the street, she had become so angry she stalked
off and returned to New York.

In Swindle's office, with Frances gone, the discussion took a
new tack. Now that their father was dead, was there some way
Elaine and Marilyn could protect their mother from Frances's
constant pressure for money? Berenice, they explained, was unable to say no to her daughter. "Is that true, Mrs. Bradshaw?"
the bland young lawyer asked. He was meeting these bereaved
Bradshaw women this afternoon for the first time. "Would you
give Frances anything she asked? *Could* you say no to her?"

Berenice thought a long time. "No, I don't think I could."

A $3,000-a-month dependent's allowance was arranged. Later
Frances petitioned for and won an increase to $5,000, citing
heavy medical expenses for emphysema and other ailments. Berenice received a $10,000-a-month allowance, and Marilyn made do
with $1,500. Elaine took nothing for now. Soon each would re-
ceive a $136,000 lump sum in oil money.

With Frances gone, Marilyn and Elaine and their mother had a
couple of relatively nice days together. "Really the last good
times we ever had," says Marilyn. "Elaine and I were talking

about how are we gonna help Mother, get her on her feet, deal with all of this?" They decided the best idea would be to rent her an office, "so that Mother would have a place to put her papers," and to make clear that Berenice's ongoing business was separate from business transacted in and by the warehouse; that was part of the estate. Berenice's mail and checks would be collected where Nancy Jones, Dad's trusted secretary, could keep an eye on them. Marilyn would come back periodically from New York "and help keep Mother's records straight." Important mail would not pile up at Gilmer Drive if Berenice were off on a cruise. They trooped over to the old Ketchum Building, near the warehouse, and rented some cheap office space. They took a few old desks from the warehouse and supplemented them with filing cabinets from a second-hand furniture store. There would be no more orange crates.

The daughters went home. Marilyn was in New York making arrangements to quit her job in the Trust Division of Manufacturers Hanover Bank, in order to be able to devote full time to her mother's affairs, when Berenice called and said she'd decided to cancel the office lease and had returned all the furniture. Obviously she had been speaking to Frances. But Marilyn was not yet worried. Perhaps the office plans *were* a bit premature.

Berenice called again and said she needed Marilyn's help right now. The problem was Larry. He was continually pressuring her for more money for flying lessons, camera equipment, and so on, and she was finding it impossible to say no to her grandson. Marilyn put in for the two weeks' paid vacation she was owed and hastened back to Salt Lake. She too was worried about Larry, as was Elaine. The sisters thought their mother was harboring a psychotic killer, a boy so desperate to recover his mother's love that he would do anything she asked. Worse, he would do anything he decided might please her and do it *without* being asked. With Larry in her basement, Berenice could be in mortal danger.

From New York, Frances was keeping in touch with Swindle by phone, assuring him she would return as soon as possible to familiarize herself with estate matters, as he had politely suggested. She was also in daily contact with her mother, soothing and smoothing from afar.

A week after the funeral, Marilyn and Berenice picked up Franklin's ashes from the mortuary and drove down to Lehi, to the family burying ground. Larry came along to take pictures. They chose a pleasant spot under a tree, a Lehi funeral director said a little Mormon prayer, and Franklin's grandson and wife and eldest daughter put the metal container of ashes into the ground and covered it with earth. Later Marilyn said she thought it looked just like a safe-deposit box.

A trip to bury her father in the company of the nephew she believed had murdered him was more than Elaine thought her heart could take. She had already gone back to Oregon. But her mother was soon on the phone: "Frances is up to something. I need your help." Like her sister, Elaine dutifully returned to her widowed and bewildered mother but found Berenice unwilling to say much. She just kept repeating that she *could not* let Marilyn run things, yet she was unable to say *why*. This in itself was sufficient to tip off Elaine that Frances already had Mother's ear and was beginning to stir the pot. She would trickle the poison in against her two sisters until she could be sure that she, and she alone, ruled Berenice. Elaine returned to Oregon and tried to figure out what was really going on in Frances's brain.

Larry was hanging around Salt Lake until he could take his pilot's license exam. Meanwhile he was happy enough to submit to a polygraph test at police request. The results indicated that he was being truthful when he denied killing his grandfather, but untruthful when he denied "possession of undisclosed knowledge" of the crime. The outcome of Larry's flight test was less ambiguous. He left for Lehigh University on August 22, a fully licensed pilot. He drove his latest used car, a '68 Impala, and this time he had been careful to tell nobody about his plans. Nobody raided his trunk, and nobody knew anything about the few souvenirs from the warehouse he had tucked inside before taking off.

In Reading, Pennsylvania, broke again, Larry had to pay his freshman enrollment fees with a bum check. He swiftly became very active and moderately popular on campus. Back in Salt Lake, Granny and Aunt Marilyn happily threw away his "stinking mattress."

Marilyn returned to New York, quit her job "to be free to assist my mother," and took an exam to qualify as an IRS examiner. Two weeks later she was back in Utah. Berenice was standing at the gate smiling and waving when she got off the plane. But when Marilyn had collected her luggage and brought it out to the curb, she saw that she had dallied too long. Curled in the back seat of

Frances Schreuder and Attorney Michael Rosen
(Copyright 1983 Heather Nelson)

Marc at Kent School
(Courtesy Salt Lake County Attorney's office)

Marc Francis Schreuder 1981
(Copyright 1981 Wide World Photos)

head 1981

(SLKd-July 6) SCHREUDER -- Marc Francis
Schreuder, 21, shown here in a police file
photo, was convicted Tuesday of second-
degree murder in the 1978 shooting death of
his millionaire grandfather, Franklin
Bradshaw. (AP Laserphoto) (gt31050d-n file)
(OEd: This is a 1981 file photo.) 1982
....schreuder.

Larry, December 20, 1979
(Courtesy Bethlehem Police Dept.)

Franklin Bradshaw
(Courtesy Salt Lake
County Attorney's
office)

Berenice Bradshaw
(Courtesy Salt Lake
County Attorney's
office)

Myles Manning
(Courtesy Salt Lake County Attorney's office)

Richard Behrens
(Courtesy Salt Lake County Attorney's office)

Doug Steele
(Courtesy Salt Lake County
Attorney's office)

Clive Davis
(Courtesy Salt Lake County
Attorney's office)

The Bradshaw Auto Parts Warehouse
(Courtesy Salt Lake County Attorney's office)

Michael George
(Courtesy Salt Lake County Attorney's office)

Mike Rosen with murder weapon
(Copyright 1983 Heather Nelson)

Frances
(Courtesy Salt Lake County Attorney's office)

Berenice's car, holding two containers of black coffee and smoking a cigarette, was her youngest sister.

Marilyn knew when she was beaten. A few days later she went home. But first she and her mother and sister called on yet another attorney, Steve Anderson, for a formal briefing on details of the estate. To Marilyn, Frances's questions indicated that her sister's understanding of wills and estates was minimal, extremely primitive compared to her own, and she returned to New York unemployed but reassured and resigned to the fact that from now on she and Elaine would have to operate from a distance and under cover. But their objective was clear. Although they suspected the wrong grandson as the triggerman, they agreed that the real villain was Frances.

The murder of Franklin Bradshaw and the developing warfare over the spoils would affect the survivors in different ways. Frances seemed energized by the stress, and sometimes Berenice did too. But at other times she broke down. She began to suffer angina attacks, and she had several surgical operations in the next few years. But such things were to be expected; she was approaching eighty. Her nerves and equilibrium held up remarkably well. Elaine Drukman would first harden, then soften, as her damaged heart again broke down. Marilyn went in the other direction: first softened by grief, later she became hardened and implacable. Larry's response was difficult to read. Marc fell into a heavy depression which lasted about a year.

Slowly the older sisters would come to feel that the ultimate villain was Frances-and-Berenice. As they saw it, Franklin's death had removed a certain boundary between mother and daughter and had allowed them almost to merge into one. "Mother and Frances have always had a symbiotic relationship. And now Berenice *is* Frances. She has *become* Frances," Elaine has said. "After Dad died, Frances began living out part of Mother's fantasy, living the high life that Mother always wanted. That was what she married my father *for.*"

Marilyn observes that in cutting down her father, Frances also set Berenice free. "Since Dad died, Mother has no call whatever to *be in* Salt Lake, and Frances has had Mother's *full attention.* Before, it was split." Before, too, "Mother and Dad were always at odds over what to *do about* Frances." Now the deadlock was broken. Eventually Marilyn would work her way around to a position where she blamed her mother as the person ultimately

responsible for her father's death. Was it not Berenice who had
brewed the broth which nourished Frances's dreams? What else
had she accomplished with her constant harping on how much
money her husband had? How tight-fisted he was? How if only
she had it, she would give it all to the Schreuders? "I always
knew she hated my father," Marilyn says thickly, choking up.
"But I never knew she hated him *this much!*"

By fall Larry was at college, Marc was a senior at Kent, and
Ariadne had transferred from Episcopal to Marc's old school, St.
Hilda's & St. Hugh's. Perhaps only a nun can smell chocolate on
the breath of a five-year-old. But on her first day of school, Ariadne was questioned about her breakfast, and when she replied
that she had found a glazed chocolate doughnut in the kitchen,
proper breakfast instruction was once more begun. No one at the
school associated the enchantingly behaved and dressed Ariadne
Schreuder with grubby, rowdy Marco Gentile of eleven years
before. Indeed, the school knew virtually nothing about this new
little girl. They sent out the usual form letter to her previous
school, asking for financial, health, and other records. The form
included the stock question about why the child is changing
schools—a discreet way of inquiring why the student has not
been invited back. When Ariadne's form was returned by Episcopal, this was the *only* question answered. In large block letters
someone had written: "WE HAVE MET MRS. SCHREUDER."

One day Marc went down to Crazy Eddie and spent some of
his stolen funds on a big new Audio-Technica mike and Akai tape
deck. He began surreptitiously taping scenes of the Schreuders'
home life. His first tapes, made in the fall of 1978, seem to have
been done for the hell of it. A year later he would make tapes of
and for Ariadne, to show her the reality of their lives, how she
was being abused and brainwashed by Mom, just as he had been.
But these first tapes were for himself. They were fun. They probably relieved his depression and could be a rich source of future
blackmail.

On one tape Frances offers Marc gleeful suggestions on how to
torment younger boys at Kent and to enjoy watching their "secret fears" as he causes them to "be churning inside." On another
she giggles about the rats in the walls at EMA and about the "big
thick-lipped nigger pictures" of Larry's graduation that Marc
sent to Granny. One tape makes fun of Behrens and his filthy

apartment furnished with other people's sidewalk discards. Frances imagines "some filthy old bed."

"Oh God! Swarming with cockroaches!" Larry exults. Frances becomes ecstatic. "Some dead man's bed. Full of pee or something. Ugh!"

She brags about coaching Marc to shoot straight. She had said, "It'll be easy as shooting fish in a barrel! Oh, it was done properly —thanks to me . . . I even told Marc the strategy. How to do it. Larry, you have to always go like this. Up—and down."

LARRY: That's the way they do in the movies. The cops.

MOM: You have to!

LARRY: And you hold it with both hands, right?

MOM [patient]: Preferably. And you always go up and down. You never go like *that*—because then you'll miss. Up—then down. 'Cause otherwise the trajectory goes off . . . That's the way you're supposed to do it.

Larry brags about the tapes *he* made of Granny last summer and gave to Mom. "Granny was furious about those tapes . . . She just *hates* the fact that you have those tapes! . . . She has no idea exactly what's on those tapes. We taped her so many times, she doesn't remember."

Frances describes her newest game. "Well, I'm letting her imagination go wild. [Frances has told Berenice that] I've got a whole library of tapes, Granny! Categorized and filed! By date! . . . You know, it's blowing her fucking mind! I've used it as a club over her. Whenever we have a fight, I bring up the tapes. *And that immediately stops her in her tracks!* Oh, it's beautiful! It just *paralyzes* her . . ."

Dropping her voice to a gleeful whisper, Frances hisses, "You know what I did? I . . . let . . . her . . . lie! I was never gonna tell her about the tapes. Then she kept pushing me. This winter. She kept pushing me. My back to the wall. Then I let her lie [let her tell me] *a big bunch of lies!* Then I said, 'That's awful! To lie like that!' She said, 'Yes.' I said [terrible, smiler-with-a-knife hiss]: *'I've got it on tape!'* "

LARRY [laughing]: That must have blown her mind!

MOM: She said, 'What do you mean?' I said, [loud screaming] 'I can't repeat everything you said! How can you say you didn't say it?' I said, [hissing] *'I've got the tapes! You wanna hear yourself, Granny?'* Dead silence. It was like someone hit her over the head! With a club . . . there was, I swear, five minutes of dead silence. She was in shock! Completely stunned. *She did not talk.* Dead silence!

MARC: Pure ecstasy.

Frances's tape fantasy builds, batted back and forth between them like an evil balloon, ever expanding. "I have them in my bank vault!" she croons. "What's she gonna do—blow up the bank? [Chuckling.] This little old seventy-five-year-old lady gonna come in like a mad bomber . . . gonna chop through Madison Avenue and Seventy-second Street, all that cement!" [Wracking, gargling coughing.]

Later the Good Old Schreuder Household congratulates itself on past exploits, taping Granny and Gramps, getting Gramps "all worked up . . . about our going to Harlem . . . the black-ies and the coons . . . he's wild and vicious about it! Then he got Granny all hopped up about it."

MOM: I mean, they had us all set up! Granny doesn't know how we survived during the winter . . . They expected us to go broke at any moment! Well, the fact that we could s-t-r-i-n-g those checks out saved us!"

MARC [childish]: It literally blew . . . her . . . mind. BLAM!

MOM: She couldn't understand why we weren't broke either in May . . . or June . . .

LARRY: How we were still surviving! Yeah, she musta been really scratching the old head.

MOM: A solution a day keeps the doctor away! [Sound of thigh slap, crazy cackling.] The Good Old Schreuder Household and our sense of humor!

MARC: Boy, if it hadn't been for our resources last sum-mer . . .

LARRY: *My* resources!

MOM: *My* resources!

MARC: And mine!

MOM: *And Mommie's brains!*

Twice a year the New York City Ballet sends out thousands of letters inviting a select public to buy seats at benefit prices to its Fall and Spring galas. In the fall of 1978 a "Champagne Gala" was promised, and the house was scaled from $150 a ticket down to $5. In time-honored manner patrons were asked to indicate their preference by marking the appropriate box and enclosing a check, and there was also a box which said, "I am unable to attend, but enclosed is my check in the amount of . . ."

That summer the thrilling Soviet dancer Mikhail Baryshnikov had defected a second time, abandoning his showy perch at the American Ballet Theater for the ensemble environment of George Balanchine's New York City Ballet. The young red Russian and the aging white Russian—each a champion in his field—had never worked together. Baryshnikov had never even been seen by the sophisticated Manhattan ballet audience. Rumor had it that he had been rehearsing the Ruby Cavalier role in Balanchine's *Jewels* and might make his New York City debut on the night of the Gala. The mailing was an instantaneous sellout. It was the hottest ticket in town.

One of the form letters which came back to the ballet office was unusual, indeed unique. The respondent had checked the form in two places and enclosed two checks. One, for $300, reserved a pair of top-price seats. But the sender had also checked "I am unable to attend . . ." and had enclosed a contribution of $2,000. Both checks were signed "Frances Schreuder." Not one of the half dozen people opening the envelopes—some professional fund raisers, some volunteers—had ever heard of her. "So this was interesting," says one, "because between us we know who everybody in New York City is." Buyers sometimes sent in contributions in excess of the ticket price, "but not *six times* in excess! We did some quick eyeballing of old records, and discovered that this person has made some small contributions in the past, but nothing so interesting as a couple of thou."

The new name was added to the master list of major gift prospects, and in due course the prized tickets were mailed out. On the magic night of November 14, 1978, Frances Schreuder was among the crush of spellbound balletomanes who saw the bright figure in pearly tights leap and hang weightless for an instant against the bejeweled sky.

Outside the blazing gilt-and-crystal theater, in the real world of Frances Schreuder, the weather had begun to darken. On November 9, Elaine Drukman had done what her father had refused to do. She had notified the FBI that Frances was a thief, a forger, and an embezzler. She described the theft of her Mountain Fuel stock and charged that either Marc, Larry, or Berenice had "acted under pressure from my sister Frances . . ." She provided the FBI with photographs of each of the suspects and with photocopies of Franklin Bradshaw's stop-payment order to the State Bank of Lehi, and of the eight forged checks. Marilyn Reagan also obtained photocopies of the bum checks, along with a letter from her father acknowledging them as his daughter's handiwork. She turned over her evidence to attorneys Swindle and Anderson, saying that Frances was a crook, and her sisters were determined to prevent the IRS from charging the estate a gift tax on the stolen funds. Together, checks and stocks totaled $50,000.

The split within the Bradshaw family had become a chasm. The following day Berenice Bradshaw, at the firm suggestion of her two older daughters, signed papers acknowledging that her own wants were amply provided for under the marital trust, and formally disclaimed any interest in the family trust. At that point five large Utah law firms were involved in the Bradshaw estate matter. Berenice and her three daughters had each retained separate counsel, in addition to Swindle who represented the estate. The disclaimer was a device to forestall further depredations by Frances, working through her mother. Unless some kind of legal, binding brakes could be applied, it was at least conceivable that Frances might wipe out the entire Family Trust.

That same week in New York, an unkempt school teacher who moved with a crablike, belly-first walk, visited the Empire Savings Bank on West Fifty-seventh Street. Richard Behrens was planning to drop out of teaching for a year of graduate work, he explained, and he arranged a $5,000 student loan, which he agreed to pay back at $58.05 a month over ten years.

Three weeks later Marc came home from Kent on his Christmas vacation. A day or two after that, Larry was back from Lehigh, howling and barking at the apartment door. The weather was unusually cold that year. Larry was "really *begging!*" Marc says, while Frances lay in bed yelling "No! Don't you *dare* open that door!" and Marc ran back and forth between her bedroom and the front door feeling like his old friend Pepe the bellhop. Soon Marc too was begging. If Mom refused to let Larry in, at least she could give him enough money to stay at the YMCA. At length Frances phoned the Y and was told a room would cost $60 a week. She came to the door and counted out $180 for three weeks. No money for food, nothing for Christmas. That was it.

Marc remembers "feeling just so *sorry for* Larry. Him locked out and me enjoying the luxury of the house. Because I'm Mom's pet." But Frances did not seem unduly upset. She walked back to her room, selected a sheet of her pale blue, engraved Tiffany stationery, and climbed into bed. Ariadne was in the bed too, curled up with the family's other pet, a rare red Persian cat with eyes like black opals. The $500 cat had been a present from Frances to Ariadne on her fifth birthday, and the children called him Ginger. Frances had renamed him Tiffany. "More chic, more elegant," she explained. Now Frances uncapped her new gold-and-ivory Tiffany pen and commenced a polite note to the New York City Ballet.

Gentlemen:
I was rather surprised not to receive a personal acknowledgement of my gift of $2,000 . . .

She sealed the envelope. In a corner lay her old ballet shoes. She got out of bed, put on the slippers of faded pink silk trimmed with white lace, and did a few simple movements, a *demi-plie*, a *port de bras.*
"I was meant to be a dancer, Ariadne. But Dad made me give up ballet and go to Bryn Mawr."

At the ballet offices Frances's gentle note of rebuke provoked an embarrassed letter of apology and an invitation to Mrs. Schreuder to please get back in touch if she were at all interested in further involvement. Planning for the Spring Gala was underway, and to attract a wider range of patrons, the benefit committee had decided on a two-tiered ticket-pricing system, which also meant two cocktail parties. It was now becoming apparent that nobody wanted to attend the "Juniors" party. "Hundred-dollar people have no social cachet," one planner explained later. "They just have their hundred bucks. So the problem was—how to market the second party? The one nobody wanted to go to?" The committee had decided to throw in a dinner, and was discussing how to pay for it, when the phone rang. The caller was the mysterious Mrs. Schreuder, effusively thankful for the letter inviting more "involvement," and eager to do something else helpful *right now.*
The one unforgivable error in fund raising is to ask for $10,000

—and get it—from someone who might have been good for $50,000. So the person who took the call suggested lunch a few weeks hence. That would leave time for the necessary financial homework. But Mrs. Schreuder said she wanted to make a commitment right then on the telephone. This had not ever happened before.

"So I'm winging it," the planner said later. "And I take a chance and mention this hundred-dollar-a-person dinner, and how if we only could get somebody to underwrite it, then we could say to people: Every cent of your hundred dollars goes to the Ballet. I tell her all about how the Gala ties in with our challenge grant from the federal government, how someone making this gift would really be doing something very useful and would become involved with a committee. Because it was my sense that this woman, whoever she was, very much wanted some hands-on involvement. And then I say again, can I take her to lunch in a week or two and discuss all this?

"She says two things. One, she thinks the dinner party is a terrific idea, and could she just say right now that she'll pay for it? She doesn't like to discuss money while eating; it doesn't do much for good food. At lunch we can talk about what she really likes to talk about, which is ballet. Two, she says, 'I don't mean to be rude, but I have an account at the Côte Basque, so would you be offended if I took *you* to lunch?' "

The planner hung up feeling slightly dizzy. "I mean—this is the fund-raising coup of the year around there! People don't normally call you up and pledge $10,000 to $15,000 out of the blue. You're meant to *work* for it!"

The notion that the great artist requires a great patron has been around since the Pharaohs. That the born patron also needs an artist to patronize is a less-studied phenomenon. Frances Schreuder would turn out to be a born patron—selfless, unequivocal in her enthusiasm, bottomless in her resources. The artist whom she chose to receive her bounty had not the slightest idea who she was. It was the ideal artist-patron relationship.

Frances Schreuder would become George Balanchine's last patron at a critical moment in his history as well as in her own, and also in the history of cultural philanthropy in the United States. Unknown to all but a very few intimates, by 1978 the great choreographer had begun to suffer severe angina attacks. The following year he would require triple heart bypass surgery. His disability was especially crippling for an artist who worked the way he did, "making" his ballets directly on his dancers, like a sculptor working in clay or Bach tempering his clavichord. He did not tell them what to do. He took them behind the closed doors of a mirrored rehearsal hall and moved their bodies around, indicating all the lifts himself, dancing all the parts, making every tiny adjustment until he found the effects he wanted. It was incredibly strenuous physical labor, especially for a man of seventy-four.

The secret of his infirmity had to be closely guarded within the Company, as well as from the public. "Ballet *is* woman," Balanchine had often said, and he had loved ballet with fierce and singular ardor since 1914 when he was a ten-year-old boy dancing in *The Nutcracker* in St. Petersburg. He had married five times, to five dazzling ballerinas—Geva, Danilova, Zorina, Tallchief, LeClercq. He loved ballet still, with undiminished passion, and it is not an exaggeration to say that his ballet company was *en masse* in love with "Mr. B." He was the genius they served, their only beloved master. He was their father, their unattainable lover, their *beau idéal*. Word of his infirmity would devastate Company morale.

Another of Balanchine's famous Delphic remarks, to a too eager stage mother, was: *"La Danse, Madame, c'est une question morale."* To him, hence to them all, the ensemble mode was a moral imperative. Famous soloists and lowly chorus dancers practiced daily together at the *barre* in humble pursuit of the perfectly unnatural technique their art required. Balanchine himself had taught daily class for thirty years. In such a sublimated atmosphere—part training gym, part temple—the notion of individual star dancers, in the manner of opera divas, would be not merely vulgar but immoral. That is why the names of soloists, even Baryshnikov, were never announced beforehand. But nature abhors a vacuum, and human nature seems to demand superstars —in ballet no less than in football. So an ironic situation had evolved wherein, more than any of his soloists, the choreographer himself had become his company's biggest star. His brilliance was legend, his work celebrated, his elegant form and White Rabbit face known worldwide, and his firm, glowing presence in the NYCB driver's seat was the major reason for his company's stunning artistic and box-office success.

Until quite recently dance in America was the ragged Cinderella of the arts. The Puritans thought dancing lewd, the Devil's business, and this heritage had lingered. Terpsichore was condemned to the chimney corner, and there she languished until the early 1930s, when Lincoln Kirstein, founding father of the New York City Ballet, stole Balanchine from Europe in the manner of Prometheus stealing fire.

In the next half century, a dance revolution occurred. Due chiefly to Balanchine's work, both as a teacher and choreographer, due to his remarkable range of styles, his superb musicality, and the sheer abundance of his creative output, an artificial style of dance confected for eighteenth-century kings evolved into a popular American art form. Today this nation has nearly 1,000 professional ballet companies, at least 10,000 trained professional dancers, and unknown millions of ardent, knowing fans—an astonishing development for what until recently had been considered manna for aesthetes only, the quiche of the performing arts.

By the time Frances Schreuder appeared on the scene in 1979, George Balanchine was nearly seventy-five, and Lincoln Kirstein was seventy-three. But both men were still very much in charge. The reclusive, patrician, and mercurial Kirstein, a tall, shaven-headed man, once greatly handsome and still impeccably austere, still invariably dressed in black, listed himself as NYCB's general administrator. The title is deceptive. He was always the shadowy *éminence noir* behind the whole show. Kirstein's wealth derives from a family fortune in department stores. His distinction derives from the often subtle, sometimes outrageous way he has utilized wealth and power to encourage whatever is finest among arts and artists. Kirstein has spent his life as a sort of invisible Lone Ranger of the arts, riding out in defense of culture and in search of the gold to support it against the Yahoos and Philistines. His most stunning accomplishment among many was to recognize the genius of Balanchine and offer it ideal conditions in which to grow and flower. Kirstein, like Balanchine, knew that a first-class ballet company could not exist without a first-class ballet school to carry on the old traditions and assure a steady supply of properly trained young dancers for the performing company. In czarist Russia, the Imperial Ballet School had been a national service academy, comparable to Annapolis or West Point. In 1934 Balanchine and Kirstein cofounded the School of American Ballet, today chartered under the Juilliard School of Music and presided over by Kirstein still.

As always, the difference between revenue and expenses of

both the School and the Company had to be made up by private contributions, and Kirstein himself had always served as chief benefactor, fund raiser, and one-man bail-out squad. NYCB was mostly "in Lincoln's pocket"; and when, as frequently happened, emergency financial help was needed, Kirstein rang up one of his famous "LLL's"—Lincoln's little ladies—rich women cultivated by the master patron over decades. Only in 1963, three years before the company moved from the grunge of Mecca Temple, the old Masonic hall on West Fifty-fifth Street, to the glitter of just-built Lincoln Center (which, it should perhaps be made clear, was named for *Abraham)* did Kirstein at last persuade the mighty Ford Foundation that a ballet company was as worthy an object of corporate philanthropy as an opera company, say, or a symphony orchestra. In that watershed year, the big automotive foundation, spurred by W. McNeil Lowry, Ford's vice president for the humanities and the arts, gave NYCB over $6 million.

The Sugarplum Fairy herself could have made no grander gesture. But eventually Ford would turn its fickle head, and new pockets would have to be found. Enter Uncle Sam. By 1977 the National Endowment for the Arts had set up a system of challenge grants known as "three-to-one matching grants." The arts institution must raise $3 million in "new funds" in order to get $1 million of taxpayer money. The first wave of grants went to established, high-profile institutions—the New York Philharmonic, the Metropolitan Museum of Art. Kirstein, once more riding to the rescue, obtained a challenge grant for NYCB. The point of specifying "new funds" was to democratize philanthropy, to reach out to thousands of unknown, anonymous pockets way beyond those of Kirstein, Ford, and the LLL's. It is a safe bet, however, that whoever thought up this good idea, "new pockets," did not envision the dark and fathomless pit that was the pocket of Frances Schreuder.

Like many arts groups, NYCB had been somewhat slapdash in the conduct of its fiscal affairs. Only in 1977 did Kirstein and Randal R. Craft, Jr., the gracious, successful, arts-minded Wall Street lawyer who serves NYCB as general counsel, get around to incorporating NYCB as a tax-exempt charitable organization and forming a real board of directors. A professional development office was set up and assigned specific goals. One of these was to double the revenues from "special events" such as the Spring and Fall galas. Like the other business objectives Craft laid out, this has been accomplished with spectacular success. The Company has stayed in the black for the past seven years—a remarkable record for an arts organization—during which time its annual budget has risen from $10 million to $17 million.

One of the tinier slipups along the way had been the failure to do the routine acknowledgment on Frances Schreuder's major gift. "Frankly," a knowledgeable person admits, "nobody was terribly interested in doing it. People are not on the boards of ballet organizations for altruistic purposes. You get a check from Walter Annenberg, and you can find plenty of people who want to have lunch with Walter Annenberg. They want to have lunch with . . . er . . . Grant Tinker. They even want to have lunch with Jerry Zipkin. But they don't want to have lunch with somebody they've never heard of, or somebody they cannot connect with a lot of money, or with the Jet Set, or with social cachet, or the Fortune 500 list."

After the Côte Basque lunch, people in the NYCB offices were eager to hear what the hot prospect was like. "Fun to be with," they were told, and "a passionate balletomane" who "looked sort of like Lily Tomlin." In truth the woman had seemed a bit eccentric, "but eccentricity is the norm around that place. Normal people are the exceptions. So she didn't really stand out at all. In some respects Frances was more than eccentric; she was weird. But everyone we dealt with was in different ways weird. None of them was weird like Frances, but I never met anyone who was exactly like Lincoln Kirstein either.

"Craziness does not stand out around here. Whoever met anybody like John Samuels?" Samuels is the Gatsby-like financier who until recently was chairman of the entire Lincoln Center complex. "The rich are not the same as everyone else. There are things they can get away with doing in public that others simply can't. So sure Frances was confused at times. Pretty spacy. Vague. No eye contact. Didn't complete her sentences. We thought maybe she was taking drugs. Her hands and head trembled. I thought maybe Parkinsonism. But I'd seen other society women the same way and other business people. And persons in the entertainment business."

The mysterious Mrs. Schreuder was intelligent, seemed generally knowledgeable about ballet, and was clearly well educated, though there were surprising lacunae in her awareness. She talked about the many things she wanted to do for "Mr.

Balanchyne," which she mispronounced to rhyme with "shoe shine." Normally it is pronounced to rhyme with "smithereen," though the name is in fact a Frenchification, acquired during his Paris-London-Diaghilev period, of the choreographer's true Georgian name, Balanchivadze.

Mrs. Schreuder mentioned Bryn Mawr and her life in Europe. She spoke good French. A staff member drove over to York Avenue to inspect the return address on her letter, and "it looked okay." A lawyer friend of NYCB put her name through LEXIS, a legal computer search. Nothing turned up. When the name Bradshaw appeared on one of her checks, she murmured something about being a distant cousin of Arco's and later RCA's president Thornton W. Bradshaw, and she let it be known that she expected soon to come into some family money herself. Through her father, she said, and said no more. But if Mrs. Schreuder was close-mouthed about her private life, so were many ballet patrons. The New York City Ballet was much newer than some of the other not-for-profit performing arts organizations which shared space at Lincoln Center—the Metropolitan Opera, for example. The money behind NYCB was *mostly* new money. *Nobody* knew where it came from; nobody cared. The NYCB board's current president, Gillian Attfield, a British-born woman from Binghamton, New York, is entirely unknown outside of ballet circles, invisible on the Manhattan social horizon, unlisted in Who's Who. Many people think her money comes from mortuaries. It does not, but the point is that it comes in to NYCB at about $75,000 annually, and always has, and in an emergency Mrs. Attfield always seems able to write a check for any amount.

By May Frances was invited to visit the company's offices in the New York State Theater and to meet some of the people who were really running things. She had by then made good on her first $15,000 pledge, for the dinner party, and was beginning to be talked about as a "Live One." People were curious about her. Frances did not stay long that first day. In a soft, timid voice she apologized for her raddled appearance, her tremors, and grimaces, explaining that she was still suffering the effects of a dreadful Christmas accident on the Triboro Bridge in which several people had been killed.

As soon as she left, one person present was "overwhelmed with the feeling: We have just had a conversation with madness. She had those wild eyes; she had the *intensity* of a lunatic." But no one else had seemed to notice.

Overall, Frances Schreuder was making a favorable impression, particularly among other so-called Live Ones. "You must remember that most ballet patrons are either socialites or businessmen," explains an observer of Frances's progress. "Neither group knows anything about how artists or creative people function. So this Mrs. Schreuder—who just wanted to give money and to talk about ballet—she was *refreshing*. So what if her fine tuning was off? So what if she pronounced it "Balanchyne"? At least she wanted to talk about ballet, and she would go to see the ballet, and she would discuss the performance last night."

In short Frances was intensely interested in what fund raisers call "The Product." Some other patrons often seemed not to care. "If you'd sit down and talk to most of those ladies on the Board about what the performance should be at the next Gala, they'd tell you the performance should be very short. Because a lot of husbands are going to be dragged there by their wives."

Belgian-born Oleg Briansky, a former NYCB dancer who with his dancer wife, Mireille, now operates the excellent Briansky Ballet School, is a seasoned, sophisticated observer of the ballet world. Although he did not meet Frances until later in the game, he read her exceptionally well. "I don't know how much Mrs. Schreuder really knew about ballet," he says. "But she had a very uncanny sense of . . . of how to *get to* people. She knew what people wanted. She . . . felt people's needs. She had sort of x-ray eyes, and could gauge a person, sense what that person hungered for, and then—*move in on them!* Feed their needs, out of this uncanny knowledge she had.

"I've seen how good the woman was at it. She always had a strategy. She approached only people in the top positions. And then somehow—I mean, you cannot say that the woman was charming. Not beautiful. Not a seductive person at all. Yet through her compulsive, constant talk, and keen sense of observation of *other people's insecurities*—she was able to get to them.

"The world of art—not just of the ballet, but all art—tends to attract unstable people. It is a world which tolerates eccentricity. And it is a world always in need of money, and usually crazily financed. I mean: The New York City Ballet has been in existence forty-odd years, it is the greatest dance company in the world, and it still has no permanent subsidy! They still don't know, at the end of each year, how they will come out.

"So this very pushy woman, who is pushing her way to *give them money,* who starts trying to push Mr. B into restaging a *Sleeping Beauty*—which has got to cost a million dollars—they don't think of her as an eccentric. You must remember: the New York City Ballet has more than one hundred dancers, an extraordinary payroll. Mrs. Schreuder gave them money, and asked nothing in return. To them the money was God-sent. It was not from a crazy lady. It was from a Good Fairy named Frances Schreuder!"

But Briansky was an outside observer. Inside NYCB, they were mostly mesmerized. After the Live One's first visit to the back-stage offices, one senior staff person did take a few key people aside. "If we have anything to do with this woman," he warned, "I promise you it will mean more trouble around here than she could possibly be worth." He might just as well have said the Emperor wore no clothes. No one paid any attention. In hindsight, it is not hard to understand. Some primal link has always appeared to join Dionysus and Apollo—the madman and the artist. Extreme individualism is valued throughout the art world. And the phantasmagoric world of ballet in particular has always been a magnet to the mad, and a kind of haven.

"Over the years, George had experiences many times with strange people," says a close friend. "*Many* oddballs felt a special kinship to him." Love letters to Balanchine arrived regularly at the NYCB offices from men and women around the world. From time to time mental hospitals telephoned Company headquarters to inquire about a patient claiming to be a wife or daughter of the choreographer. Other claimants sometimes approached Mr. B on the street, asking for money. A top NYCB executive, "always afraid something awful was going to happen," began quietly to keep a file on such people. Nothing serious did happen, but at the time of the choreographer's retirement, the file contained records of forty bizarre episodes of one type or another.

"Frances was not at all alone in this regard," the executive is quick to point out. "Certain people *attract* nuts. George was one of them. An awful lot of people incorporated George Balanchine into their fantasy lives. It's a special kind of charisma people like him have. The Kennedys had it. It's what Hinckley felt about Jodie Foster. George was *loaded* with it!"

There was another factor. Balanchine himself, though not in the least mad, was emotionally fluid. His feelings lay very close to the surface. He was easily moved—not just by music or painting, but also by bravery, nobility, or human suffering. He once sought to give the opening night receipts to aid Italian earthquake victims he had just seen on television. Another time he wanted to use NYCB benefit money to buy bullet-proof vests for Central Park policemen. Like most creative persons, he was extraordinarily open to experience. He did not wear commonplace armor *against feeling.* Whenever a friend, trying to shield him from the attentions of some of his more obviously unbalanced admirers, would suggest, "Why do you waste energy on so-and-so? Don't you realize he's crazy?" Balanchine's answer was the same.

"How do you know he's crazy? Maybe he's the sane one and you're crazy!"

Another close friend says, "There was always something about George that was slightly mad. He always defended the mad. And he was always himself afraid of madness."

But his friend Rouben Ter-Arutunian, the stage designer, and one of the few who could converse with Balanchine in Russian, the only language in which the master was entirely comfortable, disagrees. "Balanchine was supremely practical and logical, a man who all his life was drawn to harmony, to beauty—never toward disharmony, disorder, or aberration."

Nonetheless, more so than the bookworm or the music lover, the opera buff or the sports nut, the balletomane has elected to inhabit an ultimate fantasy world. At its center, spinning in a white-hot spotlight, drilling holes in the floor with diamond-hard toes, is a perfect female figure of matchless grace and electric intensity who is also in perfect balance. The male figure is equally fantastic: an impossible amalgam of weightlessness and strength, control and flight.

The backstage ballet world is also a very *family-like* environment; its emotional compass can swing wildly between fury and love. This potential was intensified at the New York City Ballet, where George Balanchine had become a kind of fantasy father-figure for all the women attached to the Company which he had fathered and now led. He himself loved women. He especially loved daughter-figures. He fell in love with, and five times married, only women younger than himself. More than Picasso, assuredly more than Stravinsky—the two other artistic geniuses to whom he is most frequently compared—Balanchine was the greatest daughter-lover of the era. Fantasy is a two-way looking glass, and more than anyone else whom we can bring to mind, George Balanchine devoted his life to the romanticizing, celebration, and apotheosis of the eroticized female child.

The new found Mrs. Schreuder seemed to development people not just eccentric but highly skittish. They did not want to risk scaring her off. So they swiftly came to see her as "a woman who values her privacy intensely," and to admire her for her extreme reticence in certain areas. "Frankly, I found this aspect of her odd personality delectable," says one. "She was so unlike the usual publicity hounds. I mean: somebody brings Aldo Gucci in here, and for $25,000 he wants his name on *everything*. In contrast, here was a woman eager to give us money who, from the start, has only one stipulation: She wants 'no publicity whatsoever of any kind.' Having dealt with some people on our Board who are obsessed with dropping names and dollar signs on you, and flashing rocks at you, I found someone who only wanted to have lunch at La Côte Basque and talk ballet utterly charming. Get the picture? A bunch of us around here *loved* Frances!"

Those people who recognized Frances's value as a "Live One" struggled to win for her the kind of hands-on involvement they sensed she wanted. They encouraged her to attend planning meetings for the Fall Gala dinner party she had agreed to pay for. She did not show up. Again they thought she was shy. "But she is doing odd things, the most memorable of which is—she decides we have to serve a 'really great dessert!'" one of her admirers recalls. Should it be a superb chocolate cake, or the Côte Basque's very special strawberry tarts? Frances discussed the matter interminably, yet she did not want to make so critical a decision herself. One Friday a uniformed messenger arrived at the stage door with a $25 Côte Basque chocolate cake in one hand, a box of strawberry tarts in the other, and a note suggesting that people take them home to taste over the weekend.

A Board member with professional connections in the catering world pointed out that identical cakes are available wholesale for $12.50. "Yes, but this woman wants to become *involved*," the others explained. "She *wants* to call the chef herself. She wants to order the cakes for 150 people herself. She does not *want* a bargain!"

The weird part was that Frances already was paying for the dinner, and a budget had been set. "So why is she also giving us $500 or $600 worth of cakes?" On the other hand many patronesses seemed to the staff chiefly to complain, and this one was sending over desserts to taste.

As Frances moved into a new and different world, a new and different personality—a second Frances—seemed to emerge. The ballet's "Live One" was the apparent antithesis of Bryn Mawr's bad, bold Frankie Bradshaw: she was never raucous, disobedient, angry. She was gracious, mannerly, thoughtful, reserved. The one uninhibited thing about her was her generosity. Instead of an enraged baby in a state of perpetual tantrum, most ballet people in those early days saw Mrs. Schreuder as an eccentric but extraordinarily selfless lover of the arts.

All that separated Frances's two worlds was the great damask curtain pleated in golden swags. Frances had the ability to move back and forth on either side of the curtain as readily as a dancer moving downstage to take a bow. Behind the curtain, in the magic land of ballet, the former Frankie Bradshaw had at last found a world in which she was comfortable, a place where she could be accepted, could dream her own dreams, and—soon—could exercise her passion for control. She fit in because, to many people in the ballet world, emotional disorder simply did not matter. Only the bankbook was required to be in balance. Naked social climbing did not matter either. Says one staffer, "An arts institution is *therapy* for climbers. Who cares why some people invent a new section of the Jet Set just so they can be *in it?* This is America!"

What did matter, especially within the development office, was to get some advance notice of what new ballets the choreographer was thinking of making for next season, so that they had some idea of how much money would be needed. Such information was almost impossible to come by. A seasoned fund raiser, not at NYCB, explains the difficulty: "You have a rational assignment. You are being paid a salary to raise money. Effectively, logically, without offending anybody. But in your job you are surrounded by artists, people whose creative process is in no way rational. You wake up, you have this idea for a ballet, and you go into a rehearsal room, and you make this ballet on people. You're not being rational, you're being creative. Fine. But because of that, there is no particular respect among artists for rationality. Why

should there be? So the development office is always considered a
sort of step-child by these people."

At NYCB this problem was especially severe because the people in charge were "still the first generation of leadership, the
founding fathers, and mothers. Not just Balanchine and Kirstein,
but all the top staff people were first generation. They'd all been
there thirty years, and the development office had been around
only two or three years. So you did not have a lot of respect for
the development office." And this generation gap, between Old
Guard and Young Turks, only tended to exacerbate the familylike
quarrels, the vacillations between fury and love.

In Frances's real family, on the other side of the great golden
curtain, similar vacillations proliferated. In January 1979, the
same week Frances had received the NYCB's belated letter of
apology and thanks, Berenice had arrived back in New York
from the round-the-world cruise she took to recover her equilibrium after the shock of what she called her husband's "death"—
Berenice Bradshaw does not use the word "murder."

Frances was waiting on the dock. She told Berenice that her
sisters had been trying to "blackmail" her for her sons' thievery
the summer before; that Marilyn had denounced her to the executors; and that Elaine had actually called in the FBI. These low-
down tactics were further straining Frances's precarious health,
she added, and she intended to petition the estate to raise her
monthly allowance from $3,000 to $5,000 to cover her new medical bills.

She invited Berenice to spend a few nights at 1675 York Avenue. Ariadne's room was available; the child still slept with her
mother. The rent on the three-bedroom apartment had recently
been raised from $1,000 to $1,200 a month, and in the five-and-a-
half years the Schreuders had occupied it, the place had become
dingy and hopelessly cluttered. After Berenice had spent a couple
of uncomfortable nights on the small child's bed, Frances suggested they take a little walk. She wanted to show her mother a
"fabulous investment."

1675 York Avenue is not a chic address, merely East Side rich.
It is faced with beige brick and has a curving carriageway entrance, lots of pretty flower beds, and uniformed doormen. A few
blocks to the northeast lies Gracie Square, a serene, two-hun-
dred-year-old enclave of old New York money at the quiet dead

end of East Eighty-fourth Street overlooking the East River. To
the north is Carl Schurz Park and Gracie Mansion, the mayor's
residence. To the south stands a fortress-like, triple-towered
apartment house known as 10 Gracie Square, a landmark building of immense grandeur and respectability, cooperatively owned
by its distinguished tenants. Apartment 6, in Building III—the
"fabulous investment" Frances brought Berenice to see—is a
fourteen-room duplex apartment with a two-story living room,
several woodburning fireplaces, and staggering views of the East
River. But the apartment itself was in terrible shape and could be
bought for a mere $525,000. Another half million or so would be
necessary for refurbishing and repairs. Berenice glanced around
at the peeling paint, scarred parquet, crumbling plaster, rusting
plumbing, and said nothing. She returned to Salt Lake City for
some necessary bladder surgery.

The ballet's spring season was on, and Frances rarely missed a
performance. The word was out on the newest Live One, and
board members and assorted LLL's went out of their way during
intermissions to greet and chat with Mrs. Schreuder. Some were
put off by her mispronunciation of "Balanchyne," others by her
physical appearance. She reminded one woman of *Gone with the
Wind*. "She was like Tara—completely neglected. She was too
fat. Her clothes appeared . . . scuffed, and her white mink
looked secondhand."

Most of them noticed her handbag, which invariably was
stuffed with hundred-dollar bills. One lady bountiful observed,
"A woman who was really brought up with money wouldn't
wear a long white dress with black shoes and an old bag."

"Maybe so," said her husband, "but you don't argue with the
color green."

Not surprisingly this was the view that prevailed, and Mrs.
Schreuder was next invited to join the Ballet Guild, an organization which encourages middle-level givers. She began showing up
regularly at Guild fund raisers, parties, and lectures on ballet
history. Often her comments were informed, occasionally rambling. Her appearance at the Galas was never quite right: her hair
was overdone, and she wore 1950s-style strapless gowns which
made her look dowdy, older than her forty-one years, the very
opposite of fashionable women like Bianca Jagger, John Samuels'
frequent companion on Gala nights. But as time passed,

Frances's appearance improved; she began to slim down and smarten up. More importantly her pledges were invariably generous and invariably lived up to—not always the case in those days with other bigtime pledgers. Best, Frances was that rarest kind of Live One who did not want anything in return for her generosity. "You'd ask her for money, and she'd say okay," one person recalls. "Not okay if I can be chairman of the event. Not okay if I can get my name on the program. Not okay if I can sit next to Suzanne Farrell. I mean, she was about the finest prospect I'd ever seen in my entire professional career."

Kirstein himself characterized Frances Schreuder as "an extremely intelligent and generous woman . . . as highly strung as a creative artist, [who] therefore . . . understands the creative process as few people can or do."

What did Mrs. Schreuder really want? What was driving her? Some thought she wanted only to become NYCB's new Fairy Godmother. Others disagreed. An arts patron and lawyer of much experience along the city's philanthropic byways feels certain that "Frances Schreuder was very much a social climber, and she knew precisely what she was doing when she alit on the New York City Ballet. I'm not saying she may not have been flaky in some areas. She did not have the slightest idea of the impression she made on other people, for example. But as a social climber, she knew exactly where she was going—she was going to get on that Board."

This observer, a man who views himself not incorrectly as an anthropologist among New York's culture savages, came to know Frances Schreuder rather well. She had very carefully surveyed New York City's cultural landscape, he says, "and she figured the NYCB Board was the most prestigious thing she could get near. It offered her the greatest opportunity for advancement *because* it was a weak Board, *because* it was not well organized. In a sense this made the ballet's Board militarily indefensible.

"Mounting such an assault was plausible there," our anthropologist says. "It wouldn't have been possible at the Met. Frances could be accepted at the ballet more readily than at other places because the place is *used to* odd behavior. I mean: the resident genius-in-charge was George Balanchine, not a man who behaves like Tony Bliss. Furthermore some of the people on that Board could be described as 'avid to fund-raise.' Getting money from

Frances Schreuder was a quick and sure way to enhance one's own position among one's fellow Board members."

People who met Frances during this period tend to remember the encounters with extreme clarity. An elderly banker-balleto-mane can recall five distinct occasions, the first at a small black-tie dinner at the home of a Board member. "She tried to pick me up!" he says. "I don't mean she said—'let's go to bed.' What she said to me, quite loudly, in the middle of dinner, so that everyone could hear, including my wife and the butler, was, 'Let's get out of here and go listen to Bobby Short.' "

Other similarly awkward encounters ensued. The last this couple heard from Frances was a telephone call at 1:30 A.M. "She kept apologizing for awakening us and said she knew it was inappropriate, but she insisted that somebody on the Board was following her."

Frances not only spoke of her fear of being followed, she said her telephone was tapped and her building under surveillance. She described a close brush with death at lunch. Five minutes after she and her guest that day left the restaurant, the woman's husband—a noted gun collector—had turned up looking for her.

Not all Mrs. Schreuder's social encounters with Board members were sinister. She could be a very animated and amusing conversationalist, and she sometimes projected an intense, exotic sexuality. New York is full of fashionable women, another lawyer says. "After a while, they all look the same. Frances was a true original. I found her fascinating."

A Ballet Guild party was held at the Carlyle Hotel. Frances and her escort grew raucous enough to drown out the entertainment. When a patroness tried discreetly to hush them, Frances huffed loudly that she was a close personal friend of Lincoln Kirstein. The next day the woman checked. Kirstein said he had never heard of her. In truth the entire inner circle knew about Frances by now, and it was becoming apparent that her dinner-party money was just the tip of a green iceberg.

The financial details of each new ballet mounted by NYCB are complex, arcane, and jealously guarded; it would scarcely do for some givers to know what other givers are, and are not, giving. But some financial facts are available regarding Frances's first really big benefaction, which was not to a new ballet but a new book. This was a mammoth *catalogue raisoné* entitled *Choreography by George Balanchine*, to be published by a not-for-profit foundation. Mrs. Schreuder was first approached about it during the spring or summer of 1979. In time she received a lofty letter from Winthrop Knowlton—then president of the NYCB Board, as well as president and CEO of Harper & Row—inviting her to contribute to the $75,000 estimated cost.

"Providing the basic information in concentrated form, the book will illuminate Balanchine's growth and adumbrate his career and influence by outlining in factual form the essential details of place, occasion, and personnel which, while emanating principally from America for the past forty years, remain directly connected with the beginnings and first triumphs in St. Petersburg, Paris and London," Knowlton wrote. His letter continued in like vein for three single-spaced pages, eventually coming out with it: what Köchel did for Mozart, what Gesellschaft did for Bach, Frances Schreuder was hereby invited to help make possible for the man whom her new friends placed alongside Picasso and Stravinsky as one of the three surpassingly artistic geniuses of the twentieth century.

Did Frances come through? Does a duck take to water? When finally published, in 1983, the huge book weighed nine pounds, sold for $75 a copy, and had cost $420,000 to produce. $105,000 of this came from earned income, and the remaining $315,000 came from individual contributors, who are thanked in the book by name. It is heady company. In a single bound, plain Frankie Bradshaw of Gilmer Drive had vaulted onto a list which includes Mr. and Mrs. Sid Bass of Fort Worth, Texas; the Lila and DeWitt Wallace Foundation; the Eugenia and Henri Doll Foundation (a Schlumberger family fund); the Lassalle Fund (a Julius Rosenwald family fund) and the Ford Foundation. Unstated, but not unknown in backstage and boardroom circles, was that an impressive 65 percent of the grand total of $315,000 came from Frances—in reality, of course, from Berenice. Mother and daughter had ponied up $150,000 in cash for this heady endeavor, as compared to the paltry $25,000 kicked in by the Ford Foundation. Poor Franklin must have been doing entrechats in his grave.

At around this time Frances began telling people she had been invited to join the Board. She had not—yet—but maybe she thought she had. Maybe, even, she had been told she had. Others, later, have suggested such may have been the case. Many odd things were occurring. Frances had taken to phoning Board members late at night, talking lengthily about her late husband, a "wealthy Belgian diplomat," and promising large gifts. The gifts came through. In the outside, nonballet world, Frances paid bills late or not at all. But as the ballet's fairy godmother, no pledge was unredeemed, and no check ever bounced.

At this time, too, she began to speak guardedly of a personal friendship with Mr. B, and to mention occasional private dinners. This was obvious fantasy, palpable falsehood. Offstage, Balanchine saw only artists, Russians, and other dancers. But no one much minded what she said. The green river washed other considerations away.

What seems to have happened when Frances Schreuder careened into the New York City Ballet was that she was misperceived by almost everybody. The only ones who had an accurate fix on her were those who were strictly after her money, who saw her as a Live One and didn't care about anything else; people who found her "selfless generosity" not addled, or calculated, simply "refreshing"; people who saw her as the all-time golden goose, source of unlimited golden eggs.

The misperception led them to see her not only as a Live One but as a reasonably sane one. This impression was perhaps strengthened by Kirstein's personal attentions, which were real. He invited her to lunch. He invited her to dinner. So did W. McNeil Lowry and his wife, and one or two of the others. Kirstein occasionally accompanied her to Ballet social functions. He may have misperceived her madness as the divine madness of the artist, rather than the mundane madness of the streets. Or he may just have seen her as newest and potentially most bountiful in a long line of LLL's.

Who knows precisely what Kirstein saw? He hesitated to speak about Mrs. Schreuder at all, he told one journalist, "as I have seen so many recent examples of devilish malice magnetized on her, that one's notion of the world's justice is only reinforced. No one can trust anyone; as Oscar Wilde said when he got out of gaol, one has no friends, only lovers."

Kirstein's quixotic moods are well known. In the words of one respected ballet authority, a man of rigorous scrupulosity: "You must remember, Lincoln speaks the truth when he's at his lowest ebb. His bad spells often occur on his birthday. He had one at age seventy, another at seventy-five. He's quite pulled together right now. You can't believe a word he says."

One of the few who did not misperceive Frances was George

Balanchine; he scarcely saw her at all. "Who was *that?*" he had been heard to mutter, in Russian, when the big jack-o'-lantern grin beamed out at the great choreographer as he hurried along a backstage corridor like the White Rabbit: *I'm late! I'm late!*

In the real world outside the theater, Frances's strange association with Richard Behrens continued. On April 18, 1979, the two old friends appeared at the East End Avenue branch of the Chase Manhattan Bank, N.A., and opened joint checking account #030-1-050738. Their initial deposit was $4,100. Of this, Frances contributed $400 and Behrens $3,700, all that remained of his $5,000 loan. He wished to conceal his assets in a joint account, he later explained, because he had by then accumulated $6,000 in scofflaw parking tickets and feared the city might seek a judgment against him. In April, Frances withdrew $1,200 from their account, in May another $1,500, and another $1,200 in June. By October, the balance on hand was $14.70.

Frances was moving into a new world of culture and beauty. Expenses were rising. By June her request to her father's estate to raise her monthly allowance to $5,000 was granted. But her most important and creative financial stroke that spring was to persuade her mother to transfer all of her assets out of Salt Lake City and put them into New York's Morgan Guaranty bank. It probably was not difficult for Frances to convince Berenice that her wealth was in better, even safer financial hands in New York than in Bradshaw-dominated Salt Lake City. Here in the East it would receive sophisticated management from Morgan Guaranty's elegant Mr. Goodfellow, "a Jew not a Mormon," Frances pointed out, and it would be watched over by the bank's lawyers, Rogers & Wells, headed by former Secretary of State William Rogers. Once the money moved East, Berenice's and Frances's affairs would be looked after by the same institutions. And, if the Ballet wanted to check on whether Frances was good for the increasingly large donations she was pledging, likely a discreet peek could be arranged.

Marc was now a senior at Kent School, and his fortunes too had begun to vacillate. William Hart Perry, the muscular, gray-haired new dean of students, formerly the crew coach, thought Marc Schreuder was "brilliant," particularly at any academic subject or sport or pastime which required a sense of strategy and tactics. His history teacher, Theodore F. Morse, thought Marc

was "possibly the brightest history student Kent has ever had."
Another teacher called him "frighteningly smart," and admired
his ability and willingness to challenge teachers in their own
fields. He took many Advanced Placement courses and won high
marks in Latin, Constitutional Law, Math, Asian Studies, and
Chemistry. His only real problem was with a class called "Theol-
ogy and Ethics." He could never score higher than a D. He did
not really seem to grasp what the class was about.

But Marc's personal habits were atrocious. He stank, he didn't
bathe, he never had his shirttail tucked in for more than ten
minutes, and his table manners were nonexistent. He never went
to bed on time. He liked to study past curfew, until 3 or 4 A.M.,
which repeatedly made him sleep through breakfast and morning
classes and earned him a great many demerits.

His mother's one- and even two-hour phone calls to her son
were legend. Marc talked to her from the pay phone outside the
administration offices, and everyone could hear him arguing,
screaming, sometimes shouting, *"Go to hell!"*

"What goes with you and your mother?" Dean Perry once
asked.

"Oh, we just don't get along," the lad replied. But the phone
calls became so abusive, the counseling office began to keep a file.
Their records show that on May 21, 1977, Marc was overheard
talking "with elation" to his mother on the pay phone and
"whooping with delight" at the news that his grandfather had
cancer.

The school had been aware from the start of Frances's eccen-
tricities but chose, like the Ballet people, to overlook them. The
day the Schreuders visited and Marc was accepted, a counselor
had written in his file, "The mother is sometimes in another
world. She feels Marc may be the next Einstein."

Frances had told the office that Marc's bill would be paid by
his grandfather. He was "senile," she said, adding, "I will soon be
in a position to make a substantial contribution to Kent's endowment fund."

By his third year, Marc was sleeping through many classes and
had piled up hundreds of hours of demerits. He had few friends,
and was often taunted by the other boys. Says Dean Perry, "He
looked like a pigpen, but it was hard to stay angry with Marc
very long, because he was so much like a misbehaving puppy."
But the puppy was turning into a very difficult dog.

By the time Granny got her money transferred East, her grandson's prep school graduation had come and gone. Marc did not take part. On the other hand, neither did he go to jail. One moonlit night in May, Marc and another student had broken into the school store and made off with assorted stationery supplies, sneakers, "cute little Parker pens," and about fifty dollars in cash. They got away with it. To relax after taking a math makeup exam, which brought up his precollege grade to A—, Marc broke in again, alone this time, and was again undetected. Then, unable to sleep the night before he was to return home to Frances, he was strolling the campus at 1 A.M. and was again near the school store when a vice-principal encountered him there and "chewed me out for lurking."

Later that night Marc's room was shaken down. Loot worth $730 was discovered, as well as a set of duplicate keys to every door on campus. Marc named the other boy, his partner on the original raid, but this did not save Marc from prosecution. Frances tried unsuccessfully to keep the story out of the local papers. The school was furious at the flouting of its Christian ideals, and removed Marc's picture from the senior yearbook. Ultimately Marc was permitted to make restitution of the stolen school property, plead guilty to breach of the peace, a Class C misdemeanor, and pay a fifty-dollar fine. Still only eighteen years old, he also was able to have the matter expunged from his criminal record under Connecticut's liberal-minded Young Offenders Statute. Kent School was not as forgiving. Although the miscreant had fulfilled his academic requirements, Kent embargoed his records for a year and, by refusing to forward a transcript to any college, effectively enforced a year of academic probation.

When summer came, Frances was back in another rented Southampton house, less grandiose but more private than Dragon's Hall. The new, two-story stucco villa on Ox Pasture Road was surrounded by ten-foot-high hedges, and it had a bigger pool. This time Frances invited Granny to visit, and pushed her to pay the bill. Before mother and daughter left for Southampton, they took another look at the Gracie Square apartment. Here Granny could have a permanent room of her own, and bath, Frances said, and it was a "real ritzy" address, a fitting place to raise Ariadne, and Marc. The building was nowhere so exclusive as the Huguenot Society, but neither would the co-op's board of directors accept just anybody. They had turned down Diana Ross and Liza

Minnelli. But Lily Pons with her husband André Kostelanetz
had occupied one of the penthouses, and upstairs from the very
apartment they were looking at lived Mme. Chiang Kai-shek.
True, she was Chinese, but very rich Chinese: she had thirty-five
servants. Berenice agreed to think it over.

Once reestablished in Long Island, Frances took on new re-
sponsibilities. George Balanchine's triple-bypass heart surgery
had taken place at New York Hospital in mid-June, and he was
now convalescing in his modest Southampton condominium. It
was surrounded by high walls, but a portion of the big yellow
umbrella on his sundeck was visible from the street. Everyone at
NYCB and SAB (School of American Ballet) was worried about
him and avid for news. Frances took to driving by daily. If the
umbrella was open, it meant to her that Mr. B was probably
feeling well enough to sit out of doors. A closed umbrella, therefore, was cause for concern. Frances took to phoning in bulletins
based on these observations. All this left her less time than usual
for her own family, and Berenice for the first time was free to
enjoy a certain amount of uninterrupted fun at pool and beach
getting to know her grandchildren.

Larry was on his own. Earlier in the year he had changed his
name legally to Lawrence Bradshaw. He didn't want a "foreign-
sounding" name, he explained later, especially if he should decide
one day to run for President. He was proud that he had taken
care of the paperwork himself and not wasted money on a lawyer.
It had been a simple matter to steal from Frances's voluminous
locked files the ten-year-old documents which had changed his
name from Gentile to Schreuder. He had stayed up all one night
typing up a similar set of papers, and at dawn had driven from
Reading to New York and found the same courthouse, even the
same courtroom, Frances had visited before. There were minor
errors in his handiwork, and he had to retype the papers and
make the drive five or six times more before he got everything
perfect. But eventually, as he wrote in his *Occupier*, "The Judge
complimented Larry on his fine legal work."

This summer Larry was in Dallas, working two jobs. He had
driven there after reading in his favorite magazine, *U.S. News &
World Report*, that Texas had the highest employment rate in the
nation. For the first three weeks, while earning enough money to
rent air-conditioned quarters, he slept in his car. He was employed as a maintenance man in a lead-refactoring plant, but the

job he liked best was working for a pharmaceuticals company interested in compiling statistics on teenage drug and alcohol use. The questionnaires were long, and Larry was paid fifteen dollars an hour to find people to answer the tedious questions. He learned to work poor black neighborhoods, where the supply of idle teenagers was limitless and other pollsters were reluctant to visit. Larry worked as hard at this canvassing as he had done when canvassing for wheatbacks. He is strong for his size—height, five feet ten, weight about 180 pounds—and seems to have limitless energy. Like his grandfather, he can make do with very little sleep. In Texas, he banked $6,000 in six weeks, sometimes putting in eighteen-hour days, and still found plenty of time to hang out at topless bars and X-rated movies, and sometimes to drive to El Paso and Juarez across the border. He recorded his extraordinary earnings and erotic adventures in his *Occupiers*. His Dallas girl cost thirty-five dollars, the Mexican girls only twenty. Larry Bradshaw was having the best summer of his life.

The summer gave Berenice Bradshaw time to contemplate anew and at close range the disorder of her daughter's domestic life. In mid-August, Larry called Granny from Texas and learned from his grandmother that Frances was again in Southampton, this time on Ox Pasture Road. Larry drove east without stopping except for brief catnaps in his car, and had no difficulty locating his family. He found his way to the Southampton post office. There he waited and watched for his mother's big new blue Delta 88 Olds, the car she bought after Freddie's car got demolished on the Triboro Bridge, the car she had proudly paid all cash for—$8,000 her sons stole from the Bradshaws the summer before the murder. The car showed up, with Marc at the wheel, and Larry followed his brother home. His ROTC scholarship paid only tuition, he said. He had no money to pay for his sophomore-year room and board at Lehigh. Frances acted cold and disinterested, but Granny wrote him a check. Then, just as he was leaving, Frances handed Larry one of his own checks, from his F & B trust fund. He left feeling "pretty good." His mother seemed to be growing "less hostile."

Now what Berenice later called her "brainstorm" struck. Why not buy this disordered family that big duplex on Gracie Square? *Why not!* She had the money, by God, and if Frances owned her own apartment, then at least the Schreuders could never get any more pesky eviction notices. Perhaps at $525,000 the place was a good investment. It might even be a steal. In any event, if her grandchildren did have to live in New York, it was a good atmosphere in which to raise kids, not just respectable but safe. It was, in fact, a true Walled City, an enchanted and locked enclave guarded by twenty-four-hour squads of uniformed doormen instead of by a dragon, and protected by the East River instead of a moat.

Berenice instructed her new bankers to come up with the necessary money. She made her offer and in time was accepted by the co-op's board. The directors might have rejected Liza Minnelli, but Granny Bradshaw was another matter. She appeared before them alone, and, as she said later, "We didn't tell them about our naughty boys." She was simply a rich widow from Salt Lake City who just happened to keep her assets in the Morgan Guaranty Bank. She intended to occupy the apartment herself, she said, and anticipated frequent visits from her daughter and grandchildren. Berenice had no more difficulty with the co-op's board than Frances did with the Ballet's Board. Moral: dough unsticks all doors. This Christmas, Berenice told herself, twenty years of bailing Frances and her brood out of an unending series of domestic crises would finally come to an end. This Christmas she could confidently expect to have her much misunderstood and abused youngest daughter, her brilliant grandson Marc, and her adorable ballerina granddaughter Ariadne all snugly installed in the best damn address in New York City.

The previous spring, Ariadne had begun taking ballet lessons several times a week after she came home from kindergarten. Shortly after Ariadne started first grade at St. Hilda's and St. Hugh's, Frances dropped in to chat with the nuns. Adroit at reading moods from faces, the sisters had developed a reliable system for judging the volatile Mrs. Schreuder before she opened her mouth. If she was smiling broadly, as she was now, all would be well. On some occasions her lips were compressed in a straight line that crossed her face like a zipper—a surefire tip-off that she was enraged, and endeavoring to hold in her anger.

Today she had stopped by to arrange that her daughter continue her study of ballet during regular gym periods. The Schreuders were a particularly arts-minded family, she explained; she herself was a Board member of the New York City Ballet. Perhaps, then, one of the nuns suggested, Mrs. Schreuder might enjoy the nativity pageant which the children were preparing to put on at Christmas, at the Cathedral of St. John the Divine? On hearing this, Frances offered, with a generosity which bordered on insistence, to arrange that her "close friend" Beverly Sills sing the Virgin Mary part. That the school did not want an opera star, that it wanted one of its own students in the role, seemed beyond her comprehension. Nor did she appear to understand that the former Bubbles Silverman, famous as the Brooklyn Jewish girl who made good in the world of grand opera, might not leap at the role.

The real trouble set in later, when Frances dropped in on first grade and discovered that Ariadne was not quick at learning to read. The star reader in her class was a small Nigerian boy. That night at home, when the shouting began in his mother's bedroom, Marc recognized in her voice the same cold anger, the same bullying repetitions, the mounting fury and threats, the tears and hysterical pleading which had once been directed at him. He camouflaged his big new Audio-Technica mike inside a piece of folded cardboard and placed it just inside the bedroom door. Marc never again listened to the so-called "Ariadne Tape," the hour-long cassette he made that awful night. He put it where he knew even Frances would never find it, in his special hiding place behind the baseboards in the back of his closet. Later, he hid other tapes there.

Marc's tapes are a window on true domestic Bedlam. They show how dangerous it was to be a child in this disturbed household. They are the "flip side" of Franklin's *Pleasant Memories* and Berenice's "100-year Autobiography." They are the reality which sanctimony and Huguenot Society hauteur had so long covered up. They document the horror of Frances's "mothering." They show how, always, she used her children as an excuse to do exactly what *she* wanted. Nothing, really, was for their good, their protection, their advancement; everything was for her own. Frances Schreuder is far from unusual in this regard, though she was surely extreme. In using her children, she dreadfully abused them. Yet many parents do much the same—parents who are not crazy at all.

Fall was an unusually eventful season, even for the Schreuder family. Over the summer, the big money had been moved East. By mid-September the written invitation to Frances to become the modern Köchel and Gesellschaft had arrived. Ariadne had

started first grade. At Lehigh University, Larry had been elected
to "Student Forum," as student government was known, and put
on the Discipline Committee. Marc, temporarily sidetracked
from his pursuit of higher education, had gone to work, first as an
A&P delivery boy, then as a four-dollars-an-hour bonded messenger boy for Mitsubishi International. Traveling the city by
subway, he delivered "strictly financial stuff . . . stocks, bonds,
cash, letters of credit, bills of lading." He did not steal anything,
he says, "because this was my first experience in the business
world, and I wanted to prove myself."

On Halloween, while Frances was out at the ballet, Berenice
and Marc sat together at the dining-room table having a few
drinks and reviewing the floor plans for 10 Gracie Square while
they waited wistfully for trick-or-treaters to ring their doorbell.
Both Granny and grandson were somewhat depressed. Marc
wished he were off in college, and Berenice wished—what? Tonight was her fifty-fifth wedding anniversary. She was worried
about her family, about the money, about her health. A few
weeks earlier, in Salt Lake, she had been hospitalized with chest
pains. As soon as Frances heard about it, she had insisted that
her mother return immediately to New York, where better care
was available. That Berenice's money was in New York now, and
that the Bradshaw estate was still in probate, and that Berenice
had not yet made out a new will must have made Granny's ongoing good health a matter of special concern to them all.

That fall Berenice and Marilyn took a long walk through Riv-
erside Park. Berenice was careful not to talk much about her
troubles, particularly her fears for her granddaughter—whom
Marilyn had not seen since her swift visit to the maternity wing
of Doctors Hospital. Berenice knew that Frances was being "very
hard on Ariadne, riding the child" unmercifully, often "ranting
and raving" into the wee hours. One night Frances had kept the
whole household awake until 4 A.M., bullying and badgering the
child about "what is a sentence," while Ariadne whimpered in
the corner. Berenice had heard it all. She knew that a six-year-old
should have a chance to sleep quietly in her own room, not in her
mother's bed. She knew she should be weaned from the nightly
nursing bottle that Frances still insisted on. But if Granny tried
to interfere, that made things worse for everybody, Ariadne especially. The consequences of saying no to Frances had become
truly dreadful. Yet it seemed nothing could be done. Berenice

could not seek advice or comfort from her oldest daughter. Marilyn would only say, "I told you so." So Berenice walked in near silence, letting Marilyn do the talking while they scuffed along through the autumn leaves.

Richard Behrens's student loan was nearly gone; soon he would be on welfare. He had been trying with no success for some months to reach Frances by telephone. She refused to accept his calls and had instructed her children and Granny to do the same. He decided to launch a letter-writing blitz. His first letter to Frances, dated December 11, is a polite three-page request begging her to return his money. He does not use the world "steal," but, as he figures it, his old friend is now into him for $4,778.43, including interest.

On November 13 the Ballet's fall season had begun, and Frances stepped back through the gold curtain once more. Around the New York State Theater, the word was out. In the first-tier boxes and Promenade Bar, where Board members and Guild members and ballet cognoscenti gathered to gossip during intermissions, everybody knew there was a new person on the scene. She was a Mrs. Schreuder, née Bradshaw, Bryn Mawr '60, and a college classmate of Anna Kisselgoff, dance critic of the New York *Times,* and of the writer and balletomane Renata Adler. She was a distant cousin, as a matter of fact, of Thornton W. Bradshaw, the industrialist who had just been named president of RCA. When these Bradshaws moved from Pasadena to New York, Mrs. Thornton W. Bradshaw was herself invited to join the New York City Ballet's Board, and thereafter she and her husband became frequent ballet-goers. Not one of these four people, who saw one another often at performances and parties that fall, could remember ever before meeting, or even being aware of the existence of the uncomfortably intense, chain-smoking woman who approached them now during intermissions and doggedly repeated in her childlike voice, "Don't you remember me? *Surely* you remember me . . . We all lived together in Rhodes Hall . . . I'm Bradshaw too, you know . . . *you must* remember me . . ." It was easier to say yes than no to so terribly insistent a person, harmless except that once she got started you could never interrupt her. So they all smiled politely back at her and murmured yes, of course they remembered. Of course.

One balletomane who did not have to pretend, who was sure he had never met Frances in the past, and sure too that he could not take much of her in the present—but was certain of her value to the board nonetheless—was Board member Robert Gottlieb, editor-in-chief of Alfred A. Knopf.

Gottlieb is a man passionate about ballet. Working for Balanchine, he says, "is a supreme privilege, like serving Mozart." And Gottlieb found Frances Schreuder "extremely intelligent, an extraordinary person with a real instinct for quality. She felt, as I do, that our civilization can be defined by Balanchine's genius. If you're a serious person about art, you must realize that Balanchine is one of, if not *the* great genius of our era. It's a litmus test for me."

Frances passed the test. Nonetheless, Gottlieb acknowledged that "despite her brilliance, she is an extremely peculiar woman, a seething mass of disorder. There are certain people whose psychic energy is so powerful, you are uncomfortable in their presence. Her tension was overwhelming. She stalks, prowls, corners people like a cat."

Gottlieb continues, "People were loathe to work with her because she was so odd, so emotionally charged. But that doesn't mean she was a murderess. I like her, although I wouldn't want to spend more than ten minutes with her. She affixes this glittering eye on you. Words pour out in torrents. She is obviously a tragic person—tragic because she has a mind locked up in that caldron. Whether it is a real intelligence or a gorging dementia— who knows? She is simply more than you need." As he speaks, Gottlieb's face contorts, he grits his teeth, strains his facial muscles, shudders as if trying to swallow a foul draft.

Backstage, and in the Ballet offices, Frances was regarded as a sort of harmless pest—"not a pest to Mr. B, because Mr. B had no idea who she was. But we all soon realized that a major difficulty with Frances Schreuder is simply that she takes up a great deal of time." Partly this is because she will not be interrupted. Break into her train of thought, and she simply starts over. From the top. It is like trying to hold a conversation with a cassette. Soon a new development specialist, a Harvard-trained lawyer, was assigned to look after the precious "Live One," and satiate her needs. "That's the best you can hope to do with Frances," someone observed, "satiate her needs. You can't ever hope to *satisfy* her." Part of "satiating Frances's needs" was to send her numerous books on ballet, as well as recordings of ballet music, particularly music which someone thought might be under consideration by one of the choreographers. In 1949 another brilliant and much younger, jazzier choreographer, Jerome Robbins, had accepted an invitation to join the staff, and, over the years, a lot of backstage and very much behind-the-hand talk concerned who, and particularly which Board members, preferred the work of which choreographer.

To be clear: Balanchine always said the dancer he respected most was Fred Astaire. The choreographer he respected most—indeed the *only* choreographer he respected—was New York–born Jerome Robbins. In Europe, which NYCB tours annually, audiences and critics sometimes respected Robbins more than Balanchine. They relished the American's energy, verve, inventiveness; they found the Russian a bit old-fashioned at times. It goes without saying, but needs to be said in this context, that Balanchine and Robbins themselves understood and respected one another entirely. Both were artists. Only non-artists made comparisons, had favorites, took sides.

The advent of new-style business practices which Mrs. Schreuder exemplified was deplored by members of NYCB's old guard. "For years we were a deficit operation!" they said with pride. In the old days, whether or not something was "best for the Company" was the sole standard for accepting a gift, no matter how thin the purse, how fat the cat. The heiress Rebekah Harkness had offered to commission and herself pay for an entire new ballet—something which rarely, if ever, happened—but only if she could write the music. NYCB declined. The impresario Sol Hurok had offered an immense bounty, but he wanted to book Balanchine's dancers on a grueling series of one-night stands. The strain on bodies, feet, limbs might prove too great. NYCB didn't accept his money either.

"When George and Lincoln started this Company, they had a dream. They didn't want to do the old chestnuts, *Scheherazade* and *The Nutcracker,*" a starchy old-timer recalls. "And in the same years the Company developed, ballet became a respected, mainstream art form. I mean: the Ford Foundation gave us nearly seven million bucks! Who in America before that had even heard of 'dance grants'? We'd made it! So why, now, having made it, do we knock ourselves senseless in order to include a madwoman on our Board of Directors? For what? For *money?*

"Of course there is great pressure for money. That's what a board *does*. The most prestigious boards in this town are the

Metropolitan Opera, the Metropolitan Museum of Art, and maybe the Museum of Modern Art. The people on them talk endlessly about 'What makes a good board member.' The answer is always the same: Someone who contributes a six-figure amount on a yearly basis."

Most rich people find asking other rich people for this kind of money distasteful. One or two don't find it distasteful; they relish it. Such persons are rare, and today they are exceedingly valuable additions to the board of any arts institution. Least valuable board members tend to be corporate executives who, with rare exceptions, hate calling other CEO's to ask for contributions. Indeed, big corporate money is so difficult for a nonprofit institution to obtain, says the starchy old guardsman, "that the lure of private-sector contributors can become overwhelmingly tempting. That's what happened to us."

Secretly, Larry Bradshaw had just bought another car, a '72 Impala, blue with a black top. It had 56,000 miles on it, had cost $1,000, and was to Larry a source of immense pleasure. When his Thanksgiving vacation came, he drove to New York and rang the Schreuders' doorbell. Granny admitted him to the apartment. Frances was spending most of her nights at the ballet, and her days in bed trying to stay out of Granny's way. She particularly hated having her mother around the house during holidays. Berenice's attempts to "take over" and wrest control from her daughter seemed most odious to Frances on those occasions. The tug-of-war over Ariadne was always stronger then. Frances accused Granny of trying to "indoctrinate" the child. Now Granny was once again carrying on about a turkey, cranberries, yams, despite the fact that Frances had already announced her Thanksgiving menu—stuffed striped bass—and had bought the huge fish. Granny enlisted Marc's support in her pro-turkey rebellion, and together they went out cruising supermarkets for last-minute supplies. Larry decided to take Ariadne to see Macy's Thanksgiving Day Parade the next morning. This would get them away for a few hours from the mother-daughter free-fire zone.

Thanksgiving afternoon, with her mother out for a walk and all her children at home, Frances made another melodramatic suicide attempt. She was in bed sipping a gin-and-tonic from the small bedside tray cluttered with glasses, papers, pill vials, coffee cups, cigarettes, ashtrays, and bottles of Schweppes tonic which always sat atop her bedside table. Marc was also in the room. Gradually he became aware that his mother was methodically swallowing Tylenol pills, two by two, along with her drink.

"What are you doing, Mom!" he shouted. By the time he realized what was happening, she had gulped ten or twelve.

She had Marc's attention and now "started just *guzzling* them down. Really stuffing them in." Marc began to slap and pound her bulging cheeks. "Mom! What are you doing! Spit 'em out, Mom!"

Begging and screaming this way, he became almost as hysterical as his mother. "Surprisingly, she did spit some out," he said later. "But she'd still ingested a shit-load, pardon the expression. I said, 'Well, I've gotta call the ambulance!' "

"Don't you dare call the ambulance! First call Loughran!" Jack Loughran was one of her lawyers at Rogers & Wells, a singularly patient man whom she sometimes called several times a day, using him as a kind of indentured shrink.

"No, Mom! I wanna call 911!"

"Call Jack Loughran!"

Marc thinks he must have dialed 911 first, because he remembers Larry admitting the paramedics to the bedroom while Mom and he were still arguing about what to say to the lawyer. "It was shocking to me—what she wanted to talk to Loughran about was her *will!"*

Frances refused to speak to Loughran herself, so Marc relayed her messages blindly, praying the ambulance would come soon. "I kept saying, 'It's okay, Mom. The ambulance is coming!' And Mom was saying, 'Tell Jack that I like the will the way it is, and to get it signed off. Get it executed!'

"Mr. Loughran was asking, 'What's going on, Marc?' and Mom was feeding me the lines. I'd say, Mom, Mr. Loughran wants to know this! He wants to know that! And she'd tell me what to say back. Because I was panicked. And I was *still* on the phone with Mr. Loughran when Larry let the paramedics in with the stretcher. By that time, when Loughran would ask me, 'What's going on, Marc?' Mom was saying, *'I'm dying! Tell him I'm dying!'* "

The paramedics asked what had happened. "Mom took a bunch of pills," Marc said. But when they asked to see the bottle, Frances signaled her son not to say anything. They were putting her onto the stretcher when she slipped the bottle into Marc's hand.

"Hide it!" she whispered.

"I quickly ran out, hid the bottle in my cupboard, and ZOOM! I was back. Then they carted her off to New York Hospital."

While Marc was out of the room hiding the pills, Frances had also whispered to Larry to hide her locked briefcase and make sure that Marc did not steal it while she was gone. Her older son took this as a vote of confidence, another tiny sign that his mother's feelings toward him had begun to thaw.

Berenice became extremely upset when she got home. But Larry was so happy about the briefcase that he turned the evening into a celebration and cooked his special spaghetti dinner for the others, the one Vittorio had shown him how to make years before.

No one was allowed to visit Frances until Sunday. Marc and Granny walked over to the hospital first, and bought four bunches of pink and red roses on the way. "Mom didn't even want to *talk to* Granny. She was superpolite, saying, 'Yes, Granny,' 'No, Granny.' But she whispered in my ear that she didn't want Granny around, only me," Marc recalls.

It was the first time she called her Granny the Croc. "Get that crocodile out of here! With her crocodile tears!" she whispered to Marc. Berenice found some excuse to leave, Marc says, and then his mother sent him down to the deli. "She had a craving for ham and cheese sandwiches, egg salad . . . wanted me to bring six or seven of them!"

That afternoon Larry drove Ariadne to the hospital. His little sister was the only one to know about his newest car. Later, driving back to Lehigh, he thought it was a good omen that Ariadne had been his first passenger. He felt happier than he had been in some time.

When Frances came home a few days later, she seemed fine and talked about how exciting it had been to see the Shah of Iran in the hospital.

At Lehigh, Larry met Nancy, a biology student. "She was a little shorter than me, real skinny, red hair, green eyes, white, and *very* smart." He called Nancy his "first love." For the first time in his life, Larry had sex without paying for it. It only happened once, but Larry was pretty sure she would have remained his girlfriend if the other thing hadn't happened. He invited Nancy to spend Christmas vacation with him, driving back and forth to Texas in the Impala. When she declined, he started to worry again about where he was going to spend Christmas. The dorms would be locked, Nancy had rejected Texas, Salt Lake City was out because Granny was in New York, and New York might be out for the same reason. Or it might not. He wasn't sure how his mother felt about him any longer. She had been sort of nice to him in September, and there had been two nice days in November, before she had tried to commit suicide. And even then she had trusted him—not Marc—with her briefcase.

Larry now started to become increasingly preoccupied with the possibility of war between Russia and the United States. He called his mother and she invited him to meet her for dinner in New York. He recalls being in a restaurant on Madison Avenue that night, and talking a lot about the "imaginary war," which by now had begun to seem quite real to him, and in the middle of it all he blurted out some mention of Nancy, and also asked if he could spend Christmas at home.

"We'll talk about that if and when Granny the Bat leaves."

Larry drove back to Pennsylvania. He shared his dormitory room with Farid Salloum, a transfer student from State University in Buffalo whom Larry thought of as a "big hairy Lebanese." When Larry's name had been Lorenzo Gentile, he had hated being called a Dago, or a Wop. He now thought of Salloum as a kind of super-Wop. The coming war with Russia was looming larger and larger in Larry's consciousness.

The next day was bitterly cold. He used the latest F & B check that Mom had given him to pay his Lehigh bill, and withdrew all his savings from his bank. He had decided to spend Christmas in his car, driving to Texas and back alone. That day it snowed heavily. By nightfall the hillside he lived on was iced up. The tires on his newest car were totally bald. It was impossible to leave, so he parked at the bottom of the slippery slope, planning an early morning getaway.

He fell asleep in his car, and woke about 3:45 A.M. Chilled and frantic, he climbed the hill to his dormitory room. Salloum was asleep. Perhaps Larry fell asleep too; he is not sure. All he remembers is Salloum jumping up, suddenly, surprising him, and Larry finding himself with a big hammer in his hand. He could not think what to do with it, he said later.

What he did was smash in Salloum's skull and jaw and leap

out the window into a snowbank. Inside, other students screamed
and banged on the locked door. Campus police picked Larry up
immediately. At his arraignment the cops said they had been
unable to interview the victim, but the perpetrator claimed Salloum had been bombarding him with secret alpha waves "with
the purpose of turning him into a female." They said Larry told
them he had slept in his car until the waves "invaded" the Impala. Then he had "ruined" Salloum.

Police also said they had found a heavy, blood-and-hair-cov-
ered, metal-bladed mason's hammer lying on Larry's bed. They
did not know that the weapon had been stolen from Bradshaw
Auto Parts, or that Larry had carried it back from Salt Lake City
in the wheel well of his Impala, or that the date of the assault,
December 21, was Larry's brother's birthday.

Marc recalls the night well. When the call came, Mom was
sitting on the couch. "Oh my God!" she shrieked. Then she said,
"Sit down, Marc. I have some very bad news to tell you." As
usual, it was taking his mother half an hour to come to the point.
Marc had gritted his teeth and kept silent. He thought at first
that Granny had died. Then he thought "they had found out
about us." Then he thought "it must be something else bad about
me." When it turned out to be about Larry, even that "Larry had
hit a guy with a hammer, had some kind of a psychotic episode
and was in jail," Marc felt relieved. This time the responsibility
was all Mom's. "She *knew* he was unstable, but she'd treated him
like dirt anyway."

Maybe Tricky was right, Marc thought. He'd always said that
Frances knew how crazy Larry was, and that she was frightened
of him, especially when he barked.

Larry Bradshaw was charged with attempted homicide, aggravated assault, and reckless endangerment. The hearing was post-
poned because the victim was in too serious a condition to be
interviewed. He had six skull fractures, a broken jaw, and multi-
ple head wounds. That day, a week after the crime, Frances visited her son for the first time.

Larry was transferred for evaluation to the state psychiatric
hospital at Allentown, Pennsylvania, and received a preliminary
diagnosis of "Explosive Personality. RULE OUT: SCHIZOPHRE-
NIA." There were several more postponements; Salloum's condition did not stabilize until mid-January. Not one member of Larry's family visited or made inquiries, save for a call from a Salt

Lake City attorney who seemed concerned lest the public defender assigned to Larry's case attempt to make some claim for funds on the Bradshaw estate.

Frances visited her son for the second and last time February 7. When Larry called Nancy and told her where he was, she told him never to try to find her again. By February 19 the hospital decided Larry was "nonpsychotic, but dangerous if crowded." They gave him a final diagnosis of Explosive Personality Disorder and sent him back to prison to await trial.

By the end of the month, the Schreuders were finally ready to occupy their expensive new home. Moving precipitated new fights over control between Frances and her mother. Granny wanted to pack boxes in an orderly manner; Frances screamed that Granny was trying to "take over my property" until she reduced Berenice to tears. Packing or unpacking silverware, plates, books—anything could trigger a new explosion. "Any time Granny wanted to pack *anything,* Mom would just go off into a rage, scream at Granny, try to make Granny feel guilty," says Marc.

The new duplex contained a large formal living room, dining room and library, kitchens, and pantries on the first floor, and a curved stair in the foyer led up to four or five bedrooms and baths above. Frances took up residence in a very large bed in the center of the huge master bedroom. She used it for sleeping, eating, reading the papers, receiving, telephoning, and all other at-home activities. Ariadne and Tiffany shared the bed, which was made up with sheets of ivory silk, and draped in elegant Chippendale-patterned chintz.

Granny remained downstairs unpacking books onto the library shelves. The scene was surreal. Now and then Frances descended the staircase like an enraged Japanese Kabuki actor, thundering, *"What have you been doing!"*

"Well, I've been unpacking. Why not, Frances?"

"I told you not to unpack. *I told you!* Why did you disobey me?"

Childlike: "Why can't I unpack. I just want to help."

"You destroy everything you touch! You will ruin all my property. *It's mine!* Yeah, you may have bought this place . . . but then I might just as well move back out . . . I WILL move back out!" Frances screams. Granny dissolves in tears.

On March 3, in Bethlehem, Pennsylvania, Larry's public defender lawyer, Stanley Vasiliadis, entered a plea of not guilty. Courtroom observers described his client as filthy, stinking, out-of-contact, unkempt, with black fingernails, bleeding gums. A request for lowered bail was denied, and Larry was returned to prison to await trial.

Marc Schreuder began keeping a diary.

March 13: Mom is lazy. I came in after being locked out; the kitchen is a pigsty: coffee is spread all over the counters, and a broken cup is smashed on the floor. I have to clean up, made dinner as usual.

Tricky [Behrens] agrees that Mom was sick to lock Larry out; this destroyed him. Mom buys cats for $500 apiece (Ginger & Fluff-fluff) as a birthday present for Ariadne. Yet I have to return Fluff-fluff. I have to feed them and change their litter.

March 14: Mom says Lehigh is shit. She always sets unrealistically high goals: only Harvard/Yale for her kids. She pushes her kids to the limit. You cannot tell Mom she is wrong.

March 15: Mom picks her nose while reading the paper . . .

In the spring, Kent School finally disembargoed Marc's academic records, and he applied for admission to Yale, Wesleyan, Trinity, and Vassar. Yale and Wesleyan turned him down and, after the usual interminable round of conversations, Mom turned Vassar down as "a bit too feminine and artsy" for her son. Happily for Vassar, Marc wound up at Trinity College in Hartford, Connecticut.

Frances was also preoccupied with Ariadne's education. She had come to dislike the nuns at St. Hilda's and St. Hugh's, and regarded their school as a kind of minor-league holding pen for her daughter until something opened up at a "better" school, that is, Spence, Brearley, Hewitt, or Chapin. In the next few months she found time to visit them all, with Ariadne in tow. Three of these schools said a very fast no. But Chapin—Frances's first choice—put Ariadne on its second-grade waiting list. Mother and daughter had two more interviews before, ultimately, Chapin too decided that this mother might be more trouble than she was worth.

There followed yet another La Côte Basque lunch with another somewhat bewildered guest. This time she was one of the Episcopal school mothers, a wealthy woman married, Frances had surmised correctly, to a Roman Catholic. To her way of thinking, parochial school education was essential, Frances announced as they sipped their white wine. Public schools were foul bedlams of violence and disrespect, filled with "niggers, Jews, and dirty white trash." Even St. Hilda's and St. Hugh's was proving not quite the right atmosphere she wanted for Ariadne. The school was too West Side, too intellectual, too liberal-minded, and accepted far too many Third World and Jewish children. Frances asked her guest to write a letter of recommendation to a fine East Side Catholic girls' school. Ultimately Ariadne was accepted, and she has been a student here ever since. She is well liked by both teachers and pupils, and her academic record is excellent.

At 10 Gracie Square, Berenice was now a regular part of the household, and Marc and his grandmother were becoming friends. Like a solid marriage, their relationship was based on a community of interest, a common problem: neither one of them knew how to say no to Frances. Much later, in prison, where Marc had learned to overcome this handicap, he spoke about it to a visitor.

"Mom's relationship with Granny was interesting. On the one hand, Mom wanted Granny dead. On the other hand, Mom wanted . . . well, it seemed like she was putting up a front, a façade, of overly caring for Granny. Because Mom hated Granny. She waited for the day she was going to die. She told me so often. If Granny died, Mom was gonna get *everything*.

"One day Granny wanted me to go with her to the Ninth Avenue Food Fair. Spring 1980. Mom said, *Go ahead!* I said, 'Right on!' I like to take Granny places. She's my grandmother. Yet I didn't like to hang around Granny too much . . . because Mom didn't like that. It's a stigma on me, when Mom calls me a 'Granny's boy.'

"But this time she gave me permission. Then, while Granny was getting ready, Mom whispered, 'Try to get her to stuff herself! Try to get her to eat lots of salty foods, so she'll have a heart attack.'

"I said, 'Come on, Mom!' I was really upset. To me this was like overkill. I mean, what does she want to do—kill off everybody that's close to her? *Am I next?* I was thinking.

"Anyway, when we went to the Food Fair, my orders were, get Granny to stuff herself; select lots of salty foods. So I made sure I did the very opposite. That is, I said nothing. I let her select whatever she wanted. I went off by myself. I thought, *Man oh man! What am I supposed to do . . . just bump off everybody? This is ridiculous.*

"When I came back, Mom was just sitting all happy, like a cat that swallowed a canary, smiling, giggling over how Granny had stuffed herself. Because she *did*. And apparently Granny had some chest pains that night. Somehow I now became really mad —I don't know why—that Mom had actually sent me to *do this again*. Of course I didn't. But the point was, I felt sorry for Gran, and I felt angry at Mom. And Granny did still have chest pains. But I had been trying to steer her clear of it.

"Granny still doesn't have any idea what's going on! She can't accept it. She's deluding herself. And maybe rightly so. Maybe if I were a little old lady, I too would delude myself. Maybe it would be very hard for me to accept reality—that your daughter is out to get you—LITERALLY! And that's sickening.

"That really changed my perception of Mom. That was the turning point. From now on, I was looking out for myself."

By spring Richard Behrens was getting desperate. Five months of phone calls and certified letters had done no good. Frances was never at home. Once her door was opened by Berenice. The strange man thrust a fistful of photocopies of Frances's withdrawal slips into the old woman's hand and sidled away. It was the only time she and her daughter's friend ever laid eyes on one another—until they met in court. Once Behrens waylaid Frances on the street while she was taking Ariadne shopping. With Behrens trotting alongside, Frances related all her latest family troubles, acted offended when he demanded she return his money, and again disappeared. Next day Behrens heard from his father, the doctor. Some woman had called him and complained that she was being harassed by his son.

Behrens wrote to the probate court handling the Bradshaw estate. He wrote the trust officer at the Utah bank. He wrote Swindle. He complained to the lawyers at Rogers & Wells. They said Frances was going through some sort of crisis but would soon settle up. He wrote to Mr. Goodfellow at Morgan Guaranty. One day Marc turned up at Behrens's door to explain to him that his mother was just out of the hospital. She intended to straighten out her affairs as soon as possible. Meanwhile Marc borrowed Behrens's American Express Card to buy a ticket to

Maine for a college interview. Behrens knew Frances was now
receiving $60,000 a year from her father's estate, in addition to
the boys' trust funds, yet she seemed as broke as ever. His dozens
of letters were polite but increasingly bewildered. He had known
Frances much longer than all these lawyers and bankers and doctors now involved in her life. How could his friend of fifteen years
move into the costliest apartment building in the neighborhood,
fleece him of his savings, then cut him dead? He even wrote to the
Utah Bar Association and the Legal Aid Society. He reminded
former Secretary of State William Rogers that he and Behrens's
mother had once been childhood friends in Plattsburg, New
York. He sent copies of his letters to everybody, including Berenice, reminding them of the "David and Goliath" aspects of his
situation. Frances lived at 10 Gracie Square or Southampton; he
lived on welfare. He even tried filing a civil suit in New York
City. Nothing worked, and his own bank continued pressing for
repayment of his $5,000 loan.

Behrens finally called up Marilyn Reagan. She was astonished
after all these years to hear from the peculiar man she and Frances had met at church so long ago. Marilyn listened in silence to
Behrens's tale of woe. Then with cold finality she told him that
she could scarcely be held responsible for her sister's bad debts,
and hung up.

At home, Frances was growing increasingly ill-tempered. Marc
tried in vain to learn what was the matter. One day he came
home and found Frances out of bed, seated on the couch in the
little chocolate-brown-painted library that looked south down the
East River. It was the only furnished room on the first floor of
the grandiose apartment. "Mom, tell me what's wrong. What's
bothering you?" Marc said.

"No! Get out! Get out of this room. You *know* what's wrong."

"No, Mom. What is it? *Please* tell me."

Frances glared balefully, saying nothing. She had refused to
speak to Marc or Ariadne for two days. They knew well enough
what was wrong: Ariadne had begun to love her brother more
than she did her mother, and Marc had deliberately brought
about this unacceptable state of affairs.

Marc hated the silent treatment. He lost control and shouted,
"God damn it! Tell me what's wrong!"

"Oh! Oh!" she was screaming now, drawing away from him to

the corner of the couch, her face contorted. "There are witnesses you tried to kill me. I have *witnesses!*"

Marc turned away in disgust. He went upstairs to his own room. A few minutes later Frances stood in the doorway. She carried a pair of scissors in her hand. "If you touch me, Marc, I'll *stab you!*"

Berenice returned to Salt Lake. Ariadne was frightened of Mom without Granny around, Marc says. When she was frightened, she tried to act supersweet. The next morning she and Marc were both waiting in the big bedroom when Frances woke up. Ariadne smiled. Her mother glared at her, without making a sound.

"I love you," Ariadne said.

Still silent, Frances got up and went into the bathroom. Ariadne turned and raced down the stairs to the foyer to wait for Marc to come down and take her to school.

"Where's Ariadne?" Frances snapped as she crawled back into bed.

"She just left. I don't know why," Marc lied.

"Why doesn't Ariadne love me?" Frances began to cry. Suddenly she shouted, "You have trained her not to love me!" and leaped out of bed.

Frances ran down the stairs, Marc following. Frances grabbed Ariadne and began shouting, "You're mean! You're a mean little girl." When Marc tried to pull them apart, Frances whirled and pushed both children out the door, onto the elevator landing.

Tock! Tock! Tock! While they waited for the elevator they could hear the three big locks on the front door being bolted shut. This episode occurred May 28, according to Marc's diary. On June 5, at a sanity hearing in a Pennsylvania courtroom, Larry Bradshaw was ruled fit to stand trial for attempted murder.

That winter and spring, in the ballet world, two things had become known. George Balanchine had recovered sufficiently to have begun making a new ballet, and Frances Schreuder had agreed to underwrite the entire production, whatever the cost might be. Even in balletland, not a notably unruffled environment, excitement was running high.

Over the years, Balanchine had tried his hand at choreographing absolutely everything; he had set twenty-eight circus elephants in pink tutus twirling through Madison Square Garden to strains of Stravinsky. But stunts and games aside, Balanchine's best work tended to be his most abstract. He normally avoided "storytelling" ballets such as *Romeo and Juliet,* or even *The Nutcracker.* As he often said, "There are no daughters-in-law in ballet, no grandfathers." Dance can deal only in primal relationships, not plot.

Whatever he attempted, his work always grew directly from the music; it *was* the music, embodied by this centaur-artist—half musician, half choreographer—in dance. And now the music which lay open on Balanchine's piano was Schumann's *Davidsbündlertänze,* a suite of eighteen piano pieces which many consider one of the composer's masterworks.

Balanchine, a formally trained musician, had known it all his life. Schumann was one of his favorite composers. Yet, before his illness, he had never made a ballet on his work. But he had begun playing the *Davidsbündlertänze,* studying it, and consulting with musician friends about matters of tempo and interpretation, while still convalescing in Southampton the previous summer and fall.

"This work seems ideally to have suited his present state of mind as an aging artist, aware of his mortality," says one who knew him well. "George was in no way an embittered man. He never read the critics. But as he aged, he became vulnerable to illness. He was also very religious, and knew a great deal about religions other than his own—Sufism, and the anti-Christ movement, for example. His interest in nineteenth-century German Romanticism had also greatly increased. And so he rediscovered this score."

All that winter and spring of 1980, behind the golden curtain, hundreds of thousands of dollars of Franklin Bradshaw's money were spent rehearsing, mounting, and costuming the important new work. The original budget was $185,000. The eventual cost would be $327,000. But by that time Frances had pledged $360,000 and had said, in effect, keep the change. It was the largest lump-sum contribution to NYCB ever made by a single individual. Her elevation to the Board of Directors seemed imminent.

Robert Schumann, a flower of nineteenth-century German Romanticism, was a most literary composer, and *Davidsbündlertänze* is the distillation of all his poetic aspects. Schumann thought and wrote of himself as a double personality, as literally two people, with two names, Florestan and Eusebius. Florestan represents the strong, stormy, passionate, active side of his nature, Eusebius the poetic, lyric, sensitive side. Every movement of the eighteen dances in *Davidsbündlertänze* is signed by either "F" or "E," or sometimes "F *und* E." The entire suite, in the words of his first biographer, is "a formal thinking out, and writing down, of his own heart-life." It became something similar, in dance, for Balanchine.

His new piece was different in tone and color from what had come before. It was darker, more elegiac, an old man's brooding on an old man's concerns: loss of his powers, episodes of Romantic love and devotion intertwined with melancholy themes of madness and death, wild with all regret.

The *Davidsbündler*s, a poetic invention of the German Romantic writer, Jean Paul, were Schumann's most elaborate literary conceit. They figure in his allegorical writings, notebooks, manuscript notations, and published compositions, and the *Davidsbündlertänze* is their anthem. Members of a mythical secret society of artists, the Band of David, the *Davidsbünd,* they express Schumann's passionate belief that the artists of the world must always band together to fight off the Philistines, the anti-artists. His own Philistines were the smug, pedantic German music critics, scornful of the new Romanticism. But, he knew, it had been ever thus, and so the *Davidsbündler*s are *all* artists, throughout history. Mozart, dead twenty years before Schumann was born, was of course one of them, Schumann wrote, as indeed was the biblical King David, the psalmist-harpist-warrior, for whom his *Bund* was named.

All of these ideas come together and find expression in the morbid, disturbing, but magnificent work which Frances Schreuder paid for. Ter-Arutunian's phantasmagoric stage set is an *hommage* to the haunted, brooding landscapes of Caspar David Friedrich, the nineteenth-century German Romantic painter whose famous dictum was: "Feeling is the only law."

The curtain rises to reveal a claustrophobic *allée* enshrouded by gigantic flapping white curtains suggestive of the hospital curtains which in nineteenth-century sanatoriums were placed around the beds of the mad and the dying; a moonlit ruined chapel and a few ripples of water are sketched in the background. Schumann's own mental illness seems to have been a creative springboard for both designer and choreographer.

Through slits in the curtains four couples appear, the men in nineteenth-century formal evening dress, the women in ice-blue tulle. They are in a mysterious relationship. Two dancers seem to be Clara and Robert Schumann, or perhaps they are each aspects of Clara and Robert. Although this eerie ballet does have a Schumann figure who bids farewell to a woman who seems to represent his wife, Clara, the work is more an allegory about the artist in society, and in particular about the artist as one who is always —by virtue of his nature as an artist—alienated from society; one whose feeling is his only law.

Balanchine always resisted invitations to discuss the "meaning" of his work. On this occasion he was willing to break his own rule and go so far as to tell an interviewer that two of his dancers were indeed Robert and Clara Schumann, and that the gloomy setting was "not a real room . . . [but] . . . a space in the past." He had made Schumann "strange," he said, "because a normal person could not be so great.

"You have to be strange to do great things."

Schumann composed his *Davidsbündlertänze* in 1837, while bitterly feuding with his piano teacher, Friedrich Wieck, over his engagement to Wieck's seventeen-year-old daughter, Clara. Schumann had first seen his beloved, and fallen under her spell, when she was an enchanting child prodigy pianist of nine. They married, despite Wieck's furious opposition, the day before Clara's twenty-first birthday. Robert Schumann, then thirty and at the height of his powers, had a family and personal history of mental illness. Sixteen years and eight children later, after a life of prodigal creativity interspersed with increasing episodes of derangement and suicidal despair, Schumann leaped into the Rhine, was fished out, and spent his final two and a half years in a private asylum, where he died raving mad. His biographers disagree as to whether his torments were due to congenital insanity or terminal syphilis.

The four couples in the ballet seem to be expressing something to do with love, something to do with frustration, something to do with devotion, with passion, with fear, and madness, and death. The dancer who plays Schumann is given a powerful mad scene at the ballet's end. Midway through his solo, he is interrupted by five grotesque, black-clad figures who appear through the flapping curtains in plumed black hats, cloaks, and beards. They wear pince-nez, and carry long quill pens. These apparitions represent "critics and society people"—*his* Philistines, in fact—as Balanchine would later acknowledge.

The ballet's many admirers find the work exquisitely romantic, mysterious, heartsick, bathed in sorrow. Its detractors—far fewer in number—see it as the work of an aging master gone soft; they find it death-haunted, weary, sentimental, overly revealing. But both sides are in agreement that, in making *Davidsbündlertänze,* a great artist was consciously choreographing his own farewell.

While the new ballet was still in rehearsal, someone suggested to Balanchine that Schumann's title would be difficult for Americans to pronounce. "If they can't pronounce it," he said, speaking like the lifelong *Davidsbündler* he himself had always been, "they don't have to come."

But they came, and they raved. The piece was received as a late-period Balanchine masterwork, nothing less, trumpeted the New York *Times,* than "one of the twentieth-century's great neo-Romantic works of art."

At the bottom of the printed program, a chaste acknowledgment said: "A deeply appreciated gift in support of George Balanchine and the New York City Ballet has made this production possible." Only that and no more. But every member of the inner ballet world, the entire peerage-pantheon of high culture-bearers, ladies bountiful, fiscal bigwigs, serious artists, jet-set sprinters, fading Tsarists, prima donnas, prime aesthetes, busting stuffed-shirts, and the whole train of strenuous social mountaineers puffing uphill behind them all knew that Frances Schreuder was the great work's sole, albeit anonymous underwriter. Surely the presentation of *Davidsbündlertänze,* "her" ballet, was her finest hour, the master patron's major gift to the master artist, and all the world could now see who Frances's "real" father was. Not pinched, dreary, stingy Franklin Bradshaw in his soiled orange polo shirt with penguins. Her *"spiritual father,"* as she spoke of him, was none less than the greatest living genius of the age, George Balanchine himself.

On June 7, 1980, in the little green conference room of the New York State Theater, Frances Schreuder was elected to the Board of Directors of the New York City Ballet. This event took place two weeks prior to the world premiere of *Davidsbündlertänze.* It took place despite an urgent plea the day before from a top staff member to Board president Winthrop Knowlton: *"Please* don't do this. This woman is not in her right mind. You will pay in spades for this money!" The words fell on deaf ears. Having found its very own Sugar Plum Fairy, the Board had promptly fallen under her magic spell and forgotten the first lesson of all fairy tales: a great gift always carries a great price.

At the Board meeting, Frances Schreuder's election was not even discussed. No credit, or background, or any kind of checkup had been done. The woman lived at an acceptable address. Her previous pledges had been generous, her current pledge was breathtaking, and the Schreuder-Bradshaw pockets appeared to be wide open and bottomless. W. McNeil Lowry, now a Board member, said he thought a woman like Mrs. Schreuder could be extraordinarily useful on the Finance Committee. A motion was made and seconded. There was no discussion. They didn't even count the votes. She was chosen unanimously, by acclamation.

Whether or not Frances Schreuder thought of it that way, she had just made a bargain buy into New York's cultural ruling class. A seat on the Metropolitan Museum of Art Board, they say, then cost a cool $1 million.

On June 20, the morning after the premiere, Frances lay dreaming in her disheveled tower bedroom. Noon sunlight streamed through the great windows above the river. She awoke and sat up in the center of her thronelike bed, eager to savor anew the critical hosannas. She lit a cigarette and opened the New York *Times.* "George Balanchine has created a ballet that is very moving, very deep and very great . . ." wrote Anna Kisselgoff, the paper's prestigious critic. Her review spoke of the ballet's "shattered world . . . a world of love but not without pain, and when that pain is depicted, it comes through with a knifelike thrust previously unknown in any Balanchine work." She mentioned "the Schumann figure's poignant leave-taking, into death or insanity," and ended up proclaiming the mad solo at the ballet's climax to be "the creative artist's archetypal angst."

More than any other of the performing arts, Frances knew, choreography without performance does not exist. As she mused in the great bed, it must have been a transcendent moment for the woman who had single-handedly paid to bring such a masterpiece into being. Perhaps the music itself was playing now, on the phonograph, as she smoked and slowly savored the critic's every rapturous word. The grateful NYCB management had presented her with a recording which she had listened to daily for months now, unable to cease, even had she wanted to . . . Yes, *single-handedly*. Not too strong a word.

"You have to be strange to be great."

"The artist's feeling is his law." His only law. *How true,* thought Frankie, lost in reverie on her frowsy, four-poster throne.

Midway between June 7, when Frances was elected to the Board of Directors, and June 19, the night her ballet opened, Larry Bradshaw was tried and convicted of attempted murder by the Commonwealth of Pennsylvania. He was represented by a public defender who had met his client only an hour before. But when the lawyer asked for a postponement to give him time to study the case, his client spoke out. He knew that the Constitution guaranteed him the right to a speedy trial, Larry said, and he demanded to have one. No one objected, and the proceedings got under way.

The prosecutor said the defendant had brought the murder weapon to the dorm from its normal resting place in his car, parked some distance away. Therefore his crime was premeditated. Salloum, the victim, said he scarcely knew Larry. He could recall nothing between going to bed at midnight and waking fourteen days later, in a hospital in Syracuse, New York, with six skull fractures. He had undergone three brain operations so far, he told the jury, and the doctors said he would need another.

Testifying for the defense, a well-known psychiatrist, Dr. Robert Sadoff, who had twice examined Larry, assured the court he was "psychotic" at the time of the crime. A young woman student who witnessed Larry's capture in the snowbank described him as gray-faced and delirious. When it came time for Larry to testify, he was asked *why* he had attacked his roommate with a mason's hammer? Smiling, the defendant replied that he would "rather not say."

Throughout most of the farcical, two-day trial, Larry had sat curled in his chair in a fetal position, sometimes with his thumb in his mouth. The jury deliberated only an hour and a half before finding Lawrence Bradshaw guilty on all counts: attempted third-degree murder, aggravated assault, reckless endangerment. His bail was revoked and he was sentenced to serve two and a half to five years in prison, pending further psychiatric examination.

Part Five

The Closing In

DURING THE SUMMER OF 1980, Frances and Marc had continued their raids on Berenice's bedroom. At first, they were looking for a diamond ring which Frances accused her mother of stealing. Later Berenice found a ring in her apron pocket and returned it. On another occasion, Frances loaned Berenice some jewelry, then forgot she had loaned it, and accused her mother of stealing *that.* It would have been hard to tell, Frances kept her jewelry "all jumbled up together in her jewelry case," Marc says, save for those pieces which might happen to be in hock. Tiffany purchases which Marc still can recall today include a pair of $40,000 clustered large diamond earrings, a $10,000 thick gold bracelet, and a $10,000 short gold necklace with fancy, curved links. Her other jewelry included "a platinum ring with one very large diamond"; a large emerald ring surrounded by small diamonds; earrings which each had "a large, single diamond set in platinum"; an antique ring with little rows of emeralds, sapphires, diamonds, and rubies; an 18-K gold chain "so long that Mom had to wrap it around her neck twice"; and a second gold chain, not so long but fashioned of thick, "fancy" links. He is certain there was "much more." He estimates his mother spent $60,000 on Tiffany jewels alone.

There were also occasions, Berenice says, when her daughter stole *her* jewels. And Frances once borrowed a $10,000 mink coat from her mother which she has yet to return. Berenice's catalogue of goods stolen by her daughter includes a $20,000 pair of Tiffany earrings. The web of interfamily theft among these people is years old, and impossible to disentangle. Suffice it to say that they were both a family *of* thieves and family thieves. Stealing from one another, raiding each other's strongholds, and forging each other's signature was an old family custom, not too different from searching each other's pockets and reading one another's mail. That first summer at 10 Gracie Square, Frances and Marc raided Berenice's room on several occasions. Granny complained that she could never keep anything secure, not even in her own half-million-dollar apartment. Once she even pried up the wall-to-wall carpeting and tacked her valuables underneath. Still, they were gone the next day.

"Me and Mom were raiding Granny's room, looking for jewelry, and I said, 'Ooh, Mom! Look at all those checks! And you're always so broke.' Cause even though Mom was getting $5,000 a month now, she was still always broke. So I said, 'Why don't you forge 'em off? You've done it *before.* Granny's done it to Grandpa.' It just seemed like a family thing to do—you know?"

At first Frances feared getting caught, says Marc. Later, she gave him carte blanche to work alone and get what he could. Frances's main interest in their raids that summer, her son says, was to find a copy of Granny's new will and be sure that Frances was in it in an important way, "for the big hunk," to use Marc's term. On the night that Frances finally found it, she took it to her own room and stayed up most of the night reading it aloud and crooning over the provisions. "Ah, yes! Here I am! And here . . . look! I'm getting about seventy-five percent of everything!"

On July 10, at a closed hearing, Larry Bradshaw was committed for a ninety-day evaluation period to Farview State Hospital for the Criminally Insane at Waymart, Pennsylvania, and treatment with the antipsychotic drug Prolixin was begun. By August the hospital had completed its evaluation. Larry was diagnosed as "paranoid schizophrenic with acute exacerbation; very confused, suspicious, delusional, bewildered, chronically ill."

Each year the Ballet goes on tour overseas, and at some point there is always a fete to honor, and entertain, the heavy givers. Arrangements are handled by the International Committee, and Frances had been an extremely active member of this committee ever since her elevation to the Board. She was passionately involved in even the smallest details. She was present at every rehearsal. She went along on shopping trips to prop and costume shops. She attended all the parties. "She showed up for *everything,*" said one observer. "This was obviously the main part of her life." She gave the others a feeling she had never been a part of anything before. So of course she talked too much, asked too many questions, and alienated many by styling herself an expert on everything from the cost of tulle to ticket-pricing. "She wanted so much to be a part of things . . . and yet you couldn't talk to her! She wouldn't listen. She was impossibly overbearing. She afterwards misquoted what you had said."

The new Board member not only babbled and misrepresented and at times asked ridiculous questions; she was at bottom ineffectual. Old-timers on the Board identified the problem straight off. Frances Schreuder did not know anyone. She had no contacts in the corporate world or in big business—the major source of development funds. Her only source of funds was Berenice Bradshaw.

This year's great occasion was to be a "Festival d'Automne À Paris: Hommage à Igor Stravinsky," in honor of the centennial of the composer's birth. It would be memorable more as a social occasion than a choreographic one. After the committee had already settled on its theme, it became evident that Balanchine had already choreographed the best Stravinsky scores; only odds and ends remained. In August, Frances dervished nonstop through Bendel's and Bergdorf-Goodman's, outfitting herself for the grand event. But she did not fly over with the rest of the group, and was a day late arriving in Paris for the September 16–22 festivities. It turned out that Frances's jewelry was in hock at the Provident Loan Society, the society pawnshop on West Fifty-seventh Street, and she had refused to leave town without it. In Paris, it would be important to "look rich," she said. Berenice wrote another check, and Frances flew off with eleven pieces of luggage for her ten-day tour.

Marc had begun his freshman year at Trinity College, in Hartford, Connecticut, so Granny had been summoned back from Salt Lake to look after Ariadne, who had just started second grade. For the next week, Berenice and her little granddaughter had a wonderful time by themselves at 10 Gracie Square. They made fried chicken almost every night, and ate candlelit dinners for two on the terrace while they watched the river traffic below. And one day while Ariadne was at school Berenice invited Marilyn out to lunch in a nice French restaurant. "I remember Mother wore a lovely yellow chiffon dress, and I've always been sorry I didn't tell her how nice she looked," says Marilyn. Mother and daughter never saw each other again.

One of the ballet professionals who traveled to Paris with the Company that fall was David Richardson, a muscular, intelligent, unflappable man in his late thirties who is considered the topnotch trainer-teacher of classical ballet to young children. His main responsibility was to select and coach child dancers from the School of American Ballet to perform the various children's roles with the professional Company, a job requiring exceptional powers of observation, tact, control. On his flight to Paris, Richardson noticed an eccentric-looking woman, about forty, with severe, pulled-back hair, and a very large antique gold watch hanging around her neck.

"That's the woman who paid for *Davidsbündlertänze,*" his traveling companion said. "She's on the Board." It was not at all surprising that Richardson had never seen her until now. Professionals and Board members rarely mix socially. If anything, they strain to keep out of one another's way. The dancers are usually too busy, and too tired, and Board members are careful to avoid even the appearance of meddling in Company affairs. Their job is to raise money only.

Richardson first thought it strange to see an obviously wealthy ballet patroness traveling alone. Such women usually brought a mate, friend, or companion. "But this woman was almost always alone in Paris. She was shy around other people, and others didn't seem to gather around her." Frances was looking a good deal better these days. Richardson found her "a strange mixture of unattractive and attractive . . . not certainly a beautiful woman, but she *was* stylish, well coiffed, and she looked like she took care of herself. She looked kind of like Lily Tomlin dressed up.

"Also, she has a dignified quality in her stance; a certain elegance about her, I thought. Then the next moment she'd start furiously chain-smoking. It negated that elegance; the dignity was gone. Another thing I noticed: when she stands still she looks much better than when she moves. She has a very strange, funny waddle in her walk. In sum, the package looks fine until it starts operating. Then it doesn't look so good."

In Paris, a glamorous fortnight of festivities had been arranged: parties round the clock, lunches at embassies, dinners at Maxim's, showings at Chanel, exhibitions of furs, cocktails at fabulous boulevard apartments, VIP tours of the Louvre, suites at the Plaza Athénée. Frances swirled through them all, chattering nonstop, earrings a-jangle. She was often eccentrically dressed, in a series of expensive costumes which never quite went together. Around her neck she almost always wore a heavy antique gold watch. Although she did not realize it, it was ticking away her last days of peace. More than two years had passed since her father's murder, and the case seemed closed or forgotten. But in New York, Richard Behrens's frustration was reaching intolerable levels. Soon it would overflow, and eventually extinguish Frances's flickering flame. The catastrophe would have been so easy to prevent. All Behrens wanted was his $3,700 back, less than the value of the watch ticking now at her throat. But Frances could never say no to money. She could never have enough.

A glittering cocktail party was under way at the Hôtel de la Ville, given by the mayor of Paris. George Balanchine sat at a round table sipping champagne. Leaning over him was a flat-chested woman in bare-shouldered, bright-red crepe, long, dangling earrings, a clunky watch on a chain. She had high cheekbones and her hair was pulled back behind her ears in a severe "prima ballerina" style. "That's the new woman. She pays for all his new ballets," the others whispered.

Frances chattered with great animation. Balanchine's grave expression did not change. "She was trying to look intelligent, glamorous, and seductive all at once—and she wasn't making any of it. She looked like a party crasher," said one observer.

Frances often looked out of place. She frequently misplaced her ballet tickets. She sometimes seemed stupefied, almost comatose. At an elegant diplomatic dinner, her neighbor was forced to whisper, "Either eat your dinner, Frances, or let the butler take away your plate."

At other times she was highly irritable. One day at a fashionable luncheon, the chic Parisian hostess inquired, "And how do you spend your afternoons?"

"None of your business!" Frances snapped.

Richard Behrens had first sought help from Marilyn Reagan in early May. As months passed, rebuffs accumulated. Bradshaw family lawyers and bankers all took the same attitude: anyone foolish enough to trust Frances Schreuder only got what he deserved. Behrens could not generate concern, let alone sympathy. Most of his calls and letters were not even acknowledged. Meanwhile, he was sinking deeper in debt. Marilyn at least gave him time on the telephone.

Probably she considered Dick Behrens a harmless eccentric. She talked to him not because she thought it would help to nail her father's assassin, but because it eased her hurt somewhat to talk about it, and opportunities had become pitifully few. Nobody but her husband and Elaine and maybe Doug Steele even seemed to care much any longer about what had happened to Franklin Bradshaw. So she was willing to supply Dick with the names of additional bankers and lawyers he might write to in connection with what she regarded as an essentially fruitless quest. And she was willing to share whatever tidbits of information on the Schreuders she had.

Later Marilyn and Behrens both would become prosecution witnesses. This would involve a prodigious amount of testifying. In their various statements to police officers, in their testimony under direct and cross examination at two preliminary hearings, and two trials, and in their assorted statements to lawyers, reporters, and others, both of their stories modulated somewhat. They shimmered in the glass of memory, or perhaps forgetfulness, or possibly self-interest. To put the matter in Marilyn's plain, dressmaker's language, the patterns of both stories are essentially the same, but the edges do not always quite match up.

Among their assertions: Behrens said he learned for the first time from Marilyn in the spring of 1980 that Larry was in prison for attempted murder. This seemed to her to confirm her suspicion that Larry was the one responsible for her father's death, even if they could never prove it because nobody could find the gun.

Marilyn said that in one of Behrens's summer calls she learned for the first time that, a year before her father's death, Frances's sons had tried to kill him by putting poison in his oatmeal. Marilyn then suggested to Salt Lake City police that they exhume her father's ashes, to look for traces of poison. They told her it was too late for definitive tests to be made.

By now, the investigation of Franklin Bradshaw's murder had been relegated to a back burner, and appeared likely to stay there, just another unsolved case. The trail was cold. It had never really been warm. There had been plenty of talk, no leads. Marilyn Reagan was still talking, but, lacking any new evidence whatsoever, the cops gradually were coming to regard Mrs. Reagan as a pathetic, spiteful, jealous crank. In fact, her endless talk would soon produce the first break in the three-year-old case.

In subsequent phone conversations with Behrens that summer, Marilyn learned that the boys had stolen $150,000 from her father a year before his death. She heard about Frances's lavish South-ampton estates. Behrens told Marilyn her sister had once asked him to try to find a "hit man" whom she could hire to kill her father, and that he, Behrens, had introduced Frances to "a fellow he knew that was talking big stories." Then Dick had walked away, and could not report on what had happened next.

Marilyn later told the Salt Lake police she had written down the "hit man's" name, but lost it before she could pass it along to them.

Behrens seemed terribly afraid of Frances. His dunning letters, though increasingly frantic, always speak of and to her in respect-ful tones. His calls to Marilyn were made from pay phones. He believed his home phone was tapped, probably by private detec-tives employed by Frances.

Marilyn believed Dick was paranoid. By fall, he was calling her two or three times a week. Whenever they spoke of the mur-der, Marilyn accused Larry. Behrens told her two or three times that she was after the wrong person. But Behrens was a flake, and Marilyn did not pay much attention to anything he said. Now Behrens decided the time had come to act, before the wacky Schreuders tried to pin the murder on *him*. And so the next time Marilyn on the phone accused Larry of killing her father, Dick Behrens told her she was after the wrong brother.

"It wasn't Larry," he said. "It was Marc." Then he added, "I've got the gun."

Marilyn called Elaine to report this startling development. She also notified Salt Lake City detective Joel Campbell, the police officer originally assigned to the case. He was the same nice young man who had taken the statements of all the family mem-bers and warehouse employees three years before. Campbell went to see Ernest W. Jones, a quiet-spoken, overworked member of the Salt Lake County Attorney's office. Jones is a lanky, pale, low-key lawyer in his forties with a disarming *"aw shucks . . . gee whiz"* Jimmy Stewart manner, and an always overcrowded desk. His office handles seventy felony cases a month. In the increasingly unlikely event that an arrest were made in connec-tion with the Bradshaw murder, Ernie Jones would be in charge, and would prosecute the defendant if the case came to trial. Jones instructed Detective Campbell to tell Marilyn Reagan to try to get her friend to hand over the gun he claimed he had, and to stay in touch.

When Behrens phoned the next day, Marilyn mentioned the original $10,000 reward which had been posted by the Bradshaw family for information leading to the capture and conviction of the killer. Turn in the murder weapon and surely the reward money was his for the claiming. She also reminded Behrens that New York had just passed a tough new gun law: anyone found with a handgun who did not have a license to carry one was subject to an automatic one-year jail sentence.

Behrens told Marilyn he would give her the gun only if she promised not to say how she got it. He knew he could not hope to remain permanently anonymous, but he wanted to be invisible for now in order to "force the police to do their homework." The anonymity was meant to protect him from Frances. Unless the police "did their homework," it was sure to cost him far more than the $10,000 reward money to "get out of what Frances will do to me."

Marilyn agreed to keep his name out of it, and assured him the family would take care of his legal fees, should that become necessary. In Behrens's next call, he said he was in a phone booth across the street from her apartment house on West End Avenue. It was early afternoon, October 16, 1980. Marilyn came downstairs, and Behrens was still huddled in the booth. He crossed the street to join her, carrying a paper shopping bag. Together they walked to the Burger King on Broadway. Behrens placed the bag under the table and they both ordered cocoa.

Had Marc actually told Behrens that he had shot her father, Marilyn asked.

Yes, Behrens replied. "He said it was easy. He just did it." Behrens also said that it was Marc himself who had given him the gun, or to use his curiously insistent phraseology, "Marc dropped it off on me."

Marilyn put down her cocoa and picked up the shopping bag. Without looking inside it, she marched directly to the nearest police station, the 20th Precinct, on West Eighty-second Street, and asked to speak to the highest ranking officer. She said she had just been handed a parcel which she believed contained the gun that had killed her father in Utah. She turned over the bag, answered a few questions, gave the police the name of Detective Campbell, and went home. The New York Police Department telexed the information to the Salt Lake authorities but refused to surrender the weapon until proper identification was made.

A week later, in yet another phone call, Behrens supplied Marilyn with the name and address of the Cavenaugh family in Midland, Texas, and said they were the people through whom Marc had bought the gun. Marilyn duly passed this information on to Campbell, but she still did not give him Behrens's name.

The Salt Lake police had checked the gun's serial number with the Federal Bureau of Alcohol, Tobacco and Firearms and learned it had been sold by Colt Firearms to Texas ex-Sheriff Jerry Register. Campbell flew to Texas and attempted with little success to interview Register and the others involved in the gun sale. Their memories were vague, their attitudes uncooperative. He came on East. Marilyn still would not tell him how she got the gun. He decided to drive the ninety-three miles to Hartford, Connecticut, drop in on Marc's freshman math class at Trinity College, and ask the young man point-blank if he had killed his grandfather. Marc denied everything. Campbell's only success was in identifying the weapon. When he test-fired it on the NYPD range, and compared the results with the slugs recovered from Franklin Bradshaw's body, the bullets matched.

The moment Campbell left campus, "ZOOM! I raced right to the pay phone in my dorm and called Mom. Ringing and ringing. Mom's never home when you want her. I finally got her two nights later, and when I told her Joel Campbell was here, she said, 'Oh my God! Don't talk over the phone!' "

She ordered Marc to come to New York that weekend and meet her in a coffee shop. She didn't want him anywhere near Gracie Square. Marc was panicky. "Look, Mom, somebody must have cracked. It's been *two years!* It must be Tricky. I know it wasn't Larry."

Frances appeared strangely unworried. She said it probably was Larry; perhaps he had let something slip to Farid Salloum. She would make some calls, ask around. Marc was positive it was Behrens and could not understand why his mother was resisting the idea. "It *had* to be Tricky! Because he was the one who'd been calling and calling. And *I* was the one who'd had to answer the phone and say things like: *Mom's not home, Mom's asleep, Mom's not here, Mom's not there, Call back later.*" Frances had been so afraid of wiretaps, Marc had been under orders all summer not to stay on the phone longer than five minutes. Yet now she was telling Marc to relax, there was nothing to worry about.

Marc had always been worried about the gun. He never even

wanted to bring it back to New York, but Mom had insisted, he
said. He had been especially unhappy about caching the gun at
Tricky's. But both his mother and Behrens seemed "very protective of it. They really didn't *want* that gun out of there," he said.
He understood Behrens's motives, but not his mother's. "I *know*
he had other uses for it! That's why he bought the cleaning rods.
He was worried about the barrel rusting out."

Marc believes Behrens wanted to use the gun to kill his stepmother. He had already offered Marc $1,000 to "bump off
Joanie." He claims he told Behrens, "Are you out of your mind?
Boy, if Mom heard you talking like that to me, she'd never talk to
you again. That's outrageous!" But ask Marc why it is any more
outrageous to bump off Joanie than bump off Gramps, and he can
only sputter. "I dunno. Never thought about it." He looks sheep-
ish and says, "Just because Mom wouldn't like it, I guess."

Indeed, Frances had not liked it. She had been furious with
Behrens when she learned about his $1,000 proposition to her
son, Marc says, and refused to talk to him for several weeks. "It
was incommunicado time. Lockout. Like with me. It's very effective."

After Marilyn received the gun from Behrens, she stopped
hearing from him. His sudden silence was uncharacteristic. She
wanted to reestablish contact because she "became concerned
about Dick's well-being." A good way to do that would be to
reimburse Behrens for all the letters and photocopies and phone
calls he had paid for which eventually had led to the recovery of
the murder weapon. She knew he needed money. A true daughter
of Franklin Bradshaw, she mailed him twenty dollars. He mailed
back what he said was a Xerox copy of a sheet of Kent School
stationery that he had discovered in the shopping bag, alongside
the gun, a few days before he turned the weapon over to her.
After making the photocopy, he had burnt the original. On the
Xerox, in what he said he recognized as Marc's handwriting, had
been the name and address of Jon Cavenaugh in Midland, Texas.
This had been his source for the Cavenaughs' name which he had
given her some weeks earlier. Marilyn sent the Xerox to Campbell.

It was mid-November, 1980. Campbell said he could proceed
no further without knowing where Marilyn got the gun. She finally told him, and once more Joel Campbell headed for Texas.
Armed now with snapshots of Marc and Larry and Frances sup-

plied by Aunt Marilyn, he got a positive ID on the purchaser of the gun.

On December 3, in New York City, Richard Behrens was visited in his apartment at midnight by Joel Campbell and Detective Ed Regan from the NYPD. In a rambling, sometimes incoherent statement, he told the officers that Marc Schreuder had "dropped the gun off on me" and told Behrens he had used it to kill his grandfather. He was giving Behrens the gun to keep, he said, because "maybe a relative was in the house," and Behrens's apartment was safe.

Asked the motive, Behrens said, "I think the whole thing is money."

Q: Did he say anything about anyone else being involved?
A: I think he just played the hero and did it on . . . his own . . . it seems to me he said he was alone.
Q: When he told you . . . was he cocky or did he act like he was sad or . . .
A: He acted very, very goddam jumpy . . .
Q: Do you remember Marc talking about the homicide in front of [Frances]?
A: Ya, ya. She was a weird girl . . . I don't know if she planned it or who planned . . . the kid's very headstrong, he could have been a . . . a . . . see there's no father in the family, and he's tried to assume an adult role, and she put a lot of pressure on him.

Why, after more than two years, had Behrens decided to tell his story to Marilyn?

When he realized Frances did not intend to pay her debt, "I figured she was perhaps really flipping out, bananas, crazy, and . . . I was the only person that really knew about this. And that isn't a very good position to be in if suddenly somebody who has a record of turning on husband, fathers, sisters and—you know, a really strange psychiatric record . . ."

Behrens could not explain *why* he had kept the gun, but he did indicate great fear of Marc, who had "buzzed down that next weekend," after Campbell had confronted him at college, in October, and had called Behrens from his mother's apartment. Certain that Frances tapped her own phone, Behrens had refused to

say a word and simply "holed up . . . stonewalled" for a couple
of more months until Officer Campbell had rung his doorbell.

Two days later, Campbell and a Connecticut cop went to Trinity College, found Marc Schreuder in his dormitory basement
playing Pac-Man, and arrested him on suspicion of murder. Since
he was under eighteen at the time of the crime, he could only be
held on a ninety-day juvenile warrant. The plump college freshman spent a miserable long weekend in Hartford's Morgan Street
Jail until Berenice Bradshaw, then en route to New York City to
spend her first Christmas at 10 Gracie Square, could be rounded
up and induced to post her grandson's $125,000 bail.

Convinced that it was all a big mistake, that this grandson, at
least, was not a murderer, Granny was happy to have the boy out
of prison and home for Christmas. Frances had found an excellent Connecticut attorney, Hiram Bissell Carey III, and he was
working hard to straighten out the mixup. As Frances told her
mother, "Cuckoo Behrens" and probably Marilyn were behind
the whole thing. She was especially thankful that the New York
papers had not picked up the story.

Four nights after Marc was locked into what he calls "that
horrible cesspool of a county jail," he was taken to the visitor's
room where Ted Carey was waiting. The lawyer drove him to his
downtown office and grilled him for two hours. Marc told the
lawyer the same pack of lies he and Frances had concocted two
months earlier, after Campbell's campus visit: that Marc and a
school friend had planned a bicycle trip out West. When the trip
was canceled, Mom said Marc could take a trip by himself, to
make up for the "lost fun and adventure of the missed trip." So
he'd called up Jon Cavenaugh, who invited him to visit. Marc
bought a bus ticket to Midland. He'd had a wonderful time with
the Cavenaugh family, but he dreaded the bus ride back, so he
decided to fly. Jon had even driven him to the airport. Marc did
not mention the gun to Carey. If he were ever asked about it, he
intended to say that, yes, he had discussed guns with Jon, but
that was just to be polite. Guns were something Texans liked
talking about.

The story was a complete fabrication, but if Carey had doubts
he kept them to himself, checked his squirrelly-seeming client
into the Sonesta Hotel, and told him to come back to the office
first thing in the morning.

Three days before Christmas, at Allentown State Psychiatric

Hospital, a nurse's aide approached inmate Larry Bradshaw. "Do you know who killed your grandfather?"

It sounded to Larry as if she was trying to trap him, so he simply said, "No-o-o-o-o-o," drawing out the one syllable as long as he could, and keeping his eyes fixed firmly on the TV game show he was watching.

"Well, your brother's just been arrested," she said. Ron Madsen, Frances's Utah lawyer, had phoned the hospital from Salt Lake City. (A few months later Madsen, who was very close to Frances and Berenice, continually counseling them by long-distance phone in their legal war against Marilyn and Elaine, and who is a frequent speaker on Marc's homemade tapes, was quietly advised by his law firm that he could represent either Frances or Berenice, but not both. Madsen discreetly left town for a while and joined the Washington staff of Utah Senator Orrin G. Hatch. He is now back in Utah, managing the Senator's at-home office.)

The moment her son was arrested, Frances began working on Richard Behrens to recant his confession. She warned him he was in very serious trouble, that he was liable to a twenty-year prison term as an accessory to murder, that the only way out of the mess he had put them all into was to change his story and try something else. She suggested a new tack: put the blame on Marilyn. She worked and worked on him, increasing the pressure, building up his terror, until Behrens was simply unable to hold out any longer. It was easier to say no to himself—to deny his own confession—than say it to Frances, and on Christmas Eve, he finally did.

Saturday morning, December 27, twenty-four days after his statement to Campbell naming Marc, Richard Behrens took the train up to Hartford. He brought with him a laborious document allegedly setting forth the "true" facts of the matter. He had spent all Christmas day and night typing it out.

In Carey's office, under the lawyer's bland but relentless questioning, Behrens gave his deposition to a waiting stenographer. The burden of his document and his deposition was the same: neither Marc nor his mother had anything whatsoever to do with the crime or the gun. It was in fact *Marilyn Reagan* who originally "dropped off" the gun on Behrens, and it was Marilyn who had mentioned Texas to him, and later had gone to Texas, and Marilyn who told Behrens she believed Marc had murdered her father. ". . . she defamed Marc as a deceitful liar, lazy, and very bad epithets and she indicated . . . that maybe they both were in on it."

Marilyn was so obsessed with the death of her father, Behrens claimed, that she had asked Behrens to make up a story about Marc buying the gun in Texas, shooting his grandfather, and giving him the gun. If Behrens would tell this story to the Salt Lake cops, he said, Marilyn had promised him $10,000 and free ski vacations in Utah. Depressed, broke, "mixed up," angry at Frances and intolerably pressured by Marilyn, Behrens had caved in.

Q: Did Marc Schreuder ever come to your apartment and bring a gun there?
A: Absolutely not.
Q: Did Marc Schreuder ever tell you that he had killed his grandfather?
A: Absolutely not.

And why had Mr. Behrens now decided to change his mind and tell the truth?

". . . several reasons. I felt that an innocent boy was being railroaded. I felt that I was doing it for reasons that were not honorable. And I felt that I had a lot of pressure and inducements put on me . . . by Miss Marilyn Reagan."

Armed with the Behrens recant, and with the unlimited budget Berenice Bradshaw was prepared to put at his disposal to prove her grandson innocent of murder, Carey hired an investigator to go out to Utah to see what he could turn up that might be helpful.

The investigator trudged up the sagging steps to Bradshaw Auto Parts warehouse. "Come on in," Doug Steele said. "Have a cup of coffee." He motioned toward the electric percolator.

"Mr. Steele, what reasons do you think Marilyn Reagan might have had for wanting her father out of the way?"

As soon as his visitor left, Doug called Marilyn.

"Talk about hurt!" she said later. "Your own mother pays for *that!*"

One spring day in 1978 Berenice Bradshaw had gone to a luncheon meeting of the Huguenot Society of Utah. The speaker was a natty, beaming, balding sixty-year-old retired airline executive and nationally known genealogist. She found his remarks so fascinating that she contrived to sit near him during the lunch itself and learned that he was from Washington, D.C., that he had been regional manager of the Eastern Region of TWA, that he had never been married, and had recently been retained by the Ford family to research their ancestry. His search had been so successful that two hundred similar requests followed, and he had been forced to get business cards printed up, and to change his telephone to an unlisted number.

He handed Berenice a small ivory card. "Grahame T. Smallwood, Jr.," she read. His mild eyes twinkled behind rimless glasses. "My friends call me Chips," he said.

After her husband's death, Berenice Bradshaw became one of Chips's best friends. She thought him beautifully mannered, a good conversationalist, an excellent dancer, an attentive escort— the opposite of Franklin Bradshaw in every particular. She had gone alone on her winter, 1978, round-the-world cruise. But soon after she returned to Salt Lake, Berenice and Chips began going every place together: dancing, drinking, wining, dining, card-playing, sight-seeing. Berenice was impressed with Chips's always-correct dress and manners, and his ready ability to make friends.

By 1981 she was inviting him along on her sight-seeing trips. That year they took three, and Chips handled all arrangements and reservations. Berenice was delighted. "I'd never had anything like that before! I've always said: I had a husband, but never a *companion*. A course, I also had a freedom not many women have had."

Chips was in no sense a husband, but he proved a superb companion. The new friends spent springtime in Mexico, went on a midsummer's jaunt to England and Ireland, and in October flew to Lisbon for a tour of Portugal, Spain, Morocco, and Madeira. She didn't give a damn what people like Franklin's pious sister Bertha Beck thought. "They say he's a wino. They say he's a homo. They say he's sixty-five and I'm eighty. I say, *So what?*" she chortled. "I say I'm finally gettin' some fun out of life. 'Bout time!"

In January 1982, Berenice and Chips set sail on the *QE2* for South America. They wore funny hats and danced and sat at the captain's table and gave nice cocktail parties in their cabins. "One must never give up," Berenice believes. "Never give up anything on account of age. My husband and I gave up square dancing, and we could never get back to it."

Berenice and Chips had a marvelous time boating up and down the Amazon, and climbing the heights of Machu Picchu. Returning, they cruised the Caribbean islands. Back in New York, there was even more to celebrate. Ariadne, still two months shy of her eighth birthday, had been accepted as the youngest student at Kirstein and Balanchine's School of American Ballet. It was run by two old Russian ballet mistresses whose own training went all the way back to St. Petersburg, but Balanchine himself taught daily classes. Kirstein was president of the Board—a separate entity from the Ballet's Board.

School of American Ballet has 350 students, and Ariadne Schreuder had joined them in the same manner as the rest: she auditioned. Frances's presence on the NYCB Board of Directors had nothing whatever to do with Ariadne's presence among the students—though it would in time have consequences.

SAB accepts children as young as eight, but they are not really weeded out until thirteen. Until then, bodies and feet are too immature to make the lifetime choice—to be or not to be a ballet professional. The choice itself, the rigors of the training, and the odds against success all are excruciating. Out of every thousand eight-year-olds who seriously take up ballet, the Company has calculated, "we will get one good dancer." Ariadne's thirteenth birthday will occur in April 1986.

Larry Bradshaw's twenty-first birthday was approaching. The one present he wanted was a glimpse of his family and a peek at the wonderful new duplex apartment he had heard so much about. The first necessity was a transfer out of the escape-proof Farview State Hospital for the Criminally Insane. He had managed that back in mid-October, just about the time that Behrens was turning in the gun. But he had returned to Allentown State Psychiatric Hospital completely out of money. He took a menial job, and eventually a small check came in. On February 9, three days after his birthday, Larry—in the parlance of such institutions—eloped. He carefully washed and shaved and trimmed his hair, put on clean clothes, and at dusk he strolled out onto the hospital grounds, caught a taxi to the bus station, took a Greyhound to New York, a subway uptown, a crosstown bus, and by 8:30 P.M. he had got past 10 Gracie's downstairs doormen and stood with his broad thumb on the doorbell of Apartment 6.

The door was opened by Paulette Tueller, the capable and savvy Frenchwoman, active in the French Resistance during World War II, who now had charge of feeding Ariadne and running the Schreuder household. The family had acquired their "French maid" from her former employer, Lily Pons, who had once occupied the penthouse. Larry identified himself and Paulette showed the visitor up the curving stair to the master suite. Here he found his entire family, all snuggled together in and on the big rumpled bed.

"Granny was shocked! Mom was shocked! They looked at me like I was a dead person," Larry laughs. "They thought I'd risen from the grave!" He thought they seemed happy to see him, though, and he himself was overjoyed, especially at catching sight of Ariadne nestled deep down in the pillows cuddling Tiffany. Marc took Larry down the hall to see *his* room and, not more than five minutes later, the doorbell rang again and four big cops hurriedly summoned by Frances came pounding up the stairs. His mother told Larry that, with Marc out on bail, she could scarcely take a chance on harboring an escaped criminal. The cops took Larry away. He and Marc have not seen each other since.

Larry hated the next twelve days on Rikers Island. "I'm a college person. I can't relate to any of these weird mental patients and those thousands of blackies and jailbirds." But when the Pennsylvania cops arrived to escort him home, he rather enjoyed the leisurely drive. While Larry was imprisoned in New York, his plea for a new trial had been denied, and he was now placed in Northampton County Prison where he would remain until Christmas. By that time he had deteriorated so severely, neglecting to eat or care for himself, and refusing to talk, that he was sent back to the psychiatric hospital at Allentown. There he was again put on antipsychotic medication, and again began to show some improvement.

Richard Behrens's recantation had put the Salt Lake authorities in a very difficult position indeed. They had the weapon but no material witness. Less than a week after Larry was released from Rikers Island Prison, Behrens was locked up for three weeks in the same institution, charged with criminal possession of a weapon, obstruction of justice, and tampering with evidence. Then, in Connecticut, ninety days after Marc's arrest, Utah's juvenile warrant expired. On March 5, 1981, all charges against the twenty-year-old youth were dropped. Berenice Bradshaw's bail money was returned to her. Marc Schreuder was completely free.

Marc should have been elated, but he was not. He felt the charges might be reinstated at any time. He was terrified of getting caught. His mother was pushing him to reapply to Trinity, and other colleges, "as if nothing had happened." But the lawyers were telling him something quite different. They warned that eventually the Utah authorities would probably figure out a way to get Marc certified in absentia as an adult. If this happened, Marc could be rearrested in New York, Connecticut, or any other state.

Marc tried to explain all this to his mother, but she refused to listen. "At this point, Mom was the eternal optimist. She just kept saying, 'Reapply!' I said, 'Why? I'm just gonna get yanked out of college and go on trial for murder anyway. I'm fighting for my life, and you want me to go back to college as if nothing had happened!' "

But Frances refused to look at the bad side. Marc can still hear, and imitate, his mother's voice repeating like a manic parrot, "No problem, Marc. No problem! You'll get off! You'll get off!"

"But, Mom! What if they . . ."

"You'll get out of it, I promise you. We've—got—the—money!"

Berenice was begging Marc to leave, to run while he could. "Go to South America! Go to Europe! Mexico! Go to Switzerland! Go to Canada!" She was right, of course. If her grandson had left the country, it would have been far more difficult to catch and extradite him. But, instead, he went into hiding. Why?

"Whew. SH-Z-Z-Z-Z-Z. That's a good question. I think the reason was I didn't want to leave Mom. I couldn't face life in another country. I could not face leaving home. I knew if I ran, and wanted to be successful at escaping, I'd never be able to see Mom again. Because I knew they'd always be watching. And I felt like—damn, there's my whole life in there! That apartment. That was the biggest thing with me: life with Mom. I couldn't live with her, couldn't live without her.

"You see, I loved my mother. I still love her, in a way. I mean, she was my whole life! Mom was my only friend . . ."

Marc's reasons for not fleeing the country are complex and contradictory. He was both afraid and overconfident. In his mind, he was James Bond. He wore an imaginary trench coat, dealt in international high finance, played the stock market, speculated in foreign exchange, putting together a grubstake. In reality, he was a mama's boy, the damaged victim of his mother's abuse. But there was another reason he didn't leave. In the few months he had been away at Trinity, he had noticed a change in Ariadne. When Marc lived at home and worked for Mitsubishi, he could go to the store for Frances, and did, every night after work. "But now Mom was beginning to have Ariadne take over my role in the house. *She* was going to the store and getting Mom's food. *She* was becoming Mom's confidante. It was already starting to happen, and she was still only seven years old!"

Even when he was home for the weekend, it seemed to him, Mom now *preferred* to send Ariadne, not Marc, down to the deli. "On the ballet thing, Mom was pushing Ariadne really hard, too. *Everything* Mom did was really geared for Ariadne." Frances wanted Ariadne to fulfill her own fantasies of becoming a ballerina, a perfect, tiny, adorable female, and Marc thinks, "Mom really drummed it in. I think Mom was pushing Ariadne really, really hard. I think, initially, Ariadne was very much the same as I was—very devoted to Mom. She was a mommy's girl, like I was a mommy's boy. She would do *anything* Mom asked . . . and I think she also wanted to *copy* Mom. There's a lot of attachment between the two. A lot of love, and a lot of hate."

Probably there was also a lot of sibling rivalry developing. Marc, although the overwhelming favorite son, had always become irrationally jealous of the least attention his mother paid to Larry. Now another, more serious rival was appearing on the scene. For whatever dark combination of motives, Marc decided the best thing he could do for Ariadne was to capture her tangled feelings about her mother on tape, so that later he could show her how she too was being used, and abused, just as he himself had been.

And so he tenderly asked his half sister to tell him about her life with Mother. He made tapes in which the little girl told him that every day her mother slapped, kicked, hit, punched, and screamed at her. Tearfully, she said that she liked her mother, but didn't like her when she punched and kicked and screamed at her. She did not like her mother's threats to push her out of the window if she did not stop crying. Sometimes she *could not* stop. Her mother knew that, and still "she screams me. She *loves* screaming me! And she loves kicking me! Loves punching me. She just *loves* it!"

It made Ariadne feel as if "Mom hates my guts," she told Marc. She dreaded coming home from school, she said, because her mother might put a knife in her stomach or in her throat. The worst part was riding home on the school bus *knowing it was going to happen.* She wished things were only as bad as last year, when Mom used to beat her with a hairbrush. One day she had had to go to school painted with Mercurochrome to cover brush marks on her forehead, arms, knees.

"What is *that?*" Sister had asked, but Ariadne had quickly covered up. "I said, 'Oh, nothing. I just fell down.' " It wasn't true, Ariadne said, but she didn't want Sister to know the truth. Then she would tell Reverend Mother, and something even worse might happen.

Marc laughed. He knew just how she felt, he said.

That spring, shortly after Ariadne's birthday, another troubling incident had occurred. Berenice had invited Ariadne to the circus, and she was seated in the foyer when Frances came storming down the stairs shouting, "Don't you dare take my daughter anywhere! I want to have her at home. I do not want to have you *brainwashing her!*"

Berenice had begun shouting back when Ariadne appeared and stepped into the middle of the fight. "You stop that! You stop shouting at my mommy, you bad old witch!"

It was too much. *"You* stay out of this!" Berenice cried out, and angrily shoved the child away. It was a push with her forearm, not a blow, but it caught Ariadne in the midsection and she burst into tears.

Frances raced to the phone and reported to the New York Society for the Prevention of Cruelty to Children that her mother was abusing her daughter. Then she gathered up the weeping child and rushed to Lenox Hill Hospital where she demanded that Ariadne be examined and treated for stomach injuries. Although the hospital kept the child several days, the real purpose, says Berenice, was to observe the eccentric behavior of the mother.

Nothing physical was the matter with Ariadne, but doctors recommended that the family seek professional counseling. A therapist was suggested, and Berenice and Frances paid him one visit.

"Are you sorry you reported your mother as a child-abuser?" Berenice recalls the psychiatrist asking Frances.

"No," Frances replied.

He prescribed some medication for Frances, and they stopped at the pharmacy on the way home. Berenice says she does not remember the name of the doctor or the drug, but after they got home, Frances withdrew to her bedroom with her new medicine and Ariadne, and locked the door. Ariadne still slept with her mother, and ever since the "shoving" episode, Frances had taken to locking her in at night, ostensibly to protect Ariadne from her grandmother.

"About six o'clock in the morning I heard all this moaning and groaning in there," Berenice recalls. "I started knocking on the door, but Ariadne wouldn't let me in."

Berenice knew that Ariadne always got up and went downstairs to make her mother's coffee, so she waited, "and as soon as she opened that door, I tore in. I found Frances in the most horrible condition! Unconscious. She had chewed her tongue all night, and the blood was running down, and she was just—her eyes. And moaning. Oh, she was *thrashing!*

"I said, 'Oh, Ariadne, you should have let me in.' But at that point, it was war, and she probably thought she was protecting her mother."

Berenice woke up Marc and told him to try to reach Frances's own doctor. Meanwhile Paulette, who occupied one of the ground-floor servant's rooms at 10 Gracie, came upstairs and helped Berenice hold down the thrashing, unconscious Frances. In an hour or so Frances's regular physician arrived, sent for an ambulance, and Berenice and the doctor accompanied Frances to New York Hospital.

Berenice believes what caused this episode was a bad drug reaction, although she cannot be sure. Frances all her life has been careful not to tell her mother whatever drugs she might be taking. What stands out most in Berenice's mind is that the New York Society for the Prevention of Cruelty to Children automatically filed a report with Ariadne's school alerting them that the child had a dangerous grandmother. Eventually it was necessary for Berenice, accompanied by one of her lawyers, to visit the headquarters of the child abuse society to have her name expunged from their records.

In June, Ernie Jones had a second stroke of luck. The Utah Legislature enacted a new statute which enabled the police to have Marc certified as an adult in absentia. They no longer needed to bring him back to Utah to process the necessary papers. The next time they went after him, he would not have to be held on a juvenile warrant.

That same month Berenice retained a Utah criminal defense attorney, Paul Van Dam, to represent her grandson in that state, should it become necessary. Van Dam, about forty, is a gentle, rumpled, professorial type, whose bald head is counterbalanced by a thick, gray-streaked black beard. He is a lapsed Mormon given to corduroy jackets and rumbling baritone pronouncements. If the Marc Schreuder case ever did come to trial, he expected it to be the biggest case of his career.

Over the spring and summer, Frances locked out Marc permanently from 10 Gracie Square, lest the neighbors somehow find out that her son was the object of police surveillance for grandpatricide. One evening the husband of a Board member drove her home from the ballet. As they approached Gracie Square, Frances grew fearful and agitated, reluctant to permit their limousine to approach the building. An important diplomat lived there incognito, she said, and armed guards patrolled at all hours. "I got the feeling she was terrified of something, and that security was a very important factor in her life," said her uncomfortable escort. When he got home he told his wife, "I never want any responsibility for that woman again."

Marc was living in "that crummy Sloane House YMCA on West Thirty-fourth between Eighth and Ninth Avenue . . . the place is a gutter! You have a little tiny room, half as big as a regular jail cell. Built about 1930. Roaches all over. Filthy . . . !" He moved to the moderate-priced Hotel Seville. He lived under aliases like Alexander Bentley and David Zablonski and was pleased when his mother said the latter was "a good lower-class Jewish name."

In August, according to Richard Behrens, he met with Marc in Carl Schurz Park. Here, for the first time, Marc gave Behrens details of the murder, including the crucial detail that it had not been his own idea: Frances had ordered him to do it.

Early in 1981, Ernie Jones finally got the biggest break in his nearly three-year-old unsolved case. Sergeant Michael George, a young investigator in the Salt Lake County Attorney's Office, stopped by Jones's office and told him that an unexpected lull had developed in a case he was working on. "I'd like something more to do," he said. Ernie tossed him the Bradshaw file.

At twenty-eight, Mike George, a lanky, handsome cop with olive skin, Afro hair, and a placid disposition, already had five years' solid experience working narcotics, and the high confidence which comes from a recent big win. In the early 1970s, dope dealers had discovered Salt Lake City, and liked the place for the same reason the Mormons had. It was isolated and safe. It was also so clean and virtuous it did not even have a police or sheriff's drug unit. The dealers made Salt Lake a "free city," a center to which couriers could bring raw heroin from Mexico to be cut, diluted, packaged, and shipped elsewhere. The dealers had come to like the place less after five years of pursuit by Mike George.

He often worked disguised behind a beard, mustache, bandanna, and gold earring, posing as a major dealer himself. It was a fervid, dangerous life. One woman had almost sliced him open with a knife. But Mike loved his job and was very good at it, spirited but stubborn, inventive but never rash. He was a prudent, self-made cop who wanted only to go on being a cop. He was married to Elaine Meppen, a brainy and pretty medical technologist. As children began to come along, Elaine suggested it might be time to get out of narcotics and into something safer, like homicide.

While he worked undercover, he had called himself Mike Frustraglio. He thought it had "a nice Italian ring to it." Besides, it was his mother's maiden name, and Mike's mother had been the key figure in molding his unusual persona. Mike's father, John George, had been a laborer at the Hercules Powder Company in northern Michigan near the Canadian border. When the Michigan mines closed, Hercules transferred John George to Salt Lake City, where he worked on Poseidon missiles. When Mike was twelve, his mother was told she had cancer and less than a year to live. Mike's mother determined to use the time she had left to show her son everything she knew about running a house. Then the miracle had happened. Her cobalt therapy actually worked, very rare in those days, and she is still living.

Mike George grew up to become a high school athlete who lettered in football, basketball, and baseball, and doubtless was the only one of his teammates who could also without embarrassment dust the house, darn socks, and bake lasagna. He had developed a winning combination of boldness and modesty, self-confidence and faith, and he was also a kid who knew exactly what he wanted out of life. "I just always had this burning itch to become a cop."

At that time the Lyndon Johnson administration had just launched a national plan to diminish police brutality and community tensions by upgrading police education. It was called Project LEEP—Law Enforcement Education Program—and it advanced prospective cops full college tuition and board. Mike George applied. Working eighteen-hour days, he completed four years' work at the University of Utah in two and a half years, supporting himself with a night job in a grocery store. He had to give up his beloved sports and, looking back, he says, "College was just no fun at all." But LEEP and the former Signorina Frustraglio had produced a very good and unusual cop, probably the only one in America who makes blueberry pies, raises bonsai trees, irons his own shirts, and has built a full-size mosaic-tiled swimming pool in his backyard. He and Elaine now have two daughters, ages five and seven, and a two-year-old son, and every birthday Daddy bakes them an Easter Bunny cake.

To admire such abilities may be merely sentimental—Bluebeard probably ironed shirts—but Mike George brings to his work a striking blend of gentleness and manliness, and utter equanimity. "Is that right?" he murmurs quietly to the most outlandish bits of information. He also has a rare understanding of where the levers are inside people, himself included. He knows, for example, that he never wants to be anything but a cop, and has several times turned down offers of a year's salary to do two or three months' work investigating a case for a defense lawyer. "I'm just prosecution oriented," he says, baffled and quietly contemptuous of those legions of rationalists and opportunists—the hired guns of the law—who can happily work either side of the street.

George was a 1960s liberal who campaigned for George McGovern, and before that for Bobby Kennedy. But his bedrock notions of morality and integrity, plus five years working narcotics, turned him into an ultraconservative in many matters. He opposes marijuana use, and speaks frequently at clubs and schools. His first homicide case after he left narcotics in 1980 was the notorious Joseph Paul Franklin affair. Franklin was a white racist who spotted two young black men not long out of high school jogging in Liberty Park with two white women. It was a Sunday afternoon; the joggers had just come from church. The sight moved Franklin to homicidal frenzy. He waited outside the park in a field until nine-thirty at night, riddled the men with nine shots, and escaped in a speeding Camaro.

Mike George worked on the investigation of the Franklin case. It took nine months. Eventually the car was discovered in Kentucky. Mike George found a Kentucky girl who remembered Franklin's hatred of blacks. The FBI followed the trail to Tampa, Florida, and found a man in a queue trying to sell his blood whom they were able to identify as the killer by the tattoo of the Grim Reaper on his arm. The Franklin case was stalled awaiting trial in early 1981, which is why Mike stopped by Ernie Jones's office looking for more work.

The case against Marc Schreuder was then in disarray. Behrens had recanted and would speak to nobody. Campbell had unwittingly put too much muscle on the Texans, and they had turned uncooperative. They confirmed that Marc had come to Midland and bought a gun, but the dates of their statements ranged across an entire year. "There's no way I can go into court unless we can put Marc in Salt Lake on July 23, 1978, and also tie him to the gun in Texas," Ernie said.

Mike studied the case, quickly concurred, went to work. "I've been in airline searches before," he said. Mike had worked on two major heroin conspiracy cases that were ten years old before he started investigating them. He had had to search out evidence of plane trips made a decade earlier—tedious, boring but vital work. His experience in narcotics had made him realize the overwhelming extent to which ours has become a "society of records." Wherever we go, whatever we do, however we pay for it, somebody—or, more likely, somebody's computer—has almost certainly made note of it. Mike George immediately subpoenaed all telephone, bank, and other financial records even remotely connected with Franklin Bradshaw's business enterprises, or with his estate. He also asked family members for personal documents and correspondence. Bushel baskets of stored-up documents began to pile up in his tiny office. Marilyn and Elaine and other

Bradshaws relinquished massive amounts of family correspondence; even Berenice turned in some letters.

In 1978 only two airlines, American and United, flew between New York City and Salt Lake. Mike George assisted by Joel Campbell started checking through the manifests of every direct flight into Salt Lake City on the day of the murder, the day before, and two days after, looking for a passenger named Schreuder or Bradshaw or Jewett. Then Mike learned from the NYC Bureau of Vital Statistics that Marc had been born Marco Gentile. He looked again. They still found nothing. Then: United did have a record of a reservation for an "L. Schreuder," on a flight from Salt Lake to New York two hours after the homicide. But no ticket had been picked up.

Computers were the problem; computers were also the solution. United's "record" was in fact a signal from Continental's computer. Continental stores its passenger name records in Los Angeles. George and Campbell flew there, and searched through 25,000 names before they hit the jackpot: on July 22, an "L. Gentile" had flown on American Airlines from New York to Dallas; on Texas International from Dallas to Midland; on Continental from Midland to Phoenix, and there switched to a Hughes Air West flight into Salt Lake. The ticket itself had been purchased in New York City at an American Airlines ticket agency. Hughes AW stored its old records in San Mateo, California. George flew there and found his essential missing link: a corroborating record that somebody had actually made the Phoenix to Salt Lake leg of the journey. Since Larry already was in Salt Lake, this suggested to George the possibility of a plot by Marc or Frances to frame her other son.

Mike George worked over all of the various records he had subpoenaed, using a police technique called VIA (Visual Investigative Aid) which charts and connects seemingly unrelated events. Other patterns emerged. He began to feel that July 13 had been a critical day. Frances had called each of her parents on that day, both times at the warehouse and, fortunately, both times collect. Otherwise Mike would not have been able to examine the phone bills. (His authority covers Mountain Bell only; he can subpoena only records of phone calls paid for in Utah.) These would have been the calls in which Marc borrowed the final $3,000, and promised never to ask Gramps for money again, the calls that produced the $3,000 check payable to Ariadne which helped to buy the gun and plane ticket—the calls which showed how Franklin Bradshaw had paid for his own assassination.

VIA analysis of bank records made clear that Frances and her children were entirely or heavily dependent for funds on her father. Phone records also showed numerous calls to Frances, or to Marc, from Gilmer Drive, calls which must have been made by either Berenice or Larry. There were also a number of calls from Gilmer Drive to Behrens. These had to be from Larry. Berenice and Behrens had never met.

Studying these patterns, and reading through the voluminous family correspondence, Mike began to feel that Marc was not really the person he was after; or at least not *the only* person. He saw no motive for the boy to come to Salt Lake on his own and kill his grandfather. One day he blurted out, "Christ, Ernie, we're after the wrong person! We oughta start chasin' Frances."

"On what evidence?"

No evidence yet, Mike said. Only a "gut reaction. The relationship between this boy and this mother is strange."

And there was one other thing. Marilyn Reagan and Elaine Drukman were helpful and courteous when Mike telephoned seeking information; Berenice was sometimes hostile and rude; Frances flatly refused to talk to him. But in a sense, her letters spoke for her.

The sum of the correspondence, dating back to the early sixties, showed the duration and depth of the family friction over money. "The feuding between Frances and her father is what tore this family apart," Mike said later. "It was not so much that Marilyn and Elaine feared Frances was after their share of the inheritance. They just didn't like what she was doing to their father. In her letters, you could see Frances pit people against each other. She pitted her mother against her father. She would pit Marilyn's husband against Elaine's husband. She was a great conspirator, a master manipulator. The further she went, the more friction she caused."

Mike George longed to meet the other members of this family, especially Frances. He had already interviewed Marilyn on one of her visits to Salt Lake. Since he was in San Mateo checking airline records, he decided it would be worthwhile to drive up to Berkeley, California, where the Drukmans were then living, and talk to Elaine.

On this trip he understood for the first time how deeply divided a family the Bradshaws had become. Elaine turned out to be the most bitter of them all. She saw her mother as literally "enslaved" to Frances. She believed Frances had used Ariadne as a "hostage" to obtain more funds from her mother. She was jealous of Berenice's extreme concern for Frances's well-being, and relative disinterest in her own. Before returning from New Zealand, Elaine had been paralyzed for a month with a back injury; she had developed skin cancers from the strong sunlight. But at the family reunion which occurred at the time of her father's funeral, her mother had not even asked her about these illnesses. Berenice seemed only able to think about Frances's auto accident on the Triboro Bridge. "Frances! Oh, my poor Frances!" was all Berenice could say, even though her sister had "no crutches, no braces, no canes."

Elaine believed that her mother hated her, it appeared to Sergeant George, and hated her most "for what I did to Frances"— denouncing Frances to the FBI and forcing her to return the Mountain Fuel stock she had stolen from Elaine's sons. Elaine even believed that Berenice's spontaneous blurt at the time she first heard of her husband's murder—"I believe in capital punishment, so help me!"—had been a deliberate attempt to mock Elaine's long-standing political opposition to the death penalty.

After Marc, not Larry, had actually been identified as their father's murderer, apprehended in Connecticut, and then released on a technicality, the bitterness of both sisters had greatly intensified. Marilyn had fired off letters of Hamlet-like grief and rage to the governor of Utah, the attorney general, and both of the Salt Lake City newspapers, taunting the authorities for being unable to hold on to her father's assassin, even though "the murder weapon has been recovered and directly connected to the victim's grandson."

Elaine's fury was directly aimed at her mother. As she saw it, Berenice was openly financing Marc's ability to avoid arrest, and she was doing it "by feeding huge sums of Dad's money to Dad's murderer."

"Now I know everything," she wrote to her mother at about this time. "You helped them murder Dad." These were the last words Berenice would ever hear from her daughter Elaine.

By the time Mike George returned to Salt Lake, his conversation with Elaine had confirmed his own gut feelings. "Frances Schreuder, not Marc, was the brain behind this murder," he told

Ernie Jones. "Marc was the executioner, but she was the mastermind." About Berenice, Mike was not prepared to go so far as Elaine and Marilyn. By this time the sisters were so bitter, they had convinced themselves that their mother too was somehow involved in, or aware of, the plot. They even thought she might have found and destroyed evidence of a second will. Mike George disagreed then, and still does. He saw the old lady chiefly as a victim of the family warfare around her.

More than anything, Mike wanted to meet Frances Schreuder. He wanted to spend time alone with her, establish a relationship, sense what she was really like. The only way this could possibly happen would be if he were sent back to New York to arrest and escort her to Utah. Such an eventuality lay far in the future. For now, he had to content himself with a visit to Larry Bradshaw at Allentown State Psychiatric Hospital.

Even for a tough cop, their three-hour meeting in April 1981 was uniquely depressing. For years, Frances had denied Larry's existence, and she had instructed Marc and Ariadne to deny it. None of their schoolmates or their parents even knew they had a brother. As Marc puts it today, "Larry has been officially nonexistent for as long as I can remember." Sometimes, on Larry's rare visits home, he would answer the telephone, and pass it to Marc. "Who was that?" the caller sometimes asked.

"Oh just some guy," Marc would reply.

In the psychiatric hospital, Frances's prophecy seemed to have come true. Said Mike George later, "He was very pathetic. Dirty and skinny. He didn't take care of himself at all. His gums bled profusely, from poor hygiene. He stank and his fingernails were long and black. He was just a pathetic human being—but very sharp, with an outstanding memory for facts and details. He could remember his exact route to Salt Lake in the summer of 1978, the buses he took, the cities he stayed in, even the names of cafes where he ate." Larry confirmed stealing auto parts from his grandfather's warehouse but declined to talk about stealing checks, cash, or securities. "Talk to Marc about that," was all he would say.

The poisoned oatmeal was just a joke, Larry insisted, something the boys had made up to entertain, or perhaps confuse Behrens. But Mike George was not so sure. Several warehouse employees told him that one day Franklin had come to work very upset. He spoke of waking at three o'clock in the morning and

finding Marc standing over his bed. Marc had said he could not
sleep and had come into his grandfather's room to open a window. But the expression on Marc's face had frightened Franklin,
he told his employees the next day. And at the warehouse, he was
dizzy, vomited, had to lie down on his desk for a while. Larry
denied all knowledge.

Mike George was in Midland by mid-July. He needed to regain
the Texans' confidence that "they were on our team, they weren't
suspects." Instead of summoning them to police headquarters for
questioning, he invited them out to dinner. Later, he began attempting to refresh their hazy memories. Again, his narcotics
training paid off. "It's hard for people to remember dates, even
last week. But start to link the date you're after with other events,
and it will usually come back." Jerry Register proved the theory
sound. The ex-sheriff had originally placed Marc in Midland on a
Saturday in May—not at all helpful since the murder occurred in
July. But now Mike George encouraged the shy sheriff to talk,
free-associate, remember. Suddenly Register said, "Wait a minute! My son was shot right after I sold Marc the gun. That's *why*
I sold it, to buy my son some new clothes . . ."

He had bought the boy some expensive Western boots, and
nine-year-old Richard Register had been wearing them and playing on the living room floor with his still-younger cousin, fooling
with one of the guns in his dad's collection, when his cousin
pulled the trigger. The bullet shattered Richard's spine and made
him a quadriplegic.

"When was your son shot?"

"August 4, 1978."

Mike George had brought along a calendar. Working back-
ward, it was now easy to peg the date of sale: July 22, 1978.

From mid-July of 1981 until the end of September, Mike had to
put aside the Schreuders for the trial of his white racist killer
Joseph Paul Franklin. The jury split ten to two and Franklin
drew a life sentence, not the death penalty. Two jurors held out
because the evidence was circumstantial; Mike had been unable
to produce the murder weapon. The verdict was a major disap-
pointment to the fervent champion of law and order, and he
vowed to do better next time.

Now Ernie Jones called a staff meeting on the Bradshaw case.
A new warrant for Marc's arrest as an adult had been issued in
mid-June but never acted upon. Marc's lawyers had meanwhile

made preliminary overtures: Marc would surrender voluntarily in return for a promise of bail, and certain other stipulations. But Ernie did not want to bargain; he wanted to "deal from strength."

"Once you have the kid in the slammer, the more pressure you put on him, the more mistakes he is going to make." The prosecutor gave Mike George thirty days to mount an all-out search for Marc.

In New York, the Schreuder matter was in the hands of the 20th Precinct, where Marilyn had turned in the gun. These cops were now all tied up on the John Lennon murder. Mike George decided to bypass the NYPD and seek help from New York District Attorney Morgenthau's office. He drew a crack blue-eyed cop with a gaze like an icicle. His name was Steve Klein and, like George, he was young and enthusiastic; this was the most important assignment of his brief career.

They had little to go on. Mike gave Steve Klein the Gracie Square address, and they started another phone records search. Acting on a hunch that if Marc *were* still in New York, Granny was probably supporting him, they subpoenaed Berenice Bradshaw's bank records and canceled checks. And there it was. A check made out to "M.T.B.", and at the bottom, a notation in a different handwriting—*Re: Marc Schreuder.*

M.T.B.—Manfra, Tordella & Brookes—deals in foreign exchange from offices in the World Trade Center, the same building Marc had worked in as a messenger boy for Mitsubishi International. Mike assumed when he saw the check that Marc had skipped the country and was somehow having money sent to him overseas. He telephoned M.T.B. and asked if he could arrange to send money to a brother in Italy.

"Of course, sir. We can transfer money to any bank in the world."

But Marc had not fled the country, or even New York City. In June, Berenice was involved in a minor traffic accident in Salt Lake City, and police spotted Marc running from the scene. He was in town to collect his passport, police surmised, and probably had raised getaway money from his grandmother. Klein and George had no idea that Marc had spent the summer in New York, occasionally, furtively visiting Mom, but mostly living in crummy hotels, and, when necessary, forging another of his grandmother's stolen checks to finance his trading in stocks and gold coins.

In fact, Marc Schreuder embezzled $90,000 from Berenice Bradshaw during the ten-month period between his release in Connecticut March 5 and his recapture October 27 in New York City—scarcely the work of a "naughty boy." Not even a doting grandmother could turn a blind eye to so large an amount. But Marc had not even attempted to run. "He never could have done it," Berenice later acknowledged. "He's too much a mama's boy. He needs to know where he's gonna sleep every night. He's not like Larry."

Now came another lucky break. Steve Klein knew the wife of an M.T.B. executive who had once worked in the New York D.A.'s office. Klein persuaded her to arrange a peek into Marc Schreuder's account. It bore an address: 205 E. 85th Street. This was a private "postal supermarket," CITIPOSTAL, which consolidates several kinds of delivery services under one roof—U.S. Mail, United Parcel, Federal Express, Purolator Courier. Marc knew the place from his messenger-boy days—a tiny, step-down room banked with the sort of locked brass mailboxes seen in old-fashioned post offices. Now he was using CITIPOSTAL as a mail drop for his foreign exchange and stock transactions.

Klein learned from M.T.B. that Marc had just ordered still another gold coin. He discovered the magnitude of Marc's dealings—$90,000 since July, all of it accomplished, it would turn out, with the checks he had stolen from Granny's bedroom. As a thief, Marc showed himself his mother's son. As a foreign exchange trader he was less skilled. M.T.B. clerks had nicknamed him "The Magician" for his ability to make money disappear. M.T.B. management agreed to stall delivery of Marc's latest purchase, a $12,500 Canadian 1912 $10 gold piece in gem-brilliant mint condition, until a proper police surveillance could be set up.

Monday morning, Steve Klein stationed himself across the street from CITIPOSTAL, between the Star of India Restaurant and a bicycle repair shop. When the chubby, slovenly blond-haired youth arrived to pick up his mail, Klein made the collar.

"The kid about died. He just about passed out," the investigator said jubilantly, reporting the arrest to Mike George an hour later. It was October 26, 1981—four days before Ernie Jones's deadline.

As Marc's arrest became known, lawyers began heading for 10

Gracie Square. Paul Van Dam had to fly from Salt Lake City, so the first legal meeting could not be held until Monday night, October 26. Marc spent the night at Metropolitan Correctional Center, the federal holding tank. When the lawyers gathered at Apartment 6, they were astonished to see the contrast between the extreme grandeur of the layout and its meager, shabby contents.

Downstairs, 10 Gracie Square is cold, old, expensive, and fortresslike: one square block of solid wealth arranged in duplex apartments topped by penthouses. Upstairs, the lawyers stepped into a small, dim foyer of dark old Chinese lacquer and peeling wallpaper with an ornate, grimy mirror cockeyed on one wall. A large, triple-locked door, lacquered Chinese red, opened onto an astonishing space—bare ruined choirs, two stories high. Fifty thousand dollars' worth of huge new steel-framed picture windows overlooked the East River. They were set into the old masonry walls, but the work was half-complete, unpainted, not even plastered. The vast space was empty of furniture. Two twelve-foot couches newly reupholstered in "vanilla velvet," still in protective covers of heavy transparent plastic, were pushed up against one wall. Chinese rugs were rolled up tightly at their feet. Dark "good" wood floors gleamed dully, reflecting river lights. A huge old French mirror above the fireplace reflected a dusty chandelier. The whole place looked like a ballet set of some abandoned ballroom, an old *valse noble et sentimentale* almost audible in the wings.

Frances had planned to refurbish her castle with all-new marble bathrooms as well as new windows, then abruptly halted all work midway, lest one amid the small army of plasterers and plumbers turn out to be a private investigator or police spy. This had left the ballroom-like living room in an incongruous state worthy of Magritte: three ten-foot crates, two lying down, one standing, occupied the middle of the otherwise empty room. They resembled giant sarcophagi stored in some dusty, unused chamber of the Cairo Museum. In fact, each crate contained a solid onyx bathtub drilled for gold-plated fittings. Because Frances had stopped the workmen, all but one of the apartment's bathrooms still looked like raw survivors of the London blitz, while the great, shadowy, and mysterious living room resembled a storehouse of loot from an Egyptian tomb. Atop one of the packing crates, as if placed there by Magritte himself, rested a pair of vivid watermelon-pink silk ballet slippers, long pink satin ribbons dangling down over the crate's edge in an attitude of chic abandon.

Off to the left was an empty dining room, to the right, the one furnished room on this floor, the small dark brown library, its bookshelves still mostly empty. To the rear was an old-fashioned, gloomy kitchen that smelled faintly of gas leaking from the expensive new restaurant range. The giant new restaurant refrigerator contained only skim milk and Campbell's soup. No desserts, no bread or butter. Ariadne must stay slim for the ballet. A new ice maker dripped unused in the old butler's pantry where very expensive roaches scurried. A laundry room off the pantry was jammed with metal filing cabinets bought on sale, bright green or yellow, all locked.

Two interior staircases, front and rear, ascended to four bedrooms on the apartment's second floor. Granny's room, down the hall, was carpeted in new purple shag and had the only decent bathroom installed before all work had been halted. "My Cinderella room," Berenice Bradshaw called it, because it was so plain compared to her daughter's and granddaughter's quarters. The window looked out on a blank wall. The room had a flowered bedspread and family pictures on the bureau. The portraits of Marc and Larry showed them in short pants, Easter outfits, and had been taken when they were only four or five years old.

Had the lawyers been invited to tour the family's private quarters—they were not—they would have been dumbfounded by the master-bedroom, lair of their client's mother. It was a *Great Expectations* chamber, gloomy and huge, the floor so completely covered with stacks of boxes, newspapers, dusty piles and mounds of other files and boxes that to walk across it would be like crossing a large pond on stepping stones. Rising dead center in the middle of the rubble was an astonishing canopied bed reaching almost to the ceiling. The bed table was stained with coffeepot marks and cigarette burns, as was the portion of floor visible between the stalagmites of rubble. This was where she sat, slept, smoked, phoned, ate, lived. It resembled a ruined pagoda improbably rising out of the stacks of bills, boxes, cans of floor wax, and wobbly towers of shoe boxes on all sides. A literal wall of boxed ballet shoes stood in the dressing room—as if the room had been papered in a repeat pattern of the magic word CAPEZIO. Clothes closets were jammed, crushed full of costly garments.

The bathroom was a disheveled osprey's nest of brushes, tools, bottles, jars. Reigning dead center of the whole mess, on the bed, amid the billowy mound of ivory-silk-covered pillows, sat Tiffany, the red Persian cat, black opal eyes blinking slowly.

To the rear on this floor was a disorderly twin-bedded room and bath for the boys. Down the hall was a small two-room suite of immaculate and cheerful perfection. It looked like a magazine illustration of an ideal little girl's room. Dozens of stuffed toys sat on child-sized furniture. Schoolbooks, pencils, and paper lay on the writing table like surgeon's tools. All the bathroom porcelain gleamed, and small bottles sparkled in graduated sizes on the glass shelves behind the mirror. The small ruffle-trimmed bed, perfectly crisp and smooth, sat dead-center in its own doll-size sleeping chamber off the larger room. On three sides of a large, well-lit closet hung rows and rows of small dresses and coats and ballet tutus, in perfect order above dozens of pairs of ballet slippers and polished party shoes aligned on freshly painted shelves. Open the closet door and a light went on automatically, illuminating what appeared on the upper levels to be an enchanted toyshop. Rows of new-looking, richly costumed beaded, wimpled, pearl-encrusted, armored, satin and silk and velvet and gold-thread Storybook Dolls stared blankly at one another from the three sides of the closet with unseeing dolls' eyes.

Downstairs, in the little brown library, mother and grandmother—in their way no less surprising than their habitat—sat down with their three lawyers. The purpose of the meeting was to formulate strategy to get Marc out of jail in New York and keep him out of jail in Utah. From MCC he was headed for Rikers Island, and doubtless would remain there unless or until bail could be arranged—always a difficult matter in capital cases. Ted Carey had come down from Connecticut to join Van Dam. But the New York lawyer was new to the case.

At the time of Marc's Connecticut arrest, the cooperating New York law firm had been Ostrow & Grand. But Paul Grand is a son-in-law of New York District Attorney Robert Morgenthau, and as a matter of policy his firm does not work on cases that fall within Morgenthau's jurisdiction. Grand had therefore called in Michael Armstrong, the very able former Queens district attorney who had served as counsel to the Knapp Commission during its inquiry into police corruption in the city. Armstrong was busy Monday night—his daughter was leaving for Botswana to join the Peace Corps—so his firm was represented by a sturdy, red-haired, and studious twenty-eight-year-old attorney named David Frankel, one of the bright young men at Barrett, Smith, Schapiro, Simon & Armstrong. As luck would have it, Frankel had recently made a special study of extradition law, a thorny subject. He had no experience in a capital case.

Since the passage by all fifty states of the Uniform Criminal Extradition Act, a state-to-state extradition request can be challenged only on narrow technical grounds. Either you are the wrong person, or you were not in the state at the time of the crime, or the extradition papers themselves are not in order. Point three had saved Marc from Utah's clutches in Connecticut. Now Marc's only hope was point two: he would have to show that he had not been in Utah on the day his grandfather was killed. This requirement made it somewhat more important than usual that the lawyer know the full truth about exactly what his client *had* been doing that day, since the burden of proof in such matters is on the defendant.

On Tuesday morning lawyers Van Dam, Carey, Frankel, and his boss, Mike Armstrong, went en masse to MCC, where Marc was waiting to be arraigned. They saw a down-at-the-heels twenty-year-old who appeared quite self-confident for his age and predicament and flatly denied any connection with Franklin Bradshaw's murder. It took the lawyers a week, and $150,000 cash bail posted in full by Marc's grandmother, to secure his release from Rikers Island. But once he was free, Frances absolutely refused to let him come anywhere near her apartment.

By an incredible stroke of luck, news of Marc's arrest had gone unreported by the New York *Times.* True, a big story had appeared in the New York *Daily News.* It described Marc Schreuder's arrest for his grandfather's murder. It named Berenice Bradshaw and listed the suspect's address as 10 Gracie Square. But—miraculously—Frances Schreuder's name was not mentioned by the *News,* and the people who mattered in Frances's life—the New York City Ballet peerage—relied for news on the New York *Times* and its promise of "All the News That's Fit to Print." The *Times* evidently had not found the Schreuder story fit. Thus it happened that, for six more months, not a soul around the New York State Theater, or at the New York City Ballet directors' meetings, had the slightest idea that their very own Sugar Plum Fairy was intimately connected to a

notorious Utah murder case; nor that her father's recent murder
was in fact the source of her prodigious wealth; nor that her son
had been charged with the crime and was almost certainly facing
trial.

Marc took a hotel room on East Eighty-sixth Street, as near to
his mother as she would allow, and spent most of his time downtown in the office of David Frankel. As the days ground on, the
older lawyers came to hope that Frankel's youth might prove an
asset in the delicate task of obtaining Marc Schreuder's confidence; that this odd young client, so very obviously in need of a
big-brother figure in his life, would come to see Frankel in that
light. Marc was telling the lawyer the same rambling, phony
story involving a visit with the Cavenaughs that he had first used
a year earlier on Detective Campbell. He said he had been at
home with his mother in New York and had first heard on the
radio about the shooting in Utah. He spoke of a long visit that
same Sunday afternoon to the neighborhood delicatessen. But in
a week of interviewing his client, Frankel was unable to come up
with witnesses, bus tickets, plane tickets, or any other evidence to
support Marc's story.

Furthermore, the more time he spent talking to Marc, and to
his bizarre mother, the less Frankel believed any of it. Very soon
it dawned on him that Marc was not telling the truth. He liked to
play games. He was sly, or thought he was. Marc's story had
developed into a rambling, complicated account of a two-week
Texas bus trip, and when Frankel sought to trap Marc in inconsistencies, he responded like a Dungeons and Dragons game
player attempting to outwit his opponent

At other times he spoke of running away. "I'm innocent, but
nobody believes me," he would say. "I'm gonna have to disappear to South America." He liked to employ spy jargon. He
talked about "going incognito, into deep cover." Frankel could
see his client donning an imaginary trench coat as he spun out his
yarns. But yarns they almost certainly were, and every time Frankel got close to the truth, Marc would threaten to bolt.

Frankel tried calling his bluff. "Fine, Marc. Run away. If
you're not gonna cooperate with me, not gonna deal with the
truth—then run."

"I will."

"Then go!" Frankel shouted, pointing melodramatically at the
door. Marc did not move. The game would begin again. The

young lawyer was getting no place. One afternoon he dropped into Armstrong's office, and they talked until well past midnight, discussing every aspect of the case. Did they even want to know the full truth? There was no other way, they concluded, to challenge the extradition proceedings—which was what they had been hired to do. "So we determined to bear down, force out the truth."

For the next ten days lawyer Frankel and his client sat in his office four to eight hours a day, going over and over Marc's story. The only reason Marc did not clam up or disappear, Frankel believes, "was because he thought we were miracle workers for getting him out of Rikers on bail." Frankel teased, threatened, bullied, cajoled. He used all the good-cop/bad-cop techniques he'd seen on television.

Marc kept spinning different stories. Once Marc said that although he was "involved," Larry had done the actual killing. Another time he said Larry was merely "involved." At other times he blamed Behrens. The one person he did not blame was his mother.

"It was a pretty emotional time for both of us," Frankel said later. "It became hard for me to separate Marc from the environment he'd grown up in." Doubtless Frankel had begun to feel somewhat sorry for his crafty, shifty, fantasy-prone client. By then Frankel had seen a good bit of Frances, "and I didn't know how I was going to feel in the end if it turned out Marc *had* done it."

After ten days and seventy or eighty hours of intensive grilling, Marc broke down and confessed that he and he alone had shot his grandfather. He described the killing in some detail. And many hours after that, amid floods of tears, Marc finally sobbed to his lawyer that his mother had compelled him to do it.

Before the interrogations ended, Frankel knew a great deal more about all the Schreuders than he needed or doubtless cared to. In a safe-deposit box Marc had the eight tape cassettes that he said were secret recordings of his family life he had made between the fall of 1978 and December 1980, when he was arrested in Connecticut. Marc turned over his tapes to David Frankel. If they were genuine—as they certainly appeared to be—they offered intimate glimpses of at-home family life otherwise unknowable to anyone but family members themselves. Frances, Marc, Larry, Ariadne, and Berenice all make their appearance on these tapes, as do various lawyers and others to whom Frances speaks by telephone. Whether, and how, the tapes may have been edited there is no way to tell. Since all family members except Ariadne appear to have engaged in fairly nonstop pilferage of one another's various belongings, it is not even possible to state with certitude that Marc himself made all the tapes. They all owned tape recorders. On Marc's tapes, Larry and Frances speak of having tapes of their own. On some, but not all, of Marc's tapes, the speakers seem to be aware that a live microphone is present; they appear to be *acting*, and sometimes seem to enjoy acting. In other tapes their laughter and tears—Ariadne's tears in particular—are unquestionably real. But whatever the provenance of the tapes, taken together they offer a shocking glimpse into a human snake pit of uninhibited family discourse.

David Frankel was the first non–family member to hear the tapes. He asked Mike Armstrong to listen to a few. One of these tapes—the so-called Ariadne Tape of Frances threatening the little girl about her schoolwork—would become the key piece of psychological evidence of Frances's demonic power over her children. The background noises, interruptions, and certain internal evidence, such as Walter Cronkite's TV voice announcing the news on a certain date, make this tape at least appear to be an authentic and—so far as it goes—unedited record of the occasion. The Ariadne Tape, and a defense-made transcription of it, were part of the evidence in both trials, Marc's and, a year later, his mother's. It was heard by both judges and both sets of trial lawyers, and both times was the subject of testimony by the expert psychiatric witness, Louis G. Moench, M.D. Dr. Moench, a venerable psychiatrist of impeccable academic credentials, says the Ariadne Tape is "the worst verbal child abuse" he has encountered in over forty years of psychiatric practice. The contents of the other seven tapes have never been made public.

David Frankel's familiarity with these tapes, as well as his marathon conversations with Marc, and perhaps a half-dozen long phone conversations with Marc's mother, led Frankel to reach certain conclusions about several members of the family.

"I would be skeptical of *anything* Frances Schreuder said. I believe she is capable of saying anything, making up anything, on the spot," he told a recent visitor. "I find Marilyn's role very bizarre—that she would turn in her nephew without even a phone call. I see Marc and Larry as tragic figures, in the sense

that they never had a chance to grow up in any way other than
they did.

"The two really tragic figures in this case are Berenice Bradshaw and, of course, Ariadne. Berenice I developed a tremendous
fondness for. I thought she was a strong and caring woman who
just could not believe what had happened in her life."

By the time the marathon interrogation had ended, and Frankel and Armstrong were satisfied that they had forced out the
whole truth about their client at last, Marc Schreuder had become well known around the sprawling downtown offices of Barrett, Smith, Schapiro, Simon & Armstrong. Many people in the
big law firm had worked on peripheral aspects of the case. Not all
of them agreed with Frankel's assessment of the principals. One
who did not was Mike Armstrong's former legal secretary, an
attractive young woman who, after some years of night law
school, had herself passed the bar exam and joined the firm. She
had met Marc Schreuder several times in the course of preparing
certain motion papers on this case.

"How did he strike *you?*" she was asked.

"Let me put it this way. I would not get on an elevator alone
with him. I've met a lot of felons. But Marc Schreuder makes my
blood run cold."

While Mike George had been chasing Marc and Frances, Ernie
Jones was after Behrens. If Utah could not for the moment com-
pel the presence within its flinty borders of Marc Schreuder, it
could at least continue to grapple for the essential material witness in the case. But Richard Behrens had got himself a new and
of necessity *pro bono* lawyer. Larry Goldman is an extremely
able, amiable, pipe-smoking attorney with curly gray hair who
viewed his job as not merely to fight extradition, but to hold his
frightened client's hand and try to keep him from flipping out
completely. Goldman saw Behrens as "a schlubby guy, a little-
old-man type, lonely and garrulous. He talks your ear off, smokes
incessantly, does good dialects, Jewish accents especially. If I
wanted to pick up women, I would use Richard. He can be amusing and he talks to everybody. I mean, he starts up conversations
with *every person he meets!*

"Richard is not criminal, not venal. He's terribly naïve and
gullible. He kept the gun for Frances because he got attention out

of it, and companionship, and a little drama in an otherwise boring life."

To Goldman, Behrens was that familiar figure around every courthouse: the litigious crackpot. He saw his client as "essentially a failure in life, a guy who just couldn't quite put it together, the kind of guy who trudges through life with an armful of yellowing, frayed, legal papers, and types 'cc: Senator Moynihan' at the bottom of all his crank letters."

The lawyer seems to have become rather fond of his wacky, eccentric client. He saw that Behrens was not only scared stiff of Frances Schreuder, he was terrified of having to set foot in Utah. Frances had succeeded in depicting her native state as a Wild West place where any stranger could expect to be shot or strung up vigilante-style.

Larry Goldman fought the extradition request over many months, arguing that his client was certainly not a fugitive from Utah—he had never even been there—nor had he committed any act in Utah that was also a crime in New York. Finally, on November 17, 1981, Judge Eve Preminger complimented Mr. Goldman on the ingenuity of his argument, but ruled against him from the bench. Behrens was immediately avid to appeal. He announced grandly that he was prepared to go all the way to the Supreme Court. Goldman gently pointed out to him that he would probably lose, in which case he might be compelled to do hard time for concealing a murder weapon or even being an accomplice to murder. A better strategy would be to work out some sort of deal with Ernie Jones.

Behrens had got in the habit of telephoning his lawyer at least once a day, and sometimes more often. By December 4 he was beginning to indicate a willingness to go to Utah and testify for Jones, providing he received an iron-clad grant of immunity against prosecution. Frances had persuaded Behrens to recant in the first place by convincing him that Utah was certain to give him twenty years.

Now that Marc was released on bail, Mike George asked Ernie Jones to send him back to New York City so he could plug up several remaining holes in his case. He traveled with his chief, Don Harman. The two Utah cops visited the American Airlines clerk who had sold Marc the "L. Gentile" ticket. Carolyn Karoliszyn Morris had an amazing memory. Although she sells fifteen plane tickets a day, she remembered the strange, chubby

boy in tousled clothes with wads of cash in his pockets and identified him readily from a stack of seven photographs Mike
showed her. Later, in Salt Lake City, Carolyn readily picked out
Marc from a lineup of seven.

Mike met with M.T.B. executives and for the first time got an
idea of the magnitude of Marc's coin dealings, and the extent of
his check forgeries—$90,000 in less than three months. He vis-
ited the Schreuders' old York Avenue neighborhood and talked to
shopkeepers who had carried the family for years because they
felt sorry for the children. Except for Larry, the family was well
known. Frances's general reputation in the neighborhood was
that of a flake who lived high but had trouble paying her bills. At
times she had plenty of money, at times she was dead broke. She
had no visible means of support and no boy friends. Ariadne was
"treated like gold, and got everything she wanted always," Mike
George was told. He heard Frances described as "totally wacko,"
a deadbeat, a hedonist. At a time when the family was facing
eviction for nonpayment of rent, he was told, she had purchased
a $1,000 negligee and a $10,000 Tiffany diamond ring. Neighbors
at 1675 York Avenue described the boys' frequent lockouts, the
cardboard and newspaper nests they constructed in the building
stairwells, and "an apartment that was an absolute pigpen except
for Ariadne's room, which was spotless."

Mike made inquiries of shopkeepers, employers, neighbors,
schoolmates, looking for any kind of evidence that Marc had
confided in anyone. Again, nothing; the boy had no confidants
except his mother. After his Connecticut arrest he had nearly
broken down and confessed to one of his roommates, but the
other boy had told him, "I don't want to hear what you're about
to say. I don't want to get involved."

Mike went out to Rikers Island and interviewed Marc's fellow
inmates. He had been housed in the "homosexual tier" because
the authorities thought he might "survive better" there, and
Marc had agreed. While insisting he was not gay, Marc said he
"felt comfortable with them" and "felt he would not be beaten up
there." Mike learned nothing from the prisoners.

The two Utah cops' most emotional encounter was with a ban-
tam pearl importer in his small office in the wholesale diamond
district. They had simply looked up Vittorio Gentile in the phone
book and rung his doorbell. It was opened by "a fat, jolly Italian

man—very cooperative and hospitable. He had no idea why we were there. I told him we had come because of his son Marc."

"Marco! What's the matter with Marco?"

"Don't you know that he's been arrested?"

"Arrested! For what?"

"Murder. Of his grandfather."

Color drained out of Vittorio's face. He did not even know Franklin Bradshaw had been shot. Frances had told him that her father had died of natural causes. Vittorio told Mike he had been trying to get in touch with Frances in order to find Larry, but she had been refusing his calls.

"Can you help me find Lorenzo?" he asked.

"I have bad news for you there, too," Sergeant George replied. "But I can't lie to you." He told the little man that Larry was in prison in Pennsylvania.

Later, Mike George said soberly, "It was one of the most traumatic moments I've ever had in police work . . . a double whammy. This man had two sons, and suddenly he finds out that both are in jail. It was like we had taken half his life away. To Italian people the family is the most important thing."

Vittorio composed himself and afterward talked a little about his sons, confirming what the policemen already knew: that Marc was a loner, that Larry had a history of emotional problems. Then he broke down and sobbed.

Mike felt terrible when he left. He made it a point to arrange a second meeting, as soon as possible. Four months later, Mike returned to New York. Gentile then told him that Frances had been "the great love of my life," and he described a protracted struggle for custody of his sons "when she went off the deep end." He told Mike how Frances claimed he was an alcoholic who tried constantly to beat her up, and said he believed she was crazy. He said she had been expelled from Bryn Mawr "for stealing and for dope," and had married him because it was an opportunity to "save face." Then he repeated that he had really loved Frances, adding that he loved her to this day.

By the time their second meeting ended, the two men of Italian ancestry had formed a relationship that would have important consequences for Marc. Mike George had now spent nine months chasing down a boy he had never met, a boy who at seventeen had cold-bloodedly shot his grandfather in the back. The case consumed him. He wanted more than anything to convict Marc

Schreuder of the crime. At the same time, he had formulated a very clear picture of what he wished his own relationship to the boy to be. "I wanted to be able to say to him when it was all over with: *I hope you have a good life, Marc.*

"I never had any ill feelings against Marc Schreuder. He deserved a fair trial. But at the same time, the state of Utah deserved a fair trial."

The most important person on Mike's list that week was Richard Behrens. Unless he could be persuaded to reaffirm his original story, Utah had no case. The approach to him had to be just right. The cops were "reluctant to bust in on him, for fear we would set him off." They were unaware that they had a silent ally in attorney Larry Goldman. But within moments of their arrival in Goldman's office on December 8, to deliver papers that required Behrens to come to Utah or risk contempt of court, Goldman said, "You people seem like gentlemen. Mr. Behrens is in the next office. I'll see if he'd like to talk to you."

They repaired to a conference room. Behrens "was on pins and needles, very nervous," even though the cops had agreed not to ask direct questions about the case. Mike George tried to play on the jumpy little man's emotions. He compared Behrens's position to Franklin Bradshaw's: a mature man imperiled by a wild, unpredictable, brilliant kid. He talked about how bizarre the case was. Goldman—intrigued, or perhaps reassured—finally permitted George to ask direct questions. The response was startling. Behrens not only reaffirmed his original statement to Joel Campbell—that Marc had told him he had shot his grandfather. He vastly improved it. Richard Behrens now said—for the first time —that in fact it had been Frances, not Marc, who had "dropped the gun off" on him. He said it was she who had "ordered the killing." Even better, he now remembered the name of a "hit man" whom Frances had tried to hire to assassinate her father, after Behrens had introduced them. He was "some guy named Manning," a printer by trade.

By the time the conference ended, Mike George could barely contain his elation. That morning all he'd had on Frances was the original statement, since recanted, of Richard Behrens, hardly an ideal witness in any case. Of course, the investigator also had proof that the checks stolen in the summer of 1977 by Marc and Larry had been forged and cashed by their mother. But he could not charge Frances with any crime because Franklin Bradshaw was dead, and he was certain Berenice would not file a complaint against her own daughter. By nightfall the Behrens meeting had confirmed George's long-standing hunch: Frances Schreuder was "really the guilty party, the boss, the mastermind behind this murder."

Furthermore, in addition to having his key witness back on the right side of the fence, Behrens had unexpectedly provided the name of the essential corroborating witness. "If we could find this Manning guy, I felt we would have a really good shot at charging Frances with Murder One."

When he phoned his boss, Ernie Jones was excited but circumspect. He would require very solid evidence to charge an important woman like Frances Schreuder. The next morning Mike got out the Yellow Pages and began calling a list of print shops. He was looking for a relative named Manning, he explained; there had been a death in the family. Coming from a right-to-work state like Utah, one of the least unionized places in the nation, it never occurred to Mike to call the printers' union. Finally someone at the New York *Daily News* said that a fellow named Manning worked the night shift. When the printer showed up at 8:00 P.M., Mike George was waiting. He identified himself as a police officer.

"Whaddya want with me? I ain't done nothin' wrong." Manning was a barrel-chested man in his forties, with a big head, two-day beard, short legs, and a breezy, wise-guy manner.

Mike said carefully, "Your name has come up in a very important case. A tragic murder in Utah. Some people are trying to say you're involved. I don't believe them. I think they're probably trying to frame you . . ."

Manning appeared shaken. "I've never done anything bad in my life. You got the wrong guy, pal."

Mike handed him a photograph of Frances Schreuder. "Tell me that you cannot identify this woman."

The printer's hands began to shake. The picture trembled. He said softly, "What do you want to know?"

Myles Manning then told Mike George the same story he would repeat on the witness stand at two trials. In the fall of 1977 Behrens, a neighborhood acquaintance, arranged a meeting on the street with a woman named Frances. At a later meeting, in the woman's apartment, she told him she wanted to have her father killed. A little girl was playing on the floor while they talked. The woman reached under the couch cushions and handed Manning $5,000 in cash, mostly tens and twenties. She also gave him recent pictures of her father, his warehouse, his truck. "It was shit. She had photos, maps, sloppily written directions, times of day, how it should be done—very incomplete. If I *was* a hit man, which I'm not, I'd say that three quarters of what she gave me was useless, and I'd need a hunnert percent more than what I *did* get. She was such a jerk, she wrote it left-handed so it couldn't be traced. Let me put it another way: with her instructions, I would have been caught."

Manning never went to Utah. He took the money, got drunk, checked into a New York City YMCA for a few days, then told Frances he had been arrested in Salt Lake City before he could carry out his assignment. Manning told George he felt no guilt whatsoever for "stinging" Frances. "He thought it was the rottenest thing he'd ever heard of, to commission your own father's killing. He was *outraged!* 'A woman like that deserves to get taken,' he said."

Myles Manning is nothing if not outspoken. After receiving immunity in Utah, and testifying at both Marc's and Frances's trial, he talked candidly to a barroom acquaintance. "I never cared anything for Marc—he was so cold-blooded. *I just blew my grandfather away,* he said. Nobody is crazy all the time, but he was off the wall. Murder itself doesn't bother me. You kill somebody, rob 'em and kill 'em, I'm not gonna do anything about it. But this was different. I don't have a family, but I guess I'm a family man. And this was just wrong. Everybody's got a limit, and they went past it.

"They were *all* crazy. That Behrens, he's not wrapped too tight either. If I didn't have too much to lose by it, he'd be in the hospital by now. After he went down, he gave them my name. He didn't have to do that. No one knew about it. His back wasn't against the wall to name me, but he did."

The Salt Lake County Attorney's office has a meager budget, and by week's end Mike George and his chief had run out of money. They had already checked out of their hotel and were scheduled to return to Utah that night. But that evening they got a tip from Steve Klein's boss, Al Sullivan, the New York assistant district attorney who had been helping them all along, and who was representing Utah against Marc's lawyers in the extradition fight. Once more the Utah cops were amazed by the helpful zeal of the New York authorities. They had expected to be received in the big city like hayseeds. How much could one faraway murder mean to men who handled two thousand homicides a year? But Al Sullivan, who was also prosecuting Mark David Chapman, the self-appointed executioner of John Lennon, was proving to be a slow, methodical, and very efficient law-enforcement professional. He now told Sergeant George that, at an extradition hearing scheduled for the next day, Judge Harold Rothwax just might be inclined to surrender Marc to the Utah authorities, even though Mike Armstrong could be counted on to put up a thundering fight.

Steve Klein let the Utah cops sleep overnight on the floor of his Greenwich Village pad. Before retiring, they got Ernie Jones to wire them an extra plane ticket for Marc, should they get lucky the next day, and they made reservations back to Salt Lake City out of all three New York airports, LaGuardia, Newark, and JFK. If they did get custody of the prisoner, they would have to move fast; Mike Armstrong would be prepared to file an instant appeal.

The next afternoon Armstrong lost. Sullivan did not even have to argue. Judge Rothwax, a courtly and deceptively soft-spoken man, said that this defendant had been better represented than any defendant he could recall in a similar proceeding, "but, Mr. Armstrong, you just ran out of law . . . Are the people here from Salt Lake City?"

George and Harman stood up. "Take him," Rothwax said.

They literally grabbed Marc, lied that they were heading for JFK, hustled him out of the courthouse, and sped toward New Jersey in Steve Klein's car. Marc was stunned and frightened. He'd had no idea his day might end with a flight back to Salt Lake City. As for Mike George, he was flabbergasted by his prisoner's appearance and manner. "He wore an old, wrinkled shirt, pants three sizes too big that he had to hold up with his hands, and a floppy coat. He was a very loud talker, almost abrasive; he'd practically yell at you in normal conversation. Underneath all that was a very smart kid who just didn't have any manners, and no common sense living habits. He was plain dirty."

En route to the Newark airport, Mike was firm but gentle. "If you say a word to anybody, or act up, I'll cuff you," he said. "But if you behave yourself, nobody will know you're anything but my friend."

On the plane Marc relaxed a little, and when the attendant came around he asked her for vodka and orange juice. "Sorry." Sergeant George shook his head. "My friend is underage."

David Richardson, the New York City Ballet's specialist in child dancers who had first seen Frances Schreuder on the plane to Paris in the fall of 1980, remembers with extreme clarity each one of his encounters with this strange woman. There were four in all. "I knew on the Paris trip she was odd. The next event was a message I got a year later, in Boston. Third, I saw her smoking in the Lower Concourse, and talking. Finally I got the full-blown tantrum."

It was autumn of 1981 when Richardson heard of Frances Schreuder the second time. He was in Boston, about to leave for New York to hold the annual October auditions at SAB to cast the children's parts in the NYCB's traditional Christmas production of *The Nutcracker.* This ballet uses child dancers in several scenes—in Act II they are angels—but Act I's opening Party Scene, in which Herr Drosselmeier gives the children individual nuts, is considered the choice spot.

Earlier that fall the NYCB had visited Boston for a fund-raising Gala while Richardson was away in Japan. When he returned, he was told that someone named Frances Schreuder, a Board member in town to attend the Boston Gala, had been looking for him. At first David did not connect the message with the woman he had seen in Paris, "which later made me very, very happy," as he delicately puts it.

"Then, I didn't know Ariadne was hooked to Frances, either," he adds. But the Boston message, delivered through the School, was very clear: *Try to make sure that Ariadne Schreuder gets into the Party Scene.* Richardson had never before received such a message. He was quietly appalled. "I don't do that sort of thing," he says. "You *can't* 'get to me.' Most people realize they shouldn't even try." That she did not recognize the obvious was the second odd thing he remembered noting about Mrs. Schreuder.

But as it turned out, at the audition he was attracted to one little girl because she was so small for her age (he did not know she was in fact underage) as well as talented. "So when the whole casting was done, I found out I had indeed chosen the daughter of somebody who was on the Board." It was the only occasion

Richardson has found himself working with a dancer who was the child of a Board member, as well as the only time any Board member ever attempted to influence his casting choices.

The day the family was notified that Ariadne had indeed been chosen to appear in the Party Scene—possibly the plummiest spot for a very young dancer in the entire nation—was October 31, Halloween, Granny and Grandpa Bradshaw's fifty-seventh wedding anniversary.

November was devoted to rehearsals, most of them held in the below-stage rehearsal halls at the New York State Theater known formally as the Lower Concourse Studios. It is a strictly functional lineup of windowless spaces—practice rooms, makeup and wig rooms, bathrooms, and an adjacent "lounge area," a bare space containing only vending machines, plastic tables and chairs, and pay phones in the corridor. It is neither comfortable nor attractive, just a resting place for sweaty, tired dancers between scenes. Two or three weeks into rehearsals, as Richardson got to know one child from the next, he noticed one mother always in the lounge area, chain-smoking. "I realized this was the one. What seemed odd was: it's only a place one would go to if one had absolutely no other choice. Yet Frances used it as her hangout. She lived there." Parents are not encouraged to stick around, not permitted to watch their children in rehearsals, or watch other dancers. Most mothers and fathers deliver their children to the theater and pick them up later at the appointed hour. "Mrs. Schreuder just sat there hour after hour in this very grim, uncomfortable atmosphere."

Most striking was that she seemed to have no awareness of the inappropriateness of her own behavior. She was a stage-door Giselle whose mad generosity had bought her a privileged position within the Ballet's inner, working world, a privilege she had no hesitation about invoking. It was not a matter of wealth or breeding or even training. Things others know instinctively are "not done" were done all the time by the Schreuders.

"Frankly, all you have to do is talk to the woman to realize she's unbalanced, though she was always kind of giggly and fun too," says Richardson. She could also be regally kind. "You know, Mr. Balanchyne thinks your daughter is really very talented," she would sometimes tell another mother. It did not matter that Mr. B did not know one child from the next, that he did not know who Frances Schreuder was, let alone recognize individual children; did not matter that he never would have made such a remark. What mattered was only the power she felt flowing through her.

"I really have to hurry," Frances sometimes said to other parents while they helped their little daughters in and out of costumes and makeup. "I'm dining with Mr. Balanchyne, you know." On other occasions, she said she had given the Company a $5 million endowment, and pledged an additional $1 million a year. Again, it was not the enormity of the amount but of the braggadocio that was striking.

It looked to Richardson as if Mrs. Schreuder was lingering in hopes that "some dancers might come by and, maybe, nod and say 'Hello.'" But he thought her presence not good either for the other youngsters or for Frances. She had shown herself "simply not a woman who understood how children behaved. She never *did* get it, the way kids play. She always thought they were picking on her daughter, rather than just doing what kids do." When another child accidentally bumped Ariadne, Frances complained loudly that the child had pulled her daughter's hair.

Then came the Saturday matinee when "the people who help me take attendance came to the stage and said: Ariadne Schreuder's not here. We've phoned her home and there's no answer." The rules were well known. If a child did not show up by 1 P.M., her alternate was summoned. Richardson called a child in Brooklyn, one who had danced the part the previous year, and she and her father got on the subway.

Moments later the balletmaster was hastily summoned to the Lounge Area. Ariadne and her mother had arrived, and an all-out Frances tantrum was in progress in full view of the other children and mothers. "She was slumped on a sofa, in her big black mink coat. She didn't look, er, presentable. She was crying, *bawling,* actually, and saying very, very loudly, 'Ariadne *must dance* this afternoon.'"

"I said, 'No, Ariadne cannot dance. Because you didn't call. And you are the same as anyone else—you have to follow the rules.'

"She was screaming. She said, 'She has to!' She was . . . uncontrollable. No one else I've ever come in contact with would pull this—*frenzy!* Her story was that the grandmother had been rushed to the hospital and almost died, so they had been at the hospital all morning and couldn't get a chance to call, and now

Ariadne was so upset about her grandmother that we just could not do this to her.

"So at last I said, 'All right. Your daughter can go on the stage.' Because I didn't like the other children seeing this."

During the uproar, Ariadne had stood quietly with her head down. Richardson had a sense she had seen her mother do this before; that it was something she was used to. "But my own instinct was: I wanted to get Ariadne out of there, and put her on the stage—just so that she wouldn't be embarrassed. Maybe it *didn't* bother her. I wasn't sure."

The point was, it bothered David Richardson, it made him so acutely uncomfortable that mostly he wanted his own discomfort to end, and the only way to do that was to let Ariadne go on stage. Thus yet another shaken-up individual joined the battle-scarred legions of people who found themselves unable to say no to Frances.

Richardson had an extra costume. He told Ariadne to put it on, and at that performance of *The Nutcracker,* not seven but eight little girls in mauve pantaloons twirled and cajoled and pleaded with Herr Drosselmeier for the first nut. The Party Scene is a long one. The dancers in Act I move rapidly onstage and off as the excitement builds. All the time that Ariadne was on stage, Frances remained backstage, screaming, *"Lincoln Kirstein will find out about this! How dare David treat my daughter that way! I will have that other child removed from the School!"*

And at one point in the madness, upset dancers bumping into one another in the gloom, the other child had whirled briefly offstage right where Mrs. Schreuder was standing. *"I'm going to kill you!"* she hissed.

Mercifully, the curtain dropped. "Mrs. Schreuder's gonna have me kicked out of School!" the other child wailed.

"I don't think that could possibly happen," said Richardson, sounding calmer than he felt.

"But I'm scared she might hurt me! She said she was going to *kill me!"*

"Don't be ridiculous. That's just a . . . a figure of speech." He promised to look into the matter.

Richardson telephoned Mrs. Schreuder and invited her to join him that evening at the Promenade Bar during the regular performance. She had calmed down, was just chain-smoking though she did order a very strong drink, a double-double, to enable her to get through the conversation. So we talked, and in a way I was protecting myself . . . because I didn't really know how much power she had. I mean, I was pretty sure my job wasn't in jeopardy. But I did feel that I should, at least, talk to her, make her feel important—if that's what she needed. Which is the way I read what had happened."

Richardson mentioned some things Mrs. Schreuder might better be doing than throwing tantrums. Perhaps she could look around backstage, where the children work and dress and rehearse, and see if she could not find ways to improve their environment. A word dropped to Mr. Kirstein, or a report to the Board, might be more constructive than "just sitting down there fomenting trouble with the other kids, competing her daughter against another." *Who is better, who is best? Which one is fairest of them all?*

"You know, Ariadne *is* good. She *is* talented," he added. This seemed to reassure Mrs. Schreuder more than anything.

The following day a messenger appeared at the stage door. He had a four-page, handwritten letter on pale blue, ornately monogrammed Tiffany stationery, and a small, heavy turquoise pasteboard Tiffany box. The letter was phrased in curiously lofty language, as if penned from some remote tower room in St. Petersburg by a courtier practiced in palace intrigue, someone who understood instinctively that nothing said under such circumstances means exactly what it seems, and may mean quite its opposite.

After many weeks of observation, Frances wrote, she was in no doubt whatsoever that "there will never be another David Richardson, just as there will never be another . . . George Balanchine . . . As an artist and a private person you must always follow your own instincts . . . Unlike others you are still young and my passion and protective feelings for the N.Y.C.B. are so intense that I hope you never leave us." The letter flowed on and on, filled with threat-by-obverse, the cloven-hoof language even young children understand wherein "you are very beautiful" really means "you are beautiful only in soul; in body hideous," and "we need you" means "we don't."

"Great artists are more rare than the most precious of diamonds. Your selflessness, devotion and inspiration can never be measured by ordinary standards.

"However tense situations may get at times in our lives, you can always count upon my steadfast devotion for your rare abilities and above all for your self."

The letter was wrapped around a heavy gold Tiffany cigarette lighter, and contained two pregnant postscripts: ". . . isn't it nice to know that you also earned this on your own merit! PPS. I always prefer anonymity but it was not possible for this little gesture. I trust however that you will not mention it to anyone."

For a long time, David never did.

Marc Schreuder spent his twenty-first birthday, December 21, 1981, in the Salt Lake City jail waiting for Granny to come up with more bail money. She and her friend Chips had gone off on a Caribbean cruise, and Marc had to sit in jail nearly a month before he could reach her and ask her to wire the necessary $100,000 from Morgan Guaranty in New York to the lawyers she had retained for him in Salt Lake. By now the rumpled Utah lawyer Paul Van Dam had invited another ex-prosecutor to join him in preparing Marc's defense.

Joseph Tesch, Jr., is an aggressive bantamweight with a taste for politics, Western clothes, and pedigree quarter horses that he and his lawyer wife raise on their ranch in the Wasatch foothills. The fees of both of Marc's attorneys were being paid by their client's grandmother, who steadfastly maintained her belief in Marc's innocence. Her grandson might be a natural-born thief, but he was no murderer. Of that she was sure. As his inevitable trial approached, the defense lawyers' situation grew increasingly sticky. Their chances for winning acquittal, fame, and fortune would improve dramatically if they could persuade their client to let them attack Frances. But he would not agree, and perhaps that was just as well. Such a strategy would put them in the position of trying to pin the murder on the favorite daughter of the woman who was paying their $150,000 fee. Their only other choice, or so it then appeared to the prosecution, was to blame Larry. Ernie Jones and Mike George therefore set about doing what they could to discourage this gambit.

Meanwhile Tesch and Van Dam forked over the bail, and Marc immediately checked into one of Salt Lake's sleaziest hotels and spent three days trying to call his mother from the pay phone on the wall outside his room. The rest of the time he hung out at porno movies, gorged on his favorite food, Chicken McNuggets, and revisited old haunts. He was amazed and thrilled to find

Larry's penciled initials still legible in the gas station phone booth they had used five years before to make reports of their warehouse crime spree to Frances in New York. Carefully Marc inscribed his own initials, *MFS,* and the date, 1982, and photographed both monograms—part of the same compulsion to record their aimless lives that drove Larry to write his monthly *Occupiers* and Marc to make his secret tapes.

Unknown to Marc, Mike George had rented the adjoining room in the same "dirt bag hotel," and was spending his days with his ear pressed to the wall, hoping Marc on the phone might let something slip about the murder. But Marc spoke almost entirely in French. The only person he could reach at 10 Gracie Square was Paulette, the maid. The ballet season was at its height. Between her own ballet doings and Ariadne's performances and rehearsals for *The Nutcracker,* Frances was very rarely at home.

When Marc finally did connect, Mike was almost as happy as his suspect. For three days the policeman had been self-imprisoned in a place so filthy that he had slept in his clothes on top of the bed rather than open the sheets. He went home, showered, and drove over to Gilmer Drive to try to talk to Berenice Bradshaw. She refused to unlock the door.

When Marc got back to New York, he stayed with his mother but called on his father. They did not discuss the upcoming trial, but Vittorio told him, "This door is always open, Marco. If you need a home, this is your home. Maybe I haven't always been the best father, but you're my son. I'll be there when you need me from now on."

Mike George and Ernie Jones were delighted to learn of this development. They hoped that if Marc got a good relationship going with his father, Vittorio eventually might be useful in influencing the boy to do what the prosecutor needed most: agree to testify against Frances. Mike and Ernie were avid though not very hopeful of persuading this wretched mama's boy that there was but one way to "become a man." He would have to betray his mother. Several times, after Marc was jailed, they urged Vittorio to come out to Salt Lake and talk to his son. But Marc always got wind of the plan and pleaded, "Please, Papa, don't come!" Vittorio's manifest warmth and affection, the welcome mat into the pleasant new Gentile household—nice wife, three nice kids—must have seemed to Marc by then the only tidy corner of his own existence. He needed to keep it inviolate, a kind of sanctuary. He liked visiting Papa's world; he did not want Papa visiting his.

As soon as Marc left New York, Frances called the police and accused him of stealing $40,000 worth of her jewelry from 10 Gracie Square while he was staying in her apartment.

During his month in Salt Lake County jail, Marc had met a woman who would become the first girlfriend he'd ever had. At first glance she seemed the unlikely object of a young man's fancy. Mary Lou Kaiser was thirty-six years old, about five feet tall, and weighed at least 250 pounds. She had been born in Torreón, Mexico, one of the many children of a "saint incarnate" mother and an abusive, alcoholic father who had become a Utah copper miner and backslid Pentecostal preacher. Mary was deeply religious and worked as a cleaning woman. She was also extremely motherly, good-natured, warm-hearted, cheerful, and loving. She had creamy beige skin, beautiful white teeth, dancing eyes behind thick glasses, and a long braid down her back. Mary had survived open-heart surgery at thirty-one, and at thirty-six, much to her surprise and joy—she had been asking God to give her a baby for over twenty years—she had been blessed with a baby daughter. Mary Lou Kaiser's luck with men was different. She had been married three times, most recently to a taxi driver who had thrown her and the baby out of their home. Mother and infant wound up in a filthy, roach-infested $109 welfare apartment, and taxi driver Millard Kaiser wound up in the county jail, charged with sodomizing a nine-year-old girl.

Marc had met Kaiser in jail, and believed him innocent, and as soon as Granny came up with his own bail money, Marc set about fulfilling his promise to Kaiser to try to get him out on bail as well. During his three days in the "dirt bag," Marc had gone to visit Kaiser's stepfather, who in turn had brought Marc over to see the taxi driver's estranged wife, Mary. Maybe she would sign his bond.

"The first time Marc came through my door—bang! Love at first sight! I saw those gorgeous blue eyes and said to myself: I'm gonna hustle this boy!" Mary said later.

Kaiser's $5,000 bail required $500 in cash and someone to sign his bond who owned property and had been employed in the same job seven years. Mary did not qualify, so they all piled into Kaiser's jalopy and drove around town looking for some other relative to post bond. "But my husband was a bad apple. He'd screwed everyone." As they drove, Marc said he guessed he'd need a car, now that he was out on bail. The stepfather tried to sell him the one they were riding in.

"You don't want this piece of garbage, Marc!" whispered Mary. It was the beginning of a beautiful friendship. When Marc returned to Salt Lake from New York he went back to jail to fulfill his promise to try to help Millard Kaiser, and found Mary in the jail visiting room, baby on her enormous lap.

"Hello! What are *you* doing here? Ever the faithful wife, I suppose!"

"Whaddya mean, 'faithful wife'? I'm just here because I was asked to be."

Marc volunteered to walk her home, three blocks from the jail. He carried the little girl, Monique. Later, Mary cooked up her special treat, chicken mole.

The next afternoon he returned for more Mexican home cooking, and Mary later invited him to sleep on the sofa. Marc shuddered at the filthy apartment. He had to go call his father, he said, and she had no phone. "This place looks like a pigpen," he said. "You clean it up and maybe I'll stay."

Four hours later he knocked at her door. She was in bed in her nightgown. "Hey," he said, "am I in the right place!" The apartment was now immaculate.

"Hey, you know what? I do cleaning for a living. I'm the best cleaning woman in Utah! You wanna talk to me, come in the bedroom," she added, cheerfully bent on seducing Marc if she could. But that first night they talked for many hours, until Marc fell asleep on top of the bedclothes. "I was under the covers. Since I was extremely religious, I felt very guilty sleeping in the same bed with a strange man." She slipped out of bed and spent that night with her baby on the living room couch.

Marc's own personal habits were curious. At Rikers Island, and again in Salt Lake, he sometimes stank so badly that other prisoners demanded not to bunk near him. At other times he bathed and changed his clothes three or four times a day, and he was so neat about schoolwork that he ironed his papers before turning them in.

Delightedly he told Mary in the morning her place was so clean "you could put the rope up"—it looked just like a roped-off model room in a museum. Marc stayed. "He seemed so hungry for love and affection. There isn't one mean bone in his body," she said later. He eagerly fed and changed baby Monique, whom he called Mona Lisa. When Mary asked him why, he said untactfully that "every Monique I've ever known was fat." Marc told Mary he had been in jail on a drug rap, but otherwise their relationship appears to have been quite an honest one. Mary was frank to admit she liked Marc's money, as well as his looks. "He had those crazy blue eyes!" she would say later. "And he's such a sweet, gentle person . . . so different from my husbands. Marc opened doors for me! He pushed my baby. He bought me presents. He gave me a compliment every single day!"

When they were together, Marc did most of the talking. He could discourse for hours on any subject. He liked to work jigsaw puzzles, the tougher the better. He ate whole cloves of garlic. Vittorio had taught him it was good for health and sexual appetite. One day he said that Mona Lisa had eaten three jars of baby food. Mary looked dubious. "Okay, Babes. I'm coming out of the closet. I *love* baby food!"

The next time Marc returned to their apartment after visiting his grandmother, he told Mary he and Granny had gone apartment-hunting and had seen a $125 apartment. Berenice had pronounced it "a dump," Marc said, but she had been willing to contribute $500 for a deposit and one month's rent in advance, believing it was for her grandson alone. Marc told Mary the new place had three rooms and he was tired of living in "the Roach Hilton," looking out through holes in the walls and sitting up nights throwing glasses of water at the vermin. Marc had begun getting rid of everything Mary owned—dishes, pots and pans, linens, lamps—and replacing it little by little with good second-hand furnishings. He insisted she abandon her roach-ridden life.

Mary was thrilled but appalled when Marc went to the grocery and spent $200 to $300 a trip. "Marc, this has gotta stop. I'm a welfare mother," she protested. Sometimes she also grew jealous of Marc's five-hour visits to Berenice. "I can't compete with twenty-six million bucks," she would tell him. But she knew he had no other friends, and she could understand that his grandmother was lonely, too. The only thing he criticized her about was tithing to the Pentecostals. He didn't believe in God. "How can you let that preacher ruin your life?" he railed.

Every day for almost two months, Marc and Mary played house, choosing new furniture, taking care of Monique, snuggling at night. They called each other by the same nickname: "Babes." They were very happy.

In early February, unknown to the pair of lovers, Richard Behrens had made a critical two-day trip to Salt Lake City, accompanied by his lawyer. Now for the first time he gave Ernie Jones a full and complete account of his role in the Schreuder case, including details of his recruitment of Manning. He described a trip to Virginia in April to try to buy a gun. He had been unsuccessful, but his story checked out. He also described a chance meeting with Marc the previous August during which Marc had given Behrens additional details of the murder and had told him it was "easy," and gave him the direct quote: "Mom made me do it." He said he had spent Sunday, the day of the murder, alone riding his bike in the park. Marc was mistaken about seeing him in the vestibule when he returned from Salt Lake City. Behrens now claimed he did not see the Schreuders until later that evening when first Frances, then Marc, came to his apartment and "dropped off" the gun.

When it was time for Mary and Marc to move into their new apartment, they decided to economize and transport everything themselves, by grocery cart. They got so involved in the three-day move that Marc forgot to show up at the jail for a lineup that had been requested by his own lawyers. All hell broke loose, but Mary had no TV or telephone, and they did not know anything was amiss until the next morning when they heard on the radio that Marc Schreuder had jumped bail and was believed on his way to Belgium.

"Oh, Babes, I *hate* waking up like this!" groaned the "fugitive," home in bed not three blocks away from the jail. He needed a phone, so they went to a photo studio where Mary worked as a scrubwoman. From seven to ten o'clock that morning, while Mary was cleaning, Marc tried in vain to reach his lawyers. They were moving to another office, and the phone was temporarily disconnected. He called his mother, but the maid said she was out. Mary now asked Marc for the first time what he was really charged with. The murder of his grandfather, he admitted. "Did you do it?" she asked. When Marc said no, she asked no more questions and they strolled home, Marc carrying the baby.

The police had blocked off the street in four directions. They had expected gunplay. A neighbor had recognized Marc's face on the TV news and phoned in an anonymous tip. Suddenly four officers threw Marc to the grass, cuffed him, and hauled him away, calling him asshole and shouting that "the state of Utah just became $100,000 richer!" Mary was left standing in the middle of the street holding Monique and crying hysterically.

Back in jail and awaiting trial, Marc was housed in the same tier as Mary's estranged husband, Kaiser, who had by now decided to cop a plea on the sodomy charge rather than undergo the shame of trial. "Why don't you give her a divorce?" Marc demanded.

"Because I want to let her stew."

But Marc insisted, and eventually he lent Mary the necessary $250 to pay the lawyer.

Mary settled into a routine of cooking chocolate cakes and chicken mole to take to Marc in jail, and waiting for his trial. She believed he was innocent, and hoped that one day they might marry. She always brought Monique to visit "Uncle Marc"; later she would tell the child Marc was her father. When she got depressed, she visited her Pentecostal preacher. "He said I was a big sinner. One day he told me I could have Marc, or I could have the church. I told him I felt Marc *needed* me. I said I can't believe I'll go to hell because somebody needs me."

One early spring morning in New York City, Mireille Briane, wife of Oleg Briansky, was about to begin teaching her regular Saturday morning children's class when a woman with "very strange eyes, as if staring into a void," turned up asking for private tutoring for her little girl. The child had been studying at the School of American Ballet for about a year, she said. Other mothers were present. Frances could not seem to stop talking. At machine-gun pace, she named so many important people she knew at NYCB that Mireille grew frightened. "Don't be nervous," Oleg muttered in Russian, so Mireille proposed that Ariadne join the class then in progress.

"My daughter really wants private lessons."

"That is quite expensive."

"Don't worry about the money. Get in touch with the Morgan Guaranty Bank. Ariadne has a trust fund there."

Three-times-weekly private lessons began. "We liked Ariadne very much," says Mireille. "She was always on time, never missed a class. And she was very polite, very friendly with the other girls."

The Brianskys, both former NYCB dancers, are serious teachers; they do not accept children younger than nine. Ariadne was
eight, and small for her age, but when Mrs. Schreuder had said
her daughter was nine, the child had nodded. And when they had
asked to see her dance, they noted the positive side of her immaturity: because the child was still small, she was sturdy, not yet
weedy. Also, her feet were strong. Although she was underage,
"we took her because she was a very independent child. No problems with her. A very, very *nice* child—smart, extremely obser-
vant. She didn't miss a thing," says Mireille. "I think quite talented."

One can find other baby ballerinas, and mothers, both at the
Briansky School and at SAB, who say, "Ariadne was the worst
dancer in the whole school. Clumsy. Gawky. Terrible. And the
least popular. She was mean, and everybody hated her. And all
the mothers hated her mother. *My* mother even hated her grandmother . . . Of course, my mother hates everybody."

Such poisonous talk is in fact the lingua franca of the backstage
ballet world. Few there take it seriously. "Ballet *is* woman," said
Balanchine, and the cackle and hiss of neurotic mothers and their
anorexic daughters are merely the dark side of the impossible
dream. Ballet's image of perfection is fashioned amid a milieu of
wracked bodies, fevered imaginations, Balkan intrigue, and sulfurous hatreds where anything is likely, and dancers know it. A
well-known backstage anecdote concerns the occasion when the
prima ballerina found ground glass in her toe slipper—and every
other dancer in the Company was equally suspect. Dancers know
that almost all infant ballerinas have pushy mothers. To want
one's daughter to become a ballerina—one of the most punishing,
romanticized, and least-rewarding disciplines imaginable—itself
betrays a certain fixation. Much better to judge Ariadne and her
mother through the experienced eyes of solid professionals, people like the Brianskys and David Richardson.

Frances's newfound role in the ballet world, her uniquely powerful, heavy position of being at once ballet Board member and
ballet mother, had given her distraught life a focus at last; it had
given the madwoman *something to do*. It had also given her license to do it her own, high-decibel way. All her volatile temperament was now on display. You could hardly miss it. The back
stage scenes, the frontstage screams were becoming continuous.
By 1982 Frances Schreuder was acting on occasion as if she *owned*

the Company, as if she thought she had bought it. She sent $200 bouquets to favored ballerinas after a performance that pleased her. Male dancers received a case of wine. She arrived at a baby shower for a ballerina mother-to-be bearing gifts that had cost more than $1,000. She told others that Balanchine and Kirstein "will do whatever I ask them." She told leaders of the Company that she would pay for, and Balanchine would stage, a new *Sleeping Beauty* such as the world had not seen since the days of the Tsars. And others *encouraged* her to think this way. They sent her books on dance history—Petipa, Fokine, Diaghilev. They offered her tapes to study; they invited her to special little private dinners and teas. They wanted her to understand, to enjoy, to *endow*.

What did Frances want? She, too, wanted what she had never had. She wanted to buy friends. She wanted to buy acceptance. She really wanted to buy a *family*—not a skinflint father, parasitic mother, hateful sisters, but a beautiful, glamorous, fairy-tale family, a family as perfect as the storybook dolls in unreachable rows at the top of Ariadne's closet.

By early March, Mike George's investigation had turned up the tuition checks that Berenice Bradshaw had written to EMA, Kent School, and Episcopal Nursery School on Franklin Bradshaw's account. Far more dangerous to Marc were the prosecution's copies of Granny's letters to Larry. They did not only indicate the icy state of affairs between the Bradshaws and the Schreuders in the months before the murder. In one, Granny complained that talking to Marc was "like talking to a vegetable." His mother had him so "brainwashed," she had written, that he could not call his soul his own.

Marc Schreuder's preliminary hearing (Utah's alternative to grand jury proceedings) was held March 16 and 17. Berenice Bradshaw gave her grandson Larry the necessary alibi. By that time, the Salt Lake authorities had sufficient facts from Behrens to enable them to obtain an "information" showing "probable cause" to believe that it was Franklin Bradshaw's own daughter who had masterminded his murder. The judge issued an arrest warrant, and the following day Frances Schreuder was listed on all National Interstate Crime Commission computers as "wanted in Utah." After that, any state in the Union could arrest her. New York acted promptly. By 1 P.M. on March 18, Detective

Steve Klein was at 10 Gracie Square. When Paulette said Madame was not at home, the building's security people refused Klein admittance, so he staked out the premises until 10 P.M., then went home. At seven the next morning he got into the building with the help of a dog-walking butler, but Paulette refused to open up. He heard shouting from within the apartment. The scribbled name and telephone number of attorney Norman Ostrow was pushed under the door. Klein went downstairs and called Ostrow, who said he was talking to Frances on his other line. She sounded suicidal, he said, and she was also a potential threat to her eight-year-old daughter, who was locked in with her. Ostrow begged for more time. Tell her to open up by nine, Klein said, or he would break down the door. He returned to the precinct to get additional help.

Stationing one cop in the lobby, and another at the service entrance of the building, Klein returned to the vestibule of Apartment 6 accompanied by his partner Ernie Cruz and policewoman Annette Cimler. Inside, Frances was refusing to accept calls from lawyer Ostrow, a psychiatrist, her mother, and perhaps others. When Paulette still refused to open up, the cops tried first to remove the triple locks and then smashed the front door in. Seeing no one, they raced upstairs. Frances was in bed, shrieking, covers pulled over her head, Paulette and Ariadne alongside.

"Mrs. Schreuder was hysterical. She was screaming epithets at me," Klein later testified. The New York City Police Department was now discovering the extraordinary unpleasantness of saying no to Frances.

The phone rang. Steve Klein answered. This time it was lawyer Frankel, who identified himself as Marc's attorney. Apparently Frances was willing to speak to Frankel but not to Ostrow. This had put the young lawyer into an intolerable position: his client had already confessed to Frankel that he himself had done the murder—because his mother had insisted on it. Marc's confession was absolutely protected by the watertight legal seal that keeps so many crooks afloat: the sacred "attorney-client privilege."

Frankel could not even discuss her predicament with Mrs. Schreuder, not even in the most general way, without violating his oath to her son. He could only try to keep her calm, and silent, while groping frantically for another lawyer. Poor Frankel *had to* say no to Frances. But this scarcely stopped Frances from appealing to him. Frances had spent the entire long night on the telephone, speaking alternately to lawyers, psychiatrists, relatives, and perhaps to others. She was raving, ranting, screaming, wild-eyed.

But this morning, now that the police had actually forced their way in, Frankel was able by phone to persuade Frances to calm down sufficiently to respond to what the cops were saying. This allowed Klein to read the suspect his Miranda warnings—that she had a constitutional right to keep silent, and so on. Frances told him she understood. If Frances would get out of bed and put some clothes on, everybody now agreed, police would hold off until the lawyer rounded up by Frankel could arrive. Abruptly reasonable again, Frances requested a few minutes of privacy to get dressed and to explain matters to Ariadne. Klein posted the policewoman outside the closed bedroom door and withdrew with his partner to a bench in the foyer downstairs. The suspect appeared to him to have recovered her composure with remarkable alacrity.

Suddenly he heard a child scream, "Mommie! . . . Mommie, don't!"

The cops raced back up and found Frances halfway out of her bedroom window, seven floors above the East River. Both her arms and one leg were already outside the building. Ariadne, howling, was hanging on to her mother's right leg.

"It looked like the kid might go right out with her," Klein said. "Ernie grabbed the kid, and I grabbed her and threw her on the bed." Klein handcuffed Mrs. Schreuder and took her down to the 19th Precinct on East Sixty-seventh Street.

Lawyer Frankel arrived to find his client's mother once more hysterical and handcuffed to a chair. The police, anticipating another suicide try, had summoned paramedics. "I just want you to hold my hand," Frances pleaded.

Frankel thought it prudent not to say no again. "Okay. But don't talk to me about what happened, Frances. *Please.*" He took her hand.

Finally, to Frankel's immense relief, the other lawyer, Michael Shaw, arrived, and so did the paramedics. Frankel left. The others all went down together to Bellevue Hospital. Shaw and the cops waited on a bench while a psychiatrist spoke privately with the suspect, attempting to evaluate her emotional state.

Quite obviously, Mrs. Schreuder told him, the police had made some sort of outrageous mistake. She appeared understandably upset, particularly about the effect on her young daughter of witnessing her mother's arrest. But the doctor was unaware of the suicide try, and the woman before him was behaving in a composed and rational manner. He emerged from the interview saying he saw no reason to hold this woman for psychiatric observation. He changed his mind however, when Klein described what had just occurred.

Bellevue lacks facilities for female mental patients, so Frances was held over the weekend for observation at Elmhurst city hospital in Queens, then moved to Rikers Island. Her last words to Frankel that Friday morning as she was being led away were, "What will Mr. Balanchyne think!"

Paulette delivered Ariadne to her ballet lesson early the next morning, and Mireille noticed they both seemed upset. *"Ne dites rien!"* whispered the maid. *"Lisez le journal!"*

That Saturday morning the ballet world picked up its newspapers and learned for the first time that its all-time champion patroness was a first-degree murder suspect in Utah, now jailed in New York after trying to leap from her bedroom window. Phones buzzed madly. Dancers, staff members, and balletomanes were incredulous. The one person who received the news with equanimity was George Balanchine. His sole response to the phone call from the Ballet executive was a tolerant, amused chuckle. He appeared to view the matter, not unkindly, as some sort of cosmic joke. Never from the moment he was told of her arrest did Balanchine have any but the gentlest, most tender words for Frances Schreuder.

Lincoln Kirstein reacted to the news with a posture of militant outrage. Mrs. Schreuder was a victim of one of the most hideous frame-ups since the Dreyfus case, he said, and he promised that she would be vindicated in the same way. Her dead father, he later added, had been a beast, and her sisters had hated her since she was born. He pronounced her the victim of a political conspiracy emanating from the Salt Lake County Attorney's office and he clinched his argument with the observation that anybody who would seek to use artistic patronage of George Balanchine as proof of mental illness—as Frances's sisters were now attempting to do—left no doubt as to their own lack of moral worth.

Marc Schreuder has no clear memory of being summoned to the visiting room of the Salt Lake County jail early that Friday

evening and told of his mother's arrest. He is not even sure which
of his lawyers gave him the news. He just remembers a sense of
supreme despair, a feeling that his entire world was collapsing,
like a huge building being demolished in a silent newsreel. "They
arrested my mother. My poor, sick mother," he sobbed to Mary.
For the first time, he himself began to have suicidal ideas.

Frances Schreuder spent the five weeks following her arrest in
Rikers Island jail. On April 6, her forty-fourth birthday, Robert
Gottlieb sent the prisoner a slim volume of Igor Stravinsky's
letters. Several ballerinas sent birthday cards, and long-stemmed
red roses from Lincoln Kirstein arrived.

Frances had retained the respected Washington law firm
headed by Edward Bennett Williams. They set about negotiating
bail and gathering the necessary information to prepare an insanity plea, a strategy that they had recently used with great
success in their defense of John W. Hinckley, Jr., after his assassination attempt on President Reagan.

Few members of NYCB's Board of Directors viewed the news
in Saturday's papers as tolerantly as Balanchine and Kirstein.
The Board was deeply divided. A number of Directors wanted to
scuttle Frances at once, in hopes of minimizing the bad publicity.
Others found the fact of her arrest for murder simply inconceiv-
able. Outside observers deemed the dump-Frances movement the
same sort of irresponsible behavior it had been to romance her so
ardently in the first place. The lawyers on the board, led by new
president Orville H. Schell, took a firm stand: dropping Frances
at this point would be both morally and legally unacceptable, as
well as quite possibly counterproductive from a public relations
standpoint. The lawyers reminded the others of Frances's constitutional rights. They pointed out that the American system of
justice presumes a person innocent until proven otherwise, and
they very firmly recommended a do-nothing policy, at least for
the moment. Privately, the lawyers began subscribing to Salt
Lake City newspapers to keep tabs on the bizarre case.

The lawyers' wisdom prevailed. The Board took no official action. When Frances got out of jail, she bravely resumed her attendance at regular Board meetings, held every six weeks, as if nothing untoward had occurred. Publicly, no reference was made to
Mrs. Schreuder's difficulties. Privately, one or two Board members whispered words of encouragement. But at least two women
Board members stopped speaking to Frances. The least she could

do, they told the others huffily, would be to take a leave of absence and spare the Ballet further embarrassment. Not bloody likely. Mrs. Schreuder clung to the board room table as to a raft in a typhoon. When it was clear she had no intention of resigning, the two women took to appearing at meetings lugging stacks of heavy books, books which they then arrayed in front of themselves on the board room table as barricades, lest Frances take a sudden notion to open fire.

On April 8 bail was finally set at half a million dollars. Berenice Bradshaw put up the whole $500,000 in cash, and Frances Schreuder returned to Gracie Square. When she stepped through her still-smashed front door, the impeccable Kirstein himself stood haloed in the sunlight flooding through the dusty, ceiling-high windows. He held an armful of roses crushed against his soot-black suit, and as Frances entered he silently extended the bouquet and she, weeping, sank to her knees in an attitude of Pavlova-like obeisance and gratitude for his faith in her innocence.

That week, just as Ariadne celebrated her ninth birthday, the School of American Ballet won the all-time Bradshaw fund-raising Olympics. That very same week Frances pledged to underwrite two full four-year scholarships, at a cost of $20,000 per year. Kirstein and Balanchine *both* were willing to come to Salt Lake City and testify on her behalf, Frances told her mother. Berenice signed the check. (A year later, after Balanchine's death, and on the eve of her own trial, Frances would change, and double, her pledge through the establishment of a permanent Balanchine memorial. This gift took the form of a $400,000 endowment, sufficient to earn enough income to allow four scholarship students to study full-time.)

The week after Frances got out of jail, Berenice Bradshaw also laid out $100,000 to Williams & Connolly for its first retainer. When Marilyn Reagan came home one evening from work at Coudert Brothers, two Williams & Connolly lawyers were waiting in her apartment house lobby to question her regarding details of her sister's expulsion from Bryn Mawr. Marilyn could not recall very much. Even so, by the time they left, the two lawyers knew more about Frankie Bradshaw's brief and mottled college career than did Bryn Mawr's own trustees.

Not long before her arrest, some of the college's important alumnae had got wind that a Bryn Mawr graduate had recently become uncommonly generous to NYCB. Bryn Mawr's hundredth anniversary was approaching. Perhaps, they ventured, the Ballet's new benefactress would like to do something for her alma mater. It wasn't an official approach, just a discreet inquiry, another little lunch date. But Frances had responded with her customary alacrity and enthusiasm. She would indeed be interested in trying to help. A specially commissioned ballet might be possible; something choreographed by Balanchine, paid for by Frances, and premiered on Bryn Mawr's greensward on Garden Party Day. In view of the baroque consequences that might have arisen from this newest entanglement of culture and money and madness, it seems a pity that Mike George and Steve Klein moved as rapidly as they did.

In the coming months, George Balanchine became Frances Schreuder's main source of inner strength. Her sense of Mr. B's quiet but firm support gave her the will and courage to withstand assaults from people like Ernie Jones. Privately, Frances felt closer than ever to Mr. Balanchyne. It seemed no accident that they had become linked through the *Davidsbündlertänze,* the Band of David, drawn to it by a shared interest in the same themes—beauty, madness, love, and death, her belief that "feeling is the only law"; no accident that they were joined now in the same battle, the war against the Philistines. Mr. Balanchine, whom she thought of as her spiritual father, must know that she was innocent; not guilty of the monstrous charges lodged against her, it would seem, with the encouragement and connivance of her own son. Should it become necessary, Frances felt certain Mr. B would come to Salt Lake and rescue her from Utah's Philistines.

She hoped it would not become necessary. Balanchine was noticeably unwell. Something had been affecting his sense of balance, his essential ability to move and pirouette. Now sight and hearing were beginning to fail. No one knew what was the matter. Many diagnoses were made and discarded during his long, slow, mysterious decline. That in fact his brain tissue had been invaded by a rare minivirus that causes the condition known as Jakob-Creutzfeldt disease could not be learned until an autopsy was performed. Balanchine lingered on for another year. It was not to be a dignified or merciful death. It was cruel, prolonged, agonizing, a disease marked not just by increasing physical debility, but by the wildest of nightmares and terrifying hallucinations as the unknown virus ate into his brain.

To Frances it came to seem no accident that during this time while she was out on bail charged with the murder of her real father, she was being permitted to serve her suffering spiritual father at so agonizing a period in both their lives. At moments she believed she knew how to save his life, if only she were permitted control. She was not, of course, but she did continually devise new little ways to try to relieve his suffering or divert his attention with breathtaking gifts of flowers, special Russian foods, unobtainable caviars, rare wines.

All that year, while her lawyers were fighting to disentangle their client's future from Marc's own, and to keep Frances Schreuder out of Utah's clutches for as long as possible, Frances was fighting as best she could to restore Mr. B to good health. In Rikers Island, "I'd thought—and it was horrible—*Now I've lost everything! I've even lost George.* Instead it was just the opposite! He cried, with joy, when I was released from prison. He'd say to me, 'Frances, you're so *strong.*' I used to feel guilty when he said it. *Why* did he have such faith in me? He even offered to testify for me! He used to spend hours telling me, 'Have *courage.* Have *faith.* Be *strong.* You *are* strong!'"

And so she fought to *be* strong, to prepare herself for the coming ordeals in Utah, to "focus on evil," to "fight to win." And she fought with all her strength to keep Mr. B alive. She had already lost one father in her life. She could not bear to lose another.

Mike George stayed in fairly close contact with Marc after his mother's arrest, passing along messages from Vittorio, since Marc was not permitted to receive phone calls, and trying to arbitrate squabbles with other prisoners, most of which concerned the bad smells emanating from Marc's cell. But Sergeant George remained only a remote father or big-brother figure, careful not to elicit any confidences from Marc that he might be forced to testify about at trial. His strategy was more indirect. This troubled, jumpy, frightened boy was the key to nailing Frances. The smart cop would move slowly, with great circumspection.

Mike George went back to Gilmer Drive, now with subpoena in hand. Berenice still refused to open up. "You have no choice! I'm serving you," he shouted through the locked door. When she opened the door a crack, Mike showed her a canceled check. "By the way, did you write this?" he said pleasantly.

She examined the check and unchained the door. It was yet another of Marc's forgeries, this time for the rent and deposit money on Mary Lou Kaiser's new apartment. The old lady was furious. She talked to Mike for two hours, heaping abuse on Marc, telling Mike all the trouble Marc had caused the family, all the grief he had caused his mother. Marc had even taunted Frances that he had wrung more money out of the Bradshaw estate than she had, Berenice said. She blamed Frances for none of it. She told the policeman that Marc had forged $360,000 on her account since her husband's death, $90,000 going to coin dealers alone.

Mike heard her out, saying nothing. The main reason he had wanted to interview Berenice was to nail down Larry's alibi. Since he and Ernie suspected Van Dam and Tesch would try to throw suspicion on Larry, it was vital that Berenice say he was still asleep at the time of the murder. "We had to make Larry look as good as we could."

Until the last moment, the prosecutors could not be sure Berenice would even testify. She was dodging subpoenas, hiding out in a remote Maine fishing village with her eighty-five-year-old Aunt Bea, while her then lawyer, Kevin Kurumada, negotiated a promise that in return for her cooperation his client would not be charged with forging checks on her husband's accounts to pay her grandchildren's school fees.

Even after the agreement was signed, "our hearts were in our throats, not knowing what she would say on the stand. She could have changed her story on Larry, and cast suspicion on him at any time," George says.

Possibly Berenice thought Larry had suffered enough. Or perhaps she feared him. A few months earlier, unknown to the Utah authorities, Farid Salloum had filed a personal injury suit against his former roommate, charging permanent brain damage. At that time, just before Christmas, Larry had been transferred from his Pennsylvania prison back to the mental hospital for a third time. He was extremely withdrawn, not eating, and suffering severe tremors. A month later, in January, he would be returned to prison with an updated diagnosis: "chronic paranoid schizophrenic . . . prognosis guarded . . . unemployable at this time

. . ." Berenice's Pennsylvania lawyers would eventually settle Farid's suit for $50,000.

After Van Dam and Tesch received Marc's eight tape recordings from David Frankel, they arranged for their client to be examined by a noted forensic psychiatrist, Louis G. Moench, M.D., with a view to putting forth a defense based on his mental state. The old doctor had two two-hour sessions with Marc, in May and early June, and concluded that, while the young man was certainly not insane, he had indeed suffered from extreme emotional pressures exerted by his mother. The evidence of this was right on the so-called Ariadne Tape. Later, in court, Dr. Moench would say that he had not the slightest doubt of the tape's authenticity, and that he had never before heard anything like it.

In transcription, the tape is a more than thirty-page nonstop record of a mother goading, terrorizing, taunting, cajoling, mocking, and threatening a sniffling five-year-old for being unable to repeat the schoolbook definition of a sentence—that it is something which starts with a capital letter and ends with a period. One hears the child choking on her tears as the mother calls her a stupid bastard, threatens not to give her any more sleeping pills, says her grades are rotten, that she's not even trying. The mother mocks her for being a crybaby, tells her she will never have any friends, never go to "pretty parties" with "nice girls," just with "cheap, rotten Yids." The child is accused of being stupid, disobedient, a liar, and told that all of it is her own fault. Ariadne did it to herself. "*You* did it! You had a *choice! You* decided to talk to those little Jew girls! You won't have love from me. Or respect. Or from Mr. Balanchyne's ballet school. Or Brearley, Spence or any other nice school . . . You will be sad the rest of your life . . . I will make you *really cry!* [Terrible scorn] You expect me to put my arm around you like Granny does and say it's all right!"

Sometimes Frances's voice becomes the child. "I hate you . . . stupid!" she wails. "I'll put you in a hospital for stupid children . . . you don't come home if you're stupid. It's not like a broken neck. You live and die there. You'll never get married, never see boys, never go out and work, never see other children. You'll never see your mother again. You'll never see your house again. Or anyone else's house. They have special hospitals for children who are disturbed and cuckoo and there's something wrong.

They stay there for the rest of their lives. *They are not permitted to go out—ever!"*

Ariadne whimpers, is incoherent. She tries to speak. Her mother will not let her. "Whaddya *do* with such an idiot!" Frances shouts. "I hate your crying . . . it's disgusting . . . At ten o'clock at night you *still* don't know what a sentence is! *Well, I hate your guts!"*

"Mommy . . . Mommy . . . I *am* trying . . . [sniffles]"

"Children like you don't go to school with other children. You have to go to nigger school, where there are only poor kids . . . little Jew kids . . ."

More tears and sniffles.

In utter fury: "Just tell me what a sentence is and shut up the crap! Stop crying and stop shivering! What is a sentence—you coward! You belong in a zoo with the animals and the monkeys! . . ."

Becoming hysterical: "Mom . . . Mom . . . wait a second . . . Mom, don't hit me . . . A sen . . . Mom, a senten . . . a sentence is . . . is . . . a . . . a . . . sentence is . . ."

"I've asked you for four solid hours!"

At last it was over. Gratefully Dr. Moench snapped off his tape recorder. Later he said frankly, "That's about as abusive a dialogue as I've ever encountered."

That spring Frances spoke to the Brianskys about enrolling Ariadne in their well-known summer ballet camp at Saratoga, New York. After they accepted her, three sets of parents notified the camp directors that they had changed their minds about sending their own daughters. More than simple snobbery was involved. With Frances's recent notoriety, her Christmastime backstage threat to kill another child had taken on new gravity.

In May, Ariadne performed enchantingly at the School of American Ballet's Spring Gala, and Frances brought Berenice along as her guest to the fund-raising dinner party afterward in the New York State Theater. There were no place cards, and the two women and the little girl wound up sitting with two very nice and attractive men. When they first sat down together, nobody had expected much fun; benefit dinner parties rarely sparkled. The men figured the women were just ballet mothers; the child was indistinguishable from every other thin, pony-tailed little girl. But all five people had a wonderful time. They chattered gaily and did not even formally exchange names until midway through the evening. The two men were astonished to discover that the younger woman was a member of the NYCB Board of Directors. They had never met a Board member before; the two worlds rarely mingle socially. They found the child charming, the younger woman vivacious and amusing, especially her long, funny story about having three bathtubs in her living room. They adored the older woman's matter-of-factness. "I got tired of paying to have my lawn mowed," she said. "So I had my contractor cement over my entire yard."

The women enjoyed meeting the two men just as much. They turned out to own a house together in Saratoga, the very place Frances and her daughter would be spending their summer. What's more, one of the men, Chris Alexander, was a well-established theater and portrait photographer, and his friend was the dancer Shaun O'Brien, the very man who played Herr Drosselmeier, the very man who played Herr Drosselmeier. Who could have recognized him without his grotesque Nutcracker makeup?

Early in June, Larry Bradshaw was given a weekend pass for a home visit. But when he got to New York, Paulette explained that Frances was too busy with the Ballet to see him, and he spent the weekend at home with the Gentile family.

On June 8, at their regular annual meeting, the members of the Board of the New York City Ballet, by now champions to a man, and woman, of the Anglo-American system of justice, unanimously elected Frances Schreuder to a new four-year term. To speak to many of these people today is a little like interviewing Germans after World War II. Only "good Germans" existed. There *were no* Nazis. The same attitude prevails throughout the entire ballet world—front office, Dress Circle, and backstage. Nearly everyone professes to have been too preoccupied, too terribly busy, too focused on his or her own obsessions, too strung out, too exhausted, too inured to at least mild and at times galloping eccentricity within their own ranks to have noticed anything odd or amiss. In the same way, the woman who was sometimes bad, bold Frankie, and sometimes poor mad Mrs. Schreuder—and at almost all times an embarrassment while she was there—is an embarrassment in memory. She should not have been tolerated. Easier to pretend it all never happened.

The Board has new procedures now. There are mandatory checks, a selection committee. There is never to be a second Frances Schreuder. As for the first one, she has been folded up like an old costume. She is permanently out of the repertoire.

The day before the Ballet Board met to re-elect Frances Schreuder in New York City, pretrial hearings in the case of *State of Utah* vs. *Marc Francis Schreuder* finally got under way in Salt Lake City. The prosecution had by then been forced to abandon its original headline-grabbing dream of staging a joint mother-son murder trial. No judge was likely to permit two opposing defenses—each defendant blaming the other—in a single case.

The morning these hearings began, Marc asked Mary Lou Kaiser to bring him two books from the library. He wrote out the titles for her. One was *Crime and Punishment;* the other, *The Brothers Karamazov.* "It's about a boy who kills his father," he told her.

"Amen!" said Mary Lou.

Part Six

The Closing Down

. . . THE PLAYERS ASSEMBLED at the start of Marc's trial look like a prosecutors' convention. On the left, well brushed and sober-faced, sit the earnest prosecutor Ernie Jones and his sidekick, Sergeant Mike George. On the right, equally grave, are the two defense attorneys, rumpled Paul Van Dam and feisty little Joe Tesch, both of them former prosecutors. And seated on the bench is the most famous prosecutor in Utah. Judge Jay Banks is a deeply lined, lean, severe-looking man who brags that in twenty-two years as a prosecutor, he has probably tried more murder cases than any lawyer in Utah—thirty-three during his last year in office—before ascending the heights of judicial impartiality where he now sits like a seasoned falcon, leather hood still in place. In short, a hanging judge.

The proceedings begin with protracted legal arguments. The defense announces it is waiving its right to a trial by jury. It sounds lunatic, staking everything on the opinion of one man—*this* man. But it will turn out that the move is a desperate attempt to get a different judge. Judge Banks, who is not well, had said at a preliminary hearing that, should the defendant waive a jury, he might reassign the case.

The grubby defendant sits hunched between his two lawyers, his back to the courtroom, kicking his short legs back and forth under the table. Spectators caught only a glimpse of Marc Schreuder before he sat down. He is five feet six or seven inches tall, his dark blond hair is cut in bangs, and he has a little potbelly. The bright blue eyes are expressionless as blue marbles. He wears wrinkled jailhouse clothing, no socks, and rubber thong sandals which soon fall off from his relentless kicking. The legal wrangling, and the kicking, continue until Judge Banks, a man of his word, finally tosses himself out of the case.

June 16, 1982. Marc's fate has been reconsigned to the tender mercies of one Judge James S. Sawaya, a swarthy, bald, heavy-featured Lebanese father of six who promises he will be no less

stern than his predecessor. On the first day of testimony, Van
Dam announces his intention to waive an opening statement until
the prosecution has presented its case. The defendant, who today
has brought his copy of *The Brothers Karamazov* to court, is still
jiggling his legs, kicking his feet, tapping his fingers, scratching
his head. Jones gets to his feet and, in brief, declarative sentences,
lays out what he intends to prove: that defendant Marc
Schreuder murdered his grandfather for pecuniary gain. He
presents his first witnesses in workmanlike fashion: the early customers who found the body, the medical examiner Dr. Moore,
some cops. Then he calls grandfatherly Doug Steele.

The manager of Bradshaw Auto Parts is a rough-and-ready
type with white hair, a raspy voice. "I was with Frank for thirty-
two years," he says, and describes his boss's prodigious work
habits—seven days a week, twelve to fifteen hours a day—and the
breadth of his empire at the time of his death. In addition to the
million-dollars-a-year warehouse operation, which had twenty-
one employees, there were twenty-eight auto parts stores, six corporations, a "Jobbers' Service," and an "oil service operation."

"Fair to say he was a millionaire?"

Steele turns red-faced. "Heh, heh! He was a millionaire—*yes!*"

In the summer of 1977, Frank told Steele that his grandsons
were coming out to work under his supervision. Did Steele "experience any problems with the defendant that summer"?

"From Day One."

Steele describes the $1,400 shortfall on Marc's first day at
work. Within a week it was clear to Steele that the grandsons
"had no intention of working."

"Based on your observations, how did the defendant treat his
grandfather?"

"Terrible." He was "disrespectful . . . dishonest . . . arro-
gant." Yes, Steele was present when Frank accused Marc of
breaking into his files and stealing stock certificates hidden in
stacks of *Life* magazines. Marc denied it. Frank asked Doug to
talk to the boy. Marc stonewalled several hours more.

Steele was also present the day the two forged $10,000 checks
came back from the bank, and Marc and his grandfather had a
public "screaming match," and the old man burst into tears. So
were Larry, Berenice, Nancy Jones, Frank's secretary, and several others.

The warehouse had ten doors, five at the rear, and all were

normally locked on Sundays. The Sunday Frank was shot, the police asked Steele to look the place over and tell them if he noticed anything unusual. The padlocks were hanging open, he told them. Yes, the keys were in their usual place, a drawer in the manager's desk behind the counter.

When Steele arrived for work one morning a few weeks after the grandsons had returned to New York, his boss handed him a copy of Exhibit # 22, a curious half-page document naming Steele and Marilyn coadministrators of the Bradshaw estate, and dividing his fortune into equal thirds among Berenice, Marilyn, and Elaine.

This was the first time Steele knew the boss was thinking about putting him, a nonfamily member, into his will. Steele knew that Frank did not like his old, 1970 will; he had said so to Doug on numerous occasions.

June 17, 1982. Steele is back this morning and, at his honor's request, has brought along both of his copies of the will-change memo from the office files. The dead man frequently rerevised his old will; the witness saw him working on it, making additions and deletions, for four or five years. When his older brother Frederick, the bank president, died, Frank obtained a copy of Frederick's will and tried to "dovetail it" to his own. He bought a book, *How to Make Your Own Will,* to "show how simple it was."

Frank understood that his half-page memo was not a legal will. But he told Doug it represented "what his intent was, on his new will . . . He said he had *had it* with Frances," and intended to put Doug and Marilyn in charge. Later that morning, he asked Doug to drive him over to his lawyer's office on Main Street.

Did Bradshaw ever indicate to Steele that he was afraid of Marc?

"Yes," says Steele, before Tesch can object.

Van Dam's lengthy cross-examination seeks to establish that Steele, as a top employee with profit-sharing benefits, was himself a beneficiary under the will. Correct; but he had no part in the real money-maker, the oil lease business. "It was strictly Frank's."

Have any arguments with the old man? "We always had disagreements . . ."

"Did you ever end up arguing or yelling at Mr. Bradshaw?"

"You didn't yell at Mr. Bradshaw . . . He was the best listener in the world. He would listen you out."

Only three months before his death, Bradshaw had finally in-corporated his stores. Steele was vice president. After Bradshaw's death, he became president until 1980 when the business was sold.

In the afternoon of the day Steele drove Bradshaw to see the company lawyer, Alma Boyce, who is also a cousin of the Brad-shaws', Frank gave Steele a second will memo slightly different from the morning one. He wanted Doug to be familiar with all the nuances of his thoughts about his estate.

"Did he ever ask you, or anyone that you know of, to witness either of these documents?"

"I found that sad tale later on, when I took it to a lawyer myself to ask him what was the validity of it." An unwitnessed document is invalid.

The morning they discovered the two forged $10,000 checks made out to cash and deposited by Frances, they also, eventually, discovered another $6,000 in smaller forged checks to depart-ment stores, beauty salons, and so on.

Any proof that Frances and her sons were involved?

"Yes. You betcha!" But the police were not called, and this response is not explained.

In cross-examination, Van Dam brings out that the strained relationship between Frank and Berenice frequently made it nec-essary for Steele to act as a kind of confidential go-between. Thus, although Frank was "a very proud, private man," Steele was privy to much. When Frank told him Berenice was coming to work, he'd asked, "What the hell's going on?"

"She's broke, Doug, and she's got to earn some money. I am going to give her money for household expenses. [But] I am cut-ting off all the funds for Frances, and she knows it." If Berenice wanted to send money back to Frances from now on, she would have to earn it. Frank would pay his wife $4.00 an hour, same as anybody else.

Didn't she resent having to work for nickels and dimes? "I imagine she would."

On redirect, the witness makes clear he believed Frank in-tended to make a new will, but was killed before he could carry out his intention.

The next witness, Jon Cavenaugh's mother, was concerned enough "as a mother" to suggest they call Mrs. Schreuder when she learned that their well-dressed young visitor had come all the way out to Texas to buy a gun. "Go right ahead," said Marc. But then she decided Marc was so at ease, so "open and disarming," she hadn't bothered.

Tall, good-looking Jon Cavenaugh, now in the Navy, is a typical hell-raising West Texas rich kid, the antithesis of Marc. He was two years ahead of Marc at Kent, barely knew him at school, and had been surprised to receive his phone call. Jon identifies the heavy blue steel gun, a "Sheriff's Special" highway patrolman model, and explains how he arranged the $175 cash sale. Jon later showed Marc how the gun worked, but neither one of them fired it.

Joe Tesch on cross-examination brings out that Marc was "rather excitable . . . socially backwards" compared to the laid-back Texas youth. Didn't he tap his foot a lot? Talk very fast, in a loud, high voice? Tesch seems to be trying to paint a picture of an emotionally distraught kid, but it isn't working. Marc "wasn't abnormal, by any means," Jon says. One begins to wonder what sort of defense these lawyers will be able to put forth.

Miss Nancy Jones, in her middle thirties, wears a neat secretary's hairdo, blazer, and skirt. She is prim and soft-spoken, but it is clear she adored her boss and has little use for the rest of his family. Most of the monies sent back to the Schreuders went through her hands. On July 13, after Frances and Marc had called the warehouse collect looking for Berenice, Nancy heard Mrs. Bradshaw speaking heatedly to Frank. If they sent the Schreuders one more check, they would never be asked for money again. So "he came in and told us to type up a check and mail it."

Nancy can identify the typewriter Franklin used to type up his half-page will memo. It was his usual practice to type up his rough drafts on half-sheets of paper, then give them to one of his two secretaries for retyping on whole sheets; he saved paper that way.

For such a cost-conscious man, Bradshaw had curious business practices. Loose, unnumbered blank checks were kept underneath the parts counter in an open box. Stealing them would be easy as stealing peanuts. Yet Doug Steele, in his testimony, had said that Frank hid his cash so carefully among the parts bins that, despite all the treasure hunters who had combed through the great rats' nest of a warehouse, hidden pools of cash were still turning up three months after the old man's death. And finally, the office rubber-stamp signature would have made forging checks a relatively simple matter.

On cross-examination, Tesch brings out that Nancy wrote checks to all three Bradshaw daughters.

And how big were the checks to Marilyn and Elaine? Ernie Jones asks on redirect.

"One hundred dollars apiece. On their birthdays."

June 18, 1982. Jerry Register, thirty-four, an amiable and large-bellied good ole boy in plaid Western shirt and square haircut, has the unfailing politeness of Texas country boys. In 1978 Register was chief of police of Stanton, Texas, eighteen miles from Midland. He then owned three .357 magnums, one of which he was happy to sell in order to buy new boots for his nine-year-old son's birthday—boots the son will now never wear.

Withal, the witness does not seem at all concerned that he sold another deadly weapon to an underage boy who the next day used it to execute his grandfather. Register is a gun fancier who bought his own first pistol when he was fourteen. He can state the date of sale to Marc with accuracy because he remembers it was a Saturday, that's the day his wife worked in the finance company office, and it must have been two weekends after Old Settlers' Day, when they have the jalapeño pepper-eating contest, and the egg-throwing contest.

When the various people involved in the sale gathered in the bank lobby that Saturday morning, and Register saw the buyer for the first time, he thought he "looked kinda nervous." The big blue steel weapon was brand-new, still in its original packing, inside a paper sack. Marc peeled off $175 in small bills—a $10 profit for the sheriff—and when the exchange was completed, somebody said, "That'll take care of anything you run into backpacking in Utah."

Stephen Swindle, the attorney in charge of administering the Bradshaw estate, is a large, genial, prosperous-looking chap through whom the court learns some interesting facts about the 1970 will. The original copy of that will, the one that Berenice had told police on the day of her husband's death "Franklin never liked," has never been found. Swindle has only his yellow office file copy. Twenty-five attorneys from Swindle's firm, plus numerous clerks and paralegals, turned the warehouse upside down looking for the original. He finally was able to obtain a special ruling from the probate court that the copy was the document still in force at the time of Bradshaw's death.

Had there been even a whisper of a threat to contest the will, this would not have been possible. The law must presume that, if the original document cannot be produced, the testator may well have written a subsequent will which would invalidate the earlier one. It is precisely men like Frank Bradshaw who prove the wisdom of this precaution; Steele has already said that Frank tinkered continually with his old will.

Swindle has brought charts to explain the will and trust provisions, and he emits immense thickets and billows of legalese in the process. In sum, Berenice Bradshaw controls it all, and Swindle pegs the inventory value of the estate—much smaller than the actual value—at about $10.5 million. Three or four months after Frank's death, Berenice had formally disclaimed her interest in the family trust. The effect was to permit assets of the family trust to pass down to the grandchildren as if Berenice had predeceased her husband. Marc Schreuder, like the others, is not a beneficiary in the will. He is a beneficiary under the family trust.

Were Berenice and her daughters familiar with the provisions of the original will?

Swindle has had numerous conversations with Berenice and her daughters. Elaine didn't seem to know much about it. Marilyn said she believed her father had had a "progression of thought" concerning the original provisions. And "a rather extensive letter in our estate-planning file written by Mrs. Schreuder . . . would indicate that she had knowledge of the contents of the documents." This is the fifteen-page howl of protest which Frances wrote in 1975 saying that her mother did not understand her father's will. The legalese in Frances's letter is far knottier than Swindle's, but the underlying message seems to be that her mother is scatty and might inadvertently—or deliberately—divert monies away from Frances and her children to the Drukmans, or even to Marilyn.

Six of Richard Behrens's plaintive letters to Swindle's office regarding some sort of joint bank account with Frances Schreuder are produced. The letters bulge with documentation. The fellow apparently had hoped to recover his loss out of the estate funds. Not while the impeccable Stephen D. Swindle is in charge. He had suggested to Behrens that he get in touch with the lawyer who represents Frances, Ron Madsen of Parsons, Behle & Latimer.

On cross-examination Paul Van Dam brings out that, once Berenice had disclaimed interest in the family trust, she could not invade that trust to divert money from the Drukmans or Reagans to the Schreuders. In Swindle's words, "it became apparent to us that a harmonious relationship did not exist" between Berenice and her two eldest daughters. By then, Berenice and each of her daughters and the estate had all retained separate counsel, and Elaine's lawyer had obtained a court order "saying the admission of the will to probate is vacated. Period." This appears to have been a preliminary move to perhaps challenging the old will. It would have served to put matters on hold while the possible challenge was being considered.

Would the effect of this have been to prevent Mrs. Bradshaw from getting any money out of the estate?

No. Because, at the same time, a petition was filed and granted giving Berenice a $10,000-a-month family allowance.

But the effect was also to put on hold what otherwise would have been her freedom to do whatever she liked with the bulk of the estate? Well, yes.

What did Marilyn mean by the strange term "progression of thought"? She used it to indicate that she had "seen an outline of another will which was not signed by her father."

Yes, Swindle's firm did consider itself attorneys of record in charge of Bradshaw estate matters, though other attorneys took care of other legal business for Franklin. And no, Swindle himself never met Frank Bradshaw, nor had any communications with him. And yes, Swindle is aware of the half-page "instrument" indicating a possible change of mind, but it is undated, invalid, and in no way changes anything.

Now, how would Marc Schreuder have benefited under the existing will? He would have to survive his mother, and become twenty-one years old, before he could get anything. Or Granny or one of his aunts could appoint some assets to him. Or Marc could try to establish some compelling need to invade the principal, but he would have to do that *through* Swindle's office. (Easier to put a camel through the eye of a needle, one would think.)

What did Swindle know about the original copy of the 1970 will? Only that he was finally able to get a court order saying it had been lost or inadvertently destroyed—but not intentionally destroyed.

And suppose Frank Bradshaw had died intestate?

Ah, well, that would have changed the distribution dramatically. Berenice would then have received $50,000 plus one half of the estate. The other half, less the $50,000, would have been divided equally between the three daughters. The tax bite would have been much larger and . . .

Yes, but wasn't it also true that each daughter would have received "a great deal more money" outright than under the will? Yes.

And wasn't there not just "disharmony" but outright "hostility" within this family? "Paul, I sensed that she was a very torn mother . . . very, very hurt . . ."

And wasn't, in fact, the disclaimer on the trust she filed on November 10, 1978, a kind of trade-off, whereby if Berenice disclaimed, her daughters would agree not to contest the will?

Hack away the lawyerly language, and what we are hearing is that the elder daughters, Elaine in particular, became concerned that, unless some kind of brakes could be applied to the runaway chariot which was Frances and Berenice in tandem, "there was no ultimate certainty that the [other daughters] would receive anything . . ."

Unstated is the fact that mounting a will challenge would have been very expensive, because of the necessary fees to lawyers and private detectives. Elaine and Marilyn did not have, or else perhaps did not wish to lay out, the kind of monies necessary. More important, it would have required a united front between the sisters, and it also would have required them to challenge their mother's mental competency. In the months right after their father's death, Marilyn didn't have the heart to do this; Elaine could not afford to do it alone. Later, by the time Marilyn's resolve hardened, Elaine's health had again broken down. By the time she had recovered from the cardiac surgery, it was too late.

Unknown to anyone in this courtroom, except possibly the defendant, is the fact that the original will does indeed exist. When Larry Bradshaw was arrested, his belongings were impounded by Lehigh. About two years later they were opened by the university; a will was found. Pennsylvania and then Utah authorities were notified. On December 13, 1982, Utah would obtain a search warrant in Pennsylvania to examine Larry's belong-

ings. Among thousands of travel photos were the letters from
Berenice. There too was Frank Bradshaw's will. When he stole it,
whence he stole it, and whether anyone else knew he stole it, is
unknown.

Judge Sawaya leans forward. How much money has been distributed from the estate so far? Swindle says Marilyn, Elaine, and
Frances have each received about $136,000 plus some oil and gas
leases.

Officer Joel Campbell is a thin, sinewy cop with lots of carefully combed dark hair and a droopy mustache. Marilyn Reagan
really broke the case, he says, though Behrens's aid was vital.
However, Behrens "refused to be interviewed by police," and
only after Utah offered complete immunity from prosecution was
Behrens even ready to consider cooperating.

The fourth day of trial, entirely taken up with more gun testimony, is in every sense a bore. But Day Five produces the State's
key witness—slovenly, barrel-shaped Richard Behrens. In his late
forties, he has a steel-gray crew cut and a darting gaze as random
and erratic as a pinball machine. A nervous habit of continually
stroking his cheeks and chin further distorts his already rapid
speech. Before he can even begin to tell his story, Tesch says,
"This is the witness that we requested a psychiatric examination
on . . . He's had psychiatric problems in the past . . . and it
appears to us that he does not know what it means to tell the
truth."

But Judge Banks had already vetoed this idea. "I will not over-
rule Judge Banks," says Judge Sawaya dryly. "Proceed." In all,
the ruling seems a loss to the annals of forensic psychiatry. This
is a very odd witness. At one point the judge leans forward,
incredulous. "Am I to believe that you had a conversation with
Marc Schreuder when his *mother* dropped off a gun and said it
was a murder weapon? Is *that* what you are saying?"

"Well, it was a mad scramble . . . He came in later . . . He
had just come back in town and he had shot his grandfather. This
was put out by both he and his mother."

"I want to know the details. Did he knock on the door?"

"No. His mother initially rang the bell and rushed in with this
gun and dumped it on me and . . . within a half an hour,
twenty minutes, Marc came in." Behrens's apartment was only a
block from the Schreuders'. Marc had stopped off at the neighborhood deli, establishing his alibi. A few days later, Marc, Fran-

ces, and Behrens looked in the Yellow Pages for a gun dealer. Frances lent Behrens her Olds, and he and Marc drove down to Chambers Street and bought a leather gun cover and cleaning rods. For the next two years, the gun sat undisturbed on Behrens's kitchen shelf in a paper shopping bag. He did not realize that a note in Marc's hand on Kent School stationery was also inside. When he found the note, he Xeroxed it and burned the original, to be certain his fingerprints were not connected to the weapon.

He runs through his whole story: the joint bank account with Frances telling Marilyn he had the gun and turning it over to her; his confession, his recantation, his reconfession, after the grant of immunity, in which he now blamed Frances for the first time, and said it was she—not Marc—who "dropped the gun off on me."

"Why did you hang on to the gun so long?"

"That's a good question. I certainly meant to throw it away." Instead, he called Marilyn.

"I will have the police come to you," she said.

Behrens told her if the police came to him, "the gun wouldn't be there, and I would sue them for breaking and entering, and false arrest." Behrens wanted nothing more to do with the matter. "So she agreed . . . and walked it up to the 20th Precinct herself."

Two months later, Behrens gave his first statement. He told Joel Campbell that he got the gun from Marc. Frances then summoned the little man to 10 Gracie Square. Mother and son held him captive for hours and terrorized him into typing out a long, phony story putting the blame on Marilyn. Otherwise, they warned, he would be charged as an accomplice to murder, and he would serve twenty years. "I had a very strong motivation . . . Mrs. Schreuder told me they were going to blame it on me . . . I kept ahold of a gun, after all. I didn't come forth . . . didn't tell exactly what happened . . . Soooo, I swung it around saying that Marilyn had the gun all along." Once he had typed out the statement, Behrens and Marc drove to a Xerox place to have copies made, and notarized. Frances required a copy, she said, in order to convince Berenice to pay Marc's legal fees.

Behrens is on the stand two days. Both days he wears a dirty, frayed nylon shirt soiled with jelly stains that look like blood. For twenty years, he says, he had heard Frances talking about her inheritance. But the more he says, the wilder his story seems.

Family assassination plots! *Poisoned oatmeal!* Other lawyers drop in to hear the fantastic tale unfold. Around the courthouse, Behrens is known as "the New York twit." When it comes time to cross-examine him, lawyer Tesch rises to his full height, sucks in a deep breath, rocks back and forth in his cowboy boots. He stares a long time as if about to encounter something awful, then says, "Mr. Behrens, how much immunity for the commission of this crime have you received? For everything connected with this crime, is that true? . . . And that immunity extends not only to perhaps assisting in the murder? But also extends if in fact you committed the murder, does it not?"

Less startling than the accusation is the fact that it ruffles Behrens not at all. "News to me," he says blandly. But he does vigorously deny it when Tesch suggests he had sexual relations with Frances.

Questions turn to what the defense alleges was Behrens's true motive for keeping the gun: that he too had feared losing a share of an inheritance from his father. "Did not he write to you in fact and say that he wished to divorce his wife because she was eating up the estate?"

"He didn't use those words. He was concerned about her drinking, and was concerned, at his age, trying to go through a divorce, the strain and stress of it." These concerns have become newly moot: the day before Behrens flew to Utah to testify, he had buried his father in New Jersey.

"Do you recall that you had conversations with Mrs. Schreuder to the effect that both of you could use a hit man?"

"No. I talked to her about legality because she was an experienced person in the ideas of divorce. She had been divorced twice. I wanted to know what my father . . . would have to go through to get a divorce."

Behrens admits twice going down to Virginia and attempting to get a gun. "She wanted a gun to shoot her father." But Behrens, a nonresident, was unable to purchase a weapon there. He admits driving Myles Manning up to see his father's summer home in New Jersey, but denies that his purpose was to show Manning the person *he* wanted hit—his stepmother, Joan Bloom Behrens. He only wanted Manning along to witness that Joan was denying him admission to his father's summer home.

What made him think Manning *was* a hit man?

Here, once more, a glimpse of the "political" views of the

'Schreuder gang." "He was in the printers' union. Union types enjoy an unsavory reputation . . . I thought perhaps he might know of somebody . . . himself."

"What made you think that he wouldn't turn you and Frances n to the police?"

"I didn't think about it."

Tesch rocks back on his heels. "You were conspiring and plan-ning a murder with Frances Schreuder, and you didn't think about the fact that he might turn you in to the police?"

"No. I wanted *them* to conspire to murder her father, Myles Manning and Mrs. Schreuder."

Deadpan. "You wanted them to conspire to kill her father."

"I wanted them to discuss it to discover whether he would do t."

"What was in it for you?"

"Nothing."

He had described the defendant's mother to Manning as a woman with "evil thoughts in her mind." But once he had per-formed the introduction, Behrens waited outside.

"If you wished to remain not involved in this at all, and wished them to conspire . . . why did you allow the meeting to arrange a murder to take place in your home, if there was nothing in it for you?"

"I dunno. They didn't wanna talk on the street . . . If they wanted to do something, it was all right with me. But I didn't want to be anywhere a part of it."

Tesch is disgusted. "What grade of our children did you teach?"

Weeks later, Behrens says, Frances called him to complain that Manning had conned her.

Here one wonders if possibly she thought that he and Manning split the $5,000. If so, that could explain her motive for looting Behrens's savings from their joint account. Or perhaps she had no motive, only a compulsion. Perhaps, like her father, she just loved money.

Didn't Behrens later ask Marilyn to get him a copy of the ballistics report?

Yes, to be sure that the gun he'd been given was indeed the murder weapon.

Wasn't it true that the real reason he gave Marilyn the gun was to recover the $3,700 Frances owed him? And because he had his eye on the $10,000 reward? And because Marilyn had offered to pay his attorney's fees?

"No. It was to keep Larry Bradshaw from being wrongly accused of a murder . . . Larry didn't do it, and Marc did."

Tesch's volley of questions grows harsh, angry. His witness begins to give ground. He admits that Marc might not have given him the gun the night of the murder; it might have been the next day.

But when Tesch suggests that Behrens held back the Cavenaugh note on Kent stationery not because of fingerprints, but because he hoped to sell it to Marilyn for a higher price, the witness denies it. Tesch suggests sharply that in fact Marc never admitted *anything* to Behrens, that Behrens is concocting this story on his own, to please his new masters, the State of Utah. Tesch attacks Behrens's memory of dates, months, years—implying over and over that he and Marilyn Reagan together fabricated the entire story against his client.

Isn't it true that the real reason he recanted his story in the office of Hiram Bissell Carey III is that Marilyn had failed to come through with the $10,000 reward she had promised him. No. "Do you remember making a statement, 'Maybe Marc bought this thing for Larry'?"

The witness denies this too. But he did make the statement, it is on the police tape, and logic suggests that it could be one bit of truth in his immunized, jelly-stained tissue of truth and lies.

Carolyn Karoliszyn Morris, the American Airlines ticket clerk with the phenomenal memory, ticks off four things which made this particular sale stick in her mind for two and a half years. Ticket #0014455192945 was itself unusual; she had never written one like it before or since. The customer paid all cash. The customer's name was Gentile. And "his appearance is a little unusual . . . I remember his eyes. They were . . . piercing . . . You know . . . looking through you, almost." Asked if she sees the buyer now, she points to Marc, sitting head down at the defense table.

Joe Tesch rises to cross-examine. Has the witness "ever been told whether or not Marc Schreuder had a *brother* . . . one year older" whose name is, in fact, Larry? Or "L. Gentile," the curious name which she recalls writing on the ticket?

No, says Carolyn. She is excused. These last questions can be interpreted in only one way. George and Jones had been right

The defense is now trying to throw blame for the murder on its client's brother.

Marilyn Reagan has let her hennaed red hair go gray for this court appearance, and she moves to the witness stand with purposeful tread, as if she expects to enjoy this moment. To the matronly hairstyle she has added rhinestone glasses, gold earrings and bracelets, and has made herself a floral pink outfit, hemline well below the knee, that suggests a Hawaiian tourist. The total effect is of a well-to-do, no-nonsense Mormon matron. A handkerchief is wadded into her strong right hand.

She describes her relationship to her mother: "It was very good." To Frances: "Distant." To her father: "He was very frugal. Mother's attitude was different. She often said, If he has all this money, why can't we spend it?"

Yes, the family offered a reward after her father's death. "I suggested it to the executors of the estate, and they agreed. So I went ahead and put the ads in the paper."

She tells the whole story of Behrens and the gun with great vivacity, as if she has been looking forward to this day for some time.

JUNE 24, 1982. For her second day's courtroom appearance, Mrs. Reagan has chosen an airy, wispy, cream-colored lawn party dress which projects just the right image—not a trace of New York City. Despite thirty years in Manhattan, she's pure down-home Salt Lake. "Like Betty Crocker," one of the reporters says.

Under Paul Van Dam's cross-examination, she is icily ladylike. She flatly denies any intention to attempt to succeed to the management of her father's business after his death, or to take over the care of her mother's affairs, or any problems with her mother in this regard.

"The only problems I have had with my mother have been letters I received after I visited when Frances was here . . . The letter accused me of doing things I didn't do." The letter resulted from her sister's powerful influence over their mother.

"And do you resent that?"

"I am not a resentful person, Mr. Van Dam."

"You don't resent it?"

"I think it is very unfair not to have a mother when she is living . . . I wish she could speak to me. But she can't."

Describing the moment Behrens handed over her father's murder weapon, she says she did not open the shopping bag because she was aware that anyone carrying a gun in New York without a license "would have been arrested. [Also] In a Burger King, pulling out a gun is not a good idea."

How did she feel about the money her mother gave her sister for the ballet?

"If that's what she wanted to do with her money, that's her business . . . It's a good charitable deduction."

Any hard feelings between herself and Frances?

"Not on my part," she sniffs. Her only complaint is that Frances created tension between her parents by "always pitting my mother against my father to get more money." Yes, her parents had argued over money. That was a "way of life" in the Bradshaw household.

Myles Manning is purest Guys & Dolls, the trial's comic relief. He looks like a denizen of "Archie Bunker's Place," and talks likewise. Like Behrens, he has immunity. He describes his four meetings with Frances, two on the street, one at her apartment, one at Behrens's place. At the first meeting, she "was a little devious." But she asked me if I was willing to do it. And I said, "No, but I would have somebody do it."

At the second meeting, he named a price, $5,000, because that was the total amount of his current debts.

At the third meeting, in Frances's apartment, a little girl was present. Manning says she was "eight or nine." But in October 1977, Ariadne was in fact only four. At this meeting, Frances handed him a manila envelope containing the money, a hand-drawn map showing the location of the warehouse, and pictures of his "target." For the first time, he learned that the "hit" was her father. Scornfully, Manning threw away everything but the money and holed up in the YMCA. Ernie Jones produces the receipted bill.

At their fourth meeting, chez Behrens, Manning told Frances he had gone out to Salt Lake but got arrested before he could do the hit.

"What was her reaction?"

"She started crying and she said, 'I am going to have to take my kids out of school, go on welfare . . .' She wanted her money back."

In his cross-examination, Tesch wonders if Manning might not be liable for prosecution in New York to recover the $5,000.

A beer-bellied, genial New Yorker rises in the spectators' section to address the court. He turns out to be Manning's lawyer. "If Mrs. Schreuder chooses to prosecute Mr. Manning for five thousand dollars that she gave him with the hopes that he would kill her father, she could go right ahead and do it." Appreciative laughter sweeps the room.

Manning says that he has never seen Marc Schreuder in his life until right now, and that Marc was not involved in the conspiracy in any way. He says that Frances not only suggested he fake a robbery to confuse police as to the motive of the crime. She reminded him that he could keep any proceeds from the robbery, in addition to his $5,000 fee.

Manning says he was never a good friend to Behrens, just a street and barroom acquaintance. He admits to a severe drinking problem in those days.

What did Behrens say to Manning at their first meeting?

"He asked me if I knew anyone that would commit a murder. I said yes."

"Were you lying to Mr. Behrens?"

"Of course."

Both sides take it fairly easy on the next witness, Berenice Bradshaw, a handsome and smartly dressed old woman with an air of money about her. She wears huge sunglasses and is slightly deaf. The lawyers must shout, but they are deferential to the matriarch of this extraordinary clan, aware of the pain she must be feeling to see her grandson on trial for her husband's murder.

Paul Van Dam's cross-examination seems excessively courtly, though not perhaps for a lawyer who is cross-examining his employer. The court learns that Frank Bradshaw had had a physical examination only two weeks before his death, and "was in terrific health."

"Mrs. Bradshaw, did you ever tell your daughters, Elaine or Marilyn . . . that Larry left the house shortly after Franklin, on the morning of his death?"

"No."

What was Berenice's relationship to Marilyn? Were there problems with her after the funeral?

"Her attitude was a bit disturbing to me. She wanted to take over and I didn't want any of my family to take over. She was a bit . . . a bit . . . hostile . . . She walked into the auto parts store and said, 'I am taking over.' The manager said, 'No, you are not.' "

"What else did she do?"

"She rented this office and was going to set herself up so she could run things . . . I went along with her at first." But after Marilyn left town, "I thought it was foolish for her to rent an office, and furnish it, when right in the warehouse there were plenty of desks and phones. She could work there. So I canceled the rent . . . and sent the furniture back . . .

"I wrote a letter telling all three girls I wanted none of my family into my affairs."

"And are Marilyn and Elaine angry at you because you continue to have contact with Frances and Marc?"

"Yes."

"Did you ever have any knowledge as to whether or not Mr. Bradshaw intended to disinherit Frances and her children?"

"I heard him say once that he was going to disinherit Frances. But I never told anyone."

"You say you never told anyone? You never told Frances? Or her children?"

Pause, then, "No." But it is a very weak-sounding no.

Before her testimony that day, her own attorney, Kevin Kurumada, had invited the old lady out to lunch and been astonished and delighted by her good appetite, her enjoyment of life, her candor. She talked about her poor childhood, about raising her family, about how it was 1975 before it really dawned on her that the Bradshaws actually were rich. She counted up the auto parts stores—they then had thirty-one! She began complaining to Franklin about his stingy ways. If he did not start spreading it around, she had warned, there would be a "bloodbath." Of course she had not meant it literally, but this was how she felt. By the summer of 1977, her grandsons' behavior had become so atrocious she had begun to wonder whether her grandsons would wind up in prison or in a mental institution—"And now I've got one in each!"

She told Kurumada she was glad when she heard Marc had missed his bail lineup and had to go back to jail. It had made her nervous to have him running loose around town. The lawyer got the idea that she was not especially fond of either of her grandsons. Yet, this afternoon after her testimony, when she unexpectedly encounters Marc being escorted by a jailer through a back hallway outside the judge's chambers, she impulsively rushes to embrace him. Granny and grandson weep in one another's arms while the transportation officer—who normally does not permit his prisoners to have body contact with anyone else—mercifully looks away.

Lawyers always save their best witness for last. The assignment in this trial goes to a soft-spoken woman named Dorothy Ferguson. She identifies herself as a free-lance writer and longtime friend of Richard Behrens who lives in Lynchburg, Virginia. In mid-July, just before the murder, Behrens had made one of his regular visits to her home, and stayed about a week. She told him she intended soon to take a trip to the beach. A few days after he went back to New York, she called him to report a few more details of her planned beach excursion.

Miss Ferguson is more organized than many free-lance writers. She saves her old phone bills. And one of these, recovered by the prosecution from Miss Ferguson's attic, shows a record of a four-minute call from Miss Ferguson in Virginia to Richard Behrens in New York City on Saturday night, the twenty-second of July.

It had long ago become apparent to the prosecution that defense strategy would have to be to try to cast blame for the crime on anyone but their client. Absent permission from Marc and/or Berenice to mount a full-scale assault on Frances Schreuder, the next likeliest candidates for blame had been Larry Bradshaw and Richard Behrens. It is now apparent that, just as Berenice Bradshaw had given Larry his alibi, Miss Ferguson provides one for Behrens. If he was at home in Manhattan Saturday night, there was no way he could have made it out to Utah in time to murder Franklin Bradshaw at seven the next morning.

Doug Steele is briefly recalled to rehabilitate Marilyn's reputation as a competent businesswoman, after her mother's somewhat disparaging testimony. That done, the State rests its case.

The defense attorneys now make the usual motions to have the prosecution case thrown out for lack of evidence; the judge makes the usual denials. It is time for the defense case to begin. And then, two weeks into the trial, the bomb drops.

The astonishing turn of events starts with the defense asking for a long lunch recess after the prosecution has rested. Observers assume they are simply unprepared. It turns out they have been awaiting the arrival of wise men from the East, two of them— Hiram Bissell Carey III and David Frankel. Both lawyers had been awakened that morning at 2 A.M. by calls from Salt Lake City and told to catch the first available flight.

After lunch, Paul Van Dam addresses the court. "It is our plan, your honor, to submit several exhibits in the form of a tape and a transcript of that tape . . . for the purpose of allowing the court access to underlying information that a psychiatrist, Dr. Moench, has used in forming and arriving at [his] opinion." What does this convoluted sentence mean? Even seasoned trial observers cannot figure out what the lawyer is trying to say. "We have also asked two lawyers that have heretofore represented Marc Schreuder," Ted Carey and Dave Frankel, to come here to testify for the defendant.

Marc Schreuder, at seventeen years old, had found himself in certain extremely strange, pressing, overwhelming circumstances, Van Dam continues. One of the lawyers the defense intends to put on the stand will describe an encounter with the defendant's mother. The second lawyer, Frankel, will testify as to a period of time he spent with Marc just after he was arrested and while he was fighting extradition.

Judge Sawaya interrupts to explain for the record that during the lunch break he has conducted an *in camera* proceeding in which Marc expressed his desire to waive his attorney-client privilege so that his Eastern lawyers can testify. The judge had required Marc formally to *ask* his lawyer to testify. He had also inquired into Marc's mental state, his free will, drugs, psychiatry —all the questions one would expect a court to use to protect itself against overturn on appeal in such an unusual situation.

Van Dam begins to say that Mr. Frankel will testify "to matters that will be a revelation . . ." then stops himself, preferring "they come from his own mouth." Frankel's testimony, says Van Dam, will explain certain acts and lay important foundations. And then it comes. Marc Schreuder is going to change his plea from Not Guilty to Guilty. He is going to admit responsibility for the crime.

Hiram Bissell (Ted) Carey III is young, Waspy, athletic-looking. He was retained to represent Marc Schreuder after his arrest at Trinity College. Yes, he has spoken to Marc's mother "on numerous occasions." How often? "Over thirty occasions." He winces.

Her calls, "and the purpose of them . . . became less and less clear . . . Mrs. Schreuder had, in my opinion, a case of wanting to hear something which was always unclear, but never listening to what was said. As a result, her conversations . . . were always relatively nonsensical . . ."

Mrs. Schreuder's phone calls went on over a period of about a year. "I would attempt to explain to her to the best of my ability —and to the extent that I was allowed to, in view of the fact that I represented her son and not her—what was going on. And respond directly to her questions. The problem always was that she would . . . be silent on the other end of the line, then ask the same question again . . . any number of times . . . despite how many times you attempted to answer, or you refused to answer . . . and I will be frank to say that, after a while, I began to feel as though Mrs. Schreuder was wasting my time. And I made a conscious effort to avoid talking to her, essentially because the length of conversations became so time-consuming . . . and so nonfruitful."

So it would be fair to say "that you became well familiar with her voice"?

"There's no question about that, Mr. Van Dam."

Van Dam now shows the witness Exhibit #92, the so-called "Ariadne Tape." Can he identify the two female voices?

Yes. He is quite familiar with both of them. The adult voice is Frances. The "very young child" is Ariadne.

The defense lawyer does not yet attempt to place the tape in evidence. "How would you characterize your telephonic relationship with Mrs. Schreuder?"

"Difficult, at best. Mrs. Schreuder demonstrated to me a lack of willingness to understand . . . what was being told her, and an uncanny ability to 'corner lawyers'—my term. Mrs. Schreuder made a conscious effort in my opinion to get me to criticize [Marc's Utah lawyer] . . . and vice versa."

How many people has attorney Carey dealt with professionally in his years as a litigator?

"Well into the thousands."

As compared to the others, was Mrs. Schreuder unusual?

"In my opinion, she was the most difficult individual I have ever dealt with . . . in the practice of law, and personally, for that matter."

On cross-examination, Ernie Jones brings out that Mr. Carey only heard the tape "out in the corridor twenty-five minutes ago." The prosecutor objects that no foundation has been laid as to how and when and by whom the tape was made. Evidently, at this point, he is unfamiliar with its contents. Judge Sawaya, who has already listened to it, agrees to reserve his ruling on the matter.

Young David Frankel now takes the stand. He does not look happy. It is his unenviable role to confess his own client's guilt.

"Did there come a time . . . when Mr. Schreuder admitted to you direct involvement in the death of his grandfather?" Joe Tesch inquires.

"Yes, sir . . . After four or five conversations . . . just Marc and myself present . . . Marc said that he and his brother Larry had murdered their grandfather."

"Did he tell you why?"

". . . the gist . . . was that he was terrified that his mother was going to commit suicide. Because over the past year to year and a half, she had hysterically warned both he and his brother about the possibility that Mr. Bradshaw was going to disinherit Mrs. Schreuder . . . Between the two of them, they felt their act was necessary for the protection of their mother."

Was his mother involved?

"He said she was not."

"Did he state to you whether or not she knew about the plot?"

"He said she did not."

In the courtroom, the lawyers representing Frances and Berenice allow themselves faint smiles. It looks as if Marc has finally decided to take the fall for his mother after all.

Frankel describes the next fifteen or twenty hours he spent breaking down Marc's story, getting him finally to confess the whole truth. "His story changed . . . The meetings were at times very emotional. I was not easy on him . . . Details began to change. I continued to press him." Marc's story was consistent on only one point: that his mother was *not* involved. Then one day, deep into a three- or four-hour session, Frankel said he thought Marc's mother *was* involved. "I yelled at him. I told him I simply couldn't help him unless he told me the truth." Frankel asked him one more time.

"He put his head down and simply said: 'Yes' very quietly."

In the courtroom, Marc puts his hand over his eyes and appears gripped by private emotions.

"I simply watched as Marc tried to gain control of himself. He was shaking." Several minutes passed. I told him I thought I understood how difficult it was for him to tell that. He nodded his head."

A quarter hour of small talk went by. Then, "I pressed him for details of how he and his mother were involved . . . He told me that for the year or year and a half prior to the murder, . . . his mother had told him that his grandfather *had* to be killed because he was going to disinherit them. They were going to be thrown out on the street with nothing to eat . . . That at one point she had attempted to hire what Marc called a hit man whose name was Myles Manning . . . He simply took their money . . . At that point, Mrs. Schreuder told Marc that he was going to have to do it. And they were going to have a plan . . . his mother suggested a number of scenarios . . . eventually it was decided that Marc or she would have to get a gun, and Marc would have to go up to Utah and shoot his grandfather."

Any more details?

"In the first conversation in which he told me that his mother was the author of the plan, he also said his brother Larry participated in the planning."

Frankel gives it everything he has. He recounts in detail Marc's version of the events of July 22–23, 1978. He identifies the Ariadne Tape, and says he himself received it from Marc and turned it over to Van Dam. He says Marc brought the gun back to New York because his mother insisted. "He told her he thought they should get rid of the gun, but that she said no . . . Then his mother gave the gun to Mr. Behrens." Later Marc was banished from home anyway. After his arrest, Frances feared the poor opinions of her neighbors, and of the co-op board. Marc was sometimes permitted to eat at home, but no longer to sleep there. His grandmother paid for a small hotel room a few blocks away.

Fire in his eye, Ernie Jones rises to cross-examine. He cannot let this sudden "proxy confession" knock his case down to manslaughter. "Didn't Marc tell you that if there was any possibility of tracing the firearm, they wanted to be able to blame his brother, Larry, for the murder?"

"No, sir."

"And you don't ever recall him telling you why he used his brother's name?"

"That's not my testimony. I testified that I do recall he told me, but I don't recall what he said." Oh, the sudden, blessed blankness of the legal mind!

"Ever tell you he and his brother Larry got in arguments from time to time?"

"Yes." At first Marc said he and Larry planned the murder, and carried it out; that Larry made Marc's motel reservation, that Larry phoned Mom to confirm that Gramps would be at the warehouse Sunday morning. But later on, Marc changed his story and said that his brother had nothing to do with it.

And who else was involved in this plot? Ernie Jones has forgotten the old lawyers' rule: never ask a question to which you do not know the answer. The reply further spatters his own witness, though—raincoated in immunity—it scarcely matters. One of the things they don't tell you when they sell you the immunity coat is the mud it attracts from the other side.

"Marc had told me that Mr. Behrens had known about it."

When Jones asks Frankel about Marc's awareness "that his grandfather was making a new will which would discredit his mother?" he gets an unexpected bonus.

"He told me that his mother told him that." Until now, the prosecution had not had direct evidence of Marc's knowledge of his grandfather's will. That a defendant have a "pecuniary interest" in the crime is essential to a first-degree murder conviction. This response takes the prosecution one step closer to that goal.

Jones wonders if possibly they had kept the gun in order to dispose of Myles Manning? Frankel has no comment. But he does add another tidbit to the mounting pile of evidence scraps against his own client. Marc told Frankel he walked into the warehouse through an unlocked "side door" after he heard his grandfather arrive.

Jones asks again: "He told you this murder was committed for the inheritance or the money from the Bradshaw estate?"

"No."

"Didn't he tell you they were going to be cut off or cut out?"

"Yes."

"Mr. Frankel, the defendant told you that he felt some loyalty to his mother?"

"Yes."

"Mr. Frankel, did this defendant, Marc Schreuder, ever tell you that as late as February of this year, he had stolen forty thousand dollars in jewelry from his mother," and that she had filed a complaint with the New York police? No. "Ever tell you that he forged his grandmother's signature . . . to the tune of almost three hundred thousand dollars?"

"As I recall, he told me that he had stolen about forty thousand dollars from his grandmother."

Sarcastic. "Feel or share the same sense of *loyalty* toward his grandmother and grandfather that he expressed toward his mother?" No. "How many times did his story change?" Four or five. "How many times did he lie to you?" Many.

On redirect, Frankel says that, shortly before this trial, Frances had begun urging her son "that the best thing for everybody would be if he just disappeared." But the lawyer had persuaded Marc to stay, to return the latest $40,000 he had stolen from Granny, return anything else he might have stolen, and face the music.

Leaving the courthouse, Ernie Jones is almost smiling. Joe Tesch looks worried. "Do you think we should have rested?" he asks a friend. The defense could have put on no witnesses whatsoever, heaped scorn on the unimpressive prosecution witnesses, Manning and Behrens, and relied on the coat of reasonable doubt to protect their client.

If Van Dam and Tesch had used this tactic, Utah would probably have won a conviction for second-degree murder at best. The defense could have harped both on Jones's inability positively to place Marc in Salt Lake City, and his failure to prove that Marc had a pecuniary interest in the crime. Without an eyewitness, a motel registration, or other direct evidence of Marc's presence in Salt Lake City, Mike George's massive airline researches had merely put Marc aboard a Salt Lake-bound plane; the evidence of his presence on the ground was still technically only circumstantial. Before Frankel's testimony, Utah had still lacked a "smoking gun."

By admitting that Marc Schreuder killed his grandfather, Frankel had put the gun into Marc's hand, and spelled out the motive for the crime: not money but the desire to please his mother. The gambit would be argued for years in Utah legal circles.

Some among Berenice Bradshaw's platoon of lawyers were frankly appalled. "Before today, they weren't looked at as a capital case," said one. "Now I think they are." Others thought the best strategy would have been a united front, that mother and son should have been tried together. "Someone should have told Berenice to pay for only one defense," one of them said.

And still others descried a larger strategy at work: a grand design to protect Frances Schreuder at all costs, including the highest possible cost to her own son.

JUNE 29, 1982. The next morning the defense puts into evidence the so-called "Ariadne Tape," made by Marc when Ariadne was not yet six. The tape is offered "not for truth, but to show some of the information the next witness, Dr. Moench, had in arriving at his conclusions about Marc and his mother," Tesch explains.

Ernie Jones objects that no proper foundation has been laid on the tape's authenticity. "I can see it's a close issue," Judge Sawaya says, "but I'd like to hear the doctor's testimony, and I can't without admitting it."

Psychiatry and the law do not normally mesh very well. The two disciplines attract different types of minds. The law deals in blacks and whites, and human emotions and feelings come only in infinite shades of gray. Trying to describe human emotion in the language of the law is like trying to dissect a butterfly with a meat ax, and in the courtroom, at least, the two professions have scant respect for each other. Very few forensic psychiatrists, even old white-haired ones, are received in courts of law with the respect and gravity accorded the next witness. Louis G. Moench, M.D., is a tall, spare psychiatrist in his late sixties, courtly in manner, a Harvard-educated Phi Beta Kappa with a medical degree from the University of Chicago Medical School. His piercing blue eyes, white hair, and pale parchment skin have become rather familiar around the Utah courts; he is called upon equally often by prosecutors and defense attorneys to testify as an expert psychiatric witness, although "it is not the easiest nor most pleasant part of my work."

Dr. Moench presides over the Salt Lake Clinic, and he twice visited Marc in jail, a two-hour visit each time, he says. He interviewed no one else in the family. Yet his professional conclusions are so firm that Ernie Jones will term them "cast in concrete." Moench is not a man to doubt or hedge his own opinions, though he claims no profound knowledge of the psyche of this defendant. That is not his function. Marc Schreuder is not his patient. He is on trial in a criminal case on which the court would like to hear the doctor's professional opinion of his mental state at the time of the crime—a very different matter, as the sixty-nine-year-old witness will shortly make clear.

Before their interviews Dr. Moench had told Marc that, in a capital case, no doctor-patient privilege exists; he might well be called upon to testify. This is something of a euphemism; Dr. Moench had examined Marc at Tesch and Van Dam's request. His purpose here this morning is to tell the court that Marc was sufficiently disturbed at the time of the crime to justify a charge of manslaughter, not a capital offense. Judge Sawaya inquires formally of Marc whether he understood at the time that he had waived his privilege? A murmur, "Yes."

Moench has brought along his clinical notes, eight sheets of green paper written in a spidery hand. He consults these freely during his testimony, and often reads from them directly, preferring not to paraphrase or elaborate on his original conclusions. He relates Marc Schreuder's history: his mother's marriages and divorces, the years of family fighting, the lockouts, his relationship to Larry, whose own history is swiftly sketched in. Marc had described his mother, Dr. Moench says, as "an upwardly mobile person . . . always trying to raise her standard of living." He spoke about her $1,000 apartment, her $20,000-a-month Hamptons estate, her fondness for caviar.

"He described his mother having spent some six or seven years under the care of a psychiatrist in New York, and having an intense emotional reaction when the psychiatrist moved to Canada . . . One of the attempts at suicide . . . profoundly disturbing to Marc" occurred at that time.

"Following this, Marc related that *he* virtually became his mother's psychiatrist." He was made to "listen endlessly to her many problems . . . try to advise her . . . trying to do the man's work in the family, helping move from one apartment to another, cooking, shopping, tending Ariadne."

Marc had told the doctor of his and Larry's struggles to provide their mother with the money she believed she was rightfully entitled to—by stealing it from her parents. It was "never enough." She could "never be satisfied," not even when "she went to Tiffany's and, as Marc put it, burned one hundred thousand dollars there." Yet when Frances later complained they were going to be evicted, and Marc asked her to sell some jewelry, she had refused.

At first Marc had thought his mother was joking when she said

"Gramps would have to be killed." Marc was very relieved when he found out Myles Manning had "ripped off" his mother rather than carry out her assignment. Throughout the winter and spring of 1978, Frances increased the pressure on Marc. Her nightly calls to him at Kent School lasted two or three hours. He was unable to study, "yet she made demands that he get excellent grades. She would discourage any friendships," continued developing the murder scenario, made the air plans for Texas . . .

Shocking, horrible shrieks in the hallway interrupt this testimony. A woman has fainted, her friend is screaming hysterically. The husband had won all in a divorce suit.

"Go ahead, Doctor," Judge Sawaya says blandly as if he expects the psychiatrist to be as imperturbable as himself to this sort of unseemly outburst. The witness relates how Frances had insisted to her son that murder was the only solution to the family's problems, that "Gramps was an old miser . . . a Howard Hughes . . . destroying their family, that she and Ariadne would have to live in Harlem in the gutter if Marc didn't do this." Dr. Moench describes Marc's return to New York where "His mother embraced him and kissed him and hugged him for about ten minutes while he was sobbing. He said she had never done anything like this before in his life."

Tesch asks the witness his opinion of this particular mother-son relationship. Dr. Moench folds his long-fingered, elegant hands. "It was my opinion that . . . there was an extremely pathological relationship between Marc and his mother . . . that he had not resolved—forgive the jargon—the Oedipal situation . . . there was no male figure [in the family] . . . it was a sick relationship . . ."

What about the strength of this mother's hold over her son?

"She was an extremely controlling person . . . she insisted on having her way . . . she was always right . . . if he or Ariadne didn't do exactly as she said, or Larry . . . she would make a suicide attempt." Marc found her continual threats to kill herself "extremely terrifying . . . by far the strongest influence in his emotional development."

What conclusions can the doctor draw about Frances's personality from the Ariadne Tape? For once, the psychiatrist has no need to glance at his notes. He can describe the contents of the tape from memory, and does so at some length, concluding, "I consider this child abuse, and extreme pressure of the *worst form."* His voice quavers. "I would much prefer hearing about a parent spanking a little child. I think this is *outrageously abusive,* and . . . pretty well confirms the way Marc described how she put pressure on him and Larry to do what she wants."

Was there any doubt in his mind as to whether this mother had once hectored and raged at her older children in similar fashion? He does not know about Larry, whom he has never met. But he doubts Marc has been "abused in the same sense Ariadne was." Marc's dual role as his mother's stand-in psychiatrist and stand-in husband, her reliance and dependence on his ability in times of stress, would to a degree shield him from the total abuse showered on the helpless Ariadne.

The "profound effect" of such an upbringing, says the doctor, is that the child's "first priority is always to please his mother. And to prevent her from doing something dangerous to herself. Or rejecting or throwing him out of the household."

The doctor sees no "propensity for violence" in Marc's nature. "I think he was always trying to be the peacemaker in the family . . . But I think his efforts to please his mother, and prevent rejection, transcended any judgment about right and wrong . . . His mother's influence was so strong that nothing else mattered."

Now, a key question: What is the matter with Frances? Speaking as a physician and psychiatrist, how would the doctor characterize her personality?

Admittedly he has had little to go on, just a couple of interviews with Marc, plus the Ariadne Tape. But he is not without a double-barreled professional opinion. "I had to use two different diagnoses to satisfy my mind about her character." First, he believes Frances suffers from a narcissistic personality disorder, "which essentially means—I want what I want when I want it. And if I don't get it, there is going to be trouble." A person with a narcissistic personality disorder is pathological—i.e. sick—"in the sense that the first-person pronoun is the most important part of the alphabet." The welfare of others, their comfort or well-being, even their lives are of lesser importance. He sounds disgusted.

Second, Frances is a histrionic personality, someone who insists on "being onstage all the time, being the center of attention, feeling entitled to everything, feeling entitled to all of the attention, all of the influence, always the center of the stage, so that everyone else has to play roles around this person."

Uncannily, Dr. Moench has just limned *the* primal scene on Gilmer Drive, 1938: a baby squalling in her crib surrounded by the entire family—both parents, two older sisters, and a brother—all of them singing lullabies hour after hour as they try to quiet the howling infant.

And here it comes, the invitation to express the expert opinion the defense needs to support a manslaughter charge. "Doctor, what do these symptoms add up to? I mean, how do you describe the nature of Marc's personality? Is he mentally ill?"

"I don't see him as mentally ill. I see him at the time of the alleged event, and much of the time subsequently, as operating under extreme emotional turmoil." In legal jargon, this *defines* manslaughter. The defense attorneys pound in their point, and extract the response: ". . . Marc was operating under extreme pressure as the result of his indoctrination, or brainwashing, if you will, over a period of several years, and, in fact, over his entire lifetime with his mother."

Cross-examination is handled by young David Walsh, a boyish expert in the legal subspecialty of disparagement, derogation, flustering, and deflation of pompous shrinks. The moves on both sides are preordained. How much is the doctor being paid? No payment for testifying, the usual rates for interviewing; total about $500, less than he would earn from a private patient. Would it not be important to talk to other people besides Marc? Granny perhaps, or Mom or Larry? Not necessarily. The examination of the person himself is the most important thing. Yes, but might not Marc have a motive to lie? "I suppose he may have had a motive, but I don't think he lied to me."

Yes, of course Marc knew the difference between right and wrong. No question he knew he was breaking the law. Dr. Moench has never suggested Marc suffered any psychiatric *illness.* No, he did not bother to perform an IQ test. Marc is obviously in the normal range. What did the doctor do to assure himself Marc was telling him the truth? "I've had thirty-eight years' experience talking to people, and I think I can tell usually when they are not telling me the truth."

Mr. Walsh's cross-examination brings out that the old psychiatrist knows virtually nothing of the defendant's other dirty deeds, his prodigious thefts and forgeries—Walsh mentions a grand total of "some $365,000"—nor of his attempts to rip off his grandmother, to frame his brother for murder, to poison his grandfather. It does not matter to Dr. Moench. That four years have passed does not matter; that Marc told Behrens "it was easy" does not matter; that he wanted to kill Manning does not matter. If he knew Marc had been lying to him, it still would not matter. Nothing could change his professional opinion. The defendant's mental state is one thing, the nature of the offense which brings him before this court is another. The oil and water of law and psychiatry can simply never mix. The only thing that matters is: will the butterfly survive the meat ax?

But the testimony of Dr. Moench has come as a surprise to the prosecution; they heard about it only yesterday morning, when Carey and Frankel arrived from the East. *That* matters. The prosecutors demand a second opinion. They want to bring in their own psychiatrist to examine Marc. Judge Sawaya says sagely that he would like to hear as many expert opinions as possible. Now Tesch and Van Dam are unhappy. They prefer that the court appoint a second psychiatrist, rather than let the county prosecutors put on somebody who is certain to be friendly to the State's cause. In other words, the law permits the defense to hire an expert and, in effect, beg for mercy. But it does not permit the State to hire an expert to beg for vengeance on the part of the people of Utah. Marc is protected by the Fifth Amendment.

The defense rests. The State has asked for a continuance, in order to find its own psychiatrist. In chambers, the defense points out that this is not an insanity plea, and moves to bar a State-appointed psychiatrist from interviewing their client. When Marc waived his doctor-patient privilege, he did not also waive his Fifth Amendment privilege. If he were forced to undergo examination by a State-appointed psychiatrist, he would in effect be forced to testify against himself.

Tesch therefore objects to Jones's motion for a continuance, on ground of "potential prejudice" to his client. But the judge overrules him. "Given the importance of this case, and the surprise nature of the defense, the court would like to hear a second opinion."

By the time court reconvenes, Ernie Jones has discovered Dr. Lee Coleman, of Berkeley, California, a tweedy, spade-bearded, forceful-speaking professor widely known in forensic circles as a professional antipsychiatrist. He is a medical mercenary, regularly hired by prosecutors all over the nation to knock down the lofty, God's-word-on-stone-tablets type of psychiatric testimony with which Dr. Moench has just favored this court. "Have couch, will travel," as the reporters say.

Dr. Coleman today earns his fee several times over. Point by point, every one of Dr. Moench's certitudes is swept away: psychiatric expertise does not exist; psychiatry is not a science; it has no diagnostic criteria; all judgments about the "mental state" of another are perforce subjective. Dr. Moench's testimony has been "storytelling," not science. The Ariadne Tape could be fabricated. It is "preposterous" to make a medical diagnosis on the basis of two two-hour interviews and a one-hour tape. How about Moench's statement, "I don't think Marc lied to me." Ridiculous! Psychiatrists are no better than anybody else at determining this sort of thing. Usually, they're worse.

The defense recalls Dr. Moench. He sounds as positive as ever, his voice rattling along like dry leaves in the wind. On cross-examination, Ernie Jones draws out the somewhat surprising statement that the doctor wrote out his eight green pages after his first two-hour examination. The second meeting was merely to double-check a few points. Surely between this man's hidebound assertions and Coleman's trendy, Bay Area debunkery lies a middle ground. Doubtless Judge Sawaya will find it.

Ernie Jones offers a quiet, nail-everything-down summation, dryly expressing the State's gratitude to lawyer Frankel for confirming for the court "all our suspicions, all of our hunches . . . all of our evidence." He scoffs at the story of Marc's tearful, hour-and-a-half phone call to Frances the night before the crime begging to be let off the hook. Where are the phone records of such a call? He is skeptical of Marc's timing with Frankel: Why does Marc implicate his mother only on the eve of his extradition from New York? Is this the action of an admitted liar, admitted thief, admitted *murderer* who suddenly now wants to purge his soul? Or is it the action of someone trying, at the eleventh hour, to lay off some of the blame? Four years ago, Marc had tried to throw suspicion for the murder on a robber. If the police had actually found a thief, Marc would have let him hang. As the cops drew closer, he tried to blame his own brother. He tried to blame his good Aunt Marilyn. Finally, he points the finger at his own mother.

"She made me do it!" he whines. This is a defense made in desperation, in despair. There is no mental illness here. What you have is an extremely obedient young man who does what his mother tells him. But that is no defense for murder! "Everything about Marc Schreuder suggests a cold, calculating killer. I ask this court to return a verdict of first-degree murder."

The defendant has listened to all this with his face buried in his hands. Was he coached to sit this way? Does he hide tears, or the lack of them? When his hands come down, his eyes are dry.

Joe Tesch's summation is a rather sentimental appeal. Judge Sawaya has six children. Tesch has spent the Fourth of July weekend with his own wife and children. "It was a grand reflection to me on what children are . . . and how bizarre is the truth in this whole matter." Tesch does not mention that, for part of the weekend, he and Van Dam went off horse racing in Idaho. They might better have stayed home and worked on their summation. Trial buffs find the entire defense presentation somewhat flaccid.

Tesch turns on his booted heel, sweeping an arm toward his client. "This is not a boy on a mission of murder . . . This is a boy on a runaway boxcar, or a ship in a typhoon . . . This boy has never known a normal life . . . never had a guardian with love . . . He was entwined in a web over which he had no control." The Ariadne Tape is "an indication of the severity of the storm" in which he was trying to survive. "We know he has a brother who is certifiably insane . . ." We know from Ted Carey that Frances Schreuder was the most difficult woman he ever met. We know the same things from Behrens, from Dr. Moench.

"We live in the Christian-Judeo Western culture. Our criminal justice system says we do not ask for an eye for an eye or a life for a life—as the State asks for today. We ask for justice tempered by mercy."

Tesch does not suggest for a moment that Marc Schreuder did not intend to kill his grandfather. He suggests only that the motive was not the one required by the statute for a finding of murder in the first degree. "The motive was to keep this boy from losing his mother." And with this remarkable assertion, the strange trial winds down.

JULY 6, 1982, 10 A.M. Judge Sawaya takes less than seven minutes to deliver his verdict to a packed courtroom. He has reviewed the evidence over the weekend, and reached his decision: The defendant intentionally and knowingly caused the death of his grandfather. However, some reasonable doubt exists as to the circumstances. The evidence does not show that death was caused in the course of a robbery for pecuniary gain. It does show that the defendant caused the death of Franklin Bradshaw based upon the desires of another person. He finds him guilty of murder in the second degree.

Marc Schreuder is smiling and animated for the first time during the entire trial. But all the lawyers at both tables are visibly unhappy. Tesch and Van Dam refuse comment. Ernie Jones has gone almost white and is slumped in his chair. In the corridor, his wife is in tears. Jones's boss, Salt Lake County Attorney Ted Cannon, is the only person willing to speak for the record. "This is an election year, and I'll make a comment. If this wasn't a first-degree murder, then it's hard for us to see what is."

Mike George made it his business to visit Marc Schreuder that afternoon. They were together more than three hours. "Marc, this is the first day of the rest of your life."

The prisoner affected not to hear. "Know what the highlight of the trial was for me?" he smirked. "Seeing how disappointed you guys were."

"You're right, we were."

"You looked like you'd been hit in the face with a brick!"

Sergeant George suspected Marc was really just posturing, that in fact he was scared, terrified of what his sentence might be. Before the trial, Mike knew, Marc had never considered himself a candidate for the death penalty. Then, during pretrial motions, one of his attorneys had made some comment about Utah juveniles not getting the death penalty and Judge Banks had quickly ticked off the names of six teenagers he himself had sentenced to death.

Mike George hoped to keep Marc from dissolving in fruitless anxiety, and to encourage him to make plans about his own future that were both positive and realistic. In sum, he said, "You know, Marc, you've now got to become a man. You didn't become a man by killing your grandfather." He told Marc he would be in the state penitentiary a long time, and "You can make of it what you want to." He knew that Marc recently had been thinking a lot about suicide, that he had been put on "suicide watch" both at Rikers Island and here in the county jail awaiting trial and that he had talked with Vittorio about ending his life. Mike urged him not to be afraid of prison. He told him that both college and trade study would be available to him, and he described the "Lifers' Program," in which prisoners serving life sentences go out into the community and speak to school and civic groups. Marc seemed somewhat interested, he thought.

Mike also talked about ordinary, everyday things: his wife, his kids, his daughter's dance recital. Suddenly Marc blurted, "You know, Mike, what I really miss is Chicken McNuggets. Every time I see that commercial, I just get sick I want them so bad."

"Tell you what, Marc. If I can arrange to get you some Chicken McNuggets before you go up to the state prison, I will."

Judge Sawaya gave Marc the strongest sentence the law allows: five years to life on the murder, plus another year for carrying a firearm, plus five more for using a firearm in connection with a felony, and a $10,000 fine. Were it not for the State's inability to prove pecuniary motive, he said, Marc might be facing the death penalty. As it was, he recommended a long prison stay, and said he would oppose any move to let Marc out on parole after five or so years.

Marc appeared stunned. He had expected to serve two or three years. He knew now it would be twelve or fifteen. After Mike George heard the sentence, he dropped in on the jail commander, a buddy, and asked permission to take Marc out for a drive before he went to prison.

"If you lose him, it's your neck."

Mike and another cop went to Marc's jail cell. "What are *you* doing here?" The color drained from Marc's face.

"Well, we took off," Sergeant George said later. "We drove down State Street and pulled into a McDonald's. His face just lit up. He ate three orders of Chicken McNuggets, a big Coke, a couple of orders of fries. He was just a happy little kid."

Sergeant George knew this would be his last chance before Marc went to prison, and he decided to drive him around Salt Lake City and try for answers to a few still unexplained questions. The cop hoped Marc would show him the motel where he had spent the night before the murder. Sergeant George had already checked records and talked to room clerks at forty hotels and motels within a one-mile radius of the warehouse, and found no direct evidence of Marc's presence in the city. Now he learned that Frances had warned her son to stay as far away from Bradshaw Auto Parts as he could. Marc pointed out the Best Western World Motel, about three miles away. Later, when Mike checked the Best Western records for the night of July 22, he found someone who could have been Marc. Marc also pointed out a Ute taxi stand, half a block from the warehouse. That was where he had caught a cab after the shooting, he said. Mike had already checked out the taxi rank; now he rechecked. No cab driver could recall picking up Marc Schreuder Sunday morning.

Driving south now on Interstate 15, Mike asked his prisoner the question he had often asked Marc before, and would ask several more times over the next fourteen months: Why, in spite of everything, did he still refuse to testify against Frances?

The answer was always the same. "I can't. She's my mother and I love her. I also hate her. But I love her and I can't."

Frances had remained resolutely away from Marc's trial. Once he was found guilty, she felt justified in severing all ties with her father's convicted killer. Berenice more or less agreed. Before Marc's trial, she had maintained at least an outward belief in her grandson's innocence. Later, she said she "had to abide by the court's decision."

Mary Lou Kaiser had attended every day of Marc's trial. She had refused to believe Marc was guilty until he switched his plea and she heard the words of his own lawyer. She became bitterly critical of Frances. "His mother didn't even show up! She didn't do anything but send a dumb lawyer. I've got second sight. That woman's a witch!"

Frances was equally contemptuous of Marc's unusual girl friend, whom she probably heard about from Berenice. Long before Marc's trial got under way, Frances had ordered her son "Drop her!"

For once Marc had refused. "She's the nicest girl I've ever met!"

So Frances hired private detectives to "get something" on Mary. One night a man came to her apartment. "What's this thing with the Immigration in 1978?" he demanded, waving a photocopy of an official-looking Immigration Department document under her nose.

"Honey, I became a *citizen* in 1978," she laughed. Had she not once been arrested for harboring illegal aliens in her home? Sure she said, but no charges were ever filed. She giggled to think that the man was being paid to snoop these things out. "The old witch could have saved her money. I would have told you everything, you'd just come and asked me. I already told it all to Marc."

As soon as new Inmate #15906 was permitted to have visitors, Mary resumed her shopping and baking. Although Marc relished junk food, he refused to eat anything made with preservatives or artificial coloring. She never came to prison to visit him without bringing a homemade cake, a bagful of take-out McNuggets, some of the homemade Mexican food he loved, and sometimes a pizza too. They snacked contentedly together and played Triaminos or Monopoly (Mary did not care for Stratego) while Monique snoozed in her basket. Mary had made up her mind to wait for Marc as long as was necessary. "I already been married three times. I ain't got anything to lose," she told a friend.

Mike George had arranged for Marc to be housed in the prison's Special Services section, where there were dormitories with individual rooms, rather than cells, and where he would be somewhat sequestered from the main prison population. Marc told Mary he had decided to "pretend I'm in an all-boys' cottage at college," and to take as many college courses as regulations permitted. "Even if they opened up the gates, I wouldn't leave here until I finish college," he said. She said she thought he would make a damn good lawyer someday.

When Marc completed his freshman college year with a 4.0 average, Mike George somehow arranged a special reward. He was going to spirit him out of prison for a few hours, he said, and take him to see *Return of the Jedi*. Marc climbed into Mike's unmarked two-door Ford, and there sat Mary, squashed into the back seat. After the movie the three of them stopped at McDonald's. Marc and Mary ate almost $30 worth of Chicken McNuggets.

Another time, Mike arranged a quiet, out-of-prison meeting between Marc and his father in Vittorio's motel room. The visit, like the movies, was part of Sergeant George's low-key campaign to win the trust and respect of this untrustworthy, disrespectful, and troubled young man. He had to make Marc understand that there was only one way out for him, only one way he could stop being a "Mama's boy" and grow up. The pain would be excruciating, like lancing and cleaning an infected wound. But when it was over he would feel better. The one way Marc Schreuder could ever become a man, he said, would be to find the balls to testify against his mother at her upcoming trial. Marc listened, but he never said a word.

During their long talks in the visiting room, Marc told Mary about his life. He told her his mother threw Larry out because she couldn't manipulate him the way she could Marc. "He had a mind of his own." He described the way his mother beat him with a belt buckle, and asked her to feel the network of scars which crosshatched his scalp. He spoke about Vittorio and said he could never recall his father being mean, but that he had seen Frederik beat his mother cruelly, and that was when she had started beating her sons. Marc thought there was probably some connection.

People had suggested to Marc that his mother had liked Vittorio to smack her around a bit, that it stimulated her sexually. Did women *really* like that? he asked.

Mary told him she "understood a lot about domination," that she'd had a very strict, abusive father who never let her date, and who often beat and terrified her. "Honey, your mother don't know what beating is till she been hit as many times as I have!" Mary laughed. Then she added, "Maybe she didn't feel loved unless she got beat up."

Marc and Mary talked often about his mother's upcoming trial, and whether or not he should testify. He told her he was determined not to make the decision until the very last possible moment—even though he still had no idea what his decision would be. Mary understood without being told that Marc was still terribly attached to his mother, that underneath all, he still loved Frances very, very much. She also knew he understood the choice he was so plainly being offered: help Utah to convict Frances by testifying against her, or spend much of the rest of his own life in prison.

Marc kept asking his motherly girlfriend what *she* thought he should do. She steadfastly refused to give him any advice whatsoever. "Marc, I want you to make that decision on your own. Someday we may have a fight. And if that happens, there's three words I never want to have to hear you say: *It's your fault.* I couldn't bear that, Marc."

While Marc Schreuder was on trial in Utah, Ariadne was enrolled at the Briansky's ballet camp in Saratoga, N.Y. "We found Ariadne very delightful, very independent and very smart. But she was not like other children. She seemed to lack a certain . . . spontaneity," says Oleg. In New York, he had noted, Ariadne never smiled. In Saratoga, she did. "In Saratoga, Ariadne was like a different person. She liked to go swimming. She had friends. She liked going to ballets."

Only when her mother came to Saratoga, say the Brianskys, did Ariadne change. She stopped smiling. "She went back into her shell." Frances insisted Ariadne have her own room, no roommate—she would pay the difference. "Mrs. Schreuder didn't want Ariadne mixing any more than necessary with the other children. She always told her: *stay alone, stay in your room. You have your dolls,*" says Oleg.

Mireille adds, "We both always liked Ariadne very much. A very, very *nice* child." Also, "We take her because we see that Ariadne never had children around her, people her own age to play with. It was a very unnatural way of raising a child. She had *no* friends. We felt sorry for her."

In New York, if her mother did not personally bring Ariadne to class, she arrived with the elderly French maid. She never went to other girls' parties, nor gave parties of her own.

Frances would plan elaborate ballet-going afternoons for Ariadne and the others, then fail to follow through. She once invited a group for a Sunday benefit performance and said she would pick them up at eleven o'clock. She did not arrive until one. By then it was too late to go.

Parents were not encouraged to visit their children at camp in Saratoga, nor even invited onto the grounds; the other children became too jealous. Most parents understood. Frances was not like other parents. She telephoned her daughter nightly and "kept the child on the phone for hours." She arrived for her first summer in Saratoga, put up at the wanly elegant Gideon Putnam Hotel and demanded daily visits with her daughter. Like everyone else, the camp directors soon found it pleasanter to say yes to Frances. Mrs. Schreuder was told she could take Ariadne off the grounds and out to dinner, "in an inconspicuous way," after the other children were already in the dining hall. Inconspicuousness is not Frances's mode. On the street directly in front of the Briansky Saratoga Ballet Center is a tall, overhead streetlight. After one dinner out with Ariadne, Frances backed her rented car into the light pole with sufficient force to bring the whole thing crashing to the street in a shower of sparks.

When camp ended in late August, the children were sent home by bus. Parents were instructed to pick up their daughters at the Port Authority Bus Terminal. No one showed up for Ariadne, so another mother took her home with her own daughter. At six that evening she telephoned 10 Gracie Square; there was no answer. She reported Ariadne's whereabouts to a doorman. Frances did not telephone back until eleven.

For some time, Williams & Connolly had been recommending to Frances that she plead insanity, a suggestion the client did not find appealing. So Frances found new counsel, lawyers who were willing to enter the plea *she* wanted: Not Guilty. Berenice Bradshaw was not notified of the switch, she said later, until after she had paid the original law firm a second $100,000 in addition to their $100,000 retainer.

Switching lawyers was essential, Frances then explained to her mother. Williams & Connolly were preparing deliberately to lose her case. "You see, a lot of people were angry because that Williams & Connolly got that Hinckley off," Berenice says. Frances had become convinced her lawyers "were ready to blow *her* case to make up for what they'd done for Hinckley."

The new lawyers, Saxe, Bacon & Bolan, the Roy Cohn firm, set a total fee for their services of one million dollars, Berenice says. It was payable in advance, so she gave them a retainer, and they set about seeking as many pretrial delays as possible while familiarizing themselves with the case. Their efforts won their client another twelve months of expensive freedom during which she was able to continue without interruption her tireless pursuit of cultural affairs.

Frances had an ambitious project in the works. She now talked continually—at board meetings, lunches, private dinners, backstage during rehearsals, in the NYCB offices, at the School of American Ballet, at the Brianskys, during intermissions at the New York State Theater—about her intention to make possible the greatest production of George Balanchine's career, a massive new restaging of Tchaikovsky's four-act *The Sleeping Beauty*. This was the fabled pink-and-gold ballet of the master's youth, the period when he had danced with the Imperial Kirov Ballet and appeared at the Maryinsky Theater in St. Petersburg. People had talked for years about restaging it. But such a production would cost at least a million dollars. It would require a huge corps de ballet, a revolving stage, and other miracles of nineteenth-century stagecraft unavailable at the New York State Theater. Others had always deemed these facts insurmountable obstacles to *The Sleeping Beauty*'s rebirth. But Frances was undaunted. She appeared to regard her proposed gift as a kind of choreographic Angel Moroni glittering at the pinnacle of the magnificent edifice that was George Balanchine's career. But by fall 1982, all of Balanchine's faculties were failing, and to his intimates it was apparent that he would never again be able to walk properly, let alone make more ballets.

During the fall season, says a fellow Board member, Frances often seemed drunk or on drugs. She was noisy and "talked loudly during performance to any companion or neighbor, or to herself." On public occasions she sometimes singled out Board members she disliked and shouted, "You hate me! You think I'm a murderess!" The bizarre behavior grew so pronounced that other Board members began to forgo their special, conspicuous seats on the First Tier, preferring to sit in anonymous quiet with the *hoi polloi.* "We tried everything to discourage her from showing up. We said her tickets were lost in the mail—*everything!* We just didn't want to be bothered with her."

When the Ballet went to Washington in October for a Gala Benefit and a week of performance at the Kennedy Center, it was deemed impossible to bring Frances along to the planned Board festivities. She was told that her "State Department clearance hadn't come through," a transparent excuse which she of course recognized. "The truth is, we just didn't take her. She didn't participate with us. Didn't come to the State Department, for the lecture on antiques. Didn't come to the parties, the White House tour, the luncheons, the visits to museums. Oh yes, of course she came to *Washington!* And she came to the theater. I mean, she'd paid for her tickets. It's a free country."

When the time came to choose children for the Christmas 1982 production of *The Nutcracker,* the executive staff of the NYCB made an essentially political decision, one with which David Richardson agreed. While it certainly would be wrong to drop Ariadne from the cast because of her mother's notoriety, it would be equally wrong to make her extra conspicuous by casting her in the main child's part that year of Marie, the little girl who dreams the entire *Nutcracker* fable unfolding on stage. They decided this despite the fact that Marie was a role which Ariadne was now probably proficient enough to handle. As Marie, she would be more visible to gossip writers. She could become just the sort of lightning rod to vulgar publicity which NYCB's company policy always had been so careful to avoid. Richardson also

thought it might be cruel to spotlight Ariadne right now. Finally,
it just wouldn't "cook well" to give the leading role to the daughter of a prominent board member.

Accordingly, although Ariadne would normally have been at
least a contender for the role, Richardson was encouraged to look
extra hard for a different Marie, and he found her. Ariadne was
assigned to dance the same part as she had the previous year and,
predictably, Frances took great umbrage. She detected unseen
enemies both behind and in front of the great gold curtain. Berenice Bradshaw, deeply disappointed, laid the trouble directly at
the feet of "that scandal sheet, 'the New York' *Times*." A few
months later, when Larry Bradshaw heard about the newest slur
upon his family, he recorded it in his newspaper, *The Occupier*.
Had it not been for the malign influence of Aunt Marilyn and
Vittorio, as he interpreted the matter, his little sister "could have
gotten the lead role."

In fact, says Richardson, the second child was in some ways a
better choice because, "while Ariadne has a lot of qualities, one
thing she does not have is the true quality of *innocence* this part
calls for." Also, Ariadne was still his tiniest dancer, and Marie is
one of the dancers who have to be paired by size: Four boys in
pink pantaloons, four girls in blue dresses. Ariadne was so small
that Richardson could find no one else good enough to pair her
with.

"I was expecting, er, something . . . and lo and behold, Lincoln Kirstein calls me into his office and wants to know why
Ariadne isn't in it. Putting *no pressure* on me, you understand.
He just needed the reason. And when I explained, he said, 'That's
fine. I just wanted to check. I was sure there *would be* a good
reason. But Mrs. Schreuder wanted to know.'" To complain to
Kirstein about so lowly a matter is madly inappropriate, akin to
complaining to the Commander-in-Chief that one's son has not
made it into the Marine Corps Band.

Most truly sympathetic to Ariadne's painful position were
some of the other dancing children. They resolved to do what
they could to make her life easier, less stressful, and not to disclose their plan to any adults. The dancer Jacques d'Amboise,
very active in working with the children at the School, at length
discovered that some of them had formed a conscious cabal to
protect Ariadne from needless slings and arrows. Sympathetic
himself, he attempted gently to discuss the matter, but was re-

buffed. "Trust no one over ten" seems to have been the "baby ballerinas' " resolve.

In truth, Richardson had found a good role for his tiniest dancer in a second ballet, and on November 9 Ariadne appeared onstage for the first time in *Coppélia,* the classic E. T. A. Hoffman fable about a doll-maker who creates and brings to life a dancing clockwork automaton. The story is another variation on the theme of mechanical people breathed into life by mad scientists; Dr. Frankenstein's monster, invented by Mary Shelley, being the best-known member of the genre. Dancing dolls, lurching hunks with bolts in their necks, and other *mēchanikos* of the time reflected the era's growing obsession with the machine, the force which was transforming the world.

At the climax of *Coppélia,* in the Balanchine staging, twenty-four children appear and do a sort of fantasy Dance of the Hours, a sequence of classical steps in pink tutus. Richardson was appalled to discover that, at each performance in which Ariadne appeared, Frances sat in her Board seat with notebook and opera glasses, making copious notes on every move. Afterward she could be overheard shouting her critique to Ariadne. NYCB considers personal comparisons between dancers odious, invidious, bad manners. Like the "star system," it is understood that comparisons are "not done." Invariably, Frances could be heard telling her daughter, "Your *élevé* was not as high as Gloria's! You did not point your feet like Eleanora in the *pas de chat!*"

Asked to rate Ariadne as a dancer, Richardson is judicious, scrupulous. "She's disappointing at times, *because* she's almost really good. Ariadne is technically very proficient. She learns *very* quickly. But she doesn't speak with her face what she's feeling, as a lot of children do. And if you correct her, you don't get the satisfaction that the correction went inside of her and *meant* something. She just stares back at you.

"She *does* do it. She just needs to be more energetic. But you can't find a way to make her go that extra level. She simply won't be pushed. She's the only child I've ever met who—when you ask her to try a bit harder—doesn't change at all. Very strange. Other kids, when I push them very hard, get a certain look on their face: *you're driving me crazy. Stop it! I can't stand it anymore!* But Ariadne would just stare back at me.

"I always thought: I've never *failed* any child before, when I gave 'em my pep talk. And took my patience, and *my energy*

. . . Got up and exerted . . . put out double the amount of energy than I would use myself, in order to . . . *show it*—almost becoming a cartoon figure. Yet I still could not get her to . . . open up. I always felt bad. *Why can't I reach that girl?*"

Whatever the reason, *Coppélia,* the ballet of mechanical dancing dollies, seemed to suit Ariadne's personality better than *The Nutcracker*'s enchanted world of childhood innocence. "Ariadne does not exactly breathe exuberance and happiness when she is performing. She never looks *transcendent.* She doesn't make mistakes. But she wasn't on that special plateau. She had none of that sense of excitement and joy in her body which so many dancing children have. Though she was always very well-disciplined. Very good." In sum, a nine-year-old *mēchanikos, truly* a dancing dollie.

By December, new alliances and relationships were forming on the far side of the footlights in anticipation of the trial to come. Michael Rosen, the top trial man at Saxe, Bacon, was planning the same defense for Frances Schreuder which he had used successfully with every criminal defendant in the past eight years: put on no witness whatsoever, and rely on his own forensic skills, plus his client's presumption of innocence, to win an acquittal. As Rosen prepared himself for this trial, the darkest cloud he saw on the horizon was his client's son. On December 6, Rosen glimpsed Marc Schreuder for the first time at the preliminary hearing of Case No. 82-CRS-0795, *State of Utah, Plaintiff,* vs. *Frances Schreuder, Defendant,* Fifth Circuit Court, State of Utah, in Salt Lake City. The lawyer was not favorably impressed. He saw a "dangerous animal." Frances was not present. She was in a New York hospital, Rosen explained to the judge, with a gynecological ailment. She was required to be present for her arraignment, however, and she appeared in the Salt Lake County Courthouse for the first time on December 16, 1982. The press described a woman who looked ill, white and silent, was draped to her ankles in black mink, and spoke but two words: "Not Guilty."

To escape family pressures, always worst during the holidays, Berenice Bradshaw had signed up for another sightseeing tour, had flown alone to Cape Town, South Africa—Chips had to be in Washington, D.C., on family business—and "spent Christmas out with the zebras." Larry celebrated the holidays by attempting to place collect phone calls to every member of his family. The only person who accepted was Vittorio. Larry wished him and his family a Merry Christmas and said cheerfully, "Only ten weeks to go!" Then he expected to be paroled into Threshold, a halfway house program which helps offenders like Larry readjust to life in the outside world. A condition of his parole was that he report regularly for Prolixin injections, his antipsychotic medication. The drug made him heavy and lethargic, and Larry did not believe he needed it, but he was willing to cooperate with any plan that would get him out of the prisons and hospitals where he had spent the past two years.

In prison, Marc was carrying a full academic load and taking as many self-improvement courses as he could fit in—first aid, emergency room care, psychology, and professional culinary skills. He was not really unhappy. He is phobic about doors and lockouts and for years has feared every time he approached a strange door that it would not open or, if it *was* open, that it would slam before he could reach it. Here in prison he felt safe. "I have my own room. I have my own key. And I'll never be locked out again," he told a visitor. "In a way this place is like a blessing. My room is *mine*. Nobody's gonna ransack the place and take all my property away. Nobody's gonna demand that I go down to the commissary and get them food and stuff. I'm my own person here. I can worry about *me*. I can worry about getting my own life straightened out. So in a way, you know—I feel really—really *happy* here! In a way, I've never had it so good." He has begun to slip again into his taped "Rockford Files" dialogue. "Yeah, I'm in prison. Yeah, my freedom's taken away. In a way, though, I have more freedom here than I had at home."

Tesch and Van Dam were critical of Vittorio for refusing to testify during Marc's trial, but Marc was entirely forgiving. "It would only have embarrassed Poppa," he says, "and it would not have done any good for *me*. He didn't know me! He didn't know the *history* . . ." Marc had in fact begged his father not to come to Utah. He did not want him to see his son sitting in jail or on trial for murder.

"He's one man I really love and really respect," Marc says today. "I'm sorry I knew him as late as I did. I think that if I had grown up with him—Poppa and I have talked about this—I would never have done what I did. I think that if I'd grown up with him I'd have been at least . . . somebody worthwhile."

Awaiting trial, Marc had often been bitter, morose. Vittorio told him, "Any time you want to call me, my door is always open."

"The very opposite of Mom!" Marc points out. "I used to call him from the county jail when I was real depressed, and any time he'd hear my voice, he'd say, *'Ofa course! Ofa course I accepta da call!'* " Marc is a perfect mimic of both his parents. "All I'd ever heard from Mom was: *'No! No! I* won't *accept.'* Always with Mom it was cutting off, locking doors, not accepting charges. With Pop it's—*'My door is always open. Yes, I will accept charges.'* He's just so loving! I mean, I wasn't used to that. At first I was very embarrassed. I was very shy. I didn't know how to deal with this. Especially his love, his kisses . . . and just his open door policy." Without question, the best thing that happened to Marc during his first fourteen months behind bars was his visit with Vittorio. Once again Mike George had been almost magically helpful. Marc was ashamed to have to meet his father in the prison visiting room, and somehow Sergeant George was again able to escort Marc out of state prison to a quiet and private meeting—indeed, two of them—in Vittorio's Utah motel room.

In November George Balanchine had entered the hospital for the last time. His decline was precipitate. A poignant, prolonged Slavic deathwatch set in. Visitors arrived from around the world. One of Frances's gifts was a ravishingly beautiful floral bouquet as big as a small tree. It literally filled the room and was banished by the nurses to the corridor as hopelessly impractical. In fact, if the object of the exercise was to distract the dying man from his torment, the floral extravaganza was probably more "practical" than all the medical paraphernalia.

Alas, after Frances Schreuder had shown up two or three times at Roosevelt Hospital, it became necessary to instruct the round-the-clock nurses to deny her further access. (Since Balanchine had no family, responsibility for his care was assumed—at his request, when he was still well enough to make requests—by a dear friend whom we shall call here Giselle.)

In January, the special nurses called Giselle to report that "One of Mr. B's visitors is a very disturbed woman." She had a habit of intense staring which upset some of the younger nurses. She hung around. On one occasion, the nurses had to call hospi-

al security and ask them to escort Mrs. Schreuder from the
ickroom.

Shortly afterward, Giselle began to be awakened by anony-
nous phone calls at two or three in the morning. The telephone
arassment became so intensive that it was necessary to take the
hone off the hook each night in order to get any sleep. The all-
ight nurses were instructed that—if Mr. B took a sudden turn
or the worse, or died in the night—someone would have to come
ersonally to knock on the door and notify Giselle. The phone
vas off the hook. It was too risky to change the phone number
uring this period, lest the dying man miss some important mes-
age. Calls from Paris and even Moscow were commonplace in
ie melancholy last months.

When, predictably, the phone rang at three or four o'clock on
ie night after Balanchine's death, April 30, 1983, Giselle picked
up and said, "He's dead now. You can stop torturing me."
fter that, the anonymous calls did stop, which appeared to con-
rm that they *were* Balanchine-related. Although Frances claims
» have visited Mr. B in the hospital in November, bringing with
er the first copy off the press of the big book she had mostly paid
r, *Choreography by Balanchine,* Nancy Lassalle, the Board
ember who organized and ran this book project, says this is
ntirely untrue. "The first copy was given by *me* to George! This
hole story of her giving it to Balanchine is absolute, total *inven-
on!*—based on her hearing that we had sent a special copy to the
ospital, one that we had made up for him. It has *nothing*—but
ich—to do with her! ZILCH!"

The anecdote confirms Frances's pattern: she incorporates
eces of other people's lives into her own. It is a kind of psychic
mpirism. She eats other people's stories. One might call her a
ographage.

Although Frances speaks often of the "intense spiritual rela-
onship" which developed toward the end between herself and
r. B, and says she helped him recover long-buried memories of
e days when he was a ten-year-old, just learning to dance, this
o seems unlikely. By January—date of her first confirmable
spital visit—"he may not even have recognized her," says
iselle. After Christmas, Balanchine deteriorated greatly. He
ked less and less and no longer in English; sometimes he spoke
ench, increasingly he spoke only Russian. He suffered "strong
mentia, terrible nightmares, terrible illusions . . ."

In January or February Frances had another backstage tan
trum. Ariadne had somehow displeased her mother and sud
denly, "downstairs, where all the other girls could see and hear,
says David Richardson, Frances began shouting and waving
fifty-dollar check. "How would you like to live on only this muc
money! I'm going to leave you right here for good! Here—take i
You'll never have any more money from me again!"

She tossed the check on a table, left Ariadne standing amid th
other girls, and walked out. Again Richardson thought Ariadn
seemed strangely unfazed, "as if this had happened before."

One of the Ballet's most popular forms of fund-raising is th
Sunday afternoon *thé*. Parents love to bring children dressed u
in their Sunday best to see the special dance programs and si
wine or tea afterward at pretty little tables decorated with fres
flower baskets set up on the theater's Promenade level. France
and Ariadne attended a *thé* in late February. "We were shocke
that she would show up!" a Board member said later. "We ha
tried *everything* to discourage her." Once again, Frances was r
fusing to accept no for an answer.

"After the performance, we couldn't seat anyone with them
No one wanted to be seen with them." So mother and daught
sat at a little round table by themselves, the last time they we
glimpsed together on a public occasion. When it ended, the oth
patrons and children watched the pair of them make their caref
way down the marble staircase taking home souvenirs of the o
casion. Frances had the programs and the gift bottle of wine, an
Ariadne carried the basket of flowers.

Berenice and Chips spent January and February cruising arour
South America and ended up in Rio de Janeiro in time f
Carnaval. "Travel and dancing—that's what I enjoy the most
Berenice says. "Chips and I do ballroom dancing. We don't lil
this disco stuff. We danced every single night, all the way arour
Cape Horn!"

In March, Frances turned up in Berkeley, California. It w
early Thursday morning when Sam Drukman, Elaine's so
looked out of the window of the apartment he shared with h
girlfriend, another Berkeley graduate student, and saw a stran
woman across the street photographing his building's entrywa
and vestibule. A silver Mercedes-Benz with its motor runni
and a driver behind the wheel was parked down the block. Sa

had seen the woman once before—at his grandfather's funeral, wearing a funny little black hat and veil. When Sam came back from the grocery store Saturday morning, the same woman was just leaving his vestibule. She had some letters in her hand. Sam shouted, and started chasing her down the block.

"Give him the goddam mail, Frances!" yelled the woman in the Mercedes. Frances dropped the letters, leaped in, and the car sped off.

Utah authorities had always worried lest Frances take off for South America or parts unknown. They were determined not to be robbed of their prize before she could be brought to justice. A condition of her bail required her to telephone her whereabouts personally to Mike George twice a week. When Mike was told about the events in Berkeley, he attempted unsuccessfully to lodge a charge of mail tampering, a federal offense, in order to get her bail revoked.

When Marilyn Reagan heard about the odd episode, she concluded that Frances hoped by stealing the mail to prove to Berenice that twenty-five-year-old Sam had a live-in girlfriend. If such an impropriety could be demonstrated, Granny could be persuaded by Frances to disapprove of it, and that would drive a further wedge between the Frances-Berenice entente and the Marilyn-Elaine axis. Marilyn knew that Frances had a penchant for plotting, snooping, and scheming. She had tried to involve Marilyn in the same sort of amateur sleuthing during the Gentile divorce. During her Schreuder divorce, she had made Dickie Behrens her partner and confidante and used his apartment as a repository for her "evidence." If Marilyn was right—and Mike George thought she probably was—the woman in the Mercedes was the new Behrens.

Elaine had a more sinister interpretation. She saw a possible assassination plot by her sister against her sons. "No amount of money is 'enough' for Frances," Elaine had often told Mike. "She's a bottomless pit. The depth of her greed and avarice is not to be believed." Elaine thought Frances was now looking for ways to eliminate all rival grandchildren who might make a claim in Berenice Bradshaw's estate. She and Marilyn knew that her mother had rewritten her own will at least twice since their father's murder. She was fairly sure that Marc already was disinherited; Larry's standing had to be doubtful, at best. So if the Drukman boys could be disposed of, that would leave only Ariadne. Elaine thought the photographs were probably intended for the guidance of a future "hit man."

On March 14, Larry Bradshaw's parole came through and he moved to a Threshold Residence in Reading, Pa. In a few weeks, if he did well, he would be permitted to move from the Residence to a furnished apartment shared with two other parolees. If he got a job, stayed clean, took his medicine, stayed in touch with his parole officer—all of which he was determined to do—he could expect to be in his own apartment before Christmas. Another year, and he would be off parole entirely.

Larry's first act as a free man, as he himself noted in his March 1983 *Occupier*, was to buy "some supplies for the *Occupier* magazine, and a book on Colleges, and a 1983 Almanac." A major story in his first issue after his enforced three-year hiatus from publishing reports:

LARRY CAPTURES STALINGRAD

Larry and Marc had a game. Whoever's fortunes were furthest ahead, would have their troops furthest ahead. It refers to the fortunes of life. Right now Marc is in a Utah State penetentary. He's been their 10 months now and has 11 years to go. So he's not doing too well. Larry for the past 3 1/2 years has been securely locked up at NCP, doing equally as bad, so according to the game he was almost kicked off the earth. Now his German Panzer divisions have finally captured Stalingrad.

Larry did indeed become a model parolee. He got two jobs—working in a clothing outlet store, and doing more of the canvassing work he enjoyed and performed so well—and soon bought two more used cars. He dieted, went back to college, and began finding new girlfriends, and now that he was free and over twenty-one, started taking steps to cash out his shares of F & F stock—all of which he reported in his *Occupiers*. By Christmas, after several chats with Mr. Goodfellow at Morgan Guaranty and with numerous other family bankers and lawyers, Larry had been able to trace down and have reissued at least some of his trust fund checks which had been sent to him care of Frances and cashed by her and Marc, during Larry's imprisonment. He had also prevailed on Berenice to sign the necessary papers per mitting him to cash out completely. With his first $30,000 from F & B he bought two more cars, an apartmentful of new furniture, stereo and camera and other equipment. As soon as he was permitted to leave the state, he began working off his inexhaustible energy on furious no-sleep motor trips. Over one long weekend he drove to Nova Scotia and back. Another time he drove out to see Palm Springs and Santa Monica. These excursions too were recorded in his *Occupier*'s, well illustrated with bright colored marking pens.

On April 10, Ariadne was ten years old. And on April 30, George Balanchine died. The long, elaborate Russian Orthodox services drew thousands of mourners. Many wept in the streets. Inside the cathedral, hundreds of grieving Russian friends, and dancers, artists and balletomanes of all ages stood squeezed together amid icons and incense during the solemn two-hour ritual. Every great dancer who could attend did, including four of Balanchine's five ex-wives. Each of the mourners held a lighted taper. The satin-lined casket was open to the waist and tilted toward the multitude. One by one, the long file of weeping, candle-holding dancers and friends moved to the altar and bent to leave a goodbye kiss on the waxen cheek. It seemed to be part state funeral and part suttee as the cortege of grieving women leaned their long bodies across the master's own to bid him farewell.

The service had been intentionally planned as a public event. The burial was meant to be kept just as deliberately private. Only two black limousines had been rented to carry the closest friends behind the hearse out to the little cemetery in Sag Harbor, Long Island, where Balanchine had asked to be laid to rest.

Except that three black limousines made the journey. In the third one, a woman entirely dressed in black sat alone, weeping convulsively. Mascara ran down her cheeks. She wore elbow-length black gloves and on her head was a little black hat like a witch's cap perched in a cloud of black veil.

By July, Frances had got word of Vittorio's Utah visits to Marc. She told Berenice that sister Marilyn was paying Vittorio to "get me." The next time Larry telephoned his mother, she accepted his call. "Marc and Vittorio are out to hang me, Larry," she said.

Larry was very happy to talk to his mother. Later he told a friend, "I think my Mom's starting to like me again."

Frances rented a house in Saratoga for the month of Augus
To the Brianskys, she seemed more determined than ever to kee
other children away from Ariadne. "When Ariadne came bac
the second year, I found she had lost a little bit that spark, th
interest in her dancing," says Mireille.

Each summer the Brianskys give a demonstration for paren
and friends at camp, as they also do in spring at their New Yo
City school. That spring, Frances had sat in the front row. "S
didn't even applaud!" says another parent. "She must ha
thought her daughter was not good enough. Sometimes s
would say: *'I love you.'* Sometimes we heard her say: *'I hate yo
The child never knew. She had the life of an adult. No friends

But mother and daughter had new friends, adults to be sure,
Saratoga. Chris Alexander and Shaun O'Brien lived just a fe
houses away and soon were inviting their delightful and stran
new acquaintances over for Saturday lunch or tea. Alexander, t
portrait photographer, says, "I was absolutely riveted
Frances's expression. She had a *haunting* look, the eyes alwa
way over to one side. She looked terrified. Flora Robson cou
play the part."

The children gave a demonstration on the last day of cam
There was to be a reception after the performance, and th
Frances and Ariadne were taking a taxi to Albany to catch t
plane to New York. Labor Day weekend was coming up. Scho
would be starting next week. Jeannie Columbo, a young a
warmhearted ballet usher, had been hired to move in to 10 Gra
Square and look after Ariadne. Frances would be flying to Uta
On Tuesday morning, the day after Labor Day, she had an a
pointment in Salt Lake City.

So the reception after the demonstration at camp was really
be the end of a dream, the finale to the beautiful fantasy
which Frances Schreuder had been living with increasing inte
sity for nearly five years, perhaps longer—who knows when
began?—but certainly ever since the magical November nig
when she had first seen the bright figure of Baryshnikov leap a
hang weightless for an instant against the painted sky. As ha
pens in fairy stories, it was a happy ending. For at the demonstr
tion, Shaun O'Brien saw Ariadne dance for the first time. That
he was sure for the first time which pony-tailed little dancer s
was, and he knew that she was good.

"That kid has *got something!*" he told Chris sincerely, drivi home after the reception. "You very rarely see that *quality* in a child."

Frances and Ariadne had been invited to stop by and say fare-well to their new friends on the way to the airport, and now Shaun was especially looking forward to the visit.

"Wow! Ariadne *is* something wonderful!" he told her mother. Frances beamed. It began to rain, a savage summer storm. Later Chris told a friend, "It was very foul weather, and I heard myself suggesting that I drive them to the airport. I think because I *liked* that little girl. Normally, I don't like children much." The two men were astonished by how much luggage Frances had, but somehow they got it all stowed in their Toyota, Ariadne sitting on top, for the jolly ride to Albany.

Shaun O'Brien had felt sorry for Mrs. Schreuder's daughter ever since he'd heard her sad story and learned of the cruelty of the other backstage mothers. He had always hoped to find a way to do something a little special for the child. But frankly, before today's demonstration, he was never absolutely certain which child she was. To him, all small girls in tights and ponytails look pretty much alike. Now he knew, and he even thought he had found a way of doing it. From now on, he told Chris, no matter what the other children did, he as Herr Drosselmeier could always make sure that Ariadne was the child who got the first nut.

In the magical way of fairy tales, the weekend would prove to be a kind of happy ending for each member of the damned and doomed family. Shortly after Berenice had moved all her money East, her new lawyers at Rogers & Wells had presented her with a draft of a proposed new will, a will dividing her estate equally among her three daughters. She had not asked for a new will; it had simply been submitted for her consideration. Eventually she had signed it. It seemed the fair thing to do. Now, on Gilmer Drive, on the very eve of her daughter Frances's trial, the same thing happened again. The newest lawyers, Saxe, Bacon & Bolan, had submitted a new draft of yet another will for her to inspect and approve. This one left everything to Frances. Berenice said she wanted to sleep on it. She did not want the lawyers to know she had already made up her mind, even though she had.

Out at Point of the Mountain that weekend, a new prisoner was transferred to Marc Schreuder's cottage. He asked Marc whether he happened to know an acquaintance of his, Mike George?

Marc smiled. "Mike George? He's my best friend in the whole world."

MONDAY, SEPTEMBER 19, 1983, 2 P.M. It is afternoon now on the first day of testimony in the murder trial of Frances Bradshaw Schreuder. The lawyers made their opening statements this morning. Then the jury heard brief testimony from Ernie Jones's first two witnesses, the customer who discovered Franklin Bradshaw's body, and the medical examiner who autopsied it. By the time it was time for lunch. Now the entire cast of characters has reassembled in the round blue courtroom. Everybody, that is save the twelve jurors and two alternates; for some reason, they are still offstage. The defendant is again seated between her lawyers, Mike Rosen, John Lang and Kevin Kurumada, toying with her gold-and-ivory pen. The play is about to resume.

Bang of gavel. Judge Baldwin says quietly, "Call Marc Schreuder to the stand." Frances's camel coat is thrown back over her chair, and her hands grip the counsel table so hard that her body shakes. A baby-faced young man in prison denim stands blinking in the doorway from judge's chambers, the duck-waddles across the arena to the witness chair, sits, smiles at the prosecutors. He does not look at his mother. His blue-eyed glance appears stapled onto Mike George's face. He swears to tell the whole truth and nothing but in a firm, strong voice.

Judge Baldwin looks worried. "Is he aware that since his case is on appeal, he does not *have to* answer any questions? Has he had the advice of a lawyer?"

Marc says yes, several lawyers, "and I have come to the decision to testify at this time." He has done this in spite of the lawyers' advice that he withhold cooperation until he has something in writing from the prosecution stating what they intend to do for him in return.

Marc has nerved himself to dive off the high board. It must be now or never.

The defense lawyers look smitten. Rosen pleads for more time to prepare. Judge Baldwin permits only a ten-minute recess before the seven women and five men jurors and the two alternates come marching in, blank-faced and squinting in the glare, to take their double row of seats. The young fellow in the witness chair gives the clerk his name, Marc Francis Schreuder, and spells out. "S-C-H-R-E-U-D-E-R."

The jurors keep their poker faces.

Ernie Jones stands up and asks in a kindly tone of voice, "Marc, how old are you?"

"Twenty-two."

"How are you related to Franklin Bradshaw?"

"I am his grandson."

"And are you familiar with the defendant in this case?"

Looking right at her for the only time in two hours of testimony, "Yes, I am . . . She's my mother."

"Mr. Schreuder, who killed Franklin Bradshaw?"

"I did . . . I shot him."

"What is it that led you to kill your grandfather?"

"My mother asked me to."

"Whose idea was it to kill your grandfather?"

"My mother's." His voice is totally without emotion. He might be saying "vanilla."

She had been talking about the murder for three years. The first time she'd mentioned her plan they were alone in the apartment, or "perhaps my brother" was there. "In a joking sort of way, she said that we were broke, and we had no source of income, and that killing grandfather was the only way of assuring we would have funds to sustain the family through the years."

The first time Frances suggested that Marc himself do it was the summer of 1977. Marc and his brother "came out to steal some money for Mom, and at the same time we were also supposed to kill grandfather."

"How were you supposed to kill your grandfather?"

"Put amphetamines in his oatmeal and make him have a heart attack . . . I got them from my mother."

"Did you attempt to kill your grandfather in the summer of 1977?"

No. But they had discussed two alternative plans: "One involved burning down the warehouse, knocking him out . . . and leaving him inside. Another one involved throwing some kind of electrical appliance in the bathtub while he was taking his morning bath."

Did his mother also instruct him to steal?

Yes. In the summer of 1977, "I took stocks, checks and cash" which were either in the till, or hidden in the warehouse. He took checks from Granny's house. He and Larry got "I think approximately $200,000, mostly in stocks, but about $30,000 in checks, and $3,000 or $4,000 in cash."

"What did you do with all these stocks, and the cash and the checks that you took?"

"I sent everything back to my mother except for . . . about $500 to $1,000 I kept of the cash." His grandfather found out about some of the thefts. "He was very angry."

Defense lawyer Lang looks horror-stricken. The jurors appear stunned. Frances has got hold of herself and regards the witness with a level gaze.

Marc is describing how he called home twice daily for further instructions, sometimes making collect calls from the warehouse, or from Gilmer Drive, but most often using pay phones because such calls cannot be traced. When Marc was unable to call, his brother Larry checked in. Individual calls often lasted two or three hours.

"Did any of them involve the death of Franklin Bradshaw?"

Like an eager puppy hearing its name: "Oh yes!" Marc's broad face, Dutch-boy bangs and the blue prison shirt cut like a painter's smock give him an air both sinister and childlike, very like the *Night Kitchen* figures drawn by Maurice Sendak.

That same summer, at his mother's request, Marc took a great many photographs of his grandparents, their home and the warehouse. He brought them to Dragon's Hall, his Mom's Long Island summer home, as soon as he returned from Utah. She said she needed them to show to a potential "hit man," someone her friend Mr. Behrens said was connected with the Mafia, and who was willing to assassinate her father for $5,000. When this scheme fell through, his mother had tried to hire a second hit man. Then she told Marc he would have to do the job himself. Both he and Behrens tried to purchase a weapon in New York, New Jersey and Virginia. Finally Frances came up with the name of a schoolmate from Texas, and she stood beside Marc writing out his dialogue on a yellow legal pad while he spoke to the boys' parents from a pay phone in the foyer of the Schreuders' New York City apartment house.

She had stood beside her son again, in early July, and forced him to phone his grandparents, say they were being evicted, and plead for a last $3,000. If they would just come through one more time, he promised never to ask for money again. When the check arrived, it was made out to his half sister Ariadne. Mom cashed it and gave some of the money to Marc to buy the gun and plane ticket. They booked passage under the name "L. Gentile" because "Mom didn't want my name on the ticket. So if the police found out anything, suspicion would be cast on Larry instead of me."

"Your mother suggested you use his name?"

"She *insisted* I use his name!"

It seems an appropriate moment for recess. Reporters rush to the phones. Marc had not been expected to take the witness stand at all, certainly not on opening day. Nor had anyone anticipated such devastating testimony. The story he is telling is so unrelievedly wicked, and is related in such deadpan tones, that the spectator is moved to giggle as often as gasp. The experience is less like watching a Friday night horror movie than the kiddie cartoon mayhem on Saturday morning.

Resuming, Marc describes calling his mother from the motel the night he arrived in Salt Lake City. They talked for about two hours. "I told Mom . . . there was no way I could go through with it. She said, 'If you don't do it, don't come home again.' She made it clear to me."

Marc took a taxi to the warehouse the next morning, hid behind the loading dock until he saw his grandfather arrive. They talked about fifteen, twenty minutes. "About grandfather sending money to Mom. After the conversation, I shot him."

"Where was he when you shot him, Marc?"

"I just remember two shots . . . I waited until he turned his back because I couldn't shoot him while his face was to me."

Marc got back without incident to the Schreuders' New York apartment.

"Marc, do you remember her reaction when you told her, 'I did it?' "

"She said . . . *Thank God! Then* she ran up to me, and hugged and kissed me, stuff like that."

Frances wanted to give the gun to Behrens to take home with him that night. When he refused to take it, "she locked it up in her little white cabinet . . . little white desk."

"Do you know why your mother wanted Behrens to keep the gun?"

She was afraid of a search warrant. His mother had always confided in Behrens and previously had used him to hide other items—legal documents during her divorce, for example.

"Marc, would you have told anyone else about killing Franklin Bradshaw besides your mother?"

"Just Mr. Behrens. And a little bit my brother."

The jury sits frozen-faced, unbelieving; two rows of department store mannequins bolted into their chairs. Marc tells them about his mother's joint bank account and Behrens' increasingly frantic efforts to recover his money.

Ernie Jones says very quietly, "Marc, did your mother *have* the $3,700 to pay Mr. Behrens back?"

"Yes, she did."

"Do you know why she wouldn't pay him the $3,700?"

Matter-of-factly, "Because she was always broke."

The story moves to Marc's arrest at Trinity College, his release on bail, his return to his mother's apartment where she was already working on Behrens to recant his original statement and blame Marilyn Reagan.

His *Aunt* Marilyn! "Your mother instructed Behrens to change his story and blame her *sister?*"

The prosecutor's raised-eyebrow tone of voice is unnecessary, excessive.

"Marc, was Marilyn Reagan ever involved in the murder of your grandfather?"

"No, she was not."

"What about your other aunt, Elaine Drukman?"

"No."

In July or August 1981 Marc moved out. His mother suggested he leave the country. He did not and was arrested in October at a postal letter drop he had set up. His attorney was David Frankel and, after many talks, eventually he told him the whole truth.

"You ever implicate anyone else?"

"Objection!"

"Sustained."

Marc received no money as a result of his grandfather's death. His mother received an allowance from the estate, $3,000 a month. Later, at her request, this was increased to $5,000.

The judge interrupts to make clear to the jury that "The $3,000 a month we're talking about was not a result of the will of Franklin Bradshaw." It is not evidence of pecuniary interest.

Yes, Marc recalls talking to Dr. Moench, and he recognizes Exhibit #21. "This is one of my tapes." He made it in '78 or '79. The voices are "Mom, Ariadne, and for a moment, me."

"Marc, were you subjected to any kind of pressure from your mother, as a child?"

"If she wanted you to do something . . . it was impossible to say no . . . She just keeps harping and harping on you . . . She'd scream, or yell, or go into hysterics . . . You just don't tell Mom no."

Ever lock him out?

"Sure she did."

For how long?

"Until I'd thought about it."

"How often would this occur, Marc?"

"All the time."

"Were you afraid of your mother?"

"Object!"

"Sustained."

"Marc, what is it then that led you to kill your grandfather, Franklin Bradshaw?"

A little too quickly, "My mother ordered me to . . . I didn't really have a choice . . . Eventually, at some point in time, I knew I would have to do it . . . My biggest concern was, God, Mom would hate me forever. She would . . . never let me back in the house." She had said it to him on the phone the night before the murder. " 'Doors can be opened, and doors can be locked'—y'know?"

"Has the decision to testify in this case been a difficult one for you?"

"Object!" Rosen is snarling now.

"Sustained."

"Have you had second thoughts about testifying here today?"

"Yes, I have."

"Marc, do you still love your mother?"

Rosen leaps to his feet, shouts out, "I object to this sh-sh-sh-show!"

"Sustained."

At defense request, the cross-examination of Marc is deferred until tomorrow morning. Frances's attorneys are going to need time to prepare a cross-examination on this seemingly unexpected testimony. In the corridor, smoking their cigarettes, Rosen, Lang and Kurumada look punched out, as if they had just gone fifteen rounds with a ghost.

"Call Vittorio Gentile to the stand."

A tiny man in Coke-bottle glasses, neat gray suit, crinkly blond-tinged hair—a midget Kissinger with a Chico Marx accent —mounts the witness stand and tells the court and jury his name and address. Asked if he knows Marc Schreuder, the man says, "Datsa my second son."

The witness describes how he came home from work one day in 1963 and found his East End Avenue apartment completely empty, the furniture, his wife and two children gone. Eventually Frances got custody. By that time Marc was about four years old. As for Vittorio, "I was completely destroyed. Monetarily . . . physically . . . emotionally." In 1967 he returned to Italy. His divorce became final in 1968. Frances got it in Idaho. In 1975 he moved back to the United States. He had been married, in Rome, to "another American girl," Jacqueline Morgan, with whom he now has three children.

Yes, he had lunch many times with Frances after his 1975 return and yes, he recalls a lunch with Frances at Gino Restaurant on Lexington Avenue in the spring of 1978.

At lunch, did Frances mention something about wanting to put a contract out on her father?

"Yes, out of the blue sky! I couldn't believe it! I was speechless . . . She said it as we were leaving the restaurant." But she did not elaborate, and her ex-husband had said nothing more.

Mike Rosen's cross-examination drips with mockery thick as marinara sauce. "You 'used to go' to Gino's?" All these jurors would have to do is *walk by* Gino's, across from Bloomingdale's, any day of the week, and they'd see you sitting at the bar *every afternoon!* Won't they?

Quietly, "Yes."

"When you were with Frances, ever beat her up?"

"No . . . I slappa her to help her with her crises . . . she hav-a de hysterical commotions."

The last time he talked to his son Marc was "three . . . four months ago." They met in a Utah motel, just father and son alone, soon after Marc's conviction and sentencing. "I aska Meester George, I say, I wanna see Marco, eefa I canna see him privately."

Very overbearing now, Rosen demands, *"The court also took your name away from your sons, didn't they?"* He waves a piece of paper, the court order, signed December 31, 1968, by New York Judge Abraham Gelinoff.

"I was penniless," the little man replies. For eight-and-a-half years, "I had no contact with my children."

"By the way, Larry, at the age of four, was certified as a handicapped child by Dr. Webb, was he not?"

Vittorio does not know. He was in Italy. But yes, he was found in contempt of court, "two . . . three times. For back alimony. I am in the business which I need liquid money."

Scornfully, "What kind of business?" He went into bankruptcy, didn't he?

"She was spending money like a maniac," says the witness. In this instance the cliché seems apt.

"Did you *want* custody?" Ernie Jones asks on redirect examination.

"Very much. I even say, 'Let's do friendly. You tak-a one, I tak-a de other.' She say *no!* The children cannot be divided."

Yes, he helped with their care. "Soon as I came home from the office, I used to change their diapers." He loves children. "Like I do with my three children now . . . I take my children alone to Italy for one month every year."

It is true that he owed Frances four or five thousand dollars in back alimony, but he did always pay his child support fees. He was a good father, he insists, and a good husband too. "After the divorce, she wanted to come back with me." When Frances was living in Europe with her second husband, "She used to call me from Belgium, when I was in Rome, and spend a couple of hours on the phone . . ."

The witness is excused. Out in the corridor, before leaving, he smiles shyly and offers reporters his business card:

"Pearls are Girls most intimate Jewels"

Pearls
Borrelli

Vittorio Gentile   608 5th Avenue
importer of cultured   New York City 10020
pearls & corals   (212) 555-9790

TUESDAY, SEPTEMBER 20, 10 A.M. The faces of Ernie Jones and Mike George at the prosecution table are not quite so grim on this second morning of trial. Over at the defense table, Mike

Rosen's handsome head looks a bit grayer than it did yesterday. His client remains a terrifying portrait. Unrelieved now by a trace of makeup, she is less Hogarth than Medusa. The "seething mass of disorder" within is becoming outwardly more visible. The face has commenced a kind of meltdown.

At ten o'clock sharp with a clank of keys, the bailiff locks the double doors to the corridor and stomps back offstage. Judge and jury, lawyers, reporters and spectators are now all locked in together. The court clerk and the court reporter enter through the side door from the judge's chambers. A pair of tall and bookend-like figures, they sit just beneath Judge Baldwin's veneered escarpment and prop up the proceedings. One is red-whiskered, one gray-bearded, but they are otherwise indistinguishable, minor characters—the Rosencrantz and Guildenstern of this drama.

"Please rise!" Sound of feet shuffling. "The court of the Honorable Ernest T. Baldwin is now in session . . ." Marc is back on the witness stand. Judge Baldwin nods toward the defense table. "All right, Mr. Rosen. Your witness."

The lawyer rises, walks slowly around and behind the defendant, places both his hands protectively on her shoulders and, looking squarely at the witness, says with faint contempt, "Mr. Schreuder, my name is Mike Rosen. I represent 'Mom.'"

With heavy sarcasm, he inquires, "Hasn't the prosecutor promised to communicate on your behalf to the Parole Board, sir?"

"Yes, he has," Marc says pleasantly.

"Have any expectation that maybe the prosecutor's communication would get you out of jail a little earlier?"

"Perhaps."

"Ever go to the movies with Sergeant George?"

"Yes . . . in June or July of this year."

"Just you and Sergeant George?"

"Mr. George, myself and my girlfriend."

"You have a *girlfriend* in Salt Lake City!" "What did you go to see, *Fantasy Island? . . . What else* did you do the evening you were out with Sergeant George and your girlfriend?"

Nothing else that day. Another time, George took Marc to the University of Utah to pick up an award he'd won.

"What was the award, Prisoner of the Year?"

Judge Baldwin cautions Rosen to cut out the sarcasm.

Yesterday did not the witness mention a psychiatrist, a certain "Doctor Munch?"

"I believe I said Dr. *Moench* . . ." Marc corrects the lawyer's pronunciation, speaking the difficult name with a perfect German-Swiss accent.

"Get that camera down!" barks the judge. "Take the film out and hand it to the bailiff!" Utah law permits photographers in the courtroom, but they may photograph only court personnel. Baldwin thinks he has caught a newspaper cameraman sneaking a shot of Rosen snarling at Marc.

Did Marc's lawyers tell him to go see Dr. Moench? Yes. Was that in connection with his attempt, at his own trial, to plead extreme emotional disturbance and get a lighter sentence, manslaughter not murder?

"At the time I did not know it. Later on my lawyers told me."

Rosen fires off a sarcastic string of questions about Marc's excellent academic record, pointing out that in 1976 he had graduated with honors from Allen-Stevenson and had won still more honors at prep school. Waving a copy of the Kent School yearbook, Rosen gets the witness to acknowledge that he got good grades and was accepted by both Trinity and Vassar colleges. And is it not correct that Marc took his SAT exams twice and scored slightly better the second time, *after* he killed his grandfather? Yes. And has he not also been active in the stock market for the past several years, maintaining his own account at W. T. Cabe & Co., and trading in $10,000 blocks of Global Marine, Smith, Kline, and other stocks? "Who gave you the money for that?"

"No one did."

And the money to buy rare coins, such as his $17,000 solid gold Maple Leaf? "Moms give you the money for that?" No. "You steal $40,000 from Moms?" No. Jewelry? No. Money? No.

"Steal . . . from Granny?"

"Yes."

"How much you steal from Gramps?"

"Seventy, eighty thousand. It's a really vague figure." The response is unhelpful to Marc's cause. The figure may be vague to him, but it sounds quite specific in this courtroom. On the other hand, Rosen's bullying, hectoring tone of voice cannot be winning many popularity points with this mannerly, modest Utah jury.

Rosen seeks to blacken the young man's reputation a bit more.
The summer before the murder, when Marc and Larry were in
Salt Lake City boarding with their grandparents and working at
the warehouse, didn't the brothers spend considerable time at sex
movies? Didn't they treat their grandfather terribly? Isn't it true
he used bad language to Gramps?

No, only to Granny. The witness is keeping himself under very
tight control.

Picking up steam, Rosen demands, "Did not Doug Steele tell
you your grandfather was *afraid of you!*"

"*Objection!* Hearsay."

"Sustained."

"Didn't you tell Richard Behrens that you tried to kill your
grandfather in the summer of 1977?"

"That's right."

"You told us yesterday that Richard Behrens was Mom's
friend. Did you ever, Mr. Schreuder, take pictures of Richard
Behrens in your bed?" He hands the witness a Polaroid snapshot.

"He's *on* my bed," Marc says dryly. Rosen has implied a ho
mosexual relationship between the witness and his "Uncle
George."

Rosen seeks to place the snapshot in evidence, but Jones ob
jects that no foundation exists. He is sustained.

"Ever tell Richard Behrens that in killing your grandfather
you acted alone?"

"Well, I told him a lot of stories Mom wanted me to tell . . .
phony stories." Marc told so many stories, he is no longer sure
what he said.

"Ever tell anybody your brother Larry was involved in the
murder of Gramps?"

"Yes, I did."

"As a matter of fact, didn't you snitch on . . . Larry [the
previous] summer about him stealing some auto parts?"

"Yes, I did."

How much time elapsed between the two shots? Did Marc
shoot his grandfather the second time as he was going down?

"No, I did not."

"Shoot him in the head after he was down?"

"Yes, I did."

Rosen now crouches to the floor himself. "And when Gramps
was on the floor . . . *you actually put your hands in his pocket*

. . ." Rosen pauses to let this sink in, then pounces. "Ever tell Richard Behrens it was 'easy to kill'?"

"No. I never did."

"Thank you, Judge." Rosen spins on his polished heel and turns away contemptuously. Now it is up to Ernie Jones to rehabilitate his star witness.

In a calm, fatherly voice, the prosecutor asks, "Marc, you indicated on cross-examination . . . that Larry may have been involved in the murder . . . Was he?"

"No, he was not.

Does Marc know *why* Larry was in Salt Lake in the summer of 1978?

"Because Mom locked him out, and . . . Granny offered to take him under her wing . . . After . . . Eastern Military Academy, Mom wasn't going to have him at her house."

Jones returns to Marc's academic record. Marc says he was not really aware of being an honor student. His report cards were sent directly to Mom. But he thought he usually got A's or B's.

"What happened if you got C's or D's?

In a matter-of-fact voice: "She flew into a rage . . . she would take a belt out and start beating me."

Hoping to retouch the rather intimate picture Rosen has painted of the relationship between state prison authorities and the county attorney's office, Jones elicits the fact that Mike George drove Marc to the University of Utah because his prison-earned marks were so high that he had been elected to Phi Beta Sigma, the honor society, and Marc was rewarded by being allowed to attend the initiation ceremony in person. In nearly a year and a half in prison, he has maintained a better than 3.5 grade point average. Presumably, this will impress the jury, some of whom attended the same university.

"Did you receive any kind of financial gain . . . for killing your grandfather?"

"No."

"Did I make you any promises?"

"No promise except that you would appear at the Parole Board."

"Did anyone ever promise you that if you testified your sentence would be reduced? Promise you're going to be released from prison early?"

"No."

"In exchange for the appearance or representation to the
Board of Pardons, by the county attorney's office what are you
expected to do?"

"Tell the truth."

"And are you doing that?"

"Yes."

"No further questions."

Lunchtime. The elevator is packed with reporters, lawyers
spectators, one of whom is conspicuous both for her spherica
proportions—she is perhaps five feet tall and weighs well over
two hundred pounds—and for a smile of seraphic sweetness. She
becomes even more conspicuous when she announces proudly
addressing no one in particular, "I'm Marc's fiancée. The movie
was *Return of the Jedi*. Then Mike took us to McDonald's fo
Chicken McNuggets," she beams. "That's Marc's all-time favor
ite food."

Mary Lou Kaiser goes across the street with Mrs. Ernie Jone
to grab a quick hamburger. They have just seated themselves in a
booth when, through the plate glass windows, she spots her fianc
coming across the parking lot escorted by a prison guard. The
are stopping for more McNuggets before returning to Draper.

" 'Scuse *me!*" She leaps up from the booth with surprising
agility and is standing chortling in the doorway as the guard an
his prisoner swing through the door. "Hiya, Babes!"

The guard, a nice fellow who knows jolly Mary Lou, allow
her to bring her tray and eat with them. Marc is smiling, almost
grinning, but he is trembling too. His hands shake as he ner
vously massages his two-day stubble of blond beard. Up close
one can see that the china-blue eyes are full of tears. He appears
very troubled young man.

"Take it easy, Babes," Mary says quietly. "Think of it thi
way. You're only twenty-two years old, Marc, and already th
two hardest things you're ever going to have to do in your whol
life are both over with!"

FRIDAY, SEPTEMBER 23, 1983. At 11:35 this morning, th
strange trial of Frances Schreuder ends barely four days after
began. It has been unsettling and unsatisfying because of its shap
—a pyramid standing on its head. Lawyers normally try to stru
ture a case to build to a climax and save their strongest witnes
for last, not first. This time, the prosecution hadn't dared wai

The risk was too great that Marc Schreuder might change his mind, or lose his nerve. So the climax came first and, after Marc's testimony, almost everything else—Moench, Steele, Marilyn, Behrens, Manning, Mike George—has been mere corroboration and amplification.

The defense will be still less dramatic. Rosen now indicates his intention to pull on no witnesses whatever. No Frances, no nobody. He will rely on his client's presumption of innocence, and his own forensic ability to show in his summation that the prosecution witnesses without exception either were out to get Frances —her ex-husband, her greedy sister—or were relying on grants of immunity plus a bit of testimony helpful to the prosecution to save their own dirty necks—Behrens and Manning.

Marc Schreuder has *both* motives, vengeance and naked self-interest, it now becomes clear. As soon as the jury is excused, Judge Baldwin says the young man has just called him, from prison, to say he had forgotten to mention during his testimony something which lawyers on both sides seemingly had forgotten to ask him about: in the unlikely event that, despite all, Marc's own appeal for a new trial were to be granted by the Utah Supreme Court, nothing he has said in this trial may be used against him.

Rosen wants to be the one to inform the jury of this cozy arrangement; Ernie Jones prefers that the court do so. Irritably, Judge Baldwin says, "Look, I have no law clerk, I have no secretary. I am exhausted. We have all been working without pause or stop. We will now all recess for a long weekend. Monday, I will give my instructions to the jury. At 9:00 A.M. Tuesday, you will give your summations, and then I will charge the jury."

The jury now is invited back in. Before they go home for the weekend, the judge wants them to know that "there will be no need to brown bag it on Tuesday night. That night the county intends to feed you. Because you'll be out deliberating by that time." Poker-faced, jurors and alternates file out. What thoughts can be whirling around inside their fourteen heads? On Monday they had been told to prepare themselves and their families for a four-week trial. Suddenly, on Friday, Day Five, they learn that it is all but over. Not only will they hear no witnesses from the other side; the defense has not even bothered formally to rest its case.

It looks to courtwise observers as if the fancy, Eastern defense

lawyers may have just made a grave mistake. The difference between trying a case in New York City and in Utah, some say, i'
the difference between playing football on AstroTurf and or
grass. Wise-guy New York jurors assume that witnesses will lie
they *expect* to hear perjury. A Utah jury is more apt to assume
that people who have sworn to tell the truth are probably doing
so. A Utah jury *needs* to hear the story from both sides. These
jurors will not get that chance. Rosen has the confidence of his
own track record: no defendants on the stand, not even any de
fense witnesses, in eight years of very successful trial work.

MONDAY, SEPTEMBER 26, 9:20 A.M. Frances today wears a
trim navy suit, white blouse, freshly washed hair parted in the
middle, and looks much more pulled together than the gorgon o
last week. Berenice Bradshaw, no longer a potential witness, is in
court for the first time, seated in the shadows directly behind he
daughter.

Each juror has in hand a thick sheaf of written instruction
from Judge Baldwin, forty-two in all. His honor proposes now to
lead them through this legal boilerplate item by item. Whistling
slightly through his teeth, the judge begins to read. First, th
indictment: "That the defendant Frances Schreuder"—Baldwi
pronounces it "Shrewder"—did "intentionally, or knowingly
cause the death of Franklin J. Bradshaw for pecuniary or other
motives."

The jurors wear the solemn countenances which are predict
able at this moment of every trial, when the full weight of th
burden they bear now looms suddenly so large, the fateful mo
ment so close. Peering and squinting through blue glasses, Bere
nice Bradshaw methodically studies each face.

The judge prefaces his instructions with the usual lecture o
how the defendant is protected by the presumption of innocenc
which she wears like a cloak, the prosecutor's job being to tear
to shreds, if he can. Because of this impervious cloak, our system
grants the prosecution two chances at bat, the defense but one
The jury will first hear a summation from Mr. Jones, then
summation of the defense case from Mr. Rosen, and then M
Jones will have the last word.

The ritual instructions now begin. The only sound in the cour
room besides Judge Baldwin's whistling drone is the sound
fourteen jurors turning their pages in unison as they follow alon

Of particular interest is Instruction #18: Marc Shreuder, Richard Behrens and Myles Manning all have received certain promises from the prosecution in exchange for their testimony. Jurors may consider this fact in weighing their credibility.

Instruction #21: A person commits criminal homicide if he intentionally or knowingly causes the death of another. The homicide constitutes Murder in the First Degree if it was committed for pecuniary or other personal gain. Judge Baldwin explains the trust agreements which accompany Franklin J. Bradshaw's 1970 will. The bank is directed to set up and manage two trusts: a marital trust for the widow, a family trust for the daughters and grandchildren. "The will makes no provision for his three daughters, and they did not inherit under the will."

All income, rents and so on accruing to the Bradshaw estate flow into the marital trust, over which Berenice Bradshaw has absolute control. She also "has the discretionary power, without limitation, to tell the bank to pay the principal to any of the children, or grandchildren, at any time . . . for medical or for any other reasons." In the shadows, Berenice Bradshaw is sitting motionless, listening very hard, her chin outthrust, looking as if she is hearing this information for the very first time.

"On Berenice Bradshaw's death, *her* will can distribute the marital trust in any way she wishes, without restriction."

Hence, any funds, or family allowances, received by Frances Schreuder, are *not* the result of the will of Franklin Bradshaw. They either flow from the FJB family trust, which is managed by the bank, or they result from the very broad discretionary powers granted to the widow.

Instruction #32 on accomplice testimony is particularly important. "A conviction shall not be had on the testimony of an accomplice," Judge Baldwin reads, "unless his testimony is corroborated by other evidence which in itself and without the aid of the testimony of the accomplice tends to connect the defendant with the commission of the offense . . . The testimony of such an accomplice is corroborated, however, where there is evidence from sources other than the accomplice, which when considered together with other facts in evidence tends to show that the crime . . . was committed and that the defendant was implicated and connected with the commission of the crime."

To find Frances Schreuder Guilty of Murder I, jurors must believe five things: that Marc Schreuder intentionally, knowingly, and unlawfully caused the death of Franklin J. Bradshaw; and that Frances Schreuder knowingly solicited, requested, committed, encouraged, or intentionally aided her son; and that she did this for pecuniary or other personal gain; and that "the hope for financial gain [was] the cause of the homicide, not merely the result." And you must be "convinced of the truth of each and every one of the foregoing elements beyond a reasonable doubt."

Murder II is "a lesser included offense." That is, if you believe all of the foregoing, but are *not* convinced "that the homicide was carried out for economic gain . . ." then you may find the defendant Guilty of Murder II.

It is 10:07 A.M. by the time Judge Baldwin gives the jurors the three possible verdicts, already typed out on three sheets of paper —Guilty of Murder I, Guilty of Murder II, and Not Guilty—and calls for a brief recess before the summations begin.

At 10:21 A.M. Ernie Jones gets to his feet, moves the podium out of the acoustical dead spot, clears his throat, and begins speaking quietly. "Ladies and gentlemen . . . there is no question in this case who killed Franklin J. Bradshaw. The real issue in this case is *why*. Why would a seventeen-year-old boy kill his grandfather?

"That's why we thought it was important that you understand . . . the friction in the Bradshaw family. The source of that friction was always Frances. Frances! Frances! Frances! And the subject of that friction was always money . . .

"The motive? Marc Schreuder mentioned two: *'My mother was afraid she'd be cut out of the Bradshaw estate.'* And second: *'She hoped for a great deal of money from the estate by killing her father . . .'*

Her "fears were real . . ." Jones emphasizes. His manner is quiet, sincere. "On July 26, . . . three days after Franklin Bradshaw's death, Frances tells Detective Campbell there *is* a new will," probably prepared by the since-deceased accountant, Herman Wood.

"Ask yourselves: was there a new will? Or was this a figment of her own imagination? Well, Frances thought there was. And that is what is important!" That is why she had her father killed. As for the old will, the defense is correct when it says that Frances did not inherit under the will. "But Frances *was* a beneficiary under the trust." Jones speaks slowly, swinging at his points methodically, like a golfer with a bucket of balls.

"Frances Schreuder starts to make her own attempts to get a gun . . . Marc says that they went to a rifle store. Marc says that his mother was looking at mail order catalogs . . . She tells Vittorio Gentile, 'I am going to put a contract on my father.' The woman is serious!

"For two and a half years, we sit here in Salt Lake City with no leads on the case . . . Then Richard Behrens, October 16, 1980, brings Marilyn Reagan State's Exhibit #9—the gun, and says, 'This is the gun that killed your father.' Richard Behrens ultimately was charged with obstructing justice, with tampering with witnesses. Then he was promised a grant of immunity, in return for telling the truth. If he did not come clean, his own attorney warned him he could be charged and prosecuted as an accomplice. And he told you: 'Frances masterminded the murder of her own father.'

"Frances was so successful in manipulating people and so successful in hiding the evidence . . . There was only one flaw. She double-crossed Richard Behrens over $3,700."

Remember that "Marc said she could have paid him back. She *had* the money to pay him back, but she wouldn't. Because that's the way Frances is.

"I'm not asking you to rest your verdict on the testimony of Marc . . . You cannot convict . . . on the testimony of an accomplice . . ." But think "about last Monday and how difficult it must have been to testify against his own mother!"

And remember what Marc told you: "I did it because my mother told me to. You just don't tell my mother no."

The prosecutor has spoken for sixty-one minutes, a sober, tightly organized, impressive summation of his case. Spectators trooping out of the courtroom pass the defendant turned around in her chair, speaking with urgency to her mother, directly behind her, and trembling severely. Getting closer, one can see that Frances is crying and telling her mother excitedly, "Don't talk! Don't talk! He's listening to *everything you say!*" She rolls her scary eyes toward the prosecutors' table. Berenice, still seated, awkwardly grasps her daughter's head in her two hands and pats her hair, trying to comfort her. Frances twists away from her mother's grip and walks out into the corridor alone, in tears.

Mike Rosen has outfitted himself for his big scene in a new, expensive-looking pastel suit, above which his bright white smile gleams almost nonstop. But his words are very much at odds with his expression; the effect is disconcerting. "If Marc Schreuder can kill his grandfather, ladies and gentlemen," he begins, "he can kill his mother."

He is pacing very close to the jury, speaking in quiet, almost intimate tones. Frances, from her table across the round well, maintains her Medusa stare. "This is not gonna be a short summary," the lawyer says. "Four-to-six weeks became five, six days . . . Be patient with me now. Ernie Jones, under the rules, comes back, but . . . this is my last chance and more important . . . this is Frances's last chance."

Rosen spins a long and complex tale: the world according to Frances. The consensus among Utah lawyers will be that Mike Rosen's three-hour closing argument is the best one ever heard in this courthouse. "Frances Schreuder, as her two oldest sisters did," left Salt Lake City for good and as soon as she was able. She had two boys who were "in turmoil from the beginning . . . a very bitter divorce . . . beaten by Gentile like a meatball . . . Frances Schreuder was concerned with education. Was concerned with culture for her children. Remember that she was with her daughter at the ballet when they were trying to arrest her . . ."

This is a nice touch, but a fanciful one. The New York City Ballet was two hundred miles away, performing in Syracuse, N.Y., every night that week.

"Marc Schreuder. Let's get right to it . . . I would like to focus on the *shooter.*" The lawyer holds aloft two handfuls of trial transcript, thick as telephone books. "It comes out of here. Out of these pages under oath. Sergeant George described Marc Schreuder as highly intelligent and calculating. Richard Behrens as intelligent and headstrong. Doug Steele told you that Marc Schreuder didn't have an ounce of compassion. As cold as Toby's behind." Flourishing the transcript, the lawyer quotes with a sneer what Behrens told Marilyn at the Burger King: " '*He said it was easy!*' "

Now he attempts to strangle Marc with his own I.Q. "Nancy Jones told you that Marc was disrespectful to his grandparents, cursing at them . . . His teachers' reports revealed a sharp mind . . . Doug Steele told you he saw report cards with straight A's . . . Now we are not talking about some little dummy!" At the Kent School, one hundred miles away from Frances, Marc was still getting honors. "Some little robot, huh?" He's even gotten honors in jail!

"That's a little dummy who goes out and kills because his mother tells him? He has a stock brokerage at W. T. McCabe and Company in Manhattan where he buys and sells securities. $10,000 at a clip . . . expensive, rare coins at $17,000 a pop. Some little—as we call 'em on the East Coast—some little nebbish, huh?

"This boy, the proof shows, is totally self-destructive and irrational . . . and very, very bright. This is the little dummy that walks around with a pistol, and blows his grandfather away because 'My Mommy told me to do it'? . . . Everything he said here, *'My Mommy told me to do it!'* "

Also, consider this: if Frances *was* scheming to get money from her father, "wouldn't Frances tell these boys: Look, fellows. You go out to Utah and just be so nice to Grandma and Grandpa . . . because if she tells 'em . . . to come out here and act like the animals that they are, she knows for sure she's out of the ball game. So she would say, 'Marc, sweetheart, you act like a *little angel!'*

"Grounds for reasonable doubt? Huh? . . . You woulda seen two of the nicest little angels runnin' around wid hot auto parts yuh ever seen in yer whole life!' "

When Rosen gets worked up, he slips into tough Brooklynese street accents, as if he's playing a John Garfield part. How does this sound to a Utah jury—offensive, or just plain weird? His summation has become like a serpent's tail, severed from its brains, and lashing reflexively in any direction. It is a dangerous, loose-cannon defense, rolling around the deck, smashing into whatever is in its random path. Even Rosen's employer is not safe. Suddenly it is Granny who is getting clobbered.

Sure there was friction in the family, and sure Frances needed money. But that doesn't mean she wanted to kill. Yes, the money from the forged checks went into Frances Schreuder's account. But "who signed the front" of those checks? *"Maybe Berenice?* . . ." They certainly didn't bring in any handwriting analysts!

Now a telling point. They didn't bring in all the phone bills either. Remember: they have the phone bills for the '77 calls! "Where's the bill? The collect call, '78, Saturday night, the night before the murder? 'Hi, Mom. I can't do it, Mom. I am flipping out.' "

The loose cannon is tied down again; Rosen is back on target, making very good sense indeed. He reminds them of the law on accomplice testimony: "You cannot take the word of an accomplice to a crime, unless what he says is independently corroborated." The State claims Behrens corroborates Marc, and Manning corroborates key portions of Behrens. "But Behrens cannot corroborate Marc. And Marc cannot corroborate Behrens. That is what His Honor . . . instructed you." Rosen will list four ways in which *Behrens himself* can be seen as an accomplice, four areas in which his—uncorroborated—testimony may therefore be assumed to be unreliable. Now, the first way to find that Richard Behrens is an accomplice is: *he has immunity!* An agreement against prosecution for murder!

Second, Richard Behrens himself told them that he went to New Jersey, and twice to Virginia, trying to help Frances get a gun. Third, Marc Schreuder has told them that Richard Behrens was present at the family murder planning discussions. Fourth, and most telling, Behrens did nothing to prevent the murder, did nothing "to save Franklin Bradshaw's life."

To win this case, it is not sufficient for Rosen to wrap his client securely in her mantle of reasonable doubt. He must also try to wrap a dark shroud of criminal intent, and responsibility, around her son Marc. He returns to the matter of the airline tickets. "Mr. Jones tells you it was Frances Schreuder's idea to use 'L. Gentile' on this ticket, which is Exhibit 36. So Frances is the mastermind. It's her idea.

"No, Ladies and Gentlemen. It was Marc's idea!" Rosen picks up the actual plane ticket from the table of exhibits and brandishes it like a spear. *"This* was Marc's way of sticking it to Larry, and what he ultimately does with Larry is almost as obscene as what he is trying to do to his mother!"

But you can't have it both ways. You cannot claim both, "My mother gave me the name of the hotel to stay in," and also claim, "I can't remember the name of the hotel I stayed in," as Marc had testified.

"This is a death-penalty case! . . . *Don't buy it!"*

Then he reaches out and tickles the manifest common sense of these sober jurors. "If any one of you, God forbid, . . . had to make a real critical life-and-death decision for one of your loved ones, would *you* take the word of Marc Schreuder? Would you take the word of Richard Behrens? . . . Would you take the word of Myles Manning before you made that life-or-life decision?"

He highlights other unlikely aspects of the prosecution scenario. Feature this: Marc Schreuder emerges Sunday morning from his nameless hotel, fully packed. "Got his little toy"—here Rosen holds up the big .357 magnum and sneers—"and he is going to do what his mother ordered him to . . ." Now Marc takes a taxi. The prosecution has painted this as a precision operation. What if Marc couldn't *find* a taxi? What if Grandpa arrived early! *Where is* cabdriver Number One? "He doesn't exist!"

Rosen has begun to carom around again, striking miscellaneous points, like the ball on a pinball machine. The padlock! It was open! But *Larry* had gone there the night before. *Larry let him in!* Boi-n-n-n-g! He has bounced to a different pin. "Then Marc Schreuder, after twenty minutes of talking to Gramps, takes this *thing*, this frightening thing . . ."—again Rosen holds up the gun—"and about a foot-and-a-half away, Dr. Moore said, . . . hits his grandfather in the back! Absolutely vicious . . . ! I asked him: 'Did you shoot him in the head while he was going down?' He sez, 'No I didn't.' 'Oh! Did you shoot him in the head when he *was* down?' He sez, 'Yes, I did.' No mother, no other human being can transmit that kind of viciousness. Lying in the pool of blood, and this kid can go through his pants!"

Frances Schreuder is now shaking all over. She weeps convulsively, her great jaw pushed forward, eyes and mouth turned down. She has become a Mayan mask of horror, horror at the suggestion that her son might actually have dabbled his hands in the blood of her father. Watching her recoil, one feels certain that this dreadful aspect of the matter had not before occurred to her.

"How did he get another cab!" Rosen thunders. That's a third taxi there's no record of! "And we saw no witnesses that Marc was on the plane home." Frances is still shaking.

Rosen is doing a neat job of shining his flashlight of reasonable doubt through the holes in the prosecution case.

"Ladies and gentlemen, *it didn't happen the way the killer said it happened . . . !*

"Lunch, Judge? Would this be a convenient place to break?"

Up on his parakeet perch, Ernie Baldwin is smiling. The judge has been enjoying this lawyer's performance immensely.

An hour later, everybody is back in his blue plastic seat, and Rosen is once more on his feet. How did Marc get into the locked warehouse? Maybe Larry let him in. How did Marc get to the airport? Maybe Larry drove him. Last year, Marc was on trial in this very courthouse, charged with murder. This brings up Dr. Moench. "Now, I don't question Dr. Moench," or his purposes. But Dr. Moench spent a total of only four hours with Marc. He got his information "solely and only from Marc." And Dr. Moench was originally the *defense* psychiatrist. Extreme emotional distress—that was going to be Marc's defense. "He was hoping for manslaughter, not murder."

In Marc's trial, Rosen informs the jury, Dr. Moench was cross-examined by this same Ernie Jones. In fact, Jones even brought in his own psychiatrist, Dr. Coleman, and the State's own expert, Dr. Coleman, had testified that "Dr. Moench doesn't know what he's talking about! . . . Dr. Coleman said Marc is storytelling."

Why the defense has not spent a few more Bradshaw bucks to bring Dr. Coleman to say the same thing to this jury is not explained.

Rosen gets to the point. Marc's "Mommy made me do it" defense was rejected in the first trial, and he was found guilty. "Grounds for reasonable doubt just pours out of that set of facts."

Does it? Or is the flow in the other direction? Perhaps reasonable doubt pours *in.* The defendant's eyes are closed. Frances is asleep! If, throughout this ordeal, Frances has been supervising her own medication, this would account for her dramatic changes in aspect: grief, fury, agitation, zombie-like torpor and gusts of antic glee have played across her countenance in rapid, bewildering variety. Watching Frances these past few days has been like watching a sunset over the Grand Canyon. Clearly Frances is sick. What is the matter with her? Surely some major disorder is at work here. One has not been surprised to hear of suicide attempts and other wild behaviors; they are implicit in her general appearance. What is surprising is to find her in a courtroom at all. Or if she must be in court, why is she not getting an insanity defense? Whatever the reason, the defendant seems clearly to have been serving as her own physician, and it is apparent that she has today overmedicated or overtranquilized herself to the point of stupor.

Rosen is back at his pinball game. "What you saw in this courtroom was an outrage! Judge Baldwin should have told you that *another* promise was made to Marc," one that Marc forgot to mention: nothing that Marc said here this week can ever be used against him at future trials . . .

"He's manipulating the system like he has done for himself, like he manipulated his brother. Please don't let him get away with it. Don't let him bury his mother like he buried his grandfather!"

He even manipulates his captors! Mike George takes him down to a motel so he can meet with Pop. They ask him: whaddya miss most in jail? Marc tells 'em, my girlfriend, and going to the movies. So what happens? *"He blew his grandfather into the grave, and* they *take him to the movies with his girlfriend!*

"Richard Behrens . . . this teacher of English and science . . ." He has immunity in New York and in Utah for every eventuality imaginable. Richard Behrens! " 'What could I do?' I'll tell you what he could do. 'Hello, Salt Lake City? There's some kid comin' out widda gun. Better warn Mr. Bradshaw' . . . none of us would be here today.

". . . our friend Behrens. Remember now, Behrens says Frances gave him the gun. So what does he do? . . . For $3,700 he does the following: He writes to lawyers. He writes to bankers. He writes to Frances. He writes to Mrs. Bradshaw. He sues Frances in court for $3,700. Ladies and gentlemen of the jury: If *Frances Schreuder* gave Richard Behrens this gun, would he have done all of that to collect his $3,700? Or would he have said: 'Frances, come here. Remember dis, Frances? $3,700. Please.'

"Oh, it was tough finding Frances!" Rosen sneers. "She wouldn't answer his calls. So you live two blocks away. You wait until Frances comes home with Ariadne from Lincoln Center, and you are standing outside, and you say: 'Frances, come on!' " Rosen holds up the bank passbook from the table of exhibits. " 'You remember dis! Can I have my $3,700, please?' And if *Frances* gave him the gun, you know what she would have said? '$3,700? How about $37,000, Richard?' . . . Do you think she is going to put her life on the line here for $3,700 when she is shooting for a million-dollar estate? She could buy this gun for $3,700 in a second. Baloney! She never gave him the gun."

Boi-i-n-n-g! "And Marilyn Reagan! I wonder why she was smiling, every time she looked over at Sis fighting for her life?"

Bo-i-i-n-n-g! "How do we know for sure that Behrens is full of baloney that he got the gun from Frances?" Because when Joel Campbell first took a statement from Behrens, on December 3, on tape, " 'He gave me the gun,' " Behrens told him. " 'He,' not 'she.' Don't forget. This guy's our English teacher. I guess he can tell the difference between he and she . . . *He* said, 'Get rid of it.'" But in his affidavit, dated December 27, recanting his first statement, Behrens says that he made up the entire story implicating Marc and made it up at the request of Marc's "hate-filled" Aunt Marilyn, who was determined to pin her father's murder on her sister's two sons. In return, says Rosen, Marilyn promised him the $10,000 reward and free ski trips to Utah.

So where is this famous affidavit? Why is it not in evidence? Rosen stops pacing, turns his back on the jury, then spins on his heels to confront them. "Grounds for reasonable doubt?" he barks.

Rosen draws their attention to other grounds. "October 16, 1981. Richard Behrens gives his original statement to Joel Campbell. He swears to Campbell that Marc gave Richard Behrens the gun. No mention *here* of Myles Manning! No mention of Frances!"

On the tape of this interview, Richard Behrens even suggests, "Perhaps Marc bought the gun for *Larry.*" Boi-i-n-n-g!

In addition to his pinball attack, Rosen employs other techniques. He cites inconsistencies: "Behrens says it was his idea to buy the gun cover and cleaning rods. . . . He says he bought this cleaning paraphernalia one week after he got the gun. Marc said one year." . . . But then Rosen draws no conclusions.

He asks provocative questions: *"Why* does Richard Behrens go to the trouble of cleaning this gun? . . . with cleaning rods!" . . . but then fails to supply any answers.

He points out situations: "Behrens also told you something else: that Marilyn and Frances hated each other" . . . but fails to interpret them.

He highlights contradictions: "Richard Behrens says he knows Myles Manning since 1974, 1975. Manning says, 'I knew him three or four months'" . . . but does not interpret them.

Ernie Jones had delivered his summation like a crack marksman. Rosen is firing buckshot. One man is not necessarily better; each has a different problem. Jones needs to nail Frances. Rosen needs to sow enough seeds of reasonable doubt to raise a protective meadow around his client.

More inconsistencies: Richard "Behrens says that Frances Schreuder gave him the gun on the night of the murder. Well, Marc says Frances Schreuder locked it up in her little white cabinet," and gave it to Behrens the next day.

More nonconclusions: "Marilyn Reagan told you that her father left everything to Berenice Bradshaw. Frances had *not* been disinherited . . . Mr. Bradshaw left everything to Mrs. Bradshaw! Frances was not disinherited!"

Big-ego lawyers—and in the cockfighting pit of the criminal bar, they are probably the only kind who are any good, the last of the Lone Rangers—suffer the occupational stress of their trade, which is overkill. That is happening to Mike Rosen now. A white-haired juror is yawning in the lawyer's face. It has all been going on much too long and too randomly to follow. It has come to seem as if the defense lawyer is just winging it, reading his notes aloud without plan, just confused, confusing spouting, oat-sowing.

Rosen suggests another ten-minute recess. This time Frances is not among the corridor smokers. She sits huddled half-asleep in a back stairwell, entirely alone, arms encircling drawn-up knees, head buried between. Where are her high-priced defenders? This image of desperate sleep is familiar to hospital workers, to Parisians confronting *clochards,* and to Manhattan pedestrians stepping carefully around the city's sleeping street people self-hugged in doorways.

It is time for Rosen to deal with the little man with Coke-bottle glasses. He is not kind. "This guy is so bad that the court strips his children of his name! This guy don't have legs. He's got a bar stool for the bottom part of his body . . . With all that has gone on between Frances and Vittorio, you think she trusts *him* to keep . . . quiet" that "she's gonna put out a contract on her father, something that could put her subject to the death penalty?"

Still more rhetoric is employed to pound Vittorio Gentile into the ground. How come after Franklin Bradshaw's death that Gentile never went to the cops? Grounds for reasonable doubt here?

Recalling once more the image of the drunken wife beater, Rosen finishes, "He *coulda* killed her *then.* Don't . . . let . . . him . . . kill . . . her . . . now!"

A parting shot about the dead man's estate. Hizzoner has already told them that Franklin Bradshaw's will made no provision for his three daughters. "We know *she* knew she wasn't in the will. We know Frances knew she couldn't inherit. Maybe Marc thought he could inherit!"

Under the terms of the will, the widow "could give it all to a guru in Egypt, and no one could stop her." In her own will, she can do what she wants with whatever's left. "So Frances Schreuder got nothing under either trust. *So Frances has no motive to kill!*"

Rosen draws this idea together effectively and ties a neat bow. "Now Mr. Jones is left with this argument: she killed because of the $3,000 allowance. Absurd! . . . She couldn't even count on a judge giving her the $3,000. That's purely up to a judge! If she thought there was a new will, and she was out of it—the last thing she would do is kill him. She'd come out here and do a nice song and dance on Dad . . . As soon as you kill him, that will is final. You are out forever."

Rosen ticks off a few final inconsistencies in the prosecution's argument. Where is her bank statement showing the withdrawal of $5,000 for Myles Manning? They showed you other bank statements, why not this one? "Grounds for reasonable doubt?"

Steve Klein. Rosen says Frances's hysteria during her arrest was the response of a frenzied mother trying to protect her child from frightening scenes of cops with drawn guns. Through savage cross-examination, Klein had insisted he never drew his gun. Sneers Rosen, "What police officer makes a forced entry in a murder case and doesn't have a weapon out to protect himself? She coulda been sittin' in there widda machine gun!"

Another wild oat: if Frances Schreuder is guilty, why doesn't she run when she hears the cops have been to 10 Gracie Square asking for her?

And another: "Mr. Jones said 'escape.' She's trying to *'escape'* out of the seventh floor window. Seven floors in the sky! What was she gonna do—*fly* to Argentina?"

And a bid to leave 'em laughing: who is Myles Manning? An admitted alcoholic. He was evicted with his brother from a series of apartments. For being winos. So he had a very appropriate reason for spending three days in a YMCA!

There's no corroboration at all for Myles Manning saying he got $5,000, or even that Frances Schreuder withdrew such a sum from the bank! Now Mike Rosen wants to call the jury's attention to a coincidence, "and if it is all just a coincidence—it's the greatest coincidence in the history of mankind!" Something happened at Culver Lake, New Jersey, in the fall of '77, and it happened at the same time Myles Manning was supposedly employed as the it man for Frances Schreuder. "Dr. Herman Behrens, Richard's father, had a younger wife, Joan. And Richard Behrens feared that his father was having a change of attitude. Richard Behrens was very worried about the undue influence his stepmother Joan appeared to have over his father the doctor. Wow, what a coincidence! *Richard Behrens feared he would be cut out of his father's estate!*"

It is obvious that Behrens and Manning were up to no good. "What Behrens has done here, ladies and gentlemen, is to shift his treachery up at the lake to an identical situation with Frances Schreuder. What a package! That 'coincidence' is an insult to our intelligence . . . I don't know what Behrens promised Manning . . . split the reward? I wasn't there [and] they both have immunity . . . So don't compromise, ladies and gentlemen. You promised. Stick with your belief! There is no way back if you make a mistake. A trial is something like a jigsaw puzzle. It's all a beautiful picture when you first see it. Then some . . . pieces start falling out . . . The picture gets blurry . . . if all the critical pieces fall out, as I submit they have here, whaddya left with? *You're left with a frame!*"

It is four o'clock, time to recess. Ten minutes later, Ernie Jones is back in front of the jury to deliver his final summation in his best Jimmy Stewart manner. One can actually hear Stewart's drawling delivery in Jones's opening lines.

"As I listened to defense counsel, ladies and gentlemen, I took it to mean that all of these people who have testified . . . Marc Schreuder, Marilyn Reagan, Richard Behrens, Myles Manning, and Vittorio Gentile are liars. All . . . are in a conspiracy against Frances Schreuder." But why would Marc lie? The defense never gave a reason, a motive, for *why* Marc Schreuder would say his mother put him up to it.

Jones acknowledges that Myles Manning is a comic figure whose recollections are foggy. He uses this fact as an indication that Manning was telling the truth, pointing out that various discrepancies in his and Behrens's testimony should be a little "refreshing," not proof of perjury, or of a desire to obstruct justice . . . "Myles Manning took $5,000 in a con game!"

But what about the testimony of Dr. Moench—he came to the same conclusion in both trials. That Marc was a victim of *extreme pressure*. "If you throw out all the evidence against Frances

except the testimony of Marc Schreuder and Dr. Moench—that
enough evidence to convict!"

Marc Schreuder has *no reason* to lie in this case. "I mean—you
hate to say it. But maybe it was the best thing that ever happened
to Marc to be convicted of second-degree murder . . . to get
him out of that environment in New York City." Jones knows his
jury. This is a telling point. Now he reminds them of the history
of this case. "At the time Marc Schreuder went to trial, Frances
Schreuder had *already* been charged with murder. That was al
ready our position—that she was the mastermind—even then."

The motive for this murder was money.

"You ask yourself: what kind of a daughter would order the
execution of her own father? What kind of a mother would ask
her own son to carry out that murder? What kind of human
being are we talking about? What kind of human being . . .
makes it appear as though her own son, Larry, is the prime sus
pect? . . . What kind of a human being would then convince
Richard Behrens that he should blame her sister, Marilyn Rea
gan, for the murder?

"Members of the jury, I submit to you that Frances Schreuder
has tried to destroy everyone who got in her road. She destroyed
her father. She destroyed Marc. She tried to destroy Richard
Behrens. She tried to destroy her sister Marilyn. She tried to
destroy Larry.

"Frances is ruthless and cruel. She was . . . hysterical at
times if she didn't get her own way. She was obsessed with
money. And she kept, according to Dr. Moench, harping and
harping and harping on Marc to carry out the murder for her.

"I submit to you that Frances Schreuder almost pulled off the
perfect crime. Almost. There was only one flaw. She crossed up
Richard Behrens for $3,700.

"The defense said—the crime doesn't make sense. It's not logi
cal. *Murder never is logical.* This isn't a logical woman. This is a
woman who becomes hysterical when she doesn't get what she
wants. That's why she tells her own son on the night before the
murder—Don't come home if you don't kill Franklin Bradshaw

"I submit to you that there is only one thing standing in the
road at this point in time, and that is a verdict in this case. I
submit to you that Frances Schreuder is a party to the offense.
She masterminded this offense. She engineered it. She put pres
sure on her own son to kill her own father. Thank you very

much." It is 5:25 P.M. Judge Baldwin excuses the two alternates, and announces he will not send the twelve jurors out to eat until 7 P.M. By 5:29 P.M. the jury has retired to the jury room and is hard at work. Western judges do not waste much time.

Departing reporters and spectators straggle out of the courtroom. Nothing to do during the anticipated long wait for a verdict but find a barroom and sit there. Rounding the corner to the elevators, they come upon the defendant. She is again alone, propped up at an open, boothless pay phone in the corridor across from the elevators, and sobbing very loudly, indeed convulsively, as she waits for her call to go through. Decency compels the crowd to look away. People turn to face the elevators, their backs to the phones.

Then, from behind them, comes a high, thin, childlike wail, as if it is being torn from the crepey, middle-aged throat: *"Ar-i-a-a-a-dne!"*

10:04 P.M., JUDGE BALDWIN'S CHAMBERS. All jury waits are agonizing. His honor looks punched out, hollow. Dixieland jazz relaxes him, and he is leaning back now, eyes closed, puffing at an unfiltered cigarette, listening to his tape deck, a jazz piano medley distributed by the Book of the Month Club. He reaches under his desk blotter to fish out a hidden, dog-eared clipping.

"I've been through this thing five times now," he says, "and I don't get paid as much as a goddam plumber!" He hands the clipping to his visitor. It is a famous quote from a speech by Supreme Court Justice Robert Jackson on the solitary ordeal of the trial judge.

> The trial judge sits alone and does most of his work with the public looking on. He cannot lean on the advice of associates or help from a law clerk. He works in an atmosphere of strife, with counsel, litigants, and often witnesses and spectators bitter, biased and partisan . . .
> This lone trial judge must make a multitude of quick and important decisions . . . He must rule immediately and firmly on questions which appellate judges may deliberate for months and then decide . . .

Baldwin opens his eyes a crack to gauge the visitor's reaction. "You're damned if you do and damned if you don't," he says.

"The only thing that keeps me going is—I don't give a goddam."
He takes a long, deep drag, a double lungful from his cigarette.
Eddie Condon and Fats Waller tear into *Ain't Misbehavin'*. Suddenly the bailiff shouts through the doorway, "Your honor,
they've reached a verdict!"

The entire cast of characters has rushed back into the courtroom, everyone in his accustomed seat, utterly silent, awaiting
the arrival of the play's special audience of twelve. Frances's face
looks lumpy, white and prayerful, as if the ever-moving, molten
lava has at last begun to congeal. Beside her, Mike Rosen strokes
the sides of his nose with paired fingertips, then rubs them over
his cheeks and lips, like a blind man trying to read a face.

Breaking the stillness comes a single harsh bark of hearty
laughter, heard through the wide-open doors to the jury room.
Then the jurors march in and hand the judge their pretyped ballot. He glances at it, reads aloud, "We find the defendant Guilty
of Murder in the First Degree."

It has happened very fast. The jury was out less than five hours
including dinner. The judge announces a one-week interlude between verdict and sentencing, rejects the prosecution's *pro forma*
plea for immediate incarceration, and releases the prisoner on her
own recognizance, supervised by her local counsel, Kevin
Kurumada. The reporters have all rushed off to file their stories.
In the most recent press pool, the odds against a Murder One
conviction had been twenty to one. By 10:24 P.M. not a soul is left
in the round blue chamber save the defendant, two of her lawyers, and her mother.

Out the corridor windows, crossing the brightly illuminated
green grass lawn two floors below, a shirtless Mike George can be
seen, leaping and twisting in the air, his arm around Ernie Jones's
shoulder, two antic black silhouettes whooping off together into
the moonlight.

One week later, on Monday morning, October 3, the entire cast
of characters in *State of Utah* vs. *Frances Schreuder* and their
handpicked audience of twelve reassemble in Judge Baldwin's
courtroom for the second-to-last time. Phase Two of Frances
Schreuder's trial, the so-called referendum on her moral character, is an embarrassment. Three character witnesses take the
stand to say they do not believe that this defendant merits the
death penalty. Two of them are fund-raising officials of the

School of American Ballet: Mary Porter, now director of development and formerly private secretary to Lincoln Kirstein, and the former Ford Foundation man, W. McNeil Lowry. The second-biggest giver after the Ford Foundation has been Frances Schreuder. Her—or, more accurately, her mother's—combined benefactions to the Company and School now total about one million dollars.

The defense's third character witness is a high school classmate whom Frances befriended when she and her family came to Salt Lake City from Germany in the 1950s. Now a professor of German at Mills College, Oakland, California, the woman owns a silver-gray Mercedes-Benz, and she is believed by the prosecution to have been the driver of the "getaway car" during Frances's spring raid on Sam Drukman's mailbox, an accusation she now denies from the witness stand.

Frances has said that Mr. Balanchine himself would have come to Salt Lake City to defend her, if only he could, and she is probably right. Lincoln Kirstein did come and is seen glowering in the courthouse corridor while his two associates testify. Mike Rosen does not put Kirstein on the stand, he says later, because Kirstein is not anxious to testify, and Rosen doubts it would be of any help. The defense already has exercised its right to waive the jury in this phase of the trial and to leave the determination of its client's fate—death, or life in prison—to the sole discretion of Judge Baldwin. Given the evident state of mind of this particular jury, that seems the only civilized option the defense had left.

Throughout the morning of testimony and cross-examination, Frances sits quietly at the defense table, her hands clasped around a small, turquoise-colored Tiffany box. Protecting himself on appeal, Ernie Jones demands formal assurance from the defense that the client knew what she was doing when she waived her right to a jury and was not, for example, under the influence of drugs. Teetering slightly, Frances Schreuder gets to her feet and, for the first time in these proceedings, speaks in her own behalf. Her voice is musical, girlish, pleasant. "Within the past twenty-four hours? No. I have physical illnesses, but not in any way so as to render me incapable."

Judge Baldwin says that over the weekend he has received two letters from family members urging the court to show mercy. "Though she caused the death of my father, I do not wish her death," Marilyn wrote, and she requested "some kind of psychi-

atric care." The judge considers the plea from the defendant's
mother "truly heartrending," he says, adding later that the "real
victim here is Berenice Bradshaw."

The lawyers now make their final pleas, Rosen for a "civilized"
disposition of the case, Jones for the execution of Frances
Schreuder as an expression of society's "outrage." Judge Baldwin
says he has known for several days that he, not the jury, will have
to make this life-or-death decision, and he has no need to retire to
chambers to consider his verdict. So saying, he sentences Frances
Schreuder to life imprisonment.

Mrs. Bradshaw is expressionless. Her daughter sits with her
mouth open, a poppet with its stuffing out. A policewoman appears to take the prisoner into custody and escort her to jail. At
her approach, Frances stands up and opens her little package. It
contains a heavy crucifix. Thrusting this object out before her in
time-honored, two-handed, anti-Satan fashion, the defendant says
loudly, "I stand on my constitutional rights!" Then the poor
thing is led away.

The play was over, the stories told. The prosecutor's version had
won handily. The departing players straggled down the courthouse steps, passing the big, black Ten Commandments monument for the last time. The Schreuder affair had violated most of
the ten. The jury had heard no evidence of adultery, no coveting
of thy neighbor's wife. But of plain, garden-variety coveting there
had been an abundance, along with killing, stealing, worship of
an entire pantheon of false gods, bearing of false witness, failure
to keep the Sabbath, and sufficient dishonoring of thy father and
thy mother to gladden the black heart of Satan himself.

But here in Salt Lake City, the case had been viewed primarily
as a violation of what might be called the Eleventh Command-
ment: Honor Thy Family. Here where the family is cast in
bronze, painted in murals, poured in concrete and carved in marble, where totemic groups of Father and Mother and little children clustered at their knees dot the broad avenues and loom
down from the walls, where billions of invisible ancestors are
believed to hover somewhere in the vacant blue skies above, their
souls mingled with the infinitude of children yet unborn, where
all will one day stand up together in holy white garments in a
greater, vaster family portrait than the human mind can conceive
—here Frances Schreuder's behavior was perceived as an abomi-

nation against the family. That is the version of reality these people saw. That is the play they preferred. The jury's swift verdict made it very clear. The jury had functioned just as they were meant to, as "the conscience of the community."

Frances Schreuder had dishonored the family, they had concluded, and for this she now literally, in the biblical sense, had been cast out for her crimes.

Afterword

. . . MY WORK ON THIS book had started with a letter and, in a sense, it ended with one. The first letter had been my own to Frances, mailed to 10 Gracie Square before her trial and returned unopened.

After Frances went to prison, Berenice Bradshaw returned to New York City to keep an eye on Ariadne and supervise the completion of the renovations at 10 Gracie Square which Frances had begun and then suspended three years before.

At the regular November meeting of the NYCB Board of Directors, a brief letter of resignation from Frances Schreuder was read, moved and seconded without comment.

Ariadne was back in school and in ballet school, preparing for her third season in *The Nutcracker*. Her constant companion was Jeannie Columbo, the young former ballet usher who had been hired as a temporary au pair just before Frances's trial. Jeannie had proved to be an attentive, loving—and loved—caretaker. The child had never seemed happier.

Frances still telephoned home nightly, from prison, to discuss schoolwork, dictate menus, and generally attempt to continue her supervision from afar. She refused to speak to her mother during these calls. Berenice Bradshaw was heartbroken several times over. She had given her entire life to her family, and all lay in ruins about her. Not one of her daughters would speak to her. "How could they convict Frances of something she *didn't do?*" she asked continually. She and I continued to call one another several times a week, as we had since we met. Once when she sounded especially blue, I urged her to come and visit me in the country for the weekend. While we were there the phone rang. "Is a Mrs. Bradshaw available to accept a collect call from Utah?" Yes, I said, but the caller had already hung up. I knew enough by then about Frances to recognize that this was her way of checking up on Granny's whereabouts. She did not like where she found her.

Later Berenice invited me several times to visit 10 Gracie Square. Although she still seemed bewildered by the turn of events, she now said she had begun admitting to herself the possibility that "Frances may have done it." I had told her before the case went to the jury that I thought her daughter was probably crazy and had been for some time, in which case she belonged in the care of doctors, not jailers. Nothing I came across in my research caused me to change my mind. Eventually I found my way to a psychiatrist who works with homicidal children and often advises courts in the handling of such cases. The same doctor was also a specialist in the diagnosis of bipolar mood disorders (formerly, less accurately termed manic-depressive psychosis), which by then appeared to be the category into which Frances's illness fell. I suggested to Mrs. Bradshaw that an informal talk with the doctor might be useful, if only to make her feel less distraught.

Both she and the doctor agreed, so I drove her down to the hospital and sat in on their three-hour conversation. It sounded to me as if the doctor had the diagnosis about right. Here is the relevant passage from *Diagnostic and Statistical Manual of Mental Disorders*, Third Edition, or DSM III, the book which serves psychiatry as the Blue Book does the used car business.

MANIC EPISODE: The essential feature is a distinct period when the predominant mood is either elevated, expansive or irritable . . . Symptoms include hyperactivity, pressure of speech, flight of ideas, inflated self-esteem, decreased need for sleep, distractibility, and excessive involvement in activities which have a high potential for painful consequences, which is not recognized.

The elevated mood may be described as euphoric, unusually good, cheerful or high; often has an infectious quality for the uninvolved observer; but is recognized as excessive by those who know the individual well . . . Although elevated mood is considered the prototypical symptom, the predominant mood disturbance may be irritability, which may be most apparent when the individual is thwarted . . .

The term "hypomania" is used to describe a clinical syndrome that is similar to, but not as severe as, that described by the term *mania* or *manic episode.*"

DSM-III CRITERIA FOR HYPOMANIA

MOOD:	elevated, expansive
PSYCHOMOTOR:	more energy than usual
	physical restlessness
SPEECH:	more talkative than usual
SLEEP:	decreased need for sleep
COGNITIVE:	inflated self-esteem
	sharpened and unusually creative thinking
	overoptimism or exaggeration of past achievement
BEHAVIORAL:	increased productivity, often with unusual and self-imposed working hours
	hypersexuality
	inappropriate laughing, joking
	excessive involvements in pleasurable activities with utter lack of concern for painful consequences: buying sprees, reckless driving, drug & alcohol abuse*

When Berenice Bradshaw went home to Salt Lake City on the day before Thanksgiving 1983, she drove directly from the airport to the prison. Her daughter refused to see her. At home she found a six-page letter waiting, "a very, very vicious attack. I was completely laid low." By Saturday, she had decided to try again, this time remembering to bring along some flowers, which she knew Frances liked. She gave the flowers to a "matron" and mentioned that on her Wednesday visit Frances had refused to see her.

"Well we'll just see about that!" said the matron, and Berenice later told me that she and Frances had sat out in the sunshine all afternoon together. "She was just as nice as she could be!" Berenice said, except when the conversation turned to books. Several people were then writing about the Bradshaw murder. The books were all Berenice's fault, Frances had told her mother, and she had vowed that, "When those books come out, she's never going to speak to me again."

On Berenice's next prison visit, at Christmas, she brought

---

* Taken from *Diagnostic and Statistical Manual of Mental Disorders*, Third Edition. Washington, D.C.: American Psychiatric Press, 1980. DSM III stresses that bipolar disorder occurs more frequently in certain families than in the general population.

smoked salmon which she knew Frances enjoyed, and again the visit went well, with one exception. Frances asked her mother to smuggle in a bottle of liquor for New Year's Eve. She showed Berenice the bush it could be stashed in, and was not happy when her mother refused to cooperate.

While Berenice was at Draper, she also dropped by the men's side of the prison to visit her grandson. "I didn't tell anybody, just went to see him. I thought: After all, he's a *human being!* I took him a fruitcake. He was so happy to see me, he cried. I didn't tell his mother. I have enough problems without that. Everyone says we're supposed to discard these kids. I know Marc is sick, but you don't just throw a sick dog in the gutter. You try to do something for him. And after all, it *was* Christmas."

Although Berenice Bradshaw and I always enjoyed one another's company, I don't think either one of us deceived ourselves into believing that we could be or wanted to be "friends." "Fellow travelers" was closer, passengers for a time on the same train, one critical difference being that I could get off the train at any time. She could never get off. After Christmas, I noticed a faint chill in her voice, but we still continued to chat on the phone and to share an occasional meal. At our last one, in a Chinese restaurant, I was astonished to learn from Berenice that she had never even heard of *Davidsbündlertänze,* the ballet she had entirely paid for. I was also surprised to hear that the New York State Theater had honored Frances with a gold plaque. "Go look at it," Berenice said. I couldn't find it. I was not at all surprised when Berenice told me that she had decided in her newest will to leave every dime to her much misunderstood, much abused youngest daughter. That development had seemed to me inevitable.

It was just as inevitable that our relationship would come to some acrimonious end. I had by then been awakened several times by late night anonymous phone calls. Usually when I picked up the receiver the caller hung up. Between Christmas and New Year's, an anonymous typewritten letter arrived. The writer claimed to be "a former friend of the family," but I had by then read dozens of letters Frances had written and recognized certain turns of phrase.

Dear Ms. Alexander,

I have debated writing to you for months now. I can no longer sit back and do nothing but I feel I must come to the defense of one who has been persecuted her entire life. As a former friend of the family, I feel it necessary to bring some facts to your attention.

Frances Schreuder has many good and decent friends. She is an extraordinarily brilliant woman who has a sensitive and caring nature. She has, unfortunately, had so much tragedy in her life, it may have taken its toll in many ways. Surprisingly, it has not made her bitter or taken away her sense of humor. She numbers among her friends the very great and the very small. Not one of them would come forward to speak to you without her permission. Those who will speak, however, are those who have given Frances nothing but misery her entire life.

When you spoke to Marilyn and Elaine, I do not suppose they told you they used to lock their baby sister in closets when she was a baby and they were old enough to know better. Marilyn was always jealous of her youngest sister. Frances was the first to marry and Marilyn was frantic to get married. Their own mother has said on several occasions that Marilyn only got a husband by squawking about how much money her family had. Did either sister tell you how many times Frances invited them for holidays? Did they tell you they never showed up? I will bet they never told you they never once sent a birthday card to Frances or her children.

Did that mother tell you how she gave to all her children? Did she tell you she never once gave a thing without telling you or anyone who would listen how much it cost and how wonderful it was of her. Did she tell you she felt stuck with her own children? Did she cry about her husband working three hundred and sixty-five days a year? What a shame he isn't here to tell you he had to get away from his nagging and badgering wife. Did that mother tell you that when Frances was a little girl and went off to camp that she asked how to take care of her child's kittens. When Frances was gone she took the kittens and drowned them.

This story makes *Mommie Dearest* look like a Grimms Fairy tale.

Frances could never tell you these things because after a
they have done to her, she could never hurt them.

I wonder who really sent Marc to kill his grandfather? . .

(signed) Anonymous

In late January a second letter arrived. This one, from Ber
nice, written and signed in her hand, said I sought only to pro
from her family's misfortunes. "In some circles you have a nic
name 'the ghoul,' " she wrote. "Now I can see why. You certain
are digging my grave . . ." Once again I recognized France
epistolary style, her precision poison penmanship, although the
was no question that the actual writer was Berenice, and that h
feelings were very bitter.

But to depict the face of madness, one must show that fac
The story of the Bradshaws pierces our thin skin of sanity a
bares the madness in us all. We are helpless in our madness, a
blind in our sanity. One must strive to say no to the power
madness, and to remember that madness comes from within.
story such as this requires a telling in full. Only an honest a
seamless account is worth writing.

"Without talking to all of us who know Frances and know h
well, your book will be incomplete," the first letter, the anor
mous one from the "former friend of the family" had conclude
"Not only that. By talking to anyone within this family of ha
your book will not be accurate."

I have now talked to everyone within this family of hate a
have reached a few conclusions as to what may have happen
Nothing as coherent, cohesive, neat, and tidy as a specially wr
ten play for a jury of twelve. Just some notions that belong here
in the realm of speculation, not fact—but do I think belong.

I think it quite possible that Frances Schreuder is only tech
cally guilty. She may not have actually "solicited, request
commanded . . . [or] intentionally aided" Marc in the murd
in the words of the Utah statute on aiding and abetting—
though it is difficult to see how she could deny having "enco
aged" him. Marc may have acted entirely on his own, done
because he knew it would please his mother, or to win love fr
his mother, and she may have had little or no specific knowle
of his intention.

think the murder in Utah in 1978 could be an eerie recapitula-
n of the infamous murder in the cathedral eight hundred years
ore, when Thomas à Becket was killed by courtiers of King
nry II, not because the King had ordered the murder of the
chbishop of Canterbury, but because the assassins knew the
ereign's wishes and sought to curry favor.

t also seems possible to me that what we may have here is a
e à trois—Frances, Marc, and Behrens—or even à quatre, if
rry too was involved. In other criminal trials, though not in
s one, the experts speak about "lethality," and whether a de-
dant possessed sufficient "lethality" to do the deed. Sometimes
en I think of those three flaky, idle people—or was it four?—
ing around day after day in that lonely flat on York Avenue,
nking, smoking, and imagining murder and playing the game
nurder, ruminating hour after hour on why and how Franklin
dshaw had to be disposed of, I think that quite possibly no
of them possessed sufficient lethality to do the deed. What if
equired the confluence of three or four dreaming brains—the
oldering resentment of Behrens, the manic frenzy of Frances,
young, disturbed, abused brains of Marc, and perhaps Larry
o conglomerate sufficient psychic energy and lethality to act?
at if it was a kind of spontaneous combustion of madness?

often wonder: how could Frances for so long have evaded the
s of psychiatry, the toils of the law, the attentions of child
se authorities, and other guardians of social order? When I
ed Dr. Moench his opinion, he said, "Easy. The green poul-
." Money heals much and hides what it cannot heal. For the
st part, only the poor wind up in the madhouse, or on death
for that matter. The green poultice dilutes madness into
mless eccentricity.

think that Frances was a monstrous mother. She almost in-
ably used her children as excuses to do whatever it was that
wanted to do. I think some mothers do that to an extreme,
almost all of us do at times. But Berenice Bradshaw was not
of them. Berenice's problem was that she was literally in
ill to her youngest daughter. She forgot about the principle of
carrot and the stick. She was choking Frances on carrots.

rances told me after the verdict that she had wanted very
ch to testify. "After Marc took the stand against me, that jury
to hear from me," she said to me during that long afternoon
er locked hotel room. "I begged my lawyers to put me on.

They said no." I thought she was right. After Marc's testimor
nothing less than hearing from Frances could have helped h
And it was hard to imagine how her testimony, however bizar
could injure her any worse than her son already had.

I think Granny was more-or-less right when she wrote
Judge Baldwin that her grandson was "a born liar, a born thie
He is also a born *gamesman*. Money is the main game, as it is
others in his family. Money is one of the few things Marc see
to have genuine feelings for. His protestations about having be
entirely Mom's puppet have substance but do not always ri
true. Rather than being an "emotional cripple," he seems to ha
no real "emotions" as most people understand the term. He ‹
have his lifelong, infantile dread of Mom's anger and overwhel
ing craving for her love. But once he turned on her, he lost so
of these infantile feelings. Having proved his manhood M
George's way—by testifying against Mom—Marc may be
longer a "mama's boy," no longer an "emotional cripple."
better term for Utah prisoner #15906 might be "emotional ‹
bris." He is like the pile of tailings left behind after his mothe
lifelong, systematic strip mining of all of this young man's cons
erable natural resources.

And what of Larry? Ask Larry Bradshaw today what
thinks really happened, who the real mastermind was, and
smiles broadly and shakes his head. "I don't want to get anyc
in trouble," he says. But at other times, he has said that Franc
Marc and Behrens all were involved. Six months or so after
mother's conviction, Larry drove to New York and dropped in
Richard Behrens. They visited their old hangout, the Midr
Express coffee shop, and at one point Behrens leaned across
table, Larry says, and told him, "This is the place Frances an
planned it all out. Sitting right here."

Mike George, you see, believes that Larry was in fact Franc
designated hit man, but that at the last moment he refused
play his part. "Frances felt she could control Larry. So, if
finger ever pointed at the Schreuders, she could save Marc, a
Larry would take the fall. That's how it was meant to work. I
Larry balked." That is why Marc and his mother had an ho
and-a-half phone conversation the night before the murder. Fr
ces was telling Marc that, since Larry would not cooperate, M
was going to have to do the job by himself. That is why Fran
was insisting, and Marc was sobbing, and Frances was threat

g: *do it, or don't bother to come home.* The reason Larry was rmanently locked out thereafter was to punish him for disobe- ence.

Mike also believes that Franklin Bradshaw *had* made a new ill. He thinks Larry went to the warehouse Saturday night un- er orders from his mother to find it and destroy it, and that arry accomplished his mission.

Mike thinks that by Saturday night, when Larry opted out, he new the "whole ball of wax," but that Larry will not admit any owledge or involvement in the murder because he fears losing s inheritance, as Marc and Frances have done. By law, one nnot commit murder for money and keep the money.

Myself, I have about concluded that Larry Bradshaw, dented ough he be, is in this tale the only family hero. Undergoing ances's monumental abuse, and surviving it, toughened him. It ade him, like a mended china teacup, stronger at the broken aces. Instead of being consumed by the flames of his mother's jection, he was hardened by them. By the end, Larry Bradshaw d turned out to be the only person in the whole improbable ory strong enough to say no to Frances.

There remains the mystery of why they kept the gun. "That's e only place they screwed up," Mike George says. "The gun d them in. If he'd thrown it into the East River, or the Jordan ver, this case would never have been solved." The likeliest ex- anation, Mike thinks, is that Behrens was supposed to get rid of e gun and decided not to, and the Schreuders had no idea he ll had it. Being Behrens, he might have had any number of asons for keeping it. A gun was useful and, he knew from expe- nce, hard for New Yorkers to obtain. Behrens was very afraid Frances. Should she or her son ever turn on him, perhaps try pin the murder on him, he had the gun, and the gun was firmly d to Marc. So perhaps he kept it as several kinds of insurance. rhaps he thought he might have a use for it one day. Who ows what someone like Behrens has in his mind? Maybe, like e Bradshaws, he simply could not bear to throw anything use- away.

But why had Frances insisted that Marc bring the gun home? hat did she have in her mind? What other plots was she hatch- ? Or *did* Frances insist? Maybe bringing the gun home was arc's own idea? Or it could have been Marc and Behrens's

private game. Why else did they buy those cleaning rods and t
protective case?

Why wouldn't Frances give Behrens his $3,700? Didn't s
understand how dangerous he was? If she didn't, or couldn't,
wouldn't, then why didn't *Marc* pay him? Or Larry? It wou
have been a simple enough matter to forge another of Granny
checks. It wasn't logical.

But "murder is never logical," the prosecutor had said.

The murder of Franklin Bradshaw had started as a fam
game, a family sick joke. Then some kind of lid came off, sor
restraints blew away, and the game escaped into reality. I thi
most murders happen that way.

By Christmas 1984, Larry Bradshaw was no longer on parole. I
drove back to Salt Lake City, where he had already rented
apartment and bought furniture, and he prepared to enroll in t
University of Utah and major in political science.

His brother continues his studies at the state penitentia
working toward a paralegal degree and an advanced degree
federal income tax studies. Mary Lou Kaiser continues visiti
baking, waiting. Marc Schreuder's appeal to the Utah Supre
Court has been filed, but one of Berenice's many lawyers says
would "fall off my chair" if a new trial were granted. Marc w
be up for parole in June 1986, however, and his chances of relea
look very good.

Berenice and Chips spent Christmas touring the Balearic
lands. She had completed remodeling the big duplex, sold t
place for a tidy profit—something over $3 million—and bough
smaller apartment not far from Ariadne's school. Her gran
daughter is still passionate about her dancing, and Granny do
not want to take the child away from what she loves most. A
adne spent this Christmas as she had the previous three—twirli
and arching and leaping in the spotlight, spinning now on d
mond-hard toes, *The Nutcracker*'s enchanted child.

Earlier in the year, Saxe, Bacon & Bolan were quietly dropp
and Salt Lake City attorney Ron Yengish was retained by M
Bradshaw to handle her daughter's appeal.

In prison, Frances Schreuder has been a constant disciplina
problem since she arrived. First she was caught and punished f
trying to smuggle in whiskey. Soon after, morphine was found
her urine and she was punished again. By summer 1984, fund

the generous allowance she receives from Berenice, she was inning the prison commissary rackets. Later that summer she as severely beaten up by two other inmates. Authorities believe e mauling was somehow related to her newfound status as oint of the Mountain's leading black marketeer.

In November, United Press International reported in a small em: "Frances Bernice Schreuder, the New York socialite conicted of first-degree murder in the death of her father, is sufferg from 'culture shock,' and has been moved from Utah State rison."

Readers familiar with the case took this to mean that Frances as at last where she had belonged all along—in a mental hospil. But they were wrong. Utah prison officials had simply got fed with Frances and shipped her off to Idaho. The two state nitentiaries have a reciprocal agreement, and Utah had decided let Idaho take a crack at saying no to Frances for a while.

ew York, N.Y.
ring 1985

Index